Reaction and Reform:
The Politics of the Conservative Party under R.B. Bennett, 1927–1938

When R.B. Bennett assumed the leadership of the Conservative Party of Canada in 1926, he inherited a party out of step with a modernizing Canada. Three years later, in the early days of the Depression, he led the Tories to power with a mandate to bring back prosperity. Larry A. Glassford explores the politics of Bennett's leadership, the strategies with which he tackled the Depression, and the reception he and the Conservative party received from voters and press of the day.

Bennett's initial efforts to tackle the Depression took the form of activist reaction: raising tariffs, trying to balance the budget, defending the dollar. When these measures all failed to bring recovery, the Bennett-led government edged towards a reform program, creating such permanent institutions as the Canadian Radio Broadcasting Commission (later the CBC), the Bank of Canada, and the Wheat Board. Bennett tried to package his reforms as a Canadian 'New Deal,' a daring move but one that failed to revive the party.

The voters were confused: did the Conservative party stand for reaction or reform? Tories themselves could not decide. The Liberals swept back into power in 1935. At the 1938 Conservative convention which chose Bennett's successor, the perplexing dichotomy remained.

Fifty years after the Great Depression, the common perception of Bennett is still of the great Canadian capitalist, driving his government, his party, and the country to the never-never land of American-style high tariffs and British-style imperialism. Glassford demonstrates the inaccuracy of that caricature, and offers instead a fresh analysis of Bennett and his party.

LARRY A. GLASSFORD is Assistant Professor in the Faculty of Education, University of Windsor. He is co-author of *Challenge of Democracy: Ideals and Realities in Canada*.

LARRY A. GLASSFORD

Reaction and Reform:
The Politics of the
Conservative Party
under R.B. Bennett,
1927–1938

UNIVERSITY OF TORONTO PRESS
Toronto Buffalo London

© University of Toronto Press 1992
Toronto Buffalo London
Printed in Canada

ISBN 0-8020-2798-9 (cloth)
ISBN 0-8020-7673-4 (paper)

♾

Printed on acid-free paper

JL
197
P67
G53
1992

Canadian Cataloguing in Publication Data

Glassford, Larry A. (Larry Arthur), 1950–
Reaction and reform

Includes index.
ISBN 0-8020-2798-9 (bound)
ISBN 0-8020-7673-4 (pbk.)

1. Conservative Party of Canada – History.
2. Bennett, R.B. (Richard Bedford), 1870–1947.
3. Canada – Politics and government – 1921–1930.*
4. Canada – Politics and government – 1930–1935.*
5. Canada – Politics and government – 1935–1948.*
I. Title.

JL197.P67G53 1992   324.27104   C91–095184–5

2680744
1/4/95

Cover illustration: PC Party Papers MG 28 IV 2 Vol. 356

'Stagnation or progress? Reaction or reform? Which shall it be?'

- R.B. BENNETT to the Conservative delegates in banquet at the
  Ottawa Leadership Convention, 5 July 1938

For my parents

Contents

8
The Search for Redemption: November 1935 to July 1938 205

9
'We Have Made Mistakes': The Legacy of the Bennett Years 231

EPILOGUE 243

NOTES 247

SOURCES 289

INDEX 293

Preface

The focus of this book is on the struggle within the national Conservative Party of Canada during R.B. Bennett's years as leader, 1927–38, to adapt its program, organization, and image to meet the realities of a modernizing Canada. What had been a largely rural and agricultural society at the time of Confederation had been transformed into an increasingly urban, industrialized one by the 1920s. The party's traditional 'National Policy' of tariff protection for industry, assistance to railways, and encouragement of immigration to settle the West was proving ever more inadequate in the face of new conflicts shaped by the nation's changing socio-economic structure. The question was whether Conservatives should reach back into their past for guidance in trying times or march boldly ahead, borrowing radical ideas from other movements and parties.

When Bennett assumed the party leadership in 1927, the Conservatives were in opposition at Ottawa: strong in Ontario, the Maritimes, and British Columbia, but weak elsewhere. Three years later, aided by hard times, Liberal blunders, and stellar organization, Bennett led the Tories to power with a mandate from all regions to end unemployment and find markets. For the next five years, the Conservative administration wrestled with the Great Depression. The Tories' traditional remedy of higher tariffs was applied with vigour, but to no avail. All the traditional levers of state were manipulated in a losing bid to balance the federal budget and defend the Canadian dollar. The Conservative government actively intervened in the economy, though always to repair, not replace capitalism. Typically, federal funds in unprecedented sums flowed into unemployment relief, while federal authorities cracked down harshly on public dissenters.

Activist reaction failed to bring recovery. The Bennett-led government edged towards a reform program, creating such permanent institutions as the Canadian Radio Broadcasting Commission, the Bank of Canada, and the Wheat Board. Under the influence of W.D. Herridge, his brother-in-law and also Canadian Minister to Washington, Bennett tried to package his reforms as a Canadian 'New Deal.' This daring move, opposed by right-wing Conservative colleagues such as C.H. Cahan, ultimately failed to revive the party's re-election prospects. Bennett's plutocratic image and autocratic style damaged the reform program's credibility, as did his public quarrel with H.H. Stevens, the very man he had chosen earlier to investigate business abuses. After resigning from cabinet in 1934, Stevens went on to form the breakaway Reconstruction Party, a move that only made the Liberal sweep in 1935 even more decisive.

If the voters were unsure whether the Conservative party was a party of reaction or of reform, they were not alone. Tories themselves could not decide. Bennett himself, while maintaining his commitment to all reform policies introduced during his time as prime minister, soon lost his taste for new radical adventures. Herridge's attempt to force the party into a reformist stance, at the 1938 convention that chose Bennett's successor, failed miserably. The perplexing dichotomy remained. The Conservative party stood in 1938, as it had during Bennett's years as leader, for both reaction and reform.

It is time now, a full half-century after the decade of the Great Depression, to look again more seriously at the party that governed Canada for more than five of those ten years. Despite numerous historical and social-scientific studies of parties, personalities, and programs in the 1920s and 1930s, the common perception of the Bennett-led Conservatives is still dominated by the editorials of John Dafoe and the cartoons of Arch Dale, both appearing in the pro-Liberal *Winnipeg Free Press*. Bennett is the great Canadian capitalist commander-in-chief, leading his government, his party, and the country by the nose, to the never-never land of American-style high tariffs and British-style imperialism. The surprise election victory of 1930 was a dreadful mistake, and the decisive defeat of 1935 a well-deserved hiding. The five-year Tory reign has been most often viewed as a brief interlude in 'The Mackenzie King Era,' important mainly because it allowed King and the Grits to avoid being tarred with the brush of hard times.

This study takes the Conservative party of the late 1920s and 1930s seriously, and examines it on its own terms. The resulting picture is not always a pretty one, but it is one that deserves wide exposure. There were then, as there are now, Conservative reformers as well as Conservative reactionaries, and many, such as R.B. Bennett, who were both. To really understand Canadian Conservatism today, we must absorb the lessons of this earlier era.

Acknowledgments

This book began as a doctoral dissertation at York University. As my supervisor, Michiel Horn was unfailingly patient, wise, and helpful. J.L. Granatstein consistently challenged me to do my very best. David Bell encouraged me to look beyond the confines of traditional history. At the University of Western Ontario, Robert J. Clark made many helpful suggestions, both before and after I completed my final degree. I am greatly indebted to all of these people.

The Honourable Richard A. Bell generously shared personal recollections of characters and circumstances dating back half a century. Similarly, Mr W.R. Herridge of Toronto kindly made available to me the private papers of his father, W.D. Herridge. Staff at the Public Archives of Canada, the University of New Brunswick Archives, the Archives of Ontario, the Queen's University Archives, the Public Archives of Nova Scotia, and the Public Archives of New Brunswick assisted me in many ways to complete my work. I am also grateful for the help of library staff at York University and the University of Western Ontario. Certain sections of this book appeared in somewhat altered form in *Prairie Forum* and *The American Review of Canadian Studies*, and I am thankful to their editors for assistance. Virgil Duff, managing editor at the University of Toronto Press, skilfully piloted this publishing project to completion, while Beverley Beetham Endersby helped me immeasurably to polish the presentation. To them also, I am much obliged. This book has been published with the help of a grant from the Social Science Federation of Canada, using funds provided by the Social Sciences and Humanities Research Council of Canada.

My greatest debt is to my wife, Twyla, who has been my typist, proof-reader, counsellor, and best friend. My children – Sarah, Ian, and

Rachel – have shared with me their gifts of laughter, hope, trust, and love. This book is dedicated to my parents, Albert and Mildred Glassford, whose formative years were the 1920s and 1930s in Canada. From them I received – besides life itself – a sense of purpose, a thirst for knowledge, a practical outlook, and a sturdy set of moral values. My failings have been my own.

REACTION AND REFORM: THE POLITICS OF THE
CONSERVATIVE PARTY UNDER R.B. BENNETT, 1927–1938

Prologue

A solitary figure strode purposefully up to the platform of the steamy Ottawa convention hall. William D. 'Wild Bill' Herridge, recently widowed brother-in-law of the retiring leader, R.B. Bennett, prepared to address the restless throng. Ignoring the colourful banners promoting one leadership candidate or another, the former Canadian ambassador to Washington launched into a vigorous denunciation of the policy resolutions passed thus far by the assembled delegates.

'Mr. Chairman,' he began, 'I thank you for your indulgence to me, a comparative stranger within the Conservative party.' It was well known that Herridge, though an influential adviser to Bennett in the eight years since the election campaign of 1930, had been a Liberal prior to 1926. His privileged access, cemented through his marriage to the leader's engaging younger sister, Mildred Bennett, had long been a source of envy and resentment among the Old Guard.

'I have listened,' Herridge continued, 'with the most earnest care to the resolutions which have been presented by your committee to this Convention and I have made inquiry and have been informed as to the character of the resolutions still to follow, and I cannot see them written into the law of the Conservative party without registering my profound protest, for in my judgment, ladies and gentlemen, they fail to disclose any real solution for the fundamental problems of this country.'

The crowd began to stir. Who did this Herridge fellow think he was? Warming to his subject, the former ambassador pressed on with a damning assessment of the policy resolutions. 'They are,' he asserted, 'little more than a lot of junk. They are an insult to the intelligence of this Convention.'

'So are you!' shouted an angry delegate. 'Sit down!' cried another.

Herridge would not sit down. 'They are a treachery to the people of this country,' he bellowed, above the din of the crowd. 'They are the supreme accomplishment of reaction within the Conservative party.'

'Throw him out!' came the clear response of one incensed delegate, whose voice carried above the general hubbub.

Still, Herridge was not about to yield the microphone. He proceeded to introduce his own resolution, by way of amendment. 'Whereas the present level of consumption is far below the national capacity to produce, and whereas the task of democratic government is to raise the level of production' – the crowd was listening now to see what the reputed author of Bennett's famous New Deal radio broadcasts would propose – 'be it therefore resolved that the Liberal-Conservative party pledges itself to undertake whatever economic and monetary reforms may be required to stabilize production upon its maximum level, and to raise purchasing power to that level, recognizing that such reforms will involve a measure of government planning and control of the economic and monetary systems –'

The remainder of Herridge's resolution was lost in a cacophony of catcalls and boos. 'Go back to the States, where you belong,' shouted a delegate, unwilling to hear any more Rooseveltian reform proposals.

'Give this resolution of mine, ladies and gentleman, fair play,' the former ambassador pleaded. The chairman, John MacNicol, was forced to intervene, shouting for order, and the crowd settled a bit. A thoroughly angry Herridge went again to the attack, deriding the results of the convention's deliberations to this point.

'Your accomplishments to date have been two-fold: you have lost your great leader, God help you, because of reaction in this party; and you have stirred the passions of religious and racial strife. Now, ladies and gentlemen, if you back up these resolutions, if you put them through, I tell you this Conservative party disappears, and history will record this as the day of its funeral service.'

'You are a Jeremiah!' a delegate shouted at Herridge. The heckling began again, but the speaker pressed on, at top volume, ignoring the calls of 'Shut up!'

'Ladies and gentleman,' he concluded, 'you stand either for reaction or for reform. There is no evading the question.' With that, he at last sat down.

Not a single delegate rose to second his amendment. A befuddled MacNicol called for a vote anyway, and Herridge's resolution, despite a scattering of support, was rejected by a thunderous roar of nays.[1]

Later that day, these same delegates chose Robert J. Manion as their new party leader. A humiliated Bennett, who'd waited in vain for signs that the party wished him to succeed himself, was conspicuously not present to congratulate the new leader. While the convention's decision to dispense with Bennett's leadership and Herridge's reform policies did not constitute Canadian Conservatism's funeral, it did mark the beginning of a long convalescence. Bennett went off in disgust to Britain to become a Lord. Herridge set off on a reform pilgrimage of speech-making and organizing that carried him out of the party and into obscurity.

Try as they might to polarize the party convention of 1938 on the issue of reaction or reform, though, neither Bennett nor Herridge could have succeeded, because the Conservative party in Canada stood for both. They might better have promised reaction *and* reform. A careful examination of the party's development from Arthur Meighen's resignation as leader in 1926 to R.J. Manion's selection as Bennett's successor in 1938 will clearly illustrate the persistently dichotomous nature of Canadian Conservatism.

1 The Conservative Heritage: What Manner of Party?

The 14th of September 1926 was a dark day in the history of Canada's Conservative party. Less than one year earlier, under Arthur Meighen's leadership, it had surged back from a devastating third-place finish in 1921 to win an overall plurality of seats in the general election of 29 October 1925. Only the wily tactics of Mackenzie King had kept the Liberal government in office for several more months. In June 1926, aided by a scandal in the customs department, the Conservatives had seemed poised to assume their rightful place in office. Governor General Byng's refusal of a parliamentary dissolution requested by King, King's subsequent resignation as prime minister, and Meighen's acceptance of the post offered by Byng led to the immediate and unexpected defeat of the new Conservative government in the House of Commons. Undaunted, Meighen and his followers confidently expected vindication at the polls. At the end of a hard-fought campaign, the leader issued a press statement predicting 'a clear majority over all other groups' in the new House of Commons. At party headquarters, the back-room boys were counting on major gains in Quebec and the Prairies, and continued strength elsewhere.[1]

The ballot boxes told a different tale. 'Liberals Are Back in the Saddle' screamed the headlines in the Toronto *Globe*. The Liberal party led by King, in conjunction with its Liberal-Progressive allies, won an absolute majority of ridings. The Conservatives dropped twenty-five seats, and Meighen himself was defeated in Portage la Prairie, along with five other cabinet colleagues. The party, while still strong in Ontario, the Maritimes, and British Columbia, could elect but one member from the Prairies, and only four in Quebec. Another period in opposition was assured. Both party and leader were demoralized. Meighen resigned soon after, not just as prime minister, but also as Conservative chieftain. In three tries, he had failed to lead his party to a majority victory. Power remained in the hands of the hated Grits.[2] It was time for the Conservative party to take stock. For some, particularly Meighen's enemies within the party, the key to rejuvenation was simply a more inspiring leader. For Meighen himself, the problem ran much deeper. 'The supreme consideration is not: who shall be the leader of this party,' he would remind the assembled convention delegates in 1927. 'The supreme consideration is: what manner of party shall he have to lead?[3]

THE LEGACY OF MACDONALD AND CARTIER

To Conservatives in the 1920s, the golden age of the Liberal-Conservative Party of Canada was the three-decade period that followed Confederation in 1867. The coalition that John A. Macdonald of Kingston and George E. Cartier of Montreal had put together in the United Province of Canada (uniting Tories, moderate Reformers, and Bleus) prior to Confederation[4] reached out to include the pro-confederates of New Brunswick and Nova Scotia. The alliance that followed John A. Macdonald's leadership in the first Parliament of the new Dominion of Canada called itself the Liberal-Conservative party. The title, used since 1854, was an apt one because, over the years, the shrewd Tory premier had enticed numerous prominent Liberal and Reform supporters into his following, not least among them, perhaps, Cartier himself, a former rebel of 1837, who was Macdonald's closest political colleague from 1854 until his death in 1873. Other prominent converts had included A.T. Galt and D'Arcy McGee of Quebec (formerly Canada East), William McDougall and W.P. Howland of Ontario (formerly Canada West), Leonard Tilley of New Brunswick, and, soon, Joseph Howe of Nova Scotia. Under Macdonald's inspired leadership, this coalition of factions was welded into a party that governed Canada from 1867 to 1896, with the exception of five years in the 1870s, when scandal and depression intervened.

What were the chief elements of the Conservatives' success during this era? The first key point is the party's intimate relationship with the country's business community. In the early years, the Conservatives worked closely with the Grand Trunk Railway interests. Later, the Canadian Pacific Railway supplanted the Grand Trunk in the party's affections. The relationship in both cases was symbiotic: the party, if in power, could pull the required legislative and administrative levers to assure the company's financial success; in turn, the company could put the party in power with generous donations of funds and ample opportunities for patronage. The same relationship existed between Canadian manufacturers and the Conservative party. Begun in 1859 with the Galt tariff, then extended and legitimized in 1879 with the evocatively titled 'National Policy' tariffs, the protection against foreign competitors provided by Conservative policy soon became an essential component of profitability for many firms. They were happy to provide funds for the party that defended the tariff against the free-trading Liberals. Through many a twist and turn of party policy, the central unity of purpose between most large businessmen and the Conservative party remained a constant factor.[5]

Despite their affinity for business interests, the Conservatives managed to maintain a healthy connection with Canadian workers in the growing urban centres. Macdonald's Trades Union Act of 1872 played a part, particularly when contrasted to the *laissez-faire* principles held by many Liberals of the day, for it freed unions from any legal restrictions arising from the fact they were combinations in restraint of trade.[6] Further, the protective tariff was widely seen as the guarantor of employment for Canadian labour. Full free trade, or even reciprocity with the United States, might help the primary producer, but the urban working man feared the export of his job if such a policy were instituted.

Nation-building was an important element in the Conservative tradition. The party that ushered in Confederation soon extended the new dominion's boundaries from the Atlantic to the Pacific, and north to the Arctic. Claiming ownership of the new territories was one thing, uniting them was another. Inherent in the Conservative policies that attracted the support of business and labour was an attitude favourable to the positive utilization of the state in the country's affairs. In the case of, first, the Grand Trunk, and, later, the CPR, it meant public support for private companies to both pursue profits and serve the public interest. In the case of the Intercolonial Railway, it meant public ownership of a non-profitable line deemed essential to the national interest. Tariffs were, of course, a blatant example of state interference with the free flow of goods. They were acceptable to business on the basis that they would guarantee profits, to labour on the basis that they would guarantee jobs, and to many Canadians in general on the basis that they would guarantee the survival of a new northern nation distinct from the expanding American republic. Furthermore, they were an important source of government revenue.[7] Private interests and the national interest were seen to go hand in hand. What was good for business was good for the country. State intervention was meant to assist private enterprise, not supplant it.

When the Liberal-Conservative coalition was formed in 1854, cultural dualism was at the very heart of the accord. For the next two decades, Macdonald and Cartier, in their own partnership, embodied the mutual respect and equality of English and French. Party and government policies reflected the views of both cultural groups. Confederation ended the practice of dual premiership, and reduced the electoral importance of Quebec, but Cartier's own prestige and his standing with Macdonald prevented any serious diminution of the bicultural partnership.[8] After his colleague's death in 1873, Macdonald found capable lieutenants from Quebec, such as Hector Langevin and Adolphe Chapleau, but no one who was Cartier's equal in skill and stature. Even as English Canada was experiencing a growth of ethnic nationalism, Quebec was undergoing a Catholic conservative revival. A clash was inevitable, and the Conservative party was caught up in it. The Conservative government's decision to allow the execution of Louis Riel was widely perceived at the time as a victory of English, Protestant Ontario over French, Catholic Quebec. The hostile attitude of English-speaking Conservatives at the time of the Jesuit Estates and Manitoba Schools controversies convinced many French Canadians there was no room for them in the Conservative party as it was evolving in Macdonald's declining years.

British-Canadian nationalism, or loyalism,[9] was an essential element of the original Liberal-Conservative coalition. At times it manifested itself as anti-Americanism, and the Conservative party exploited this feeling in achieving Confederation, and, later on, to help win elections, Macdonald's 1891 campaign being the classic example. At other times, it showed up as virulent anti-Catholic and anti-French prejudice, often emanating from the Loyal Orange Lodge, a bastion of Tory support in central and eastern Ontario. The bicultural basis of the Macdonald-Cartier partnership was steadily eroded by this anglophone aggression. The solid electoral base for the party switched from Quebec to Ontario. During the pre-Confederation period, it was Cartier's Bleus who had sustained Macdonald's Tories in office. From Confederation through the election of 1882, the size of the contingents from the two largest provinces in the Conservative caucus was roughly equivalent. From 1887 on, however, the party's support in Quebec declined, and Ontario became Conservatism's most loyal supporter.[10]

In addition to the legacy of English-French partnership under

Macdonald and Cartier, this 'golden age' of Conservatism contributed one other powerful myth, the legend of John A. himself. One of the country's ablest politicians, without doubt, he was soon elevated in Conservative tradition to near-Olympian stature. Even his foibles and weaknesses became part of the heroic legend. Not only was Macdonald successful at winning elections, he was positively loved by legions of faithful followers as well. No succeeding leader could ever match the expectations generated in the party ranks by the myths of Macdonald. This nostalgic longing for a new version of the old chieftain would permeate the Conservative party for a long time to come.[11]

THE ERA OF BORDEN AND MEIGHEN

The successful Liberal-Conservative voting coalition knitted together by Macdonald had consisted of representation from the three major economic interests: business, labour, and farm; both significant linguistic groups: English and French; and both major religious affiliations: Protestant and Catholic. Holding this amorphous mass of conflicting elements together had required generous dollops of wisdom, charm, and patronage. After Macdonald's death, a succession of leaders fumbled the job, until Wilfrid Laurier grasped the opportunity in 1896 to weld a new electoral majority behind his leadership. For fifteen years, the Liberals governed Canada, while Robert Borden, elected leader by the Conservative caucus in 1901, slowly assembled the elements of a new Conservative majority. His methodical efforts came to fruition in 1911. For the next nine years, he served as prime minister, receiving increasing help and support from the man who would eventually succeed him in 1920, Arthur Meighen.

Borden had sensed the modernization of Canadian society, and he personally subscribed to many reform policies associated with urban progressivism. These were most succinctly expressed in the Halifax platform of 1907, in which he advocated civil-service appointments based on merit, controls on party fund-raising, Senate reform, tighter legislative control over government spending, and state regulation of public utilities.[12] This modern program was insufficient to win the election of 1908, however. Indeed, Borden's two electoral victories were each won by virtue of alliances of convenience with political foes. In 1911, his party linked up with business Liberals to fight reciprocity and with Quebec nationalists to fight Laurier's naval policy, while, in 1917, the Conservatives joined forces with anglophone Liberals to maintain an all-out war effort, including manpower conscription. By 1920, when Borden passed on the mantle of leadership to his designated successor, Meighen, the Union government party – soon to become the Liberal-Conservative party again – was alienated from four key elements of the Macdonaldian majority: French Canadians, farmers, organized labour, and Montreal business.

The tradition of dualism was grievously wounded during the Borden years. The Tory leader's choice to fill Cartier's shoes, Frederick Monk, resigned from cabinet barely a year into office. No credible replacement could be found. The naval issue, which had plagued Laurier, wrecked the Conservative-Nationaliste alliance. Despite an initial euphoric unity, the long, bloody world war that began in 1914 drove a deep wedge between Canada's two cultural solitudes. Borden's decision in 1917 to impose conscription for military service was strongly opposed by most French Canadians, though endorsed by an imposing majority of English-speaking Canadians. At the same time, the anti-French educational policy embodied in the Conservative Ontario government's Regulation 17 created new heights of tension and resentment. The landslide for Laurier's Liberals among French Canadians in the wartime election of 1917 was to no avail in the face of the sweep of English Canada by the Union government, whose mandate was assisted by blatant gerrymandering in the form of the Military Voters Act and Wartime Elections Act. For all these grievances, French Canada held the Conservative party responsible.[13]

The election of 1911 was fought outside of Quebec largely on the issue of reciprocity. The Laurier government had negotiated a trade arrangement with the United States that eliminated or reduced tariffs on hundreds of products, both natural and processed. A judicious blend of emotional patriotism and economic self-interest carried the day for the Conservatives, whose total opposition to reciprocity was particularly appealing in industrializing Ontario. By contrast, the newly opened grain-growing areas of Alberta and Saskatchewan had opted for the Liberals and reciprocity. High protective tariffs remained government policy in spite of the strong support for the Unionist cause across the agrarian-dominated Prairies in 1917. Furthermore, a promise during that campaign that farmers' sons would not be conscripted was soon broken after the votes were in. The farmers held the Conservative party responsible for the negative impact of the tariffs upon them, and for the broken promise about conscription.

The Borden government made other enemies, as well. The imminent financial collapse of, first, the Canadian Northern, and, then, the Grand

Trunk, forced the Borden administration into increasingly costly subsidization. To stem the losses, and prevent the chaos that might arise from bankruptcy, the two railways were nationalized between 1917 and 1920. Such drastic state intervention provoked bitter opposition from much of the business community, particularly in Montreal, where the privately owned Canadian Pacific feared the competition from a public enterprise, and had lobbied for total unification of the nation's railways under its own management. The close connection between the CPR and the Conservative party was severed.[14]

Shortly after the war's end, labour strife in Winnipeg culminated in a six-week general strike. The federal government sided with management and the civil authorities, and refused to give in to the strikers' demands. Two ministers, Meighen and Senator Gideon Robertson, travelled to Winnipeg to spearhead the suppression of a perceived revolutionary situation. After a bloody police riot, the Winnipeg strikers capitulated, and the status quo was restored. Organized labour, particularly in western Canada, held the Conservatives largely responsible for the repression of workers.

Meighen inherited from Borden the Union government's liabilities along with the prime-ministerial powers. An intelligent man, a brilliant speaker, and a master of parliamentary debate, he had had a hand in most of the controversial actions of the Borden government. In the public mind he was firmly identified with the most odious Conservative and Unionist policies. It was Meighen who had devised the closure strategem that cut off the Liberal filibuster of the naval bill in 1913. His role was critical in gaining passage of both the conscription and the wartime-elections bills in 1917. His high-profile participation in the negotiations and debates surrounding the nationalization of the Canadian Northern and Grand Trunk placed him in deep trouble with the many opponents of a state-owned railway, largely centred in Montreal. Finally, his prominent part in the suppression of the Winnipeg General Strike, and his subsequent role in seeing through Parliament amendments to the Criminal Code to curtail the rights of organized labour, ensured his unpopularity with much of the working class.[15]

Meighen chose to fight the 1921 election on the tariff issue. In so doing, he hoped to resurrect the winning voter combination of 1878, 1891, and 1911, when the 'National Policy' had carried the day. He was disappointed. The political situation in 1921 was quite different from that in the pre-war era. There were no Conservative provincial governments to aid the party cause. The agricultural West had grown immensely in population and seats, from ten in 1878 to fifty-six in 1921. The unpopularity of the Union government was tied to the Conservatives by their opponents, the Liberals and the Progressives, the latter a new political movement fuelled by farmers' discontent. Meighen had hoped the tariff issue would soothe angry voters in industrializing Quebec, conciliate the Montreal capitalists, and entice workers to vote Tory to defend their jobs. It did not. The party was decimated. Its only parliamentary seats came from the regions of solid British loyalist support in New Brunswick, Ontario, and British Columbia.

By 1925, the party's prognosis had improved immensely. The Progressives were split, and the Liberals were blamed for economic hardship. Three strong Conservative governments, in Ontario, Nova Scotia, and New Brunswick, were eager to aid the federal party. Montreal business could not yet bring itself to support Meighen, but it did endorse E.L. Patenaude, a distinguished French-Canadian Conservative who was publicly keeping his distance from the party leader. Meighen repeated the strategy of 1921, making protective tariffs the centre-piece of the Conservative campaign, coupled with some freight-rate adjustments to appeal to Atlantic and western Canada. Riding the tide of 'Maritime Rights,' the Conservatives swept twenty-three of twenty-nine seats in the Maritimes. Anglo Montreal returned four Tories. In Ontario, aided by the provincial machine of Premier Howard Ferguson, the party surged to a lopsided victory reminiscent of 1911. Even on the Prairies, thought to be wedded to low tariffs, the Conservatives elected seven MPs in Manitoba and three in Alberta. British Columbia strengthened its Tory bias. By all odds it was a tremendous victory, an amazing comeback from 1921.

Unfortunately, while Meighen stood his ground on the program he had enunciated in the recent campaign, Mackenzie King manoeuvred for time by offering policy concessions on tariffs and pensions to the Progressive and Labour MPs. Meighen did offer a new appeal to French Canadians in a major address at Hamilton, where he declared that no future Conservative government would send Canadian troops to a foreign battlefield without first obtaining a renewed mandate from the people via a general election. This departure from the Borden policy angered many prominent Conservatives in English Canada, some of whom publicly denounced it. Nevertheless, when Meighen formed his short-lived new ministry, Patenaude was prepared to enter it, and fought the ensuing election as a straight Conservative. The 1926 results were thus doubly disappointing. Both Meighen and Patenaude were personally defeated. In fact, no Conservatives were elected in any Prairie province, or in Quebec outside anglo Montreal. Strong support in the Maritimes, Ontario, and British Columbia was simply not enough to carry a majority. Meighen could read the results as well as anyone. He resigned forthwith.[16] Once again, Conservatives faced the challenge of renewal. The time had come to confront the central question later posed by Meighen: What manner of party did they wish to be?

2 Choosing a New Chieftain: The Liberal-Conservative Convention, 1927

Nova Scotian premier Edgar Rhodes's gavel banged the final session of the Winnipeg convention to order shortly after 3:00 p.m. It was 12 October 1927, and the occasion was the first national convention of the Liberal-Conservative Party of Canada. Six choices faced the delegates as they made their way to one of the nineteen ballot-boxes spread throughout the main hall of the old Amphitheatre. In alphabetical order, the candidates for party leader were: R.B. Bennett, of Calgary; C.H. Cahan, of Montreal; Sir Henry Drayton, of Toronto; Hugh Guthrie, of Guelph; R.J. Manion, of Fort William; and Robert Rogers, of Winnipeg. On the previous evening, these six men had addressed the great gathering. Now, the delegates were casting their votes.[1]

Once balloting was concluded, the convention occupied its time with several policy resolutions. All were carried as presented. The delegates' minds were elsewhere – in the counting rooms with the scrutineers and returning officers. At last, the results were ready. A hush spread over the crowd as Senator Gideon Robertson announced the totals in alphabetical order: Bennett, 594 votes; Cahan, 310; Drayton, 31; Guthrie, 345; Manion, 170; Rogers, 114 (see table 1). In a moment it was clear: no candidate had an absolute majority. A second ballot would follow. Each man decided to stay in the race.

Once again, the delegates headed for the voting-booths. Minor resolutions, impromptu speeches, and spontaneous singsongs filled in the time. When Senator Robertson at last returned to the podium, he read the names in ascending order of their support; Drayton, 3; Rogers, 37; Manion, 148; Cahan, 266; Guthrie, 320; and, finally, with a clear majority, Bennett, 780.

TABLE 1
Leadership voting results at 1927 convention

Candidate	First ballot	Second ballot
R.B. Bennett	594	780
Hugh Guthrie	345	320
C.H. Cahan	310	266
R.J. Manion	170	148
Robert Rogers	114	37
Sir Henry Drayton	31	3
Totals	1,564	1,554

SOURCE: John R. MacNicol, *The National Liberal-Conservative Convention* (Toronto 1930), 55

Pandemonium reigned, as the delegates welcomed their new leader with thunderous applause. Chairman Rhodes restored a semblance of order, whereupon Guthrie moved that the selection of Bennett be made unanimous. His motion was seconded by Cahan, Manion, and Rogers. The new leader then addressed the delegates in his stentorian voice, calling them to join a crusade for Canada and the Conservative party: 'Promise here and now, as you walk out of yonder door, that you will be missionaries for the great party to which we belong, missionaries from the greatest political convention ever held in the Dominion of Canada, and if you are missionaries your efforts will be crowned with success, and you will have a government at Ottawa reflecting your principles.'[2] It was a powerful call, answered by another huge ovation. A great crush of people surged to the platform to congratulate the new chieftain in his hour of triumph. Dozens of reporters frantically filed their lead stories by telegram. 'Bennett wins on the second ballot' read the messages sent tapping over the wires.

While 'Bennett wins' was the climactic resolution of the convention story for contemporary journalists, half a century later a deeper question poses itself: What did his victory mean for the party? In opting for the loquacious Calgarian, assembled Conservatives made a significant choice, not just between different personalities, but also between alternative futures. His selection revealed much about the manner of party that existed in 1927.

ORGANIZING THE CONVENTION

Defeat in the 1926 election had been a devastating blow to the Conservatives. Had Meighen chosen to stay on and fight, he might well have carried the majority of caucus with him, but even many of those most loyal to him had concluded he could never lead the party to victory. Typical of this element was R.B. Hanson of New Brunswick, who wrote to a friend shortly after the election that 'we probably never can win with him, nevertheless, I feel under personal obligation to him on account of my first Election, and I feel an intense admiration for his ability in Parliament.'[3] By contrast, other Conservatives, particularly in Montreal, wished to lay all the blame for the defeat at Meighen's feet. 'The essential fact is that Quebec will not have Mr. Meighen,' the *Gazette* thundered.[4]

Some party members pointed to organizational difficulties at the national level as the chief deficiency. 'Most important of all [was] the lack of proper Dominion organization,' observed Premier Rhodes of Nova Scotia.[5] There was justification for this belief. Even during the successful campaign of 1925, a Meighen aide, Harold Daly of Ottawa, had confided to R.B. Bennett that 'there is no headquarters here and every Province looks after itself ... If we win it will not be because we have organized properly.'[6] Sir Joseph Flavelle, the Toronto tycoon and Tory benefactor, took a different tack in a long, penetrating letter that was widely circulated within party ranks for years thereafter: 'I believe it will be a mistake to plan for the work of the party in the hope that it will speedily return to power. There is the same prosaic need of education that there was in 1896. Progress established through constructive planning will not come through the conventional machine.' Flavelle urged the party to concentrate on developing more progressive policies, attracting new Conservative supporters among the young, recent immigrants, westerners, and Quebeckers, and broadening the base of the party's financial support away from the small clique of protected manufacturers. 'The Conservative party,' he wrote, 'has been consistently wrong for more than a quarter of a century in being primarily interested in securing power, in place of being primarily interested in being competent to govern.'[7] Flavelle's views, though widely discussed, were not widely accepted by a party that felt it had been cheated out of office.

Meighen, aware of strong opposition to his leadership, and heartily sick of politics, made his own decision to retire. One of his last acts as party leader was to summon a special caucus meeting of MPs and defeated candidates to deal with the party's future. The special caucus, convening in Ottawa on 11 October, made two important decisions. The first was to select Hugh Guthrie, a Unionist Liberal who had remained with the Conservatives after the breakup of the wartime coalition, as their temporary party leader. The second was to call for a national convention 'at the earliest possible date following the next session of Parliament for the purpose of naming a permanent leader and for such other purposes as to the Convention may seem fit.'[8]

Why a convention? To this point in its history, the party's leader had emerged from the parliamentary caucus. Not all Conservatives accepted the wisdom of such an innovation. Months later, F.D.L. Smith of the Toronto *Mail and Empire* wrote to Ontario premier Howard Ferguson that 'many prominent Conservatives ... still entertain the view that the Winnipeg Convention is a mistake, and out of keeping with the traditions of the party, which never yet in Great Britain or Canada has filled the leadership of the party in this way.'[9] The contrary view was expressed by Sir Thomas White, the finance minister under Borden, who pointed out to Meighen, 'We live in a democratic age and a Convention will give that "equality of opportunity" for political advancement so much to be desired as a spur to effort and enthusiasm in a great party.'[10] There were some Canadian precedents for adopting the American practice. In 1919, the Liberals had chosen Laurier's successor, Mackenzie King, at a party convention in Ottawa. Ontario Conservatives had selected Howard Ferguson as their leader at a Toronto convention in 1920. In both cases, a rejuvenated party went on to victory at the next election. A national convention might well hasten the achievement of the missionary aims articulated by Flavelle, by boosting morale and garnering free publicity, while strengthening the organization and legitimizing the selection of a new leader. Yet many cautious Tories agonized over the possibility of a mass convention being stampeded into choosing a poor leader or passing unwise policy resolutions.

The caucus's action in calling a national convention did not sit well with John R. MacNicol, who felt that the Dominion Liberal-Conservative Association, of which he was the president, should exercise that prerogative. The Dominion association had been formed at a convention held in Toronto on 17 November 1924. Attended by some three hundred delegates representing the nine provincial party associations, the Toronto meeting had attempted to fill the organizational void at the top of the party pyramid. By resolution, the delegates in 1924 had directed that, 'in case of emergency relative to the Party, the Dominion association [shall] call a Dominion Convention.'[11] For a time it appeared that two parallel conventions might be organized. MacNicol summoned the national executive of the Dominion association to Toronto on 26 October where a decision was reached 'that the time had arrived to summon a National Convention.'[12] Meighen and Guthrie went out of their way to soothe the ultra-sensitive MacNicol's wounded pride, but they insisted on the primacy of the initiative launched by the special caucus. At a November meeting in Ottawa, MacNicol was included on the committee being set up to plan the convention, and the wound was closed. However, the incident did underscore the party's chaotic disorganization at the national level.

Having decided upon a convention, the Conservatives faced the question of location. In 1919, the Liberals had convened in Ottawa. Besides being the national capital, Ottawa was located on the border of Ontario and Quebec, thus permitting both English and French to feel neither favoured nor excluded. The Conservatives opted instead for Winnipeg. Their choice was intended to symbolize the party's openness to the needs of the Prairie provinces. While Winnipeg was a popular choice with western Conservatives, the selection of the grain metropolis did not impress Quebeckers. *Le Devoir* even suspected a plot to downgrade Quebec's influence: 'il semble que les conservateurs, par leur décision d'aujourd'hui, veulent éviter l'embarras d'une délégation québécoise forte et puissamment organisée, et faire des amours a l'Quest' [It seems that the Conservatives, by their decision of today, wish to avoid the obstacle of a strong, well-organized Quebec delegation, and appeal to the West]. Plot or not, the selection of Winnipeg did elevate the party's western profile.[13]

To organize the gathering, a national convention committee, consisting of nine representatives from each of Ontario and Quebec, two from Prince Edward Island, and three from each of the other six provinces, was set up. At least one of the representatives from each province was a woman, in recognition of their new electoral importance since the grant of female suffrage at the end of the First World War. The male representatives were a mixture of federal MPs and provincial party workers. MacNicol was one of the Ontario representatives. Guthrie served as the committee chairman. A number of subcommittees were established, namely: an executive or organization committee, to carry on between meetings of the full national convention committee; a finance committee, to raise the required funds; a transportation committee, to oversee travel arrangements; a local Winnipeg committee, to arrange for hotel accommodations, local hospitality, and the convention hall; and a publicity committee, to ensure prominent press coverage. At the convention, three housekeeping committees were set up: the credentials committee, to oversee delegate registration; the rules committee, to approve appropriate regulations governing convention procedure; and a nominations committee, to supervise the leadership contest.[14]

The driving force behind the organization committee was its chairman, Major-General A.D. McRae. A self-made millionaire, the quartermaster-general of the Canadian forces overseas in the First World War, and an MP for Vancouver since 1926, McRae proved to be a master of organization. After setting up a central office in Ottawa to coordinate the convention preparations, he criss-crossed the country, seeing to the details of delegate selection, publicity, finance, and travel. Most of the resolutions approved by the national convention committee were passed at his suggestion. The Conservative journalist Grattan O'Leary noted McRae's central role in the convention's success: 'Oblivious to the fears and misgivings of many of the old hands, he proceeded almost on his own account and, incidentally almost at his own expense, to organize the Winnipeg convention.' The organizational framework he evolved became the model for ensuing national Conservative conventions.[15]

REPRESENTING THE PARTY

One critical decision facing the national convention committee concerned the rules governing who would be eligible to attend the convention as voting delegates. The question was a fundamental one, for what it really meant was this: whose party was it? How much weight in the final selection should be assigned to the parliamentary caucus, the provincial association executives, or the local party notables? And what of the powerful interests who underwrote the electoral campaigns?

The organizing committee created three classes of delegates: ex officio, constituency, and at large. The ex officio category consisted of 'Conservative Members of the House of Commons, Conservative Candidates at the last Federal Election held in each Federal constituency, and Conservative Prime Ministers and Conservative Leaders of the Opposition in the different provinces.' To represent the local party workers across the country, each constituency was requested 'to select in the manner, as nearly as may be, in which Conservative Candidates are nominated for federal elections, four additional delegates, men or women or both at the option of the constituency, and also four substitute delegates.' Finally, to recognize the influence of the provincial associations, the committee authorized the selection of 'delegates at large' from each province. Initially the total number stipulated for this category was only seventy-five, weighted somewhat in favour of the more populous provinces. As the need to include more of the 'big men of the party' became apparent, the number of provincially appointed delegates at large was increased to a number 'not greater than the number of Federal constituencies in each such province.'[16] Furthermore, the organization committee, chaired by McRae, was 'empowered to select ten persons of national standing and importance in the Conservative Party as delegates-at-large.'[17]

Another factor in the decision to enlarge the number of delegates at large, besides the desire to include some of the party's 'big men,' was a determination to increase the number of female delegates (or, as many, including MacNicol, referred to them, 'the ladies').[18] The resolutions creating the constituency and at-large categories had carefully suggested the inclusion of women in each group, but then left the final decision to the local riding associations and provincial organizations, respectively. Evidently, the result was not found satisfactory by the central organizing committee. 'It is considered especially desirable that there should be a large woman [sic] representation,' T.H. Blacklock informed Premier Rhodes after a 30 April meeting of this committee. 'There is already a dissatisfaction among the Conservative women that they are not receiving the recognition to which they are entitled ... As the women voters number nearly half the electorate, we cannot afford to have such dissatisfaction.'[19] Such hard-headed realism led the committee to attach a rider to its resolution, enlarging the number of provincial delegates, such that 'twenty-five per cent at least ... should be women.' In the end, 255 women registered as delegates or alternates, or about 15 per cent of the total convention body.[20] The representation of other significant social groups such as labourers and farmers was left to the discretion of provincial and constituency associations. The party press, however, was allocated one delegate from 'each and every Conservative daily newspaper throughout Canada.'[21] Such a move was designed to involve the increasingly independent Tory dailies in the party's deliberations, and perhaps also to ensure more prominent news coverage of the convention.

In 1927, the average cost for travel and hotel accommodation was two hundred dollars per delegate, a large sum when ordinary labourers were earning perhaps five dollars a day.[22] Each delegate was expected to cover this cost personally; no subsidy was offered, beyond negotiating some group rates with the railways. These facts ensured two things:

TABLE 2
Representation at 1927 convention

Locality	Eligible votes at convention				Province's % of votes at convention	Province's % of seats in House of Commons
	Constituency	At-large	Ex-officio	Total votes		
Yukon	5	1	0	6	0.4	0.4
British Columbia	70	14	4	88	5.5	5.7
Alberta	80	15	6	101	6.4	6.5
Saskatchewan	105	21	10	136	8.6	8.6
Manitoba	85	17	24	126	7.9	6.9
Ontario	410	81	35	526	33.2	33.5
Quebec	325	60	18	403	25.4	26.5
New Brunswick	55	10	5	70	4.4	4.5
Nova Scotia	75	11	9	95	6.0	5.7
Prince Edward Island	20	3	2	25	1.6	1.6
Dominion-wide	0	10	0	10	0.6	0.0
Totals	1,230	243	113	1,586	100.0	100.0

SOURCES: P.C. Party Papers, vol. 239, 'Delegates: National Convention – 1927; M.C. Urquhart and K.A.H. Buckley, eds., *Historical Statistics of Canada* (Toronto 1965), 620

first, that attending delegates from outside the Winnipeg area were from the more affluent class; and, second, that many constituency delegates from the more distant regions simply did not attend. The final report of the credentials committee noted that 1,601 delegates had been authorized, but only 1,207 had registered.'[23] Most of the absentees were constituency representatives. To ensure each riding would have an equal voice, a proxy system was worked out whereby those delegates and alternates from a given constituency who were present at the convention could decide by majority vote among themselves 'how or in what proportion the votes of those selected to represent such constituency, who are not present, shall be polled.'[24] The result was to equalize the influence of each constituency, but also to emphasize the influence of the more well-heeled delegates able to afford the trip to Winnipeg.

Table 2 shows the relative influence of each province in the leadership vote, and compares this weighting with the one reflected in the make-up of the House of Commons. Note that the MP or defeated candidate has been included in the constituency rather than ex-officio category, since the proxy-voting rule guaranteed each constituency a weighting of five votes regardless of the attendance of the MP, defeated candidate, or all of the four locally chosen delegates. The provincial ratio at the convention was remarkably similar to that prevailing in the House of Commons, with the host province, Manitoba, somewhat overrepresented, and Quebec slightly underrepresented, in each case because of disproportionate numbers of ex-officio delegates. In neither case was the discrepancy of any real significance. If it be accepted that the MP or riding candidate was a legitimate representative of the rank and file, then constituency delegates' votes accounted for 77.6 per cent of the total. The delegate profile did reflect a disproportion of affluent males, when compared to the general population, but it probably was a faithful representation of Conservative party activists.

DRAFTING A PLATFORM

The string of twenty-two policy resolutions passed by the convention did not excite wild enthusiasm in the party ranks, or among the Canadian public. Indeed, one Conservative newspaper, the *Montreal Star*, was quite uncomplimentary. 'The loose and unrelated collection of resolutions which it has adopted – commonly with little discussion and even less consideration – come as near as such a flood of words possibly could to being the absolute zero in the way of "platforms,"' it lamented.[25] Yet, platitudes and generalities were just what many in the party élite desired from the convention. 'I do not think any convention should define with too great particularity the specific activities of the party,' Howard Ferguson suggested to Senator Smeaton White in July. 'We should deal with broad principles only.'[26] Lest the assembled delegates should overplay their hand, former leader Sir Robert Borden made the same point from the convention podium. 'You must not forestall too much,' he lectured, 'a leader who will be responsible to you, to parliament, and to the country, for the policy which is put before the people.'[27] In large measure, his words were heeded.

The resolutions committee consisted of 150 delegates, apportioned in such a way that the central provinces, Ontario and Quebec, accounted for just under half of them. Tiny Prince Edward Island was granted four members, the six medium-sized provinces had twelve each, while Quebec received thirty-three places, and Ontario had forty-one.'[28] The significance of the formula was that the Atlantic and western delegates swung more weight on the committee than would have been the case if strict representation by population had been followed.

When the resolutions committee convened at eight o'clock on the first evening of the convention, it was presented with some 150 resolutions that had been submitted by local associations from around the country. McRae had grouped and summarized them and, according to Grattan O'Leary, he 'threw scores of unwise resolutions into his waste basket,'[29] thus exercising some managerial control prior to the convention. One committee member, P.D. Ross of the *Ottawa Journal*, described the scene as the huge committee met: 'Imagine the chaos ... Well, the resolutions committee got duly busy at eight last evening, and we adjourned at 4:30 this morning with the work half done, resumed business at 10 o'clock, and while the convention was disposing of the first resolutions sent to it, the committee sat on and framed up the final ones.'[30] The committee members divided into subcommittees of about twenty, each with a particular subject area. Resolutions that reached the convention floor, then, had first been debated and passed by a subcommittee, which had perhaps based the wording on one or more of the resolutions submitted prior to the convention. Next, the full resolutions committee approved the motion, before the subcommittee chairman headed to the convention hall to propose, explain, and defend it. Where the committee spent hours agonizing over the precise wording of the platform, the full convention rushed through approval of even the most contentious planks 'with brief explanations and little discussion.'[31]

If there was a theme to the convention platform, it was contained in this innocuous resolution, simply headed 'Party Policy': 'The Liberal-Conservative Party whose founders have brought about Confederation and cemented its Provinces into an harmonious political whole, based upon common interest, common ideas, and mutual respect and affection of all its elements, stands everlastingly pledged to a policy which will at all times bring prosperity, contentment and peace to all its citizens irrespective of boundaries and of origins.'[32] The party sought, through its platform, to reach out to all the various regions and interests that made up the country, particularly those like the Prairie farmers and organized labourers who had largely resisted the party's appeals in 1925 and 1926. Unity and harmony under a Tory banner would not be created by sharpening differences and heightening emotions, but rather by overlooking divergent views and soothing hurt feelings. With three years expected before the next electoral campaign, the significance of the convention platform was not in what it said, but in what it symbolized.

A desire to woo the West was evident in many of the resolutions. The section on the tariff, for example, was toned down to such an extent it did not even mention the word 'protection.' It was presented as a policy to help the farmer preserve his Canadian markets, the worker maintain his job, and the country retain its sons and daughters who were currently being lured south in search of work. The resolution nodded in the direction of 'the welfare of the consumer,' endorsed preferential tariffs, and urged 'scientific investigation' of the policy by a 'permanent tariff commission.' The tilt to the West was also demonstrated by the transportation resolutions. Completion of the Hudson's Bay Railway, construction of the Pacific outlet for the Peace River district, development of the St Lawrence canal system, and federal aid to interprovincial highways were all popular with westerners. Furthermore, the convention pledged the party to maintain existing freight rates on grain, and subsidize the transportation of western coal into central Canada, as part of a 'national fuel policy.' Finally, the party endorsed the transfer of resource ownership to the three Prairie provinces.[33]

The Conservatives did not forget the other peripheral region, the Maritimes. A national fuel policy to subsidize coal would be as welcome to Nova Scotia as to Alberta, and it, along with the pledge to promote the use of Canadian ports, was a mainstay of the Maritime Rights movement, still a potent force in Atlantic Canada.[34] Naturally, the Conservatives endorsed the report of the Duncan Commission and pledged to enact all measures recommended by it to solve the Maritime grievances. With an empty resolution noting the 'primary importance' of the fishing industry to Canada thrown in for good measure, the Atlantic region had reason to believe, along with the West, that its presence was felt at the convention.

Significantly, there was not much in the platform to appeal specifically to Quebec. At the insistence of Sir George Foster and C.H. Cahan, both prominent anglophones, a clause was added to the natural-resources resolution on the convention floor stipulating that the school-land endowment funds set up by federal legislation in 1883 for the Northwest Territories would continue to be used solely 'for educational purposes.'[35] The implication was that separate schools would retain some public funding. The resolution on imperial relations was carefully worded to appease autonomists, some of whom were Quebeckers, by linking the mandatory pledge of 'loyalty to the Crown' with 'satisfaction at the position attained by Canada as a nation within the British Empire.' Autonomy within the empire had been in large measure an accomplishment of the former conservative prime minister Sir Robert Borden, but it was also linked to the current Liberal government of Mackenzie King. True-blue Ontario Tories had to accept a watered-down statement on the imperial issue, as well as on the tariff, to the visible annoyance of some, such as former Toronto mayor Tommy Church. He lambasted the trade resolution, for instance, as 'a weak apology for protection,' but his call for a firmer stance was not heeded.[36]

In an attempt to reach out to labour, the party endorsed a lengthy resolution based on the labour convention associated with the Treaty of Versailles of 1919. Specific reforms advocated were: employees' right of association; adequate wages; eight-hour work day; weekly day of rest; abolition of child labour; and equal remuneration for work of equal value by men and women. The resolution mapped out an active role for the government, stating that 'to promote industrial peace and human welfare is the duty of the State.' Linked to this pledge were several social-welfare proposals, which, if taken seriously, would have launched the Conservative party firmly on the path to a socially interventionist state. The delegates pledged the party, 'so far as is practicable, to support social legislation designed to conserve human life, health and temperance, to relieve distress during periods of unemployment, sickness and in old age.' However the qualifying clause, 'so far as is practicable,' was broad enough to save the party embarrassment, regardless of which approach the new leader took. A similar resolution, with a similar qualifier, had been passed by the Liberals in 1919.[37] With regard to old-age pensions, recently inaugurated by the Liberals as a shared-cost program with the provinces, the convention proposed that 'Pension legislation should be the subject of Federal Legislation only.' In this way, elderly residents of poorer provinces would be sure to receive a pension, as would those who lived in more affluent regions. These openly interventionist resolutions passed easily, with but one dissenting voice.[38] Nevertheless, the conclusion is inescapable that most delegates thought of them as election fodder, not blueprints for a social revolution.

Harmony, not consistency, was the order of the day when it came to platform-making at the convention. The difficult compromises were worked out in the resolutions committee, behind closed doors. 'You will probably have detected the skilful hand of our friend Sir Thomas [White] in the Tariff Resolutions,' J.M. Macdonnell informed Sir Joseph Flavelle.

`The sub-committee on Tariff furnished a fine example of mutual for-
bearance and concession on the part of the Manufacturing members of
the committee, Chaplin, Cockshutt and Cantley on the one hand, and
several farming members on the other.'[39] A similar mood of compromise
prevailed with regard to the St Lawrence canal, generally favoured by
the West and opposed by Quebec. As one committee member explained
to Howard Ferguson, 'Taking a position in favour of the Canal scheme
as an all Canadian project leaving the provinces free in relation to power
would unite all the provinces, give us good fighting ground and leave
the Government to get out of their own difficulties.'[40] Something for everyone but the Grits, in other words.

Only two policy resolutions provoked serious conflict on the convention floor. In the course of the debate on granting ownership of resources
to the Prairie provinces, a sharp clash arose between Armand Lavergne
of Quebec City and Dr John Wesley Edwards of Kingston. Their disagreement was fundamental, and involved two opposing views of
Canada. Lavergne favoured 'equality of races, of religion and of language.' Edwards countered with a plea that 'every person recognize the
Union Jack, and the English language, as the distinguishing marks of
our common Canadian citizenship.' Before the issue could tear the convention apart, cooler heads intervened to move the debate to safer
ground.[41] The second divisive issue was immigration, more particularly
a two-word clause that stated simply 'Oriental exclusion.' Although
many Conservatives, such as the ex-minister Sir George Foster and John
Haig of Winnipeg, found the baldly racist tone of the phrase objectionable,
their pleas were overlooked in the face of the single-minded determination of the West Coast Tories. 'Reject this report of the Resolutions
Committee,' declared Vancouver MP H.H. Stevens, 'and you put British
Columbia out of the Conservative party.' The resolution was passed, on
division.[42]

The policy platform represented a snapshot in time of what the first
national convention of Liberal-Conservatives was prepared to endorse,
in its quest to unify the party, inspire the electorate, and win the next
election. It was a moderately worded document, pieced together with
planks designed to appeal to all the major interest groups. Special attention had been paid to two classes whose support the party particularly
coveted: Prairie farmers and urban workers. Yet, when all was said and
done, the words and actions of the new leader would do far more to
determine Conservative policy than would this platform.

CHOOSING A NEW LEADER

The central function of the Winnipeg convention was to choose a new leader for the party. Much would be expected of the eventual victor. The newest heir to Macdonald would have to captain the parliamentary party; oversee the extraparliamentary organization; and stimulate public interest through tours, speeches, and interviews. The Conservatives wanted a winner, someone who would lead the party to power, and then keep it there. For such a demanding position, the list of desirable qualities was lengthy: oratorical skill, dexterity in debate, experience in public affairs, a reputation for integrity, and the ability to command loyalty and reconcile differences. As the legendary 'John A.' was dead and thus unavailable, the delegates sought their new chieftain from a list of less glittering contemporaries.

For many Conservatives, the 'dream' candidate was wily Howard Ferguson, the Ontario premier since 1923. He had taken a demoralized party from the aftermath of defeat in 1919 to a sweeping victory four years later, and kept them in power despite confronting two thorny issues: prohibition and French-language school instruction. His government's repeal, in September 1927, of the controversial Regulation 17, which had effectively curtailed French-language instruction in Ontario since 1912, was very well received in Quebec. Coming just one month prior to the Winnipeg convention, this action lent Ferguson's potential candidacy a momentum possessed by no other.[43] Ferguson had his drawbacks, however. The taint of scandal, reaching back to his days as minister of lands and forests, continued to linger, though no wrongdoing had ever been definitively established. His shrewd grasp of the realities of electoral politics made him suspect to some as being too shallow, crass, and manipulative. Furthermore, his total political experience was in Ontario. National politics took place on a different stage, before a different audience, with a different supporting cast.

Ferguson did not campaign overtly for the leadership, and, in fact, stoutly denied any such aspirations. Writing to a correspondent in May, he protested, 'Because I made two or three patriotic addresses, everybody apparently jumped to the conclusion that I was angling for the Dominion leadership, so I stopped talking.'[44] The premier's reticence was not considered much of an obstacle to his eventual selection. In this, the party's first leadership convention, there was a strong feeling that the office should seek the man (it being assumed no woman was suitable). Keeping personal ambitions hidden from view was practically a precondition for any serious campaign.

Ferguson supporters were legion, particularly in the central provinces. Typical of the exhortations he received was this bit of flattery from F.D.L. Smith, of the Conservative Toronto *Mail and Empire*: 'The legend runs that you have the John A. Macdonald touch, that you have the genius for success, that you are a statesman as well as an astute politician, that you have a passion for real public service, that you are wise in the choice of your associates and agents, that you have the persuasive power to enlist influential men in support of your policies, and that if you allow your name to go to the Convention all other contenders will fade into the dim distance.'[45] A two-page letter signed by sixteen prominent anglophone business leaders, including Ward Pitfield, J.M. Macdonnell, General E. McCuaig, G.L. Ogilvie, and W.M. Birks, similarly urged Ferguson to offer himself as leader. 'There is throughout the length and breath [*sic*] of this Country,' these men declared, 'as there is undoubtedly in the City of Montreal, an almost universal feeling among Conservatives that if you would take the Leadership of the Party we should be in a fair way to regain, in the not distant future, the enviable position which our party so long occupied.'[46]

Ferguson did his best to quell the speculation, rampant in the press as well as in party circles, that he planned to toss his hat in the ring. Only days before the convention, he denied any such ambitions in a letter to Lord Atholstan, declaring, 'I have reached the conclusion that I can give better service both to the country and the party by continuing my activities in the provincial field.'[47] Still the rumours persisted. As one Hamilton Tory put it, 'Is it going to be a case of "Saying she would ne'er consent, consented" '?[48] Many Tories thought so. From the train carrying delegates west to Winnipeg, the *Globe* reporter noted the widely accepted belief that 'if the Prime Minister of Ontario will accept the leadership of the Conservative party there will be no contest.'[49]

One other figure loomed large over party proceedings. Arthur Meighen had created the leadership vacancy by his resignation. Many Conservatives could see no one able to fill that vacancy, save Meighen himself. It was well remembered that the Quebec and Saskatchewan delegations, representing two provinces in which the Conservatives had fared very poorly in the 1926 election, had been among those at the October 1926 special caucus who strongly urged Meighen to stay on.[50] Shortly thereafter, the editor of the Tory *London Free Press* had suggested to Meighen that he might well succeed himself: 'For the present I agree with you that it was the best to retire. If you had remained there would have been grumbling and dissatisfaction in certain quarters. However, I believe that when the time for the convention comes there will be an over-whelming desire for your return as leader.'[51] Many other Conservatives continued to feel the same way. Meighen was an attractive choice for several reasons. His intelligence, his eloquence, his ability to inspire devotion in his followers, and his skill in parliamentary debate were unexcelled. And yet, Meighen had failed the ultimate test: as a leader, he had not been a winner, despite three tries. Though he could motivate those who already agreed with him, he could not conciliate opponents, reconcile differences among his followers, or convince the uncommitted to join him. Like Ferguson, Meighen denied any interest in the leadership. In a letter to the Honourable Donald Sutherland, who had suggested that Meighen would 'eventually be the choice of the convention,' Meighen sought to dispel the rumours. 'It has never been my thought to become my own successor,' he wrote, 'and in any event I have not seen throughout the country any very general desire that this should take place.'[52]

The non-candidacies of Meighen and Ferguson collided head on in dramatic fashion at the convention's first public session. Meighen had agreed to deliver 'a short address.'[53] Characteristically, he chose a con-troversial topic: the defence of his Hamilton speech of November 1925. In that address, delivered during a critical by-election in Bagot, Quebec, Meighen had committed his party to a new departure in foreign policy in the hopes of defusing some of the conscriptionist apprehension in Quebec. 'The new feature,' he explained to the convention, 'was this, that, in the event of an outbreak of war, the government would come to its decision; act upon its decision in the way of mobilization and organi-zation; and obtain the verdict of the people.'[54] Before any troops were sent into battle, a Meighen government would seek an electoral mandate from the people. In one of the most eloquent addresses of a career studded with magnificent orations, Meighen stoutly defended this policy initiative, which had provoked widespread opposition among anglo-phone Tories, and not visibly improved the party's popularity in Quebec. P.D. Ross of the *Ottawa Journal*, a man who strongly opposed the content of Meighen's speech, filed this admiring description of its style: 'For an hour and a half he waded into the convention with a speech splendid in form and fire. It was eloquent, it was picturesque, it was dramatic, it was, toward the close, poignant and touching, and beyond all doubt it won the sympathy of a majority of the convention.'[55] When at last he sat down, the ovation was thunderous.

Before the applause for Meighen had died away, a red-faced Howard Ferguson strode purposefully to the microphone. An unscheduled speaker, he did not deliver a polished address. Before three sentences were uttered, he was rudely greeted by cries of 'Sit down' and 'Shut up.' 'I never could see the wisdom of digging up a corpse that had been buried for two years,' the premier shot back, 'just for the purpose of raising a smell.'[56] A *Winnipeg Free Press* reporter caught the intensity of the moment: 'The delegates from Alberta, Saskatchewan, Nova Scotia, and New Brunswick appear to be all on their feet booing Mr. Ferguson. There are a few cries from the Quebec block. The Ontario block on the right is keeping silent.'[57] Though visibly shaken, Ferguson would not leave the podium. 'If Mr. Meighen adheres to that view,' he shouted, 'I want you to understand that I, as a Liberal-Conservative, entirely disagree with him and repudiate that view; and if this convention chooses to endorse him, I will disassociate myself from the activity of the convention.'[58] As he returned to his seat on the platform, most of the western and maritime delegates gave three cheers for Meighen, while the Ontario delegation rose in support of their premier. An ugly party split was graphically revealed for all to see, just when unity was supposed to prevail.

Any chance of Howard Ferguson becoming the national party leader ended, then and there. By contrast, 'a pro-Meighen wave of sentiment' swept the convention for the next several hours. Had Meighen chosen to run, and had the vote been held that first evening, he would have won easily.[59] By the morrow, sober second thoughts had taken hold. Meighen's triumph had betrayed his fatal weakness. He could win debates, but not without creating divisions, often within his own ranks. The local Conservative paper, the Winnipeg *Tribune*, spoke for most of the national Tory press, and indeed echoed the sentiment of most of the party élite, when it stated unequivocally in its next edition, 'Howard Ferguson saved the day, saved the Conservative party from the disgrace of silent acquiescence in a defence of the Hamilton speech.'[60] It had been from among the crowd of party bigwigs – privy councillors, premiers, and provincial leaders – up on the convention stage that Ferguson had emerged to denounce Meighen's speech. Seated next to Ferguson had been R.B. Bennett. The rank and file might love Arthur Meighen, but the élite had had their fill of him.

Despite considerable delegate pressure to change his mind, the former national leader opted not to enter the leadership fray. He had had enough of leading a fractured party. Many influential party supporters had had enough of his fractious leadership style. The ultimate result of the dramatic clash between Meighen and Ferguson was that neither would wear the mantle of Macdonald.

With these two men effectively out of the running, the focus of the convention shifted to several other prominent Conservatives. Besides Ferguson, there were two other Tory premiers at that time, J.B.M. Baxter of New Brunswick and E.N. Rhodes of Nova Scotia. Both had served for a time in Ottawa as MPs; both had benefited from the Maritime Rights wave of resentment to gain provincial office. Neither was eager to forsake power at home for the prospect of several years of opposition in Ottawa. By staying where they were, they could assist the rejuvenation of the national party through their control of the provincial patronage. 'I am not the man who should be selected as Leader,' Rhodes had informed a correspondent firmly in May,[61] and Baxter was equally resolute. Both men were nominated at the convention, as were Meighen and Ferguson, but none of this group consented to stand.

Fortunately, the caucus contained several men of ability and experience. Among these were Hugh Guthrie, the interim parliamentary leader; R.B. Bennett, the lone Tory MP from the Prairie provinces; H.H. Stevens, the Vancouver MP who had uncovered the Customs scandal in 1926; Sir Henry Drayton, former head of the national railway commission; Sir George Perley, who had represented the Borden government in London during the First World War; C.H. Cahan, a St James Street lawyer with ties to the Quebec Nationalists; and R.J. Manion, a decorated war veteran from Fort William who had served in both of Meighen's short lived cabinets. All of these men were nominated, though Stevens and Perley declined to run.[62] Perley, who was already seventy years old, had no desire to begin a new career at his age. Stevens, however, was forty-eight, in vigorous good health, and a sixteen-year Commons veteran with experience in two cabinet portfolios; trade and commerce, and customs. A major reason Stevens declined to run would emerge a few months after the convention, when a company with which he was associated, the Manufacturers' Finance Corporation, went bankrupt. Within two years of the convention, he would announce his retirement from politics in order to shore up his personal finances. Stevens lacked the material resources to forsake his own private affairs in favour of a full-time pursuit of the party's interests.[63] As a result, the field was narrowed to six candidates: five from the caucus, along with a former minister, Robert Rogers of Manitoba.

When the results of the first ballot were counted, only thirty-one delegates had cast their votes for Drayton. Yet, he was far from a nuisance candidate. After serving ably as the chief commissioner of the National Railway Board from 1912 to 1919, he was appointed to replace Sir Thomas White as Borden's minister of finance. Drayton won re-election from the Toronto riding of West York[64] through the 1920s with huge majorities. In the short-lived 1926 ministry, he had served as House leader. Unfortunately for Drayton, it was during his acting leadership of the Conservative forces in Parliament that King's Liberals successfully moved non-confidence in the new government, precipitating the Tories' rapid return to opposition. Meighen was not alone in concluding that Drayton proved 'utterly incapable of handling the leadership in troubled hours when I could no longer take my seat.'[65]

Drayton did not actively campaign. As the *Globe* reporter noted, 'He has not lifted a finger to get the leadership, and will not do so, but he will accept if that is the will of the convention.'[66] With the support of E.L. Patenaude behind him, and possessing a modest fluency in French, Drayton based his appeal on his ability to span the two solitudes. As nominator, Drayton chose Charles Duquette, the bilingual ex-mayor of Montreal, while as seconder he selected F.W. Turnbull, a unilingual Regina attorney. A woefully weak speech ended any chance he had to be a factor in the final outcome. 'Not content with being a buffoon in English,' J.M. Macdonnell reported to Sir Joseph Flavelle later, 'he tried it also in French ... I discovered many of the French Delegates, among whom I was seated, convulsed with laughter.'[67] The result was to turn a dark-horse candidacy into an embarrassment.

The fifth-place finisher, with 114 first-ballot votes, was Robert Rogers, favourite son of host Manitoba. 'The Honourable Bob' was sixty-three years old, and almost a pure example of the old political warhorse. As minister of public works, first in Manitoba and then under Borden in Ottawa, Rogers had directed government patronage with both skill and pleasure. An undisguised, unrepentant Conservative partisan, he bitterly opposed the movement to Union government, and was dropped from cabinet in 1917. An unforgiving rival of Meighen, Rogers had little role in national party affairs in the 1920s. Indeed, he was personally defeated in 1921 and 1926, and played only a minor role in the short Parliament that followed the election of 1925.

Though his contacts were a bit rusty, Rogers had hundreds of political 'IOUs' on which to draw among local party officials in every province, dating back to his days as Borden's minister of public works. His opposition to Meighen's leadership had endeared him to some of the St James Street barons.[68] Furthermore, as a native of Argenteuil County, Quebec, and able to speak passably in French, Rogers hoped for significant support from Quebec delegates. In Ontario, his candidacy was supported by 'a small Toronto group of whom T.L. Church, MP, was the most prominent.'[69] Finally, as a Winnipeg resident, he could count on strong local support, bolstered by his key role in overseeing convention arrangements. So strong did he appear in the months leading up to the convention that some urged Ferguson to run on the basis that he was 'the only man to beat the machine candidate.'[70]

As did Drayton, Rogers alternated anglophone and francophone in his choice of nominator (W.J. Tupper) and seconder (Louis Cousineau) and delivered a portion of his speech in French. In addition, he tried to reach out to another significant delegate group, delivering an elaborate tribute to the 'ladies' present. Rogers staked his appeal firmly on the bases of 'party loyalty' and the traditional policies of Macdonald, 'national unity' and 'national development,' by which he meant bicultural accommodation and the protective tariff.[71] It was a speech out of the past, delivered in a dull monotone by a white-haired veteran of political battles dating back to the previous century, heard by a convention anxious to put a fresh face on the party. The 'machine candidate' was not wanted as party leader. His courtesy vote on the first ballot largely disappeared on the next round.

The other 'Bob,' R.J. Manion, was a genuine dark-horse candidate who came from nowhere to finish a very respectable fourth, with 170 first-ballot votes. Manion confided in a private diary that he had not decided to run till the eve of the convention. '[There] was quite [a] boom for me. I held out but on [the] 10th I consented to run.'[72] A surgeon, an author, a war veteran, first elected to Parliament in 1917, Manion had served with Meighen as minister of soldiers' civil re-establishment in 1921, and as postmaster general in 1926. A lusty partisan, valiant debater, and colourful platform orator; handsome, dashing, and congenial; Manion possessed yet another asset: to his own passable French he added a French-Canadian wife. Not everyone viewed Manion's Catholicism as a plus. Though Manion was popular with most Protestant Ontario Conservatives, for many of whom he had stumped in recent provincial and

federal campaigns, the *Globe* was only being accurate when it noted ob-
liquely that 'the fact that he is a Roman Catholic may have lessened his
strength in some quarters.'[73]

Manion chose as his nominator and seconder two Ontario MLAs, the
Catholic J.M. Robb, of Algoma, and the Protestant Wilfrid S. Haney, of
Sarnia. To underscore his openness to the French factor, he delivered a
small portion of his own speech in that language. Manion's theme was
party and national unity, but his delivery was not marked by its usual
fiery eloquence. The final speaker of the evening, Manion did not begin
until after midnight, when both he and his audience were past their
best.[74] Manion's strategy on voting day was to draw on political 'IOUs' in
Ontario to make a good showing on the first ballot. 'Quebec promised
me support after first vote for Cahan,' he noted in his diary. Manion's
hopes were blocked on both counts. As for Ontario, Manion learned that
'Bennett's supporters took fright and Howard Ferguson used the whip
on many of my followers.' Meanwhile, Quebec's French-Canadian delegates stuck with Cahan, 'a hopeless cause' in Manion's view.[75] Manion
was overlooking the negative effect in Quebec of his own record as a
Unionist Liberal. Still, his candidacy had raised his profile in the party
without incurring either material expense or permanent enemies. At age
forty-five, he could easily wait for the next contest.

C.H. Cahan received 310 votes on the first ballot, in many ways an
unusually high total for a man who was nearly sixty-six, had been an MP
for only two years, and had delivered such a dull convention speech
that his audience was visibly bored.[76] To be sure, Cahan had the most
interesting *curriculum vitae* among the nominees. A native Nova Scotian,
Cahan had edited the Tory Halifax *Herald*, and then led the provincial
Conservative party while completing his bar exams. Moving to Montreal,
Cahan came to represent several blue-chip corporations in various Car-
ibbean and Latin American countries. He developed close ties with
Henri Bourassa, and played a key role in the Conservative-Nationaliste
alliance of 1911. Near the end of the First World War, he was appointed
director of public safety, and played a prominent part in the suppression
of socialist and foreign elements.

Along the way, Cahan's abrasive, uncompromising independence had
won him many enemies. In Nova Scotia, he had quarrelled in turn with
Sir Charles Tupper, Sir John Thompson, and Sir Robert Borden.[77] Twice he
had been forced to forgo a party nomination – in 1896 in favour of Borden,
and in 1917 in favour of the Liberal-Unionist C.C. Ballantyne – and he
deeply resented both snubs ever after. His record as director of public

safety did not endear him to the working class, nor did his staunch support of tariffs appeal to the farmers. As a Tory MP, Cahan proved to be 'a thorn in the side of poor Mr. Meighen.'[78] In 1925, with the Hamilton speech, and again in 1926, with the Hudson Bay Railway, Cahan publicly disassociated himself from his leader's positions. As the 'favourite son' of St James Street,[79] Cahan was the sort of ally Meighen could well do without, and indeed he did exclude the crusty though able Montrealer from his 1926 cabinet.

Cahan began his campaign early, behind the scenes. At a meeting of Quebec Conservatives, held in Three Rivers in November 1926, he was appointed chairman of a committee to organize Quebec's convention delegation. From this vantage point, he acquired considerable control over the selection of delegates.[80] His connections to Henri Bourassa and to Montreal business combined to make him Quebec's favourite son. After one ballot, he hoped to draw in the supporters of Robert Rogers. As one delegate remembered it, 'it was rumoured around the backrooms and the lobbies that Rogers and Cahan had made a secret deal. The one who fell behind on the first ballot would persuade his following to vote for the other.'[81] Cahan also attempted to woo Howard Ferguson, even travelling to Toronto to meet the premier in May 1927. In September, Cahan was reported in the *Globe* to have claimed Ferguson was supporting him, a rumour he was forced to deny.[82]

In the end, Cahan's strategy failed. Rogers did not deliver his supporters to Cahan after the first ballot, opting to stay in the race. Most of his delegates went to Bennett. Ferguson, too, supported Bennett. Ferguson's clash with Meighen on opening day did enable Cahan to retain his Quebec supporters, many of whom had gone to Winnipeg planning to vote for Ferguson, after a courtesy ballot for Cahan on the first round.[83] As neither of the front runners, Bennett and Guthrie, had bothered overly much to appeal to French Canada, the Quebec delegation had little alternative. Characteristically, Cahan blamed his defeat on a malicious plot, ostensibly organized against him because of his defence of minority school rights in the West. Manion's candidacy he wrote off as a nasty ploy to drain off his own Catholic supporters. 'It is utterly impossible,' Macdonnell informed Flavelle, 'for Cahan to realize that probably not ten people outside the Province of Quebec had ever even considered him as a possibility.'[84]

The runner-up candidate, with 345 first-ballot votes, was Hugh Guthrie. Tall and dignified, Guthrie looked the part of a prime minister. As a speaker, he had few peers in the Commons, or on the hustings. Of all the candidates, he had the longest parliamentary experience, having been first elected from South Wellington in 1900 at the age of thirty-four. The Conservative caucus had recognized his abilities in October 1926, when they selected him as their interim parliamentary leader. Guthrie proved to be an effective, if not dynamic, House leader – 'competent without being inspirational,' in the words of one commentator.[85] In view of their recent defeat and upcoming convention, the Conservatives did not mount an all-out effort to defeat the government. Still, Guthrie showed sufficient skill as interim leader that a majority of the caucus appears to have supported him at the convention.[86]

Guthrie's biggest drawback was that, for seventeen of his twenty-seven years in Parliament, he had been a Liberal. It was not until 1917 that Guthrie crossed the floor of the House, in connection with the wartime movement for conscription and Union government. In the watershed reciprocity election of 1911, he had been one of only thirteen Ontario Liberals to resist the Tory tide. As a late convert, Guthrie was suspect in die-hard Tory circles as something of a closet Grit. Guthrie compounded this suspicion by an unfortunate slip of the tongue at the official opening of the Winnipeg convention. With three raps of the gavel, he officially declared the 'National Liberal' convention to be opened. Amidst laughter from the audience, he quickly corrected it to the 'National Liberal-Conservative' convention, but the damage was done.[87] Nothing his rivals might have said could have been better calculated to renew the old doubts about Guthrie's fidelity to the Tory cause.

Guthrie based his candidacy on a specific issue to a much greater degree than any of the other nominees. His speech to the delegates sounded the keynote of his campaign. 'I have laid it down as my opinion that the first duty of the Conservative party was to cast its eyes towards Western Canada, where, unfortunately, at the present time we have little support,' he declared. In his view, the National Policy had to be made more attractive to Prairie voters, with downward freight-rate adjustments, tariff revisions, and subsidies to specific industries.[88] As interim leader, he had made no secret of the direction he felt the party should go, provoking a savage reaction from the Montreal *Gazette*, which complained in June: 'he advocates openly a sectional policy of the most extreme and extravagant kind.' Such a policy might sacrifice Montreal business interests, the *Gazette* feared. Guthrie the ex–Unionist Liberal was not popular with French Canadians either. His choice as interim leader in 1926 was termed a 'grand désastre' by *Le Devoir*.[89] His notion of 'a united Canada,' as outlined in his convention speech, was to 'obliterate class distinctions ... race distinctions, creed distinctions, geographical distinction(s).' In Guthrie's melting-pot, there would not be much room for a distinctive French Canada. As the admittedly partisan Cahan had earlier noted to Georges Pelletier of *Le Devoir*. 'Mr Guthrie by his recent speeches has disclosed that he knows nothing of the mentality, opinions and aspirations of our people.'[90] It is doubtful if any candidate had as little delegate support from Quebec as did Guthrie.

To win, Guthrie needed overwhelming support from English Canada. He did not get it. Although he received the backing of 'a large number of the Ontario members' by Ferguson's own reckoning, the rank-and-file delegates from Ontario proved more loyal to their premier than to their MPs. 'My great weakness,' Guthrie later informed Meighen, 'was in the Province of Ontario where, out of over five hundred votes I only secured something like 100 to 125. Our friend Ferguson attended to this part of the programme.' As an Ontarian himself, Guthrie had hoped for more. 'From what I can gather,' he revealed in a press interview, 'I ran well in Prince Edward Island and Nova Scotia and likewise in Saskatchewan and British Columbia,' all provinces without native-son candidates.[91] One of Guthrie's votes came from Arthur Meighen, but, unlike Ferguson, Meighen lifted not a finger to aid his personal favourite, believing his proper public role was one of neutrality.[92]

The choice of the convention, Richard Bedford Bennett, was, at age fifty-seven, the second-youngest of the six candidates. Born and raised in New Brunswick, of Loyalist parentage, he had first taught school, and then practised law, before heeding a call to the West. In 1896, Bennett moved to Calgary, where he joined the law firm of Sir James Lougheed, a well-known Conservative. Blessed with a prodigious memory, an enormous capacity for hard work, and an amazing eloquence that provoked the nickname 'Bonfire' Bennett, the young New Brunswicker was soon arguing cases before the Judicial Committee of the Privy Council, profiting from shrewd investments in concert with his Maritime friend Max Aitken (later Lord Beaverbrook), and leading the Conservative opposition forces in the Alberta legislature. In 1911, he was the sole Alberta Conservative elected to Ottawa.[93]

Bennett chafed at the limitations imposed on lowly government backbenchers. Privately, he badgered Borden for a cabinet or Senate appointment, while publicly he locked horns with Meighen over the government's bail-out of the troubled Canadian Northern Railway. For a time he occupied himself as chairman of the National Service Board, charged with wartime manpower registration. In 1917, he declined to run for re-election in face of Borden's inclusion of his old Alberta rival, the Liberal premier Arthur Sifton, in the new coalition ministry. In 1921, Bennett ran again in West Calgary, only to lose by sixteen votes. Though his political career had stalled, Bennett continued to flourish on the legal and business fronts. He was for many years the western solicitor for the Canadian Pacific Railway. From a female friend of his youth, he inherited control of the E.B. Eddy paper empire. The sale of his interest in Alberta Pacific Grain brought him in excess of one million dollars. Large profits accrued from his role, along with Aitken, in the organization and later sale of the Canada Cement, Calgary Power, and Calgary Brewing companies. By the mid-1920s, he had acquired a string of corporate directorships 'as long as his arm.' Among the prominent companies with which he was associated were the Royal Bank, Imperial Oil, Imperial Tobacco, and Canada Packers.[94]

Bennett resumed his political career in 1925, winning election in West Calgary. One year later, when every other Tory candidate across the Prairies was defeated, Bennett increased his winning margin substantially. This feat more than any other stamped Bennett as 'a winner.' Bennett played a key role in the Session of 1926, first on the committee investigating the Customs scandal, and then as minister of finance in Meighen's short-lived government. Although Bennett flatly refused to let his name stand for temporary leader in October 1926, his star continued to shine in the 1927 session.[95]

Publicly Bennett denied interest in the leadership, though privately he did concede that, 'if the Convention seemed to be going for Mr. Rogers, he himself would reluctantly step into the breach.'[96] Though Bennett later declared to his friend Beaverbrook, 'I did not seek the position,' others recollected differently. H.H. Stevens felt 'he was very active in seeking the election,' and Meighen noted that 'Mr. Bennett ... was very ambitious.' Certainly there were others who were ambitious for him. Rod Finlayson, a convention delegate and later a prime-ministerial aide to Bennett, recalled that 'the word was quietly passed along that the man for the job was R.B. Bennett.' Among those passing the word were three Tory titans: Howard Ferguson, A.D. McRae, and H.H. Stevens.[97]

As both Guthrie and Manion realized, Howard Ferguson's influence on the Ontario delegation was decisive in swinging votes away from them and into the Bennett column. The Conservative editor and organizer Arthur Ford, of the *London Free Press*, contended that Ferguson was the convention's kingmaker. 'Mr Bennett could largely thank Hon. Howard

Ferguson for being chosen leader,' he maintained. 'It was the quiet, behind-the-scenes support of the Ontario Premier which threw the balance in his favour.' Another Tory journalist, Grattan O'Leary, nominated A.D. McRae for the honour, claiming it was he 'who determined that R.B. Bennett should be the Conservative leader.' After overseeing the organization, and playing a large, though indirect, role in deciding the representation of the convention, McRae chose the very eve of the convention to make the dramatic announcement that, 'as a delegate from North Vancouver,' he was 'unequivocally in support of Hon. R.B. Bennett for the leadership of the Conservative party.' Having served in caucus and on the organizing committee with both Guthrie and Bennett, the two acknowledged front runners, McRae's public choice of the latter was nasty, well-timed, and effective. Stevens's decision to renounce his own nomination in favour of Bennett was also critical. The runner-up to Guthrie in the ballot for interim leader, Stevens was well known across Canada for his role in uncovering the Customs scandal. Bennett paid tribute to his British Columbia colleague's decisive role on the convention platform after the final vote tally. 'Harry, I owe this entirely to you,' Stevens recalled him saying. 'You are the one that put me here.'[98]

Bennett presented himself as the candidate able to unite party and country behind traditional Liberal-Conservative 'convictions and principles.' To symbolize his own roots in both East and West, Bennett chose L.P.D. Tilley, a New Brunswick MLA and bearer of a historic family name, as his nominator, and A.A. McGillivray, an Alberta MLA, as his seconder. Tilley stressed that Bennett was 'a winner,' while McGillivray lauded his magnificent rise from humble origins to the pinnacle of his profession. In the buoyant, success-oriented, business-worshipping late 1920s, Bennett's background was impressive. Missing from the nomination symbolism and rhetoric was any recognition of French Canada. Missing also was even one word of French in an otherwise effective convention speech by Bennett.[99] There were tactical reasons for the omission.

Bennett's closest rival was Guthrie, not Cahan. To win, Bennett needed the support of anglophone Conservatives, many of whom still resented French-Canadian antipathy to conscription and Borden's wartime government. There was little to be gained from catering to the minority French-Canadian bloc, when Drayton spoke better French, Rogers was a Quebec native, Manion had a French-Canadian wife, and Cahan largely controlled the Quebec delegation and commanded nationalist respect. A *Montreal Star* survey did show Bennett gaining Quebec support on the decisive second ballot. The French-Canadian delegates stayed with Cahan, but many anglophone Quebeckers clearly preferred Bennett to Guthrie, regardless of their first choice. Bennett's traditional Liberal-Conservatism was more appealing to them than Guthrie's blatant lean to the West.[100]

Bennett's victory, then, was the result of a combination of his own strengths and his opponents' weaknesses. He was a vigorous, articulate, self-assured, wealthy, successful lawyer-businessman, with personal ties to both the Maritimes and the West, who had proven both his vote-getting and his parliamentary capacities. Guthrie was anathema in Quebec, and could not carry a majority in his native Ontario. Furthermore, he was unable to shake his Liberal past. Cahan was strictly a Quebec favourite son. Manion suffered from being too young, a Catholic, and a Liberal Unionist. Rogers was too old, and suffered from a well-deserved reputation as a political fixer. Drayton was a capable administrator with very few political skills. In the end, Bennett was the most acceptable choice for the English-Canadian delegates who, far outnumbering the French-Canadian delegation, had their way at Winnipeg.

FACING THE FUTURE

The purposes of the Winnipeg convention had been fourfold: to choose a leader, draft a platform, gain publicity, and boost party morale. Generally, the new leader was hailed in the press. The *Globe* coverage was typical: 'Mr. Bennett has an abundance of energy ... His legal acumen and his business ability are of a high order. He has had long experience in legislative halls. He possesses culture and the advantages gained by much travel.' A note of caution crept into the *Ottawa Journal* editorial, where it was noted that 'there are those who hold that Bennett is temperamental and emotional.'[101] Whatever his faults, it was agreed he definitely had 'star' qualities.

The platform was not an inspiring document, but it did avoid many obvious pitfalls. The planks were sufficiently general in tone to allow the leader and his caucus wide leeway in formulating parliamentary tactics and electoral strategy. At the same time, all the major ethnic, regional, and occupational groups had been saluted with resolutions of one form or another, in particular two key target groups: western farmers and urban labourers. The party showed itself sufficiently aware of the new problems associated with urbanization and industrialization to include resolutions dealing with labour rights, social welfare, Maritime stagnation, western alienation, increasing ethnicity, and the development of new staples such as hydroelectric power.

The convention was highly successful as a publicity event. Nearly a hundred journalists filed stories to the four corners of the Dominion via telegraph, while radio coverage reached thousands of homes. The speculation about Ferguson's candidacy, Guthrie's gaffe in opening the convention, the drama of Ferguson against Meighen, the mystery surrounding Meighen's intentions, the excitement of balloting day, even the tense clash between Edwards and Lavergne about bilingualism – all were grist for the media mill.

Party morale received a tremendous boost from the convention. The decision of both Meighen and Ferguson to forgo the leadership prevented a divisive battle that would have left one winner and two losers: the defeated candidate and the party itself. As it was, Bennett's victory was hailed by all in attendance, albeit with somewhat less enthusiasm among the French-speaking delegates. In symbolic terms, however, the bicultural nature of Canada was recognized by joint convention chairmen, Premier Rhodes and Senator Beaubien; by the reading of the Lord's Prayer in French and English; by special welcomes from the Winnipeg hosts in both languages; by the immediate translation of all major announcements made in English into French; and by allowing speakers to use either of the two languages at the podium. Special meetings for women and youth delegates engendered enthusiasm among these party groups as well. The simple fact of constituency delegates from across the country rubbing shoulders and swapping stories as they shared in a historic event injected new life into a dejected party. The massive effort coordinated by McRae to organize the convention previewed the organizational efficiency required to carry the next election. As the convention ended, the party faithful were ready and eager to be Bennett's 'missionaries' in the great cause of Conservative victory.

Significantly, a number of contradictions within the party were left unresolved. A party intent on wooing western farmers and urban labourers was still in alliance with eastern business. A party looking for a breakthrough in francophone Quebec had chosen a candidate with little understanding of or sympathy for French Canadians. Bennett had carried the convention because he looked and sounded like a winner, a proven vote-getter with ties to the West and roots in the Maritimes, who nevertheless could reassure the traditional party supporters in Ontario and anglo Quebec of his fealty to their cherished principles. Still, he was a millionaire seeking the support of common people. Little was known about the degree of his personal commitment to the progressive reform measures in the convention platform. In the apparently prosperous late 1920s, that seemed not to matter. There was very little immediate public pressure for major reforms. The Conservative party's overriding priority would be organizational, not ideological.

3 Building for Victory:
The Conservatives in Opposition,
1927–1930

An air of expectancy filled the Commons chamber on 1 May 1930 as the new minister of finance, Charles Dunning, rose to speak. Canadian dignitaries and foreign emissaries filled the Speaker's Gallery. The media scribes were poised expectantly. The visitors' galleries were jammed to capacity, and long lines filled the hallways.[1] In a quiet voice, Dunning delivered his dramatic May-Day budget statement. For free-traders, he announced the extension of the British preferential tariff on a large number of items, including fresh vegetables from the West Indies, tea, and porcelain. For protectionists, he introduced a series of countervailing duties to combat rising American tariffs, embodied in the Smoot-Hawley bill. For the farmers, he served notice that the unrestricted entry of New Zealand butter would be terminated in October. For consumers, the sales tax was cut in half. Furthermore, he announced a healthy surplus of $45 million during the preceding fiscal year.[2] Dunning sat down to thunderous applause from the Liberal benches. Led by Prime Minister King, the entire cabinet came forward to shake his hand.

The din had subsided but a little when opposition leader R.B. Bennett rose to his feet to reply. Disdaining the customary motion for adjournment, he launched into a spirited attack on Dunning, his Liberal colleagues, and his budget. The Conservative members, fresh from heckling the finance minister, now seized the opportunity to cheer their own chieftain. 'It is always a matter of satisfaction to see sinners turn from their sins,' Bennett declared to noisy approval from his supporters, but, he added, 'a countervailing duty that is now to prevail in the Dominion of Canada is a policy made in Washington.' As the Liberals jeered, Bennett issued his challenge. 'The people are the final arbiters, and ... should have an opportunity to decide.'[3]

Five days later, on 6 May 1930, Bennett formally moved want-of-confidence in the Liberal government, in a motion seconded by H.H. Stevens. 'This administration, having lost the confidence of the country, he declared, 'cannot safely be entrusted with the direction of the fiscal policy of Canada nor the carrying into effect of proposals to which it has heretofore been opposed.' Moments later, the prime minister answered the challenge. 'In the opinion of the government,' he informed Mr Speaker, 'it is desirable that a general election should be held this year ... at the earliest possible date.'[4] As King sat down, Grit and Tory members alike leaped from their seats, pounded their desks, tossed their blue books and order papers into the air, and shouted themselves hoarse. Election fever had been rampant in Ottawa for weeks; now, at last, the call to the polls was issued. And, despite the initial popularity of Dunning's budget proposals with press and public, the Conservatives were very confident of victory.

How realistic were the Conservative hopes? Answering this question requires an analysis of the federal Tory party from the morrow of the leadership convention in October 1927 to the announcement of the election in May 1930. During this period the new leader, R.B. Bennett, worked very hard to burnish his own public image, rejuvenate a disheartened parliamentary caucus, and breathe life into a haphazard party organization. Special attention was directed at Quebec and Saskatchewan, two normally Liberal bastions that might respond to renewed Conservative appeals. Policy positions were chosen with the next election as much in mind as past party history. If Bennett and his associates had done their work well, then victory at the polls was a very real possibility. Two key allies, depression and discontent, would be available for service in the election campaign to come.

TAKING STOCK: OCTOBER 1927

As he contemplated the magnitude of the new responsibility handed him by the Conservative party at Winnipeg, Bennett would have mused upon the question posed by Arthur Meighen. What manner of party did he now lead? What were its strong points and shortcomings? Before moving to shore up weaknesses, he needed to take inventory of its strengths, both in Parliament and across the country.

The doughtiest fighters in the trenches of the House of Commons alongside Bennett would be three of his leadership rivals – Guthrie, Cahan, and Manion – as well as one key supporter, Stevens. Together, they would have to carry much of the fight against a Liberal government that featured such skilled parliamentarians as Ernest Lapointe, minister of justice; James Robb, minister of finance; Charles Dunning, at that time minister of railways and canals; and the prime minister, W.L. Mackenzie King. Unfortunately, the Tory back benches were rather bereft of first-rate talent. From the West, the only significant member, in addition to Stevens, was A.D. McRae, for S.F. Tolmie, a former minister, had left to become leader of the British Columbia provincial party, while Bennett was the sole Prairie Tory in the House of Commons. Ontario had sent plenty of Conservative members to Ottawa in 1926, but, after Guthrie and Manion, few were of cabinet calibre. The best of the rest were three survivors of Meighen's cabinet: Sir Henry Drayton, who had been humiliated at the convention; J.D. Chaplin, ex–minister of trade and commerce; and E.B. Ryckman, ex–minister of public works. From Quebec came but four MPs, all anglophones. Joining Cahan on the front benches from that province was Sir George Perley, a grizzled veteran of the Borden era. The Maritime contingent was strong in numbers, though diminished from the previous Parliament. The most prominent were the three who had served as ministers in 1926: W.A. Black of Nova Scotia, G.B. Jones of New Brunswick, and J.A. Macdonald of Prince Edward Island. By sheer numbers (see table 3), Ontario dominated the caucus. French Canadians and Prairie farmers would search in vain for a representative of their social groups among the Conservative MPs elected in 1926.

Bennett had some fence-mending to do with his parliamentary followers. Although Ferguson's provincial machine had swung solidly behind him at the convention, Bennett knew full well that a large number of the Ontario MPs had supported Guthrie. Furthermore, Bennett's personality, 'a bit overbearing and impatient' in Ferguson's observation, presented a serious obstacle to forging immediately a solid front with the caucus. Wisely, Bennett was persuaded to 'avoid making party addresses in public until after he [had] had the experience of [the 1928] Session.'[5] The first priority was to make believers of his House of Commons colleagues.

The central party organization was a shambles. The Dominion organizer for the 1926 election had been the BC MP S.F. Tolmie, who operated the party headquarters from his Commons office, supplemented with a few rooms nearby that had been made available by the doubling up of other Tory MPs. The 1927 convention was organized by McRae from these same parliamentary offices.[6] Through the summer and fall of 1927, the central office had been held together by the yeoman's service of a faithful

TABLE 3
The Conservative caucus elected in 1926

Provinces	Conservative MPs	Total seats
Nova Scotia	12	14
New Brunswick	7	11
Prince Edward Island	1	4
Quebec	4	65
Ontario	53	82
Manitoba	0	17
Saskatchewan	0	21
Alberta	1	16
British Columbia	12	14
Territories	1	1
Total	91	245

SOURCE: M.C. Urquhart and K.A.H. Buckley, eds., *Historical Statistics of Canada* (Toronto 1965), 620

secretary, Jane Denison. She was forced to beg the sitting MPs for any unused parliamentary stationery in order to keep functioning.[7] Financially, the federal party was, in the words of its new leader, 'without assets and still with many liabilities.'[8] The Conservative press was not the power it had once been either. As one Tory wrote Bennett, there were 'only eleven Daily [sic] papers that [could] be termed Conservative, and the support accorded by some of these [was] questionable.'[9] All in all, it was a bleak picture: no organizer, no separate headquarters, no funds, and a diminished press.

The party's strength varied province by province, largely according to the strength of the respective provincial parties. Ontario was the rock on which the Conservative house was built in this period. The Ferguson forces held 76 of the 104 seats in the provincial legislature at the end of 1927. With the exception of four years right after the First World War, the Tories had ruled Ontario since 1905. As the most populous province, Ontario exerted a crucial influence on national voting results. So long as the Ferguson machine held sway, it looked solid for the federal party.

The other two Conservative administrations were in the Maritimes. Conservative governments in New Brunswick and Nova Scotia ruled with healthy majorities. In both cases, the Maritime Rights cry had helped elect them. However, the results of the 1926 federal election, combined with a Liberal victory in Prince Edward Island in June 1927, seemed to indicate the beginning of a Liberal rebound in the Maritimes. Still, so long as the Tories controlled the provincial governments in Halifax and Fredericton, they would reap the undoubted benefits that control of patronage brought to the ruling party. Conservative hopes in British Columbia were raised by the healing of a serious split that had seen a splinter group called the Provincial Party, financed in part by General A.D. McRae, contest several ridings in the 1924 election. After the selection of Tolmie from the federal caucus as leader in December 1926, the BC party had closed ranks behind the genial farmer-politician. Nevertheless, in this province, the federal party seemed stronger than its provincial counterpart.

The situation was grim in Quebec and the Prairies, both provincially and federally. A Conservative resurgence in Quebec in 1923 raised 'Bleu' hopes, but these were dashed in May 1927, when the Liberals reduced Conservative strength to nine seats in an assembly of eighty-five. On the Prairies, the Conservatives formed the official opposition in Manitoba, but stood only third in Saskatchewan, and were a dismal fourth in Alberta.

In seeking to build a strong federal organization, the Conservatives could rely on kindred governments in three provinces; Ontario, Nova Scotia, and New Brunswick. In three others – Prince Edward Island, Manitoba, and British Columbia – the provincial parties were moderately healthy, though still in opposition. For the rest, the federal party would either have to devote considerable resources to resuscitating its provincial cousins in Saskatchewan, Alberta, and Quebec or else bypass them entirely and build an independent organization.

BENNETT AND THE PARLIAMENTARY PARTY

Bennett's strategy during his first year of parliamentary leadership was to avoid pointless obstruction, yet stop well short of endorsing the Liberal record. 'The Opposition should not volunteer its willingness to a particular thing,' he explained to Stevens, 'but rather when it is requested express its agreement with what the government proposes to do if it appeals to our judgment.'[10] In a change from Meighen, he pursued a more conciliatory policy towards the other parliamentary opposition groups, the farm and labour representatives. In part, Bennett's caution was attributable to the fact that his illustrious predecessor had cut such a wide swath through the House of Commons. As the Globe's William

Marchington noted in January 1928, 'the Conservatives, for the present, do not seem in a belligerent mood. Mr. Bennett, their new leader, is on trial.'[11] Whatever Bennett may have lacked in brilliance, he compensated for with hard work. As the session progressed and Bennett's confidence grew, the *MacLean's* observer noted, he 'showed his willingness, again and again, to leap into any scuffle and make it a major engagement.'[12] By June, Bennett had earned his spurs as far as the Tory caucus was concerned. Even Sir Robert Borden concluded that Bennett was conducting his new duties 'with excellent judgment and with his usual ability in parliamentary debate.'[13]

Bennett continued to bear a tremendous burden of work, both inside the House and out, over the next two years. In Parliament, he was given to delivering three-hour speeches on major topics, while his contributions during committee-of-the-whole deliberations filled page after page of Hansard. As time went on, his combative interventions during Liberal speeches became more and more frequent. Whenever Parliament was not sitting, he embarked on speaking tours, covering Quebec and the Maritimes in the summer of 1928, and rural Ontario and the West the next year.

To the major centres of central Canada he ventured more frequently. By 1930, the party, press, and public had become well acquainted with the new Tory leader. Generally, the reviews were favourable. 'I feel that your Maritime tour was a great success,' R.B. Hanson wrote to Bennett in November 1928. 'It cheered your followers, and I am satisfied made you and the Party many new friends.'[14] Hanson's enthusiasm was mirrored by many other party regulars across the country. The strategy, as key adviser A.D. McRae later noted, had been simple: 'As a new leader, you had to be sold to the people. As I have frequently said, you are a good seller.'[15]

Whipping the Tory caucus into fighting form took some doing. One of the prominent front-benchers, R.J. Manion, recollected his years in opposition as 'a free-lance life, with plenty of opportunity for criticism and little real responsibility.'[16] Bennett was not satisfied with this scattergun approach, but his early efforts at rejuvenating the caucus were frustrated. 'We had an indifferent attendance, and absolutely no internal organization,' he complained to H.H. Stevens, himself absent, in May 1928. 'I appointed committees to look after the Estimates, and Auditor-General's report. Many worked real [sic] well; others found it difficult to understand just what was to be done.'[17] In addition to its lack of talent and uneven regional representation, internal differences over policy hampered the caucus, for it contained reactionary as well as progressive members. Not all the Tory MPs were prepared to endorse the social and labour policies adopted at the 1927 convention. Furthermore, the air of smug superiority displayed by millionaire MPs such as J.D. Chaplin and E.B. Ryckman was keenly resented by their less affluent colleagues. 'Some of the members of our Party in Ottawa,' Stevens complained to Bennett, 'while possessed of abundant wealth themselves, do not hesitate to cast aspersions upon me because I was unable to match them – dollar for dollar – in personal wealth.'[18] It was a challenge for Bennett, himself a millionaire, to develop a team spirit that would unite and motivate both classes of MP.

During the 1929 session, Bennett successfully implemented a plan that utilized to the full what talent there was in caucus. Several internal committees were struck, one to monitor the activities of each government department. During the parliamentary recess, each committee of caucus spent considerable time investigating problems in its area of jurisdiction, and some held public hearings across the country. For example, the agriculture committee, chaired by Mark Senn, accomplished the following objectives in the second half of 1929, according to an internal party report: 'the members of the Agricultural Committee visited the six easternmost provinces of Canada and did yeoman service in the way of assuring those engaged in agricultural pursuits that the Conservative Party was vitally interested in the immediate and future needs of the industry.'[19] The net effect of the committees' work was to shore up the party's public image, while increasing the knowledge, morale, and usefulness of the Tory back-benchers. By 1930, they were an effective fighting force in the parliamentary battles, loyal to their leader and committed to a common cause: victory at the next election.

Bennett's leadership strategy was greatly influenced by the advice of Howard Ferguson. Writing to Senator White shortly after an interview with Bennett in December 1927, the Ontario premier gave this assessment of the party leader's task: 'I have always thought that in the field of public life the most important thing is the creation of an atmosphere. This is something that he must do himself. He can give a leadership and trend to public opinion that will secure the support of the press and gradually strengthen his position.'[20] Ferguson counselled patience, and the slow but steady development of a positive public image. McRae had accepted the wisdom of this strategy for Bennett's initial years as leader, but he urged the adoption of a new approach as the election approached: 'The old political school considered it bad policy for an Opposition to enunciate constructive issues in advance of the campaign ... I disclaim any membership in this school ... It is now imperative that we take active steps to convince the public of our constructive abilities, and what they may look for if the Conservative Party, under your leadership, is given an opportunity to govern this Dominion.'[21] McRae was suggesting an alternative-government image in place of the negative-opposition role. Bennett, however, was reluctant to come out with new policies too soon before an election.

Until the 1930 session, generally buoyant economic conditions had made any approach other than nit-picking criticism difficult to sustain. Major Conservative themes in 1928 had been their opposition to Canadian legations in non-British countries; criticism of the Liberals' laxity in implementing the Duncan recommendations on Maritime grievances; and demands for action to stem emigration, improve transportation, and preserve the home markets. To these traditional positions were added, in 1929, calls for an imperial economic conference in Ottawa, a comprehensive self-financing pension system, and the immediate grant of resource ownership to the Prairie provinces. Though Guthrie, the party's chief budget critic in 1929, accurately predicted that the Hoover administration's plans to raise U.S. tariff walls would cause grave problems for Canada, and though Cahan accurately attributed the latter-day prosperity to the artificial appreciation of stock values, theirs were voices crying in the wilderness. Finance minister Robb's 1929 budget had once again produced a healthy surplus, coupled with tax cuts. It was hard for any opposition, however talented, to make political headway under such conditions.[22]

New Year's celebrations in Canada rang a bit hollow on the eve of 1930. In the wake of the stock-market crash of October 1929, urban unemployment had shot up dramatically.[23] Some businesses had gone bankrupt, while many others laid off staff to weather the economic crisis. Conditions on the nation's farms were not as threatening yet, but commodity prices were down sharply, and drought threatened on the prairies. Other resource-export industries such as mining, fishing, and forestry were equally hard hit. The multiplier effect quickly spread the impact of the recession to all sectors of the Canadian economy. Political parties, accustomed to the politics of prosperity, would now have to practise the politics of hard times. The recession of 1929–30 grew into the Great Depression of the 1930s. In the first six months of 1930, however, it was not at all self-evident that this period of economic hardship would be anything more than the normal cyclical downturn, soon to be followed by a new era of growth and prosperity.

The Conservative strategy, standard for an opposition party, was to hammer away at the government with the evidence of economic decline, while holding aloft a vision of returning prosperity if the voters would only install them in office. During the Throne Speech debate, Bennett refrained from offering specific alternatives, contenting himself with ridiculing the government's claim that prosperity was still the order of the day. 'There has been great unemployment in Canada since the first of the year,' he declared emphatically. 'Do you mean to say that the Dominion government should make no contribution to provide assistance to provinces and municipalities in matters of the kind?' Bennett succeeded in trapping Prime Minister King into a dismissal of the deepening economic crisis as merely 'a few temporary circumstances prevailing at the moment ... in particular localities.'[24] A few weeks later, during an emergency debate on unemployment precipitated by A.A. Heaps of the Labour group, the Conservatives provoked King into a more damaging statement. At a time when Conservative administrations governed in five provinces, he angrily rejected even 'a five-cent piece' in federal assistance 'to any Tory government in this country for these alleged unemployment purposes.'[25] The statement was so categorical that even King could not wiggle out of it. For the Conservatives, his miscue was like manna from heaven. It allowed them to paint the Liberal government as arrogant and unresponsive, more concerned with budget-balancing and narrow partisan advantage than with helping people in difficulty.

The unemployment problem allowed the Conservatives to resurrect their traditional tariff policy as the centre-piece of an alternative economic master plan for Canada. Downgraded at the Winnipeg convention, protective tariffs now reappeared as the cure-all for the country's economic woes – the saviour of the farmers' markets and the workers' jobs. At last, Bennett was able to take McRae's advice and offer a concrete Conservative alternative. At a time of rising unemployment and falling farm prices, increased tariff protection could be portrayed, not as an undeserved subsidy for rich manufacturers, but as an aggressive defence of the livelihood of ordinary Canadians. Hence the initial Conservative consternation when the Dunning budget seemed to steal the Tories' policy, with its adoption of countervailing duties. Bennett was able to rally the Conservatives against this daring Liberal manoeuvre on the basis of three themes. First, a policy of countervailing duties left the initiative for

Canadian economic policy in foreign, essentially American, hands. Second, the British preferential tariffs, offered without reciprocal benefits, would hurt Canadian producers. Here, Bennett took a calculated risk that pro-imperial supporters would not be alienated. 'I am for the British Empire next to Canada,' he asserted. Finally, he ridiculed the Liberals for their death-bed conversion to the Conservative principle of higher tariff protection.[26]

Though King served notice, on 6 May, of an impending election, the Conservatives extended the budget debate for two more weeks, their speeches following the battle lines laid out by Bennett. Stevens demanded why there should not be 'a quid pro quo' from Britain before granting it preferential treatment. Manion called for 'a consistent, courageous, Canada-first policy' on tariffs. Cahan noted that, in terminating the preferential entry of New Zealand butter in October 1930, the Liberals were merely acceding to a request 'long demanded' by the Conservatives. When the vote on Bennett's amendment was called on 15 May, the Liberals were joined by the 'ginger group' of Labour and Farmer representatives in voting down the Tories' clarion call for red-blooded Canadian protective tariffs.[27] Sensing a winning election issue, the Conservatives were delighted to polarize federal politics in such a way that they could cast themselves as the only true defenders of Canadian jobs, Canadian markets, and Canadian national pride.

ORGANIZATION, PUBLICITY, AND FUNDING

Mobilizing the parliamentary party was just one of the challenges facing Bennett in October 1927. The central organization had to be put into shape as well. The Winnipeg convention had endorsed a resolution submitted by the committee on party organization, of which John R. MacNicol was chairman, that provided for the establishment of a Dominion council. This body, consisting of three representatives from each of Ontario and Quebec, one representative from each of the other provinces, a woman from each province, the federal and provincial leaders, and the federal organizer, was instructed to meet annually, in order to coordinate Dominion-wide organization. After much prodding by MacNicol, the first meeting was set for 21 April 1928 in Ottawa.[28]

Bennett confessed to a party insider his own misgivings about this method of organization: 'You will understand that if I were doing this myself I would not have this meeting, nor would I have approached the problem of organization from the same angle as has Mr. MacNicol, but the meeting was provided for at Winnipeg and I am bound to carry out the terms of the resolution, or meet with opposition from Mr. MacNicol. I have chosen the path of the least resistance.'[29]

As it turned out, Bennett had little to fear. Although MacNicol had organized the Ottawa meeting, and was formally thanked by resolution for his prodigious efforts, the end result was to withdraw the organizational impetus from his hands. Bennett, as party leader, was authorized to select a national director to oversee the party's organization from a central headquarters to be set up in Ottawa. To assist the new Dominion organizer and himself, Bennett was further authorized to set up a small executive committee, whose members would all be within easy reach of Ottawa. At the provincial level and below, the committee agreed, the party would rely on existing provincial associations. One of the national director's major tasks would be coordinating the efforts of the various provincial organizations.[30] Overall direction of the party machinery would be centralized in the hands of this Dominion organizer, hand-picked by Bennett, but the foot-soldiers in the next campaign would be, as usual, provided by the provincial parties.

Rumours at the time, indeed ever since the successful Winnipeg convention, had suggested that General A.D. McRae would be the choice for national director. No announcement was forthcoming for several months, however, because, just prior to the Ottawa meeting, McRae slipped on an icy sidewalk and fractured his skull. At the time of the organizational gathering, he was still gravely incapacitated.[31] As McRae was indeed Bennett's first choice, the appointment awaited the general's recovery. In the meantime, the organizational machine continued to rust. One unfortunate result was a foul-up of the arrangements for Bennett's speaking tour in the summer of 1928. His handlers kept him so long in the Maritimes that a lengthy series of engagements in populous Ontario had to be cancelled. An unamused Arthur Ford, Conservative organizer in western Ontario, complained to Bennett that 'frankly someone has badly blundered in making your summer arrangements.'[32] Fortunately, it was not an election year. There was yet time to mend fences. In November, McRae felt strong enough to accept Bennett's appointment as 'chief organizer' of the party. His duties began in January 1929.[33]

McRae proved to be a very effective national director. By 1 May, federal headquarters had been set up in the Victoria Building at 140 Wellington Street in downtown Ottawa. In addition to McRae, who retained his job as a Vancouver MP and served as chief whip of the Conservative caucus, the permanent staff included Redmond Code as general secretary, Robert Lipsett as director of publicity, and additional research, clerical, stenographic, and mechanical staff. By February 1930, there were twenty-seven full-time employees at party headquarters.[34] Permanent provincial headquarters were also set up in the following centres: Charlottetown, Halifax, Saint John, Montreal, Toronto, London (for southwestern Ontario), Winnipeg, Regina, and Vancouver. In most cases, the Conservative provincial association merely turned over its already existing headquarters to the federal party in return for financial support. Organization and campaign committees were set up in each province, again utilizing provincial party personnel wherever possible. McRae spent a good deal of the first nine months of 1929 on the road, meeting local Conservatives, cementing a federal organization together from the provincial building blocks. Only in Quebec was an entirely new organizational committee established, for the provincial and federal wings of the party were still at odds.[35]

The entire focus of McRae's organizational effort was the next general election. Both he and Code travelled extensively in 1929, instructing local party officials on organizational tactics. At the same time, they were assessing the calibre of potential Conservative candidates. Although the federal party was relying on provincial organizations, there was never any doubt who was running the show. This fact was made abundantly clear in correspondence, such as this letter, sent from Code to J.D. Stewart of the Conservative provincial headquarters in Charlottetown: 'I have just received a letter from General McRae,' Code wrote, 'asking me ... to point out very clearly that if the candidate in the last federal election gets the nomination there will be absolutely nothing doing in the way of support from here.'[36] McRae's control extended even to parts of Howard Ferguson's fiefdom of Ontario. In a letter to Code, he requested that arrangements be made so Bennett could 'see the men we want for candidates in several Ontario ridings.'[37] McRae's chief criterion for Conservative candidates was that they be the party representatives most likely to win. He recognized there were a number of ridings, particularly in Quebec and portions of the West, where Conservative chances were dim, and he resisted the allocation of party resources where no return was likely. His strategy was simple: to concentrate on ridings where victory was a realistic possibility. 'There is, of course,' the former quartermaster-general explained to his chief Saskatchewan organizer, 'no object in wasting any of this ammunition on constituencies where we have no show.'[38]

Lipsett's role was to set up and operate a research and publicity bureau. The first priority was to build up a storehouse of information about the individual MPs and their constituencies. In a form letter sent to all elected members of the Conservative caucus, Code requested a personal interview to discuss 'the political situation' in their home areas. In addition, the MPs were requested to supply party headquarters with a confidential report outlining the political history, major economic activities, racial and religious composition, and organizational details of their own ridings, as well as any adjoining ridings held by other parties. Further, the MPs were requested to supply a complete list of daily and weekly newspapers published in the constituency, broken down as to pro-Conservative, neutral, and anti-Conservative editorial viewpoints. 'This information,' Code wrote, 'is required for the use of the Director of Publicity in connection with a general publicity campaign designed to reach every part of each constituency in the Dominion.' Finally, the Tory members were asked to submit an up-to-date mailing list for their ridings in three categories: key men and women in their local organization; known Conservative supporters; and doubtfuls. The purpose of the mailing lists, Code explained, was so that the party headquarters could prepare 'sets of addressograph or multigraph plates' that would permit mass mailing.[39]

In a follow-up memo to MPs, Code explained that the Addressograph system that Conservative headquarters had installed would make possible mailing of 'letters and general literature' to Conservative supporters, sympathizers, and those who could be converted, and 'the Conservative Bulletin and special organization literature' to the key men and women of his riding organization. Code suggested the key list should contain about five hundred names per constituency, while the general list could be considerably longer. This general list was to be broken down 'into a number of different classes such as farmers, industrial workers, urban electors, rural electors, Protestants or non-protestants [sic].' Such a division would permit mail-outs on specialized themes, aimed at specific socio-economic groups. The target date for completion of the lists was October 1929, so that the publicity office could begin mailing in January 1930.[40]

In a private letter to a Conservative supporter, Code acknowledged that the Addressograph innovation had been borrowed from south of the border. 'A very careful inquiry into the methods employed in the last presidential election in the United States' had been carried out. Code had discovered that 'the old method of newspaper and magazine advertising was largely abandoned.' In its place, the American parties had substituted radio ads, and 'literally millions of letters of a personal nature,' using the Addressograph machine. Radio was still in its infancy in Canada, but the Conservatives moved quickly to adopt the personalized mass-mailing system. Their aim was to place 'perhaps 20 per cent of the electors' on their general lists.[41] Yet the system was so flexible that it could be used by Bennett to send out a personalized letter to each of the hundred or so members of caucus, simply by dictating the letter, having it typed once, then sending it to Code's mechanical department for printing and mailing.[42]

The theory underlying Lipsett's publicity bureau was that the information disseminated would not be just partisan rhetoric, but would be based on solid factual material. 'Instead of attempting to inflame with adjectives,' he explained to Bennett, 'we undertook to convince with facts. Every declaration of fact was substantiated by reference to the authority.'[43] The newspaper-clipping bureau was transferred from Bennett's Commons office to party headquarters in order to facilitate this aim. As well, the information gained by the caucus committees was shared with Lipsett's publicity office, which also researched economic conditions and legislative initiatives in the United States. Such information was circulated to the Conservative caucus, friendly newspapers, and supporters on the mailing lists. Two issues that the publicity bureau was able to exploit by late 1929 were urban unemployment and sagging farm prices. 'I think we may rightly take credit for first publicly sensing the unemployment issue,' Lipsett later stated. 'In November we commenced to exploit the issue ... As with unemployment, we utilized every advantageous figure to make the farmer unhappy.'[44] Clearly, the aim was to propagandize, to create in the voters' minds a negative image of the Liberal record and a positive image of the Conservative potential. The Conservative publicity, less emotional and more factual than was the norm for partisan literature, largely conditioned the public to accept the validity of speeches made by Conservative speakers in Parliament and across the country. As Lipsett explained, 'we placed – largely before the argument was made before the House or on the platform – the facts upon which our attacks on the late Government were made. Thus when our criticism had developed these readers had already accepted its basis.'[45]

The coordination of effort between Lipsett's publicity bureau and the Conservative caucus was no accident. Lipsett's boss, General McRae, was the parliamentary party's chief whip. The caucus set up, in February

1930, a special publicity committee to oversee the party office's propaganda efforts. McRae urged that the committee and bureau collaborate so as to ensure that the party bulletins would always have favourable Tory speeches to quote on those issues which the Conservatives could exploit: 'I am suggesting that the Publicity Committee should at an early date consider the subjects to be covered by your Bulletin and where it is found we are not as completely on record as we might wish, or where our story can be further strengthened by a pronouncement at this time, that the Committee arrange with some Member to cover the story along the lines they particularly desire and thus give you an authentic reference in Hansard that will be complete.'[46] The publicity bureau itself engaged in a great deal of research on key issues, which it fed to members of caucus. The Tory MPs then delivered speeches in the Commons that were reproduced by the publicity bureau from the pages of Hansard, and circulated to the public.[47] The relationship was incestuous, but effective.

The mailing list of Canadians who received the Conservative publicity in English numbered just 20,000 in the summer of 1929. McRae was characteristically blunt in obtaining the cooperation of fellow MPs and potential candidates. 'We haven't got a single name on our mailing list for Kent constituency,' he informed Thomas Bell, a New Brunswick MP. 'What is the trouble? In Northumberland, McDade is equally bad ... Can't you get after this?' Such persistence got results. By February 1930 there were 100,000 names on the list, and three months later that number had risen to 210,000. The Montreal office developed its own list of 60,000 names, mostly in Quebec, but also covering the francophone areas of New Brunswick and Ontario. For the Prairie provinces, the party produced literature in Ukrainian, Polish, and German, which circulated to 50,000 households.[48]

The 'state of the art' equipment at Conservative headquarters allowed the party to send a personalized letter favourable to the Tory cause to the entire mailing list, and a stronger letter to that portion of the mailing list deemed to be 'stalwarts' by the MPs and party organizers who had submitted the names.[49] Because the names were also categorized by such characteristics as occupation, gender, and religion, specific mailings could easily be targeted to the most receptive groups. Furthermore, each MP could send out a monthly mailing to those of his constituents who were on the party's master mailing list. This mailing was produced and addressed at headquarters, but mailed with his own signature, and free of charge on his parliamentary frank.[50] This approach was 'a distinct innovation in Parliamentary campaign methods' in Canada, as Code pointed out to Bennett.[51]

In addition to personalized form letters, the Conservative headquarters prepared a monthly party bulletin called *The Canadian*, and precampaign pamphlets with titles such as *Why I Am a Conservative* and *Election in Sight*.[52] The bulletins and pamphlets were mailed to the voters whose names appeared on the party mailing list. As with other aspects of the pre-election campaign, McRae designed a specific plan for the bulletin's use. He instructed Lipsett to keep it 'short, terse and to the point,' with references given for all critical statements of fact or quotations. Each monthly bulletin was to highlight a particular issue, such as unemployment, farm relief, technical education, and old-age pensions. The content would be a mix of articles, speech excerpts, editorials, and political cartoons. When the election was actually called, the collected issues of *The Canadian*, once bound together, would serve as the core of the 'speakers' handbook.' The first issue was mailed in February 1930.[53]

Lipsett developed another campaign innovation for the Conservatives: the news service. The first of these he called 'The Standard News Service.' Several hundred weekly papers – some Conservative, some neutral, some Liberal – subscribed to this service, which supplied digestible bits of national news of an outwardly non-partisan sort. Lipsett was able to use 'The Standard News Service' for the Conservative cause by emphasizing developments favourable to the Tories or harmful to the government. However, its value to the weekly publishers was that it ostensibly circulated 'non-political' news. To this end, Lipsett emphasized the need for secrecy about its real source and purpose. 'It is quite essential,' he informed Bennett, 'that it should not be understood that we have any interest.' By election time, 'The Standard News Service' was providing a news package to 645 weekly newspapers, with a circulation of 750,000 subscribers.[54]

In addition, Lipsett's bureau supplied a weekly political letter to 165 pro-Conservative weekly newspapers. Unlike 'The Standard News Service,' where non-partisanship was emphasized, the weekly political letters were 'written with a distinctly Conservative trend.' Finally, Lipsett provided 99 Conservative weeklies with 'a straight Conservative editorial,' which was delivered, by mail or telegraph, 'on the day of the week most convenient for publication.' By April, the Tory publicity bureau was 'mailing 4,500 packages – not pages – of news per month' to weekly papers in all nine provinces.[55]

This Conservative organization – the wonder of its day – was expensive to operate. Expenditures for the federal headquarters were $21,000 for the month of April 1930, for instance, and a similar amount was budgeted for May. Of this amount, $5,000 was sent each month to the party's Quebec branch headquarters in Montreal, and a few hundred more to the provincial organizations in the six other easternmost provinces. The monthly cost of the Addressograph machine was $1,800; of the monthly bulletin, $4,600; of the letter service, $2,400; of the news service, $600. Salaries, rent, postage, travel, and incidental expenses ate up the balance of the monthly budget.[56]

R.B. Bennett supplied $50,000 to the party office from his own resources in 1929. Initially, his undertaking was to contribute $2,500 per month. Once the headquarters on Wellington Street was actually launched in May, this amount proved sadly inadequate. By the end of 1929, he had advanced so much money that he was paid up all the way to August 1930.[57] Yet, the party till was empty. 'I took up with Sir George Perley our financial situation this morning,' McRae wrote to Rhodes on 4 December, 'with the result that Sir George and myself had to sign a note for $10,000 to take care of this month's expenses.'[58] Though Bennett, McRae, and Perley were all millionaires, the economic collapse at the end of 1929 reduced their ability to finance the elaborate party organization. Yet, until an election was actually called, traditional party donors were unlikely to loosen their purse-strings. In January, Perley was forced to arrange for one more month's activities to be financed on his own credit. 'This organization,' he warned Bennett and McRae, 'is in danger of collapsing any day.' Furthermore, Perley wanted out as treasurer, an unofficial, unpaid post he had been holding. 'I am no longer young enough to submit to worries of this kind.'[59] McRae would not budge. 'Looking after this damnable job and paying my own expenses is about as far as I wish to go,' he declared.[60] Bennett found himself required to pay the bills. Evidently they were paid, though not without Bennett insisting that McRae practise the utmost of economies in his supervision of the central party organization. By June, when the election campaign was finally getting under way, Bennett confided to personal correspondents that he had already spent half a million dollars on the Conservative party of Canada since becoming leader, including $100,000 in Quebec. At this point, Bennett the leader was also Bennett the chief party benefactor.[61]

For that part of his massive contribution that went to the party headquarters, Bennett obtained the services of a first-rate organization that was already functioning smoothly prior to the election call. It was innovative, effective, and far beyond anything the Liberals had in place. With victory in sight, the costs could be borne.

THE CONSERVATIVES AND QUEBEC

For years, the Conservative party in Quebec had been little more than a strife-ridden collection of feuding factions. Once chosen leader, Bennett was the recipient of prolific correspondence from party supporters in that province, much of it related to the endemic internal bickering.[62] There was an E.L. Patenaude faction, consisting of supporters of Meighen's fallen French-Canadian ally of 1926. There was an Arthur Sauvé faction, made up of followers of the long-time provincial leader, whose *nationaliste* views had alienated the business wing of the party. Other stalwarts with at least a modest following included Armand Lavergne, Henri Bourassa's former *nationaliste* ally; Senator D.O. L'Espérance, who controlled *L'Evénement* of Quebec City and *La Patrie* of Montreal, both nominally pro-Conservative papers; Rodolphe Monty, briefly secretary of state in 1921; and G.A. Fauteux, briefly solicitor general in 1926. Among the anglophone Tories, from whom came all four of the province's Conservative MPs, there was a *Gazette* faction, led by the White family, and a *Star* faction, answerable to Baron Atholstan. C.H. Cahan had been able to unite most of these factions temporarily behind his favourite-son candidacy at the Winnipeg convention. This unity proved short-lived, and jockeying for influence under the new leader began in earnest shortly after the delegates returned in the fall of 1927.[63]

Bennett was under considerable pressure to anoint someone as his Quebec lieutenant. The Macdonald-Cartier myth still burned brightly among francophone Conservatives. However, Bennett resisted the temptation to make a quick selection. 'Until these factions are united, we cannot hope for support,' he pointed out to one Quebec supporter, 'and they cannot be united if I select any person as chief-lieutenant in Quebec.'[64] Bennett did consent to attend a large party banquet in Montreal, in October 1928, on the condition that 'all sections of the party were represented.' The result was better than he had dared to expect. His theme, 'Wake Up Canada,' delivered almost entirely in English, was well received by several hundred Conservatives representing all the major factions. Arthur Sauvé, who had boycotted the federal party during the Borden-Meighen years, not only attended, but spoke from the platform, delivering 'a very admirable speech,' in Bennett's view.[65] In a province where

the Conservatives were noted for possessing 'plus de chefs que de sol-
dats,' the banquet marked an important turning-point for Bennett. Sauvé
followed up the banquet with a letter of firm support for Bennett. 'My
strongest desire,' he pledged, 'is to do all in my power to serve my party,
a cause dear to me, and to see effective means adopted by which it could
be led to victory in my province as well as elsewhere.' In his view, the
most critical needs were 'a good organizer,' and strong French-language
party newspapers in Montreal and Quebec City.[66]

General McRae was unable to duplicate in the province of Quebec his
organizing success elsewhere. He did not understand the French language, or the French-Canadian people, and found the shifting factional
alliances of the Quebec Conservative party extremely frustrating. A man
of action, he voiced his frustration pointedly to General G.E. McCuaig:
'Dissension among the Conservatives of Quebec has reached a point
which makes it very difficult to proceed ... The Chief has his own views.
I have to say frankly, that so far as I am concerned, until such time as
there is some evidence that our good friends in Quebec are going to get
together, I do not propose to trouble very much about that province.'[67]
At the same time, McRae was not well accepted by French-speaking
Conservatives. 'It is unfortunately true,' Sir George Perley informed
Bennett in May 1929, 'that the good General is far from popular among
the French Canadians. Therefore I think McRae should be out of the
limelight there as far as practicable.'[68] Expecting little in the way of improvement in Quebec, McRae was happy to comply. An effective organization in that province would await the appointment of a francophone native son as chief organizer.

The first major event for Quebec Conservatives in 1929 was a day-long
conference on organization and policy held in Montreal on 15 May. Intended as a follow-up to the successful banquet held the previous autumn,
the meeting was organized principally by L.J. Gauthier, a former Liberal
MP who had crossed the floor to support Meighen in 1921. The Montreal
meeting was initially opposed by several important elements of the
Quebec party. '[Senator Beaubien] says that Gauthier goes in to a constituency and picks out three or four men and asks them to come,' R.J.
Manion informed Bennett. 'In other words it is a packed meeting.'
Montreal financier Ward Pitfield, in touch with the White and Patenaude
factions, wrote Bennett, asking that the 'Cahan-Gauthier Convention' be
cancelled, or at least 'postponed until such time as a convention properly organized can be held.' A colleague of Pitfield's, John Hackett,
noted privately the basis for much of the objection. 'Lord A. [Atholstan]

was apparently furnishing money to G. [Gauthier] to get delegates together from the Counties.'[69]

For good or for ill, Lord Atholstan was still acting as the manipulative 'godfather' of the Quebec Conservative party. Perley pointed out to Bennett, in discussing candidates for provincial organizer, the necessity of finding someone 'who had been suggested or approved by Lord A. and Mr. C. [sic].'[70] Atholstan had his own ideas about a successor to Patenaude. 'Mr. Cahan,' he insisted, 'is your best choice for the temporary direction of the Conservative Party effort in this province.'[71] Cahan was, indeed, widely respected among francophone Conservatives. Sauvé, for instance, wrote to Senator P.E. Blondin as follows: 'M. Cahan est trop nécessaire pour que l'on gaspille son goodwill.' Lavergne expressed similar sentiments. 'We believe Cahan to be an asset,' he informed Bennett, 'and a strong one in our province.'[72] Opponents of the Atholstan group, such as McCuaig, Pitfield, and Hackett, felt differently. 'The solicitude of Mr. Bennett for Mr. Cahan and Gauthier, who are the authors of so much trouble and who have been hostile to him, is truly touching,' Hackett noted ironically in a private memo. 'The chaps who have put up the money, done the work and tried to keep him out of a hole are overlooked.'[73]

The May convention formally endorsed both the Winnipeg platform and Bennett's leadership. Its most significant result was that Bennett used his keynote speech to unveil a new organizing committee for the province, with members from all the warring factions. Bennett shrewdly passed over Gauthier, the nominee of the Montreal convention for provincial organizer, in view of Gauthier's too-strong connection to the Atholstan faction.[74] His eventual choice, ratified by the Quebec organizing committee, was Joseph Rainville, a Montreal lawyer and businessman.

An MP from 1911 to 1917, with brief experience as deputy Speaker, Rainville had served as a Unionist organizer and candidate in the divisive wartime election. A second organizer, Thomas Maher, was chosen for the Quebec district, the part of the province centred on Quebec City. Maher reported to federal headquarters through Rainville, and funds were sent to him from party headquarters in Ottawa through Rainville's Montreal office. The situation led to inevitable jealousy and conflict. (One typical incident involved a dispute between Quebec and Montreal over the best candidate to nominate in L'Islet constituency.) McRae developed considerable confidence in Rainville. 'I think he is doing very good work,' McRae informed Bennett at the end of 1929. The chief federal organizer had little use for the Quebec district organizer, however.

'Maher puts up a good front,' he wrote to Bennett, 'but I am afraid he is altogether too optimistic to be practical.'[75]

In an attempt to obtain more favourable press coverage for the party, Maher launched a pro-Conservative weekly, *Le Journal*, in December 1929. It was published in Quebec City, and began with a subscription list of 10,000 names. Maher and two colleagues, Lucien Moraud and Maurice Boulianne, put up half the funds, some $27,000. The other financing was obtained partly through Ward Pitfield, and partly from 'a friend we all know,' namely Lord Atholstan. The first editor, Louis Francoeur, had previously been employed by Atholstan's *Montreal Star*. Bennett and McRae were unimpressed, and refused to subsidize *Le Journal*, even though its circulation reached 22,000 by mid-March. Though Rainville referred to it as 'the biggest asset our Party has in the Province,' the economic climate of early 1930 rendered such a venture financially precarious. Under the pressure, Maher tendered his resignation to Bennett in May, though he withdrew it once the election campaign commenced.[76]

In an attempt to obtain more French-language press coverage favourable to the federal Conservative party, Rainville arranged a subsidy for *Le Goglu*, *Le Miroir*, and *Le Chameau*, three virulently anti-Liberal weeklies published by Joseph Menard and Adrien Arcand. The new provincial leader, Camillien Houde, had initially subsidized their publication, but, in April 1930, he renounced them. 'Je tiens à réiterer de nouveau que ni *le Goglu*, ni *le Miroir*, ni *le Chameau*, ne sont mes organes,' he declared. At Rainville's initiative, the federal Conservatives gained the dubious benefits of the nationalist, anti-capitalist, and, occasionally, pro-Fascist and anti-Semitic broadsides of these three papers.[77]

Houde had replaced Arthur Sauvé at a convention held in Quebec City, in July 1929. Any chance of the federal party gaining a measure of cooperation and support from their provincial cousins was dashed by a ham-handed attempt by Bennett to manipulate the selection of the new Quebec leader. Senator Blondin had advised Bennett to keep his hands off the provincial convention, accurately predicting that Houde would be 'the unanimous choice of that convention.' On the advice of J.H. Price and 'the Quebec crowd,' however, Bennett wrote to Dr Edouard Montpetit, a prominent University of Montreal educator, asking him to stand for the provincial leadership. Price had advised Bennett to speak to Houde, and further suggested that Sauvé would 'have to be taken care of later on.' To Bennett's surprise, Dr Montpetit, the man who Price assured him was 'ready to take on the job,' turned it down flat. 'My sole interest is with education,' he coolly informed Bennett. 'But I have in fact always been liberal.'[78] Bennett was embarrassed. Houde was annoyed. He resumed the traditional aloofness of the Quebec provincial Conservatives towards their federal counterparts.

As the pre-election preparation period ended, the federal Conservative wing in Quebec was much improved over 1926 in terms of organization, and somewhat better as regards funding and press support. Nevertheless, as Rainville conceded to Code in May 1930, there still existed 'a small group [who] do not want to obey.'[79] Factionalism, the bane of the Quebec wing's existence for decades, could not be so easily eradicated.

PROVINCIAL CONSERVATIVE STRENGTH IN ENGLISH CANADA

Ontario continued rock solid for the Conservative party during the late 1920s. Under Premier Ferguson's leadership, the party swept to an unprecedented victory in the provincial election of 30 October 1929. With 57 per cent of the popular vote, the government returned ninety-one members; the combined opposition, twenty-one. Ferguson had requested the election after only three years in office, with no burning issues, but with an eye on the expected federal election sometime in 1930. His timing was fortuitous: the stock-market collapse had not had time to develop into serious recession by voting day. Significantly, Ferguson's popularity with Franco-Ontarians was such that Conservatives were elected in all six ridings in which francophones were a majority. 'Mr. Ferguson could well go into Quebec now and speak on behalf of Mr. Bennett, and have good results,' his colleague George Henry pointed out to J.R. MacNicol shortly after the election.[80]

The provincial Conservative organization in Ontario was a superbly functioning political machine. W.H. Price, the attorney general who represented Toronto Parkdale, and Charles McCrea, minister of mines from Sudbury, oversaw the organization from their cabinet portfolios. Under them was William Clysdale, a paid organizer who ran the machine on a day-to-day basis. In addition, Gordon Reid in western Ontario and Garrett Tyrrell in the Toronto region were on salary to oversee party affairs in their regions. J.R. MacNicol, president of the provincial association, lent a willing hand as well. Looking after eastern Ontario, and presiding over all the others, was Howard Ferguson.[81]

After his own decisive victory, the premier was ready to use his potent organization to help drive the Grits out of Ottawa. The decision of the national party to rely on provincial associations wherever possible as the basis of the federal organization made this transition relatively easy.

Clysdale was a key person in both federal and provincial wings. In western Ontario, McRae's man, Arthur Ford, was on good terms with the premier as well. Following the Conservative sweep in October 1929, Bennett requested the help of Ferguson's henchmen, Price and McCrea, on the federal team.[82] Ferguson himself was a key factor in many parts of the province. 'Federal issues will play a comparatively small part in the determining of results,' a prominent Toronto Conservative with business and political connections in Northern Ontario, D.M. Hogarth, pointed out to Bennett. 'Provincial factors are all important and in every instance, I would not think of arranging for conventions without first having Mr. Ferguson's approval of the candidate who can best represent us.'[83] Party publicity continued to emanate from party headquarters in Ottawa, but control of nominations and pre-campaign activity in much of the province passed to Ferguson and his team.

Conservative fortunes in the Maritimes ebbed and flowed. A snap election in Nova Scotia, called by Premier Rhodes for 1 October 1928, nearly ended in disaster for the Tories. The government, basking in their landslide support from 1925, was nearly defeated. Besides overconfidence, the Nova Scotia Conservatives had suffered from weak organization and a 'war chest' that had been emptied 'and more in the Federal contests of 25 and 26.'[84] By the fall of 1929, a subsidy from federal headquarters to the Nova Scotia organization had been arranged of a few hundred dollars a month to cover basic expenses. Rhodes got to work building an effective organization, one that impressed even McRae, who found it 'very good,' and a model for other provinces.[85] The test came in a provincial by-election in Halifax, early in 1930. In 'a bonnie battle,' the Conservatives successfully held the seat, and hence their control of the legislature. The reversal of apparently declining party fortunes in Nova Scotia was heartening for Conservatives all across the country.[86]

The party in New Brunswick, comfortable with its large provincial majority, was slow to organize federally. McRae personally ensured that a federal office was set up there with an organizer, secretary, and stenographer on his summer trip to the province in 1929. He sought Premier Baxter's interest in the federal organization, but, in the end, turned to Bennett, who was a native son and retained many personal contacts, to help get things moving. As was the case in Nova Scotia, the New Brunswick federal office of the party received 'a little financial assistance,' amounting to a few hundred dollars a month. Similarly, in Prince Edward Island, McRae 'took steps to get an organization office started,' and secured an arrangement by which the Nova Scotia party office would assist, however needed. Some $900 was sent to Charlottetown from Ottawa headquarters to facilitate the politician organization of the province.[87]

In British Columbia, things started out well for the Conservatives, but ended badly. On 18 July 1928, affable Simon Fraser Tolmie led a united Conservative party to a decisive victory over the Liberals. Incredibly, victory at Victoria turned out to be the worst thing that could have befallen the BC federal Conservatives. Barely had the new ministers settled into their offices before Bennett began to receive angry complaints about the Tolmie government. 'Today, if the Liberal Party were in power in the Province,' Bennett wrote sharply to Tolmie after a 1929 tour, 'the fortunes of our Party federally would be brighter than they now are.' The short-lived unity of the provincial Tories had not lasted beyond the first round of government appointments.[88] The disarray on the Conservative side nearly cost the federal party Tolmie's vacated Victoria riding. Long considered a safe seat, Victoria was held by the Conservatives by fewer than a hundred votes, in a by-election held only five months after the sweeping provincial victory. The discord among provincial Tories seemed only to worsen with the passage of time. Both McRae and Stevens, each a strong MP from the province, sought to rectify the situation, but with little success. In the end, the party's hopes rested on British Columbia's traditional loyalty to the federal Conservatives. 'Our friends are hopeful,' Bennett wrote to a fellow Tory, 'that as the campaign develops provincial matters will be less under consideration.'[89]

On the Prairies, the dramatic upset of the Liberal government in Saskatchewan on 6 June 1929 boosted party morale throughout English-speaking Canada. Defeat of the entrenched regime had required an alliance with the Progressives, but still the Conservatives were the dominant element in the new coalition, and their leader, J.T.M. Anderson, became the new premier. On the surface, the chief issue in the election campaign was the excessive patronage and corruption of the Liberal government, in office continuously since 1905. The underlying issues that gave bite to the cry 'break up the machine' were schools and immigration. Both issues were steeped in bigotry. The anti-government coalition pledged to end Roman Catholic influence in the province's public schools, and curtail the influx of 'foreign' immigrants, who allegedly spoke little or no English and tended not to be Protestant. The coalition charged that a Catholic foreign bloc-vote, organized by the Liberal machine, prevented the Protestant English-speaking majority from creating the sort of province they desired, and had a right to expect.[90] Nativism provided the issues on which the Conservative and Progressive forces united. The Ku

Klux Klan, with its secret meetings and rituals, was the catalyst that brought the nativist issues to the fore, and permitted Tories, Farmers, and disgruntled Grits to work together against the government machine. The Klan campaigned openly for the defeat of the Liberals, though with no formal connection to either Conservatives or Progressives.[91]

R.B. Bennett had a hand, or more accurately, his wallet, in the Liberal defeat in Saskatchewan. As secret owner of the newly created Regina *Daily Star*, he invested $344,000 by October 1929 in the Conservative paper. The *Daily Star* had been launched in July 1928 to counteract the Liberal monopoly of daily newspapers in the province. Judged on the basis of political rather than economic returns, the investment was sound. 'Tens of thousands of copies' of the *Daily Star* were distributed free around the province, for several weeks prior to the vote. The Liberal monopoly on daily news coverage was broken.[92]

It was fortunate for Bennett that his ownership of the Regina *Daily Star* did not become public knowledge in Quebec. The scurrilously bigoted tone of the paper's editorials on the racial and religious issues of the election may have played well in the wheat belt, but they were a red flag to Quebeckers. For example, the 8 June issue featured these views in an editorial: 'Quebec, by virtue of its Liberal bloc, had with the assistance of Saskatchewan members, dominated all Canada ... The Dominion under Quebec control has been making bold efforts in recent years to bring the West under the French-Canadian subjection ... Steps have been taken to fill the entire Civil Service of Canada with French Canadians.'[93] A year earlier, Bennett had fretted over the probable effect on federal Conservatives of the adoption by the Saskatchewan provincial party of anti-Catholic policies. 'Nothing could be more injurious to this country,' he had written to a Saskatchewan Tory, 'than that religious differences· should become the line of division between political parties!' The prospect of a friendly government displacing the hated Liberal machine in Regina apparently quieted Bennett's qualms, and opened his pocket-book.[94] So long as his personal involvement went unknown in Quebec, Bennett's quest for victory would be greatly aided by the defeat of the Saskatchewan Liberal government, one of the pillars of the federal Liberal party.

The new Co-operative government led by Anderson moved quickly to fulfil its campaign promise to eliminate Catholic influence in the public schools, and restrict the amount of French-language instruction. Unpopular in Quebec, these measures were well received by the Protestant anglophone majority in the West.[95] Although the government included Progressives and Independents, it was dominated by Conservatives, who had high hopes of transferring their provincial success to the federal sphere. To further this aim, the Saskatchewan provincial party received a monthly subsidy of $300 to aid in federal party organization.[96]

In Manitoba, the provincial Conservative opposition faced a Progressive government increasingly supported by the Liberals. McRae's chief federal organizer was Dr H.C. Hodgson, who was 'doing good work,' in the general's opinion. Hodgson's party office in Winnipeg received about $600 per month to promote the Tory cause. By contrast, Alberta received no money from the central party headquarters. 'I am not paying any attention to that Province,' McRae informed Bennett, 'assuming you will do what is necessary in the four or five constituencies where we have a show.'[97] The Conservative hopes in Alberta rested on the urban ridings of Calgary, Edmonton, Lethbridge, and Medicine Hat, and on Bennett's own popularity.

TAKING STOCK: MAY 1930

In May 1930, *MacLean's* ran an article purporting to give the candid opinions of Bennett and McRae in regard to their election chances. 'Mr. Bennett,' the anonymous author related, 'expects to win.' McRae predicted Conservative gains of twenty-five to thirty seats, perhaps more. At a small dinner given for party stalwarts at about the same time, Bennett and McRae were seen to be 'very confident of victory.'[98] How realistic were their expectations?

The federal Conservative party was stronger in May 1930 than it had been in October 1927, in several ways. Bennett was a more experienced, more confident leader. His performance in the House of Commons had been vigorous and sustained, and his speech-making across the country well received. Bennett's image as a successful business tycoon was an asset in his quest for the nation's top political job at a time of economic uncertainty. Although the lacklustre Tory caucus had been altered only by a handful of by-elections since the Winnipeg convention, it was now organized in such a way as to make the most of the talent that was there. The prospect of victory had improved morale and promoted cohesion.

The major political issues played to the Conservatives' strong suits. The unemployment crisis occurred long enough before the election campaign to be blamed on the Liberals, who had taken the credit for the preceding boom years. American protectionist moves against Canadian exports, and soaring New Zealand butter imports under a Liberal-negotiated trade treaty, invited the raising of Canadian tariffs to protect

Canadian primary and secondary producers. The Liberals moved part way in this direction in the Dunning budget, but their eleventh-hour conversion to deliberate protection had not been very convincing. The Conservatives, however, had a long history of advocating tariff protection, as embodied in the party's historic National Policy of 1878. Protection was their issue. Sensing the parallel with 1891 and 1911, when anti-Americanism assisted the Conservatives in forging victorious voter coalitions, the Bennett-led party played up the nationalist angle on the tariff issue.

The party organization, led by A.D. McRae, was immeasurably stronger in 1930 than it had been in 1927. A full-fledged publicity machine, buttressed by state-of-the-art technology and Yankee-inspired innovations, was cranking out well-researched propaganda to hundreds of thousands of voters through the newspaper services and mailing lists. The provincial associations were linked to national headquarters by personal contacts and financial subsidies. In Quebec, an organization separate from the unreliable provincial party had been set up, and was duplicating in French the efforts of the Ottawa headquarters. Funds to pay for all of this were not as plentiful as McRae's people would have liked, but thanks to generous contributions from Bennett, Perley, and McRae, the organization was able to carry out its work largely unhampered by fiscal stringency. Certainly the Conservative organization was the envy of the Liberal leader, Prime Minister King, who complained bitterly of the lack of attention to campaign preparation within his own party.[99]

Provincially, the party ruled in two provinces that had been Liberal three years earlier: British Columbia and Saskatchewan. It retained office in New Brunswick, Nova Scotia, and Ontario. By contrast, the Liberals held power only in their perennial stronghold of Quebec and in tiny Prince Edward Island. The prospect of five provincial governments aiding the national party in the upcoming election campaign was encourageing.

Organizationally, the Conservative party was positioned for victory. The preparations of Bennett, McRae, and company had readied the party to meet the electoral opportunity afforded by the eocnmic crisis. Philosophically, ideologically, it was a different story. Unable to see into the future, the Conservatives dusted off their traditonal National Policy one more time. Suitably adapted, it might see them through a successful campaign. Confidently, they assumed it would bring a return of prosperity, too.

4 The 1930 Election:
Securing a Mandate

The polls opened on 28 July at 8:00 a.m., local standard time, and when they closed, ten hours later, 3,922,481 Canadians – three out of four eligible voters – had cast a ballot.[1] In the larger cities, interested citizens congregated outside the offices of the daily newspapers, which, aided by telegraph and telephone, posted results as they were reported. Those Canadians who owned a radio – in 1930 more than 450,000 did[2] – could listen to the returns at home. Prime Minister Mackenzie King settled into his East Block office for the long night's vigil, while Conservative leader R.B. Bennett chose to await results in his suite at the Château Laurier.

The Maritime provinces reported first. The Conservatives picked up a couple of seats in Prince Edward Island, where the Liberal minister, Cyrus Macmillan, was toppled, but dropped two to the Liberals in Nova Scotia. New Brunswick, where Bennett was a native son, swung three new seats to the Tories. All told, the Conservatives carried twenty-three seats to only six for the Liberals. The trend was encouraging, but they had done nearly as well in 1926, yet still lost the election. (See table 4, page 90.)

Quebec, long the bane of Conservative hopes, proved remarkably receptive this time. One supposedly safe seat after another tumbled out of the Liberal column, including those of Lucien Cannon and Frederic Kay, both ministers. Among the newly elected Conservatives were the former provincial leader, Arthur Sauvé, and Armand Lavergne, for many years a Nationalist colleague of Henri Bourassa. When the last vote was counted, Conservative representation in Quebec had leaped from four to twenty-four seats out of sixty-five.

Party standings in Ontario ebbed and flowed all evening. In the end, the Conservatives picked up six seats, leaving them with fifty-nine of the province's eighty-two. For the first time in the twentieth century, however, the Liberals broke into the Tories' Toronto stronghold, where Alderman Sam Factor upset the former mayor and long-time MP 'Tommy' Church. The Conservatives had done well, but not so well as they had hoped.

In 1926, the Conservatives had failed to carry a single seat in Manitoba and Saskatchewan. This time, the Bennett steamroller moved right into the Prairies, overturning two key ministers, Thomas Crerar and Charles Dunning, in the process. The voters returned eleven Tory candidates from Manitoba, and eight from Saskatchewan. Rural Alberta's allegiance to the United Farmers held firm, but the Conservatives added three more urban ridings to Bennett's Calgary constituency. With twenty-three Prairie seats out of fifty-four, they were assured of a majority already.

British Columbians went against the tide. Two prominent Tory front-benchers, A.D. McRae and H.H. Stevens, were upset in Vancouver ridings, and the party lost five seats overall. Still, it held eight of the fifteen ridings on the West Coast, enough for a comfortable victory. On Tuesday, 29 July, Prime Minister King advised the governor general to send for R.B. Bennett.[3]

The numbers derived from the ballot-boxes seemed straightforward. They indicated a strong swing in seats to the Conservative party headed by R.B. Bennett, sufficient for a comfortable parliamentary majority. But what had brought the Tories their victory? Was it their organization? Perhaps their platform? Or maybe Bennett's leadership? Before analysing the Conservative record in office, it is crucial to understand the basis of the mandate given to Bennett and his party on 28 July 1930.

STRATEGIES FOR VICTORY

The economic setting for the 1930 election was grim: falling wheat prices, growing unemployment, a rising business-failure rate, a collapsed stock market, and diminishing foreign markets for Canadian goods. After five years of continuous, even spectacular, expansion, the economy was in the throes of a painful contraction.[4] The winter slump of 1929–30 continued to spread during the campaign months of June and July. Conditions were not yet as bad as they would become, of course, but to people unable to glimpse the future, they were bad enough. And yet, most Canadians were unwilling to accept that the days of prosperity, illusory though they had been for many, had finally departed. As James H. Gray has noted, 'There was nothing in our experience or in our history that prepared us for the Dirty Thirties. Booms and busts there had been – four major depressions in the previous thirty years. But they had passed quickly; and the assumption everywhere was that this, too would pass quickly.'[5] Canadians were hurting, but they were not ready to relinquish their optimism about the future.

Protected by a parliamentary majority, Prime Minister King had largely controlled the timing of the election. Initially he had favoured 1931: '1930 ... will be too soon after the changes in the U.S. tariff & ours,' he wrote in his diary in July 1929, '& the question as to who it would be best to send to the next Imperial Conference could be an issue in the elections of 1931 which would help us in Quebec.'[6] Four months earlier, King had received a confidential report from his election adviser, Senator Andrew Haydon, predicting serious Liberal losses in Manitoba and Saskatchewan that would be only partially offset by modest gains in Nova Scotia and British Columbia.[7] With only a thin majority, the Liberals would have to hold their overwhelming lead in Quebec, and attract new seats in populous Ontario, if they hoped to retain power. When the imperial conference, which King saw as the key to another mandate from Quebec on 'the issue Canadianism vs. Imperialism,' was rescheduled for the autumn of 1930, he began to think of an election for the summer of the same year. The Dunning budget was carefully crafted to hold existing Liberal support in the West, while breaking into imperial-minded Ontario. 'Switch trade from U.S. to Britain,' King wrote, 'that will be the cry & it will sweep the country I believe. We will take the flag once more out of the Tory hands.'[8] Such a policy might accelerate the slow Liberal rebound in British Columbia and the Maritimes, both regions being susceptible, as Ontario was, to a pro-British appeal. Unlike 'reciprocity,' which had always proven disastrous for them, 'British preference' had served the Liberals well in the Laurier era. King would try it again.

The Conservatives' minimum target was 124 seats, a bare majority. They had come very close in 1925, with 116, but close did not count in a minority House where Arthur Meighen was outmanoeuvred for several months, then stumbled into another election that reduced his party to second place once again. With a badly faltering economy, the existence of widespread disaffection with the Liberal government was to be expected in 1930. The trick for the Conservatives was to convert the protest vote into new seats. To do so meant breaking through in at least one of Quebec and the Prairies, since they already held most of the seats in the Maritimes, Ontario, and British Columbia.

The Conservatives opted to lean to the West. The 1925 results had shown that, with a handful more Prairie seats, they could have won their majority, even without support in francophone Quebec. The Winnipeg convention had marked the beginning of the Tory attempt to woo the West, by choosing the Albertan R.B. Bennett as leader. The convention's platform had largely reflected the pro-western concerns of the first runner-up candidate, Hugh Guthrie. The Conservative break-through in Saskatchewan in 1929, ably assisted by Bennett's pocket-book, seemed to bode well for such a strategy. To A.D. McRae, Bennett wrote optimistically of 'a new Ontario–Western Canada alignment.'[9]

Critical to the success of the Conservative strategy was winning back the Ontario seats lost to the Liberals between 1925 and 1926. Fifteen in number, they were seen as a necessary though not sufficient condition for a Conservative majority. Premier Howard Ferguson and his Ontario Conservative machine held the key. Fresh on the heels of a landslide provincial victory in 1929, Ferguson was confident he could produce the numbers. As J.W. Dafoe learned, he had promised 'to deliver a minimum of seventy-two seats in Ontario.[10] By merely holding their strength in British Columbia and the Maritimes, the Conservatives could win if their breakthroughs in Ontario and the West materialized. Quebec was not written off completely, but no substantial improvement was expected there.[11] If all went as planned, none was needed.

ISSUES AND IMAGES

An important part of both major parties' election arsenals was their campaign platforms. These were carefully designed to reassure existing supporters and attract new ones. For an interested minority, then as now, the intellectual content of party policy was important. For the vast majority, then as now, the symbolic content was the more significant. The platform message, delivered either through printed literature or by party speakers and canvassers, helped to formulate in the voter's mind an image of what each party stood for. This, in turn, helped the voters decide for whom to vote.[12]

The Conservatives seized the initiative in the campaign by unveiling their platform first. R.B. Bennett launched his national tour with a major speech in Winnipeg on 9 June that was carried nation-wide on radio.

The location was symbolically important. Winnipeg, the site of the first national Conservative convention three years earlier, was the gateway to the West. Stripped of its decorative features, Bennett's speech pledged the party to four key things: 'a policy of protection'; 'the improvement of the whole scheme of Canadian transportation,' including the St Lawrence seaway, Hudson Bay Railway, and Peace River outlet; 'a plan for greater Empire trade to be based on mutual advantage'; and 'a national old age pension scheme.'[13]

Because the word 'tariff' was a red flag to many of the voters, particularly in the West, to whom the Conservatives wished to appeal, it was used but once in the party manifesto. All around it were soothing references to 'development of our national resources, our agricultural and industrial life,' 'protection for ... our consumers from exploitation,' and 'development of a foreign market.' Presumably the wealthy manufacturers needed no specific persuasion to see the benefits of Tory protectionist policies for themselves. Linking 'protection for Canadians' with 'greater Empire trade ... based on mutual advantage'[14] was a clever attempt to oppose the Liberals' British preferential-trade program (potentially harmful to many of the interest groups traditionally Tory in allegiance), without trampling on the emotional appeal of that policy for all the voters of British stock and sympathy (many of whom were also traditional Tory supporters). Emotionally, the transportation plank harkened back to the popular nation-building policies of Sir John A. Macdonald, while, practically, it promised investment, employment, and a host of ancillary economic benefits. The appeal of the old-age pension promise was most particularly for voters in those provinces – Quebec and the Maritimes – whose governments had decided not to enter the joint, dollar-for-dollar pension plan set up by the Liberal government in 1927.[15] All provinces were feeling the economic pinch by mid-1930, however, and could use more federal aid. Advocacy of a national old-age pension also helped to soften the party's image, often portrayed as excessively pro-business and uncaring.

The Liberals countered with Mackenzie King's nationally broadcast, keynote campaign address, one week later, in Brantford, a medium-sized industrial Ontario city typical of the areas the Liberals hoped to capture enroute to a new majority. The Liberals, King declared there, would stress three points: 'the record of the government,' 'the budget of 1930,' and 'a choice between the Liberal and Conservative parties as the representatives of Canadian opinion at the Imperial and economic conferences.'[16] The two most notable aspects of this platform were, first, it did not promise anything new, and, second, it took no account of the deepening economic recession. 'The record of the Govt ... is a truly marvellous one,' King declared in his diary, obviously feeling it would go a long way to ensure re-election. Furthermore, he felt Bennett's emphasis on unemployment was mistaken. 'The men who are working are not going to worry particularly over some of those who are not,' he wrote hopefully.[17] In essence, then, King and the Liberals were promising the Canadian people more of the same, a continuation of the policies, personnel, and practices that had marked their administration over the previous nine years in office. With widespread economic hardship more and more evident, it was a curious, perhaps even arrogant, approach to take.

Unfortunately for King, the chief issue of this election was unemployment, which served as a code word for the faltering state of the Canadian economy. 'The Conservative Party,' Bennett promised over and over again, 'is going to find work for all who are willing to work, or perish in the attempt.'[18] It was the perfect opposition issue. The economic crisis was widespread, yet could not be blamed on the Conservatives, who had not been in power. King's first answer to the hostile audiences was to promise to call together a conference of experts representing labour, business, and government immediately after the election, to devise a solution to the unemployment problem. 'In going over speech material,' he wrote, 'I thought of putting in an amount for an unemployment conference $10,000. This will be the answer to the 5¢ piece.'[19] Bennett was ready for this feeble response. 'Mr. King promises you conferences,' he declared. 'I promise you action. He promises consideration of the problem of unemployment; I promise to end unemployment. Which plan do you like best?'[20] Bennett's pledge to call an emergency session of Parliament immediately after the election to end the unemployment problem seemed to ice the cake. Eventually King was forced to promise that a Liberal government would match 'dollar for dollar' any provincial contributions to the emergency relief of unemployment.[21] It was too little, too late. Knowing a winning issue, General McRae urged all Conservative candidates to make unemployment 'the outstanding issue' in the final weeks. Once the battle was over, even King acknowledged that Bennett 'had stressed the unemployment issue from the start to good effect.'[22]

Liberal hopes for persuading voters that their party could handle the economic crisis rested upon the Dunning budget. It had seemed to have something for everyone: reduced tariffs for the free traders, increased tariffs for the protectionists, broadened British preferences for the impe-

rialists, countervailing duties against the United States for the nationalists, a sales-tax cut for all. Howard Ferguson was particularly worried
about its effect in Ontario.[23] In contrast, by muddying the tariff waters
and sullying the low-tariff image of Thomas Crerar, the former Progressive leader whom King had made his minister of railways, the Dunning
budget gave the Conservatives a decisive opening with Prairie voters.
At his kick-off rally in Winnipeg, Bennett directed a rhetorical broadside
against age-old Liberal and Progressive mythology: 'Listen, you agricul-
turists from the west and all other parts of Canada, you have been
taught to mock at tariffs and applaud free trade. Tell me, when did free
trade fight for you? ... You say tariffs are only for the manufacturers. I
will make them fight for you as well. I will use them to blast a way into
the markets that have been closed to you.'[24] With commodity prices falling rapidly, farmers were prepared to listen to new approaches. The
Conservative party was ready with a saleable version of its traditional
protectionist policy. 'We will go further and take the necessary steps,'
Bennett promised in a mass letter sent to Canadian farm voters, 'to
protect for our farmers the home market, and to assist them to regain
their position in the world market.'[25]

New Zealand butter was a rallying cry that proved as effective for the
Conservatives in rural Canada as unemployment was in the cities. In
1925, the Liberal government had negotiated a trade treaty with Australia, the terms of which were subsequently extended to New Zealand.
Unnoticed at the time, the treaty opened up the Canadian consumer
market for butter from 'down under,' much to the chagrin of Canadian
dairy farmers. New Zealand butter imports, insignificant in 1925 at
162,848 pounds, mushroomed to 39,744,826 pounds in 1930.[26] Dunning
had served notice in his budget that this aspect of the treaty would be
terminated in the fall, but the damage to Liberal free-trade rhetoric was
already done. The Conservatives added fuel to the flames by pointing
out that, while butter in the unprotected Canadian market sold for
twenty-six cents a pound, across the border American dairy farmers
were receiving forty-two cents a pound behind their tariff walls.[27] It was
a telling argument against Liberal trade policy, and nowhere more effective than in rural southern Ontario and the Eastern Townships of
Quebec, where Canada's dairy industry was concentrated.

Traditionally, the Conservative party was linked in the public mind
with a policy of close ties with the British Empire; the Liberals were
viewed as the party more attuned to a position of Canadian autonomy.
Over the years, each party reaped the electoral rewards associated with

its respective image. The 1930 campaign witnessed an interesting reversal. Counting upon the loyalty of Quebec voters, the Liberals reached out for the imperialist vote, concentrated in Ontario, by stressing the beneficial effects to the empire of broadened British preferential tariffs. Not to be outdone, the Conservatives, relying upon the faithfulness of Ontario voters, reached out for the nationalist vote, in Quebec and elsewhere, by emphasizing their economic protectionism. Bennett declared the Conservative policy to be 'Canada first, then the Empire.'[28] Translated into French, with the second part conveniently dropped, the policy became 'Canada d'abord,' a potent nationalist cry in the mouths of Bleu speakers.[29] The Conservatives easily won this battle of symbolic slogans, as King himself admitted. 'Canada first & Canada for the Canadians made a strong appeal,' he noted privately after the election. 'Having the imperial side of that issue was not really helpful to us.'[30]

A couple of other issues achieved some prominence. King and Premier Ferguson engaged in a public controversy over whose government was responsible for the delay of the St Lawrence seaway. The Liberal party in Quebec attempted to resurrect the bloody shirt of conscription once more. *La Presse* ran a front-page story three days before the election, alleging that, with a possible crisis in Egypt, London expected Bennett would be susceptible to a British request for conscription at the upcoming imperial conference.[31] Beyond these, there were the usual campaign charges of extravagant promises, unfounded accusations, and irresponsible rhetoric by the other side. However, the principal issues, the ones the parties used most frequently to burnish their own images and deface those of their opponents, were these four: unemployment, the Dunning budget, New Zealand butter, and the symbolic relationship of Canada and the empire.

LEADERS AND IMAGES

A second important factor in the election campaign was the contrasting styles of the two party leaders. Mackenzie King, who had bested Arthur Meighen two out of three times, now faced a new Conservative champion in R.B. Bennett. The importance of the leader as the 'chief bearer of the party's image' had been growing in Canadian politics since Confederation.[32] The 1930 campaign marked the first election in which radio played a major part. This new medium of mass communication enhanced even further the role of the party leader. For the first time, voters in numbers far beyond those who could cram inside the four walls of a smoky auditorium or steamy arena could hear the party leaders for themselves. For example, Conservative organizers expected a listening audience of more than two million for Bennett's keynote Winnipeg address, dwarfing the projected live attendance of 10,000.[33] Air time was expensive, so the parties concentrated the party's radio exposure on the leader. When added to the traditional national tour by train and, now, automobile, the effect was to focus media and public attention on the leader, at the expense of his party colleagues. No longer was it necessary to 'communicate with the electorate only through a chain of regional and local intermediaries.'[34]

Throughout the campaign, Bennett exuded an air of righteous self-confidence. The journalist Bruce Hutchison ably described his hustings performance this way: 'His manner was at once lofty and sympathetic. His radiant smile encouraged the weak and humble. As he lowered his massive head and glared over his glasses the strong quailed. Before a vast audience or a small group he struck a pose of natural sublimity. No more than King could he ever be one of the boys, but he seemed to symbolize and promise that age of abundance which, briefly lost, would quickly return under his guidance.'[35] Bennett frankly acknowledged that the country had serious problems, sternly admonished the Liberal government of nine years' duration for its failure to act, then confidently prescribed the remedy: the Conservative platform of 'Canada First' protection, great transportation projects, and universal old-age pensions. He talked of a 'fair deal' for farmers and workers, dismissed fears of a CPR monopoly with the evocative phrase 'Amalgamation? Never! Competition? Ever,' and summed up his campaign theme with this question to a Three Rivers audience: 'Are you as prosperous as you were in 1926?' It was a command performance, repeated from one ocean to the other.[36] Everywhere he went, Bennett was well received by large, enthusiastic crowds. His handlers devised a variety of meeting formats, including motorcades of several hundred cars in Quebec, an open-air meeting on Vancouver Island, a Confederation picnic for 1 July in New Brunswick, luncheons, ladies' teas, formal dinners, handshaking with railway employees, factory tours, whistle-stops, and what was still the bread-and-butter event of campaigns in that era, the evening rally in a packed auditorium.[37]

Bennett's campaign itinerary was arranged by McRae, after consultation with Bennett, Ferguson, and the provincial campaign committees. Midway through the campaign, a dispute arose, with the Ontario committee insisting that Bennett finish off in their province, while western

Conservatives requested that he wind things up on the Prairies. Bennett himself informed McRae he was 'strongly of the opinion' that the tour should finish in the West, but he was overruled.[38] His final campaign speech was delivered in and broadcast from Ottawa.

Between Winnipeg on 9 June, and Ottawa on 26 July, Bennett travelled nearly 14,000 miles, and delivered an estimated 107 speeches, sometimes at the rate of five per day.[39] It was a gruelling pace, even though he travelled on a private railway car as often as possible. Journeying with him was an entourage of three. Arthur Merriam, his private secretary, was a discreet, organized, calming influence, a good counterbalance to the second member, William Herridge. A recent convert to Conservatism, and a former family friend of Mackenzie King, Herridge was an Ottawa lawyer brimming with ideas. As chief speech-writer, he was responsible for the most memorable phrases of Bennett's campaign, including the slogan 'Canada First,' the promise to 'blast a way' into world markets, and the pledge to 'end unemployment or perish in the attempt.'[40] The third member was Bennett's younger sister, Mildred. While she served as a travel companion to her devoted brother, Mildred's feminine charm was also exploited on the public platform. 'I think they would like to see your smile,' McRae advised her at the beginning of the tour.[41] As the Conservative editor and organizer Arthur Ford noted, 'she had all the tact and diplomacy, graciousness and ability to meet the public which Mr. Bennett often lacked.'[42]

A key supporting role was played by the five Conservative premiers, who appeared with Bennett at major rallies in their home provinces. Ferguson was particularly successful in diverting King from his primary target, the federal Conservatives, by utilizing, first, the five-cent-piece gaffe and, then, the jurisdictional controversy over the St Lawrence waterway project. King became so incensed at Ferguson, whom he considered 'by nature a skunk,' that he devoted increasing attention in his final ten-day foray across Ontario to mud-slinging denunciations of the premier's alleged 'Tammany' methods, in spite of contrary advice from two of his local ministers, W.D. Euler and James Malcolm.[43] Similar charges of political manipulation against the other Tory premiers only enlivened their participation in the campaign. E.N. Rhodes in Nova Scotia, J.B. Baxter in New Brunswick, J.T.M. Anderson in Saskatchewan, and S.F. Tolmie in British Columbia, all came out four-square for Bennett and the Conservative cause.

Three other Conservatives, front-benchers from the federal caucus, played important supportive roles. Hugh Guthrie, H.H. Stevens, and

R.J. Manion were each sent on speaking tours of the West, a region crucial to the party's victory plans. Significantly, Manion, a Catholic, was kept out of Saskatchewan at Bennett's specific instruction, sent in code to McRae by telegram from Regina, 'to avoid arousing latent prejudices ... in this Province.'[44] Former prime minister Robert Borden was persuaded to chair one of Bennett's Ontario meetings, thus demonstrating his full support. Not so favoured was Arthur Meighen, who was more than willing to help out, but was not asked. Back-room gossip indicated that Ferguson, still smarting from the 1927 convention, vetoed any role for the former national leader.[45] Meighen's Quebec ally, E.L. Patenaude, was also left on the sidelines, apparently as a condition of Lord Atholstan's support. The assistance of one other prominent Conservative, Camillien Houde, would have been welcomed, but the Quebec leader opted to continue his provincial party's tradition, and stayed neutral, much to Bennett's annoyance.[46]

While Bennett was a model of supreme self-assurance, King projected an image of petulant uncertainty. In truth, he never recovered from his ill-timed declaration in the House of Commons that no Tory provincial government could expect a five-cent piece from any administration led by him. The Conservatives were able to make his own leadership virtually an issue in itself. A series of partisan cartoons generated by the Conservative publicity office depicted a prosperous, well-fed King, with a five-cent piece prominently mounted on his vest, turning a deaf ear to needy Canadians in a variety of circumstances.[47] Tory election tactics were designed to maintain the momentum derived from the final session of Parliament. McRae underlined this point in a letter to the party stalwarts. 'The Liberal Party is on the defensive from the start,' he wrote 'and there we intend to keep it.'[48] In choosing to highlight the Liberal record as one of the keynotes of his campaign, King voluntarily assumed the defensive position McRae desired for him. Jeering crowds forced King to conjure up, first, the promise of an economic conference to study the unemployment problem, and, then, the pledge of 'dollar for dollar' grants to provinces truly in need. Even this sensible policy caused the party grief, its monetary image calling to mind King's five-cent-piece statement. The Liberal leader's lack of personal popularity dragged down the appeal of his party.

Where King picked fights with the provincial premiers, Bennett stood shoulder to shoulder with them. Where King offered cautious study, Bennett pledged vigorous action. Where King defended a shaky status quo, Bennett promised a better tomorrow. Where King rationalized failure, Bennett guaranteed success. Given this choice of leadership images, there was really no contest.

ORGANIZATION, PUBLICITY, AND FUNDS

Much still depended on the rival organizations. When the election call came, the Conservative party headquarters had been in smooth operation for more than a year. The Dominion organizer, A.D. McRae, immediately sent off a 'week-end letter' to the party's nominated candidates. 'We are hard at work this week laying the foundation securely for the campaign,' he assured them.[49] His right and left arms continued to be Redmond Code, general secretary, and Robert Lipsett, director of publicity. Provincial headquarters and campaign committees were already set up and functioning.

With the aid of kindred provincial governments, the Conservatives were strong organizationally in Nova Scotia, New Brunswick, Ontario, Saskatchewan, and British Columbia. As Escott Reid learned during a research tour of the country in 1931, 'the prov[incial] machinery of gov-[ernment] is always very important to a party in a federal election,' because 'the prov[incial] patronage built up an efficient machine.' Provincial governments, not constrained by Civil Service Commission regulations, were better placed than the federal government to dispense petty jobs as patronage. Consequently, they could generally swing a small army of foot-soldiers behind the campaigns of their federal brethren. For this reason as much as any, federal parties tended to rely upon their provincial cousins' party organizations, even in federal campaigns.[50]

Though in opposition, traditionally active Conservative provincial organizations in Manitoba and Prince Edward Island guaranteed a vigorous party effort there. Even in Quebec, where the provincial party remained aloof, the Conservatives had built a new organization that would be, if not as strong as the Liberals', certainly the best one in nearly twenty years. Joseph Rainville, assisted by organizer Jacques Cartier and publicity director L.J. Gauthier, headed the Montreal office, while Thomas Maher oversaw the Quebec City district.[51] Only in Alberta was the party weak organizationally, without even a provincial headquarters. Bennett's Calgary constituency secretary, Alice Millar, directed the party's modest efforts in that province, assisted by the former provincial leader, A.A. McGillivray.[52]

Though they were the party in power, the federal Liberals did not possess a well-oiled political machine. For one thing, they held provincial power only in Prince Edward Island and Quebec. Cooperation, even in the latter province, long a firm Liberal base, was hindered by a serious disagreement between Premier Taschereau and the federal Liberals over water-power jurisdiction.[53] Furthermore, the national campaign office headed by Senator Andrew Haydon did not really move into high gear until May 1930, a full year after McRae's headquarters was launched. The result was a predictable chaos, much to Mackenzie King's dismay, though he was as much to blame for it as any Liberal. On 29 June he wrote: 'The organization in these matters is all pretty much of a "hit and miss" character. Really we have no organization. Candidates have gotten into the field here & there, but many constituencies are still without anyone, literature has not reached the candidates, speakers are not arranged for as they should be. Our opponents, on [the] other hand, have a splendid organization, own their own printing press, have been getting out literature right along.'[54] In practical terms, responsibility for the Liberal organization in each province fell to the cabinet ministers, many of whom found themselves hard-pressed to hold their own seats.[55]

The theory underlying the sophisticated Conservative publicity machine was simplicity itself. 'The more people we can get using the same arguments,' McRae lectured the party stalwarts in a campaign letter of instruction, 'the more likely we are to impress our policy on the mind of the voter.'[56] Utilizing the Addressograph system, the publicity office sent mass mail-outs to the entire list of 210,000 names, and more partisan letters to the key people. Some letters went out over Bennett's signature, some over McRae's, and some simply bore the party's imprimatur. A large number of new pamphlets were churned out, many earmarked for specific subgroups in the population. As Lipsett later explained to Bennett, 'we issued some twenty such pamphlets, some of which we printed five thousand of, and some one hundred and fifty thousand, but each directed to a definite purpose and a definite audience.'[57] Detailed cross-referencing of the mailing lists, combined with the technical prowess of the Addressograph system, allowed the party to direct *Restoring the Live Stock Industry* to farmers, *Playing Politics with the Soldier* to veterans, and *A Message to Labour* to workers. Such flexibility in a pre-computer age was impressive.[58]

Five more issues of *The Canadian*, the party's in-house propaganda journal, were published to join the four mailed out prior to dissolution.

As with the policy pamphlets, extra copies were forwarded to the candidates and the provincial headquarters. The average press run during the campaign was a quarter of a million copies. The first six issues of *The Canadian*, along with Bennett's keynote address, Manion's rebuttal of King's Brantford speech, and the most important pamphlets, were combined to form the 'speakers' guide.'[59]

Lipsett continued to utilize his various news services in support of the party's propaganda effort: the 'non-political' Standard News Service, the Weekly Political Letters, and the Conservative editorials. These weekly news services reached a combined circulation of over one million, and were 'particularly effective in reaching the rural population,' as many farm families did not subscribe to the urban dailies. During the campaign, Lipsett instituted a separate news service for pro-Conservative daily papers. In Lipsett's view, 'it vastly improved the Canadian Press reports' of Bennett's Maritime campaign, and generally buttressed the Tories' press coverage.[60]

The publicity department came up with a few other gimmicks as well. One of these was a gramophone record featuring Mildred Bennett giving a three-minute talk, on one side, and General McRae, on the other. In a letter to the candidates, McRae recommended its use 'particularly for afternoon tea parties and other functions carried on by the ladies,' as well as for local broadcasts.[61] The office also prepared matted copies of Racey's cartoons, originally prepared for *The Canadian*, and mailed out more than 2,000 copies of them to some 200 daily and weekly papers for publication.

To supplement the nationally oriented information, the research office tracked down information requested by the local Conservative associations. 'There were hundreds of these [queries],' Lipsett reported to Bennett. 'Some of them took days of digging to answer but I believe every candidate, organizer, or speaker who wrote in will attest that he got fast and satisfactory service. Where the information sought might be useful in other ridings, it was sent into them.'[62] Arthur Ford recollected in his memoirs that 'copies of Liberal pamphlets and literature were in Conservative headquarters the day they were off the press.' Lipsett confirmed this undercover research in his post-election report to Bennett: 'We had facilities for reviewing the general Liberal constituency advertising a week before it was published. In every case we furnished the reply to it to our candidates simultaneously with publication and in many instances they were able to run the reply in the same issue as the

Liberal advertisement was published.'[63] Responsibility for placing newspaper ads was left in the hands of the provincial headquarters, but the research facilities of the national party's publicity bureau assisted the process immeasurably.

The national headquarters coordinated arrangements for the major English-language radio broadcasts. R.A. Stapells, an executive with the J.J. Gibbons advertising agency in Toronto, was in charge of this aspect of the campaign. The central party office sponsored twelve such broadcasts, seven of them by Bennett, including the campaign opener from Winnipeg and the closing speech in Ottawa. The other five were by leading party spokesmen: R.J. Manion, Hugh Guthrie, Thomas Bell, Premier Ferguson, and Premier Rhodes. The radio broadcasts were promoted through newspaper ads, as well as via the party's mass mail-out system.[64]

While the Conservative organization was churning out 'tons of leaflets, pamphlets, handbooks, ready-made speeches and ready-made editorials [that] poured over the nation like a Niagara,'[65] the Liberal headquarters was stumbling and fumbling along. Where McRae had been given eighteen months to pull together his organization, Haydon was expected to throw one together in a few weeks. The inevitable result was second-rate literature, tardily distributed, and slip-ups in booking meetings, reserving radio time, and arranging press coverage. 'At every turn the Conservatives are getting ahead of us,' King lamented early in the campaign. The situation never really improved, despite Haydon's best efforts. The Liberals most effective stroke was a reactive, negative one. King ordered the postmaster general, P.J. Veniot, to cut off as of 18 June the parliamentary franking privileges, which the Tory MPs had been using to mail out vast quantities of party publicity free of charge.[66]

Funding the campaign organization was an expensive proposition. As the *Ottawa Journal* noted, 'no political party can enter an election in this country today without a central fund of at least $1,000,000 – for perfectly proper purposes.'[67] Labour MP J.S. Woodsworth was more expansive in his estimate: '$2,000,000,' he asserted, 'is closer to the actual mark, from the information I have.'[68] In addition to headquarters expenses, the party was expected to help with expenses in the local constituencies. Escott Reid learned that in 1930 the two major parties spent $10,000 to $20,000 each per riding, most of which was obtained from party headquarters.[69]

The Conservative central office operated on a $50,000 monthly budget during June and July, about two and a half times its pre-election expenditures. Additional staff and vastly increased publicity accounted for the increase. For instance, the cost of printing and mailing a sixteen-page 250,000-copy issue of *The Canadian* was $3,930. A dozen national and regional radio broadcasts featuring Bennett and other leading Conservatives, plus newspaper ads plugging the broadcasts, ate up an additional $28,900, over and above the regular headquarters budget.[70] To finance these costs, McRae secured a financial commitment from five wealthy Tory MPs. He, Sir George Perley, E.B. Ryckman, and J.D. Chaplin, each advanced $25,000, while their leader, R.B. Bennett, committed himself to $50,000. With $150,000 up front, the organizational office and publicity bureau could carry out their plans without fear of a crippling shortage of funds.[71]

The major traditional sources of party funds for both the Liberals and the Conservatives were the corporate business communities of Montreal and Toronto.[72] Bennett's predecessor, Arthur Meighen, had experienced considerable trouble with St James Street. Initially, the Bennett fundraisers foundered there as well, caught in the bitter factional enmity that centred chiefly around the controversial Lord Atholstan of the *Montreal Star*. McRae himself went to Montreal to sort the matter out in early July. 'With Perley spent balance of week Montreal struggling with impossible situation with Atholstan,' he wired Bennett. 'His final proposal was ... that all collections pass through him, otherwise he would do nothing. Much feeling in Montreal against Atholstan collecting.'[73] Meanwhile, the local riding associations were starved for funds. 'The cupboard is as bare as possible,' Quebec candidate John Hackett was informed by his Montreal law partner, George B. Foster.[74] As Montreal funds traditionally financed the Maritime as well as Quebec ridings, the situation was grave. Eventually McRae was able to bring the sides together, and the funds flowed in.[75] During the final week of the campaign, with Quebec organizer J.H. Rainville in need of an extra $50,000, the two sides cooperated handsomely. 'Lord Atholstan ... volunteered to subscribe half that amount if I could secure the other,' Rainville wrote McRae. 'I managed to obtain the Twenty-five thousand from Gen. McCuaig and friends, and within a half hour, the balance was subscribed and distribution effected.'[76] Ironically, Atholstan's cooperation was assisted by none other than Mackenzie King, who had blasted his newspaper, the *Montreal Star*, for alleged partisan hypocrisy in mid-July. 'My action may lead to his putting in money against us,' King conceded, 'but I could not resist showing up the deception.'[77]

In the end, the Montreal supporters were more generous than McRae had dared hope. He had been told to expect $300,000.[78] When the last contribution was added in, the Montreal committee had raised $565,540. The list of donors read like a Who's Who of the Montreal financial and industrial establishment. Particularly large donations included: $50,000 each from the Bank of Montreal and the Canadian Pacific Railway; $35,000 from Canadian Car and Foundry; $32,500 from Montreal Light, Heat and Power (a Herbert Holt company); $30,000 from Dominion Textile and its related companies; and $25,000 each from the *Montreal Star*, National Breweries, the Royal Bank, and Shawinigan Water and Power.[79] The funds were put to immediate use: $105,000 was sent to Thomas Maher for the constituencies in the Quebec District; $97,000 went to Nova Scotia (with some earmarked for Prince Edward Island); $46,000 was forwarded to New Brunswick; and $15,000 was kept for the provincial headquarters. The remaining $300,000 was distributed among the forty ridings in the Montreal district.[80]

Less evidence is available concerning Conservative fund-raising in Toronto. The Ontario committee in charge of finances consisted of Home Smith, a Toronto industrialist and Ferguson ally; the wealthy Toronto MP E.B. Ryckman; and J.J. Gibbons, owner of an advertising agency. Their collections were less successful than the Montreal committee's, for, in the end, the three of them underwrote a campaign deficit of indeterminate amount, 'each assuming responsibility for one-third of same.'[81] The Ontario constituencies seem not to have suffered from any undue shortage of funds, however. For instance, General D.M. Hogarth, a Toronto mining entrepreneur, 'did much, if not all, of the financing in the Federal Election for the whole of Northern Ontario,' according to R.J. Manion.[82] A city like London, Escott Reid learned, was 'self-supporting,' requiring no subsidy from Conservative fund-raisers in Toronto. Conservative control of the provincial government, Reid was told, proved quite beneficial to party fund-raisers when approaching potential campaign donors.[83]

R.B. Bennett filled the financial gap in western Canada. While the financial communities of Winnipeg and Vancouver could take care of the Manitoba and British Columbia ridings, the provinces of Alberta and Saskatchewan were left to the party leader. Through his Calgary secretary, Alice Millar, Bennett funnelled his own money to the Alberta ridings.[84] 'Bennett money' also turned up in Saskatchewan, some $70,000 in all, divided among the twenty-one constituencies.[85]

After the election, a controversy arose over the amount of Bennett's campaign contributions. A Saskatchewan Conservative MP, F.W. Turnbull, was quoted in a Regina newspaper as saying that Bennett had spent $750,000 during the 1930 campaign, a claim Bennett denied. 'As you made the statement,' he admonished Turnbull, 'it would appear that I spent $750,000 in the last election, which is not correct.' The dispute was largely one of semantics. Bennett had already spent 'one half million dollars on the Conservative party' by the time the 1930 election was called, by his own admission. Add another $250,000 for the campaign, and one arrives at Turnbull's figure.[86] In addition to the $70,000 for Saskatchewan and $50,000 for the Ottawa headquarters, he spent an indeterminate amount for Alberta, including his own riding, and doubtless paid the cost of his own national tour.

The Liberals were roughly on a par with the Conservatives in raising money, 'the sinews of war.' As the *MacLean's* correspondent noted, 'Haydon, indeed, matched McRae, national hookup for national hookup, hired as many private cars, bought as many pages of advertising and deluged Canada with as many leaflets, handbooks, pamphlets. Where all the funds came from, nobody knows.'[87] Rumours reached the Conservatives' brain trust as to the origin of the Liberal funds, but no use was made of the information.[88] Not for another year did the public learn of the massive generosity of the Beauharnois Power Company, which contributed some '$600,000 to $700,000' to federal Liberal coffers, divided between the national and Quebec offices. The federal Conservatives had been offered a substantial contribution as well, but Bennett refused to accept it. A few thousand dollars of Beauharnois money did find its way into the federal Conservative campaign in Quebec.[89] The ensuing scandal damaged the Liberal party's reputation somewhat, but it had no effect on the election outcome, of course, since the votes had been cast long before the adverse publicity surfaced.

ANALYSING THE VOTING RESULTS

The Conservatives scored a convincing victory in the 1930 election, in terms of the seats won by each party. Their total increased from 91 in 1926 to 137, while the Liberals dropped from 128 to 91. Significantly, the number of ridings carried by 'Other' candidates declined to 17, the lowest total for any election between 1917 and 1958. The Conservatives showed net gains of 2 in Prince Edward Island, 3 in New Brunswick, 20 in Quebec, 6 in Ontario, 11 in Manitoba, 8 in Saskatchewan, and 3 in Alberta, offset by net losses of 2 in Nova Scotia and 5 in British Columbia (see table 4). When related to their pre-election strategy, it can be seen that they performed as expected in the Maritimes and Prairies, fell

TABLE 4
Federal election results, 1926 and 1930

	1926						1930					
	Liberal*		Conser-vative		Other		Liberal*		Conser-vative		Other	
Province	S	%	S	%	S	%	S	%	S	%	S	%
Prince Edward Island	3	52.7	1	47.3	0	0.0	1	50.0	3	50.0	0	0.0
Nova Scotia	2	43.5	12	53.7	0	2.8	4	47.5	10	52.5	0	0.0
New Brunswick	4	46.1	7	53.9	0	0.0	1	40.6	10	59.4	0	0.0
Quebec	60	62.3	4	34.3	1	3.4	40	53.2	24	44.7	1	2.2
Ontario	26	38.9	53	54.1	3	7.0	22	43.9	59	54.4	1	1.7
Manitoba	11	37.9	0	42.2	6	19.9	4	37.2	11	47.7	2	15.1
Saskatchewan	18	56.8	0	27.5	3	15.6	11	46.5	8	37.6	2	15.9
Alberta	3	24.5	1	31.5	12	44.0	3	30.0	4	33.9	9	36.1
British Columbia & Territories	1	37.0	13	54.3	1	8.7	5	40.9	8	49.3	2	9.8
Total	128	46.1	91	45.3	26	8.6	91	45.4	137	48.7	17	5.8

SOURCES: Howard A. Scarrow, *Canada Votes* (New Orleans 1962), 62–3, 76–7; also M.C. Urquhart and K.A.H. Buckley, eds., *Historical Statistics of Canada* (Toronto 1965), 620
NOTE: S = number of seats; % refers to share of popular vote.
* Includes Liberal-Progressives

below expectations in Ontario and British Columbia, and fared considerably better than hoped in Quebec. Bennett affirmed these calculations in a post-election chat with King, who was himself much surprised, and disappointed, at the Liberals' declines in Quebec and the Prairies, and had hoped for better in the Maritimes and Ontario.[90] Popular-vote figures indicate the Liberals did increase their share of support in Nova Scotia, Ontario, Alberta, and British Columbia, but these increases were insufficient to bring many new seats, and were more than offset by major losses elsewhere.

In 1925, Arthur Meighen had come tantalizingly close to leading his party to a majority victory. Table 5 shows clearly where Bennett's Conservatives found the handful of extra seats required to put them over the top: 20 from Quebec and 13 from the Prairies. The breakthrough in Saskatchewan was especially noteworthy. Significantly, Bennett did not

TABLE 5
A comparison of Conservative results: 1925, 1926, and 1930

Province (total seats in parentheses)		1925		1926		1930	
		S	%	S	%	S	%
Prince Edward Island	(4)	2	48.0	1	47.3	3	50.0
Nova Scotia	(14)	11	56.4	12	53.7	10	52.5
New Brunswick	(11)	10	59.7	7	53.9	10	59.4
Quebec	(65)	4	33.7	4	34.3	24	44.7
Ontario	(82)	68	57.0	53	54.1	59	54.4
Manitoba	(17)	7	41.3	0	42.2	11	47.7
Saskatchewan	(21)	0	25.4	0	27.5	8	37.6
Alberta	(16)	3	31.8	1	31.5	4	33.9
British Columbia & Territories	(15)	11	49.4	13	54.3	8	49.3
Canada	(245)	116	46.5	91	45.3	137	48.7

SOURCE: Scarrow, *Canada Votes*, 48–9, 62–3, 76–7
NOTE: S = number of seats, % refers to share of popular vote.

do as well as Meighen had in 1925 in either British Columbia or Ontario. The Maritime provinces were equally generous to the Conservatives in both elections. Popular-vote analysis indicates that, in three of the provinces that contributed vital new seats to the party in 1930, namely, Quebec, Manitoba, and Saskatchewan, the party's share of the total vote had shown an increase in 1926, as well. This modest upswing in support did not result in any pay-off in seats to Meighen; in fact, he lost several in Manitoba through the cooperation of the Liberals and Progressives. However, the foreshadowing of the 1930 breakthrough is significant because the overall national swing had been away from the Conservatives in 1926. Four years later, the combination of growing regional support and a national swing to the Conservatives brought the party's share of the vote high enough to translate into a meaningful number of seats in these three provinces.

In view of the Conservatives' concerted efforts to broaden their appeal to rural voters, an analysis of voting statistics broken into urban and non-urban categories is useful. Utilizing the UNESCO definition of an ur-

TABLE 6
Conservative seats and share of popular vote by urban and non-urban classification:
1925, 1926, and 1930

Category	Total seats	1925			1926			1930		
		Seats won	% of seats	% of votes	Seats won	% of seats	% of votes	Seats won	% of seats	% of votes
Urban	67	44	65.7	51.4	38	56.7	49.2	42	62.7	51.7
Non-urban	178	72	40.4	43.0	53	29.8	42.9	95	53.4	46.7
Canada	245	116	47.3	46.5	91	37.1	45.3	137	55.9	48.7

SOURCES: *Seventh Census of Canada, 1931*, II, Table 7; *Report of the Chief Electoral Officer, 1931*; Scarrow, *Canada Votes*, 48-9, 62-3, 76-7

NOTE: The following sixty-four constituencies were defined as urban for the elections of 1925, 1926, and 1930: *Nova Scotia* – Cape Breton South, Halifax (dual-member); *New Brunswick* – Saint John–Albert (dual-member); *Quebec* – Hull, Quebec East, Quebec South, Quebec West, Sherbrooke, Trois Rivières, and these Montreal-area constituencies: Cartier, Hochelaga, Jacques Cartier, Laurier-Outremont, Maisonneuve, Mont Royal, Ste Anne, St Antoine, St Denis, St Henri, St Jacques, St Laurent–St Georges, Ste Marie; *Ontario* – Algoma West, Brantford, Essex East, Essex West, Fort William, Hamilton East, Hamilton West, Kingston, London, Ontario, Ottawa (dual-member), Peterborough West, Waterloo North, Wellington South, Wentworth, and these Toronto-area ridings: Parkdale, Toronto East, Toronto East Centre, Toronto High Park, Toronto North East, Toronto North West, Toronto Scarborough, Toronto South, Toronto West Centre, York South, York West; *Manitoba* – Winnipeg North, Winnipeg North Centre, Winnipeg South, Winnipeg South Centre; *Saskatchewan* – Moose Jaw, Regina, Saskatoon; *Alberta* – Calgary East, Calgary West, Edmonton East, Edmonton West; *British Columbia* – New Westminster, Vancouver-Burrard, Vancouver Centre, Vancouver South, Victoria.

ban area as a community of at least 20,000 people, the Canadian ridings can be grouped into two categories. The 64 constituencies in which 50 per cent or more of the population resided in communities whose population was at least 20,000 are deemed to be 'urban', whereas the remainder are classified as 'non-urban.'[91] Table 6 shows how successful the Conservatives' campaign strategy was in 1930. From a base of 91 seats in 1926, they added 4 urban ridings and 42 non-urban ones. A swing in the popular vote of less than 4 per cent towards the Conservatives in the non-urban ridings produced this large movement in seats. The successful appeal to non-urban ridings in both Quebec and the Prairies proved the difference between a comfortable majority in 1930, and a near miss in 1925.

In his post-election study of the linguistic cleavage in Canada, Escott Reid classified the ridings into three categories: predominantly French, predominantly English, and bilingual. The Conservatives won 99 of 157 English ridings, 24 of 42 bilingual ridings, and 11 of 46 French ones. From a comparative perspective, the significant factor was not that the Conservatives won so few predominantly French ridings, but that they won so many. Since 1917, their parliamentary caucus had been almost exclusively anglophone. In 1930, the party gained a bridgehead to francophone Canada.[92] Whether it could be held would be determined by subsequent events.

There were three key elements in the Conservatives' majority victory over the Liberals: superior organization, more effective leadership, and more saleable policies. Of these, the most significant was organization. Operating on an accelerated pre-campaign basis since mid-1929, the Conservative headquarters possessed a critical head start. McRae's organization was more innovative, utilizing the Addressograph machine for personalized mass mailings of publicity at an economical cost, and developing an elaborate weekly news service that placed the Conservative case effectively before the voters of rural and small-town English Canada. The Tories were assisted organizationally by five kindred provincial governments, whereas the Liberals could draw on just two. In Quebec, where the Conservative forces traditionally suffered from poor organization, an effective machine was set up under Rainville that largely negated a traditional Liberal advantage. The availability of funds during the campaign was not a decisive factor, as the two major parties each had adequate funds, and generally matched each other in their expenditures. The Conservative advantage in finances arose from the generosity of Bennett, in particular, as well as McRae and Perley, during the several months prior to the formal campaign.

Though there were no knock-down blows, R.B. Bennett clearly outpointed Mackenzie King on the hustings. Where King appeared cautious, petulant, and vacillating, Bennett seemed confident, vigorous, and decisive. Furthermore, the energetic support of five provincial premiers effectively neutralized the presence on the Liberal team of several high-profile ministers. Bennett's background as a successful business tycoon lent credibility to his prescriptions for the ailing economy. King, as the incumbent, was a natural scapegoat for those voters described here by J.W. Dafoe who were hurt by hard times: 'What they wanted to do was to hit someone in the eye, in retaliation for hard times, low prices of grain, disappointment at the failure of the wheat pool to deliver the goods, losses suffered through speculation, lack of cash, the indignity of having to put up with the old car.'[93] The Liberal leader had set himself up for this role by callously underestimating the gravity of the unemployment crisis throughout 1930, and arrogantly dismissing the possibility of federal assistance to Conservative-ruled provinces in the five-cent-piece declaration. In short, Bennett recognized the economic problems, and promised solutions. King evaded the problems and, consequently, could offer no solutions. At this point in the Depression, Bennett's image was more appealing.

The same advantage carried over into the area of policy. By stressing the beneficial effects an increase in tariffs would have for farm prices and factory jobs, the Conservatives were able to sell a traditional party policy to two targeted interest groups: farmers and workers. Furthermore, they depicted the Liberals' trade policies – countervailing duties against the Americans and unilateral preference for British goods – as rather supine and unsuited to the virile young Canadian nation. 'Canada First' and 'Canada d'abord' proved to be more effective slogans than 'British preference' and 'Rappelez-vous 1917.' Their nationalist appeal and promise of economic salvation combined to form the crucial link between traditional Tory territory in the Maritimes, Ontario, and British Columbia, and the promised lands of Quebec and the Prairies. For this one election, 'Canada First' provided the Conservative party with the makings of a country-wide majority consensus.

National trends notwithstanding, certain regional factors must be considered to understand clearly the overall voting pattern. Frank Underhill addressed this matter in a satirical pre-election piece for *Canadian Forum*:

In the Maritimes the question is simply which party will be most lavish and unscrupulous in the bribes for the treasury under the guise of 'Maritime Rights.' In Quebec the Liberals hope to return their 61 members by appealing to the racial and religious solidarity of the French against the Anderson 'persecution' of their compatriots in Saskatchewan. In Saskatchewan, in turn, the Conservatives, whose national programme (as usual) has nothing to offer the prairies, hope to profit from the religious animosities aroused by the subservience of the late Gardiner Government to the French Catholic hierarchy. In Manitoba the result depends upon how the tangle of Liberals and Progressives and Liberal-Progressives is unravelled, and this depends almost entirely upon local and personal considerations which have nothing to do with national issues. In Ontario there is no issue except whether the Tory machine will operate as smoothly and efficiently as it did in the last provincial election.[94]

Underhill exaggerated, but there was much validity in his comments.

The Conservative promise of federally financed old-age pensions was appealing in the Maritimes, a have-not region, but not more important than Bennett's own New Brunswick roots. 'I am a native son in this very clannish party of Canada,' Bennett noted. Anti-Catholic and anti-French prejudice whipped up by the Ku Klux Klan certainly played a part in the party's resurgence in Saskatchewan, a fact later acknowledged by at least two of the Tory MPs who benefited from it – E.E. Perley and F.W. Turnbull. The cause of the Conservative decline in British Columbia was, in McRae's view, 'principally the Australian Treaty, which affects particularly the business of the Port of Vancouver.'[95] The Liberal trade policies, blamed elsewhere for rising unemployment and falling dairy prices, had been a welcome boon to the mercantile West Coast.

There is some evidence that the Roman Catholic hierarchy in Quebec altered its stance from opposition to 'strict neutrality,' thus freeing Conservative candidates from the disapproving hand of the parish curés. According to A.O. Dawson, president of Canadian Cottons, Lord Atholstan had a hand in this welcome development. 'I understand that he has outlined, or is going to outline, ways and means whereby his objective in this connection may be realized,' Dawson informed Bennett.[96] Quebec Conservatives were also aided by the public support of L'Union catholique des cultivateurs, an important interest group in the rural areas of that province. With former provincial leader Arthur Sauvé and nationalist firebrand Armand Lavergne heading a list of prominent candidates, the federal Conservatives were at last able to compete on a nearly equal footing with the entrenched Quebec Liberals.[97] Finally, the Ferguson provincial machine, though stopped short of a sweep, was able to nullify the Liberals' Ontario strategy based on British preferential tariffs, thus assuring the wisdom of the Conservatives' national strategy, which had de-emphasized the traditional tariff and empire policies so long popular there, in favour of a 'Canada First' policy with more appeal on the Prairies and in Quebec.[98]

THE CONSERVATIVE MANDATE

The seeds of the Conservative defeat in 1935 were sown in the victorious campaign of 1930. Bennett had asked for and received a mandate to solve Canada's grave economic problems. He did not hedge his words: 'The Conservative party is going to find work for all who are willing to work, or perish in the attempt. It is going to call parliament at the earliest possible date after July 28 and take such steps as will end this tragic condition of unemployment and bring prosperity to the country as a whole.'[99] Bennett did more than promise; he offered the voters a guarantee. 'After I am Prime Minister on July 28,' he pledged, "I will see that my promises are carried out or the government will go out of power trying to do so.'[100] Bennett gambled heavily on the return of prosperity.

His specific prescriptions for recovery were fraught with contradictions. Manufacturers and labourers had been promised substantial and consistent protection in the domestic market, while grain farmers had been told that higher tariffs would be utilized as bargaining leverage, to 'blast' a way into world markets. It would be difficult to use the same tariffs both as a solid protection for domestic production and as a bargaining chip in negotiations with other countries. Furthermore, raising tariffs was a traditional approach not geared to the actual causes of the economic collapse. If combined with an insistence on a balanced budget, they might well exacerbate the crisis. As Robert Borden noted: 'His programme calls for greatly increased expenditure, and this in the face of diminishing revenues which will be still further diminished by exclusion of imports from which large sums are presently gathered in customs duties.'[101] Assuming the full cost of old-age pensions and launching a vast expansion of transportation facilities, as promised, would require deficit financing on a large scale. There was little to indicate that Bennett was ready in 1930 even to contemplate such a radical departure from the conventional wisdom of balanced budgets.

Part of Bennett's electoral appeal stemmed from his confident assertion that the country's economic problems were eminently solvable, and that he was the person to apply the remedies. While self-assurance is a necessary ingredient of leadership, J.W. Dafoe, for one, felt Bennett possessed it to excess: 'He is chock-full of self-confidence and conceit. If he were an ordinary politician prepared to do anything or say anything to reach office, I could make a prediction about the future by saying that once in office he would forget the extravagances of the campaign. I do not think, however, that Mr. Bennett is a politician in this sense at all. I think he regards himself as a man of destiny.' Indeed, Bennett, who was a devout Methodist, was at times given to religious metaphors that bordered on Messianism. 'There is a good time coming,' he assured one audience in Regina. 'I came to call the sinners, not the righteous.' Ominously, his predecessor, Arthur Meighen, foresaw for him not a new parting of the Red Sea, or a re-enacted calming of the Lake of Galilee, but 'oceans of trouble ahead.'[102]

Certainly Bennett and the Conservatives were justified in viewing the election as a convincing Conservative victory. With 137 of 245 seats, they could count upon a secure parliamentary majority for the length of their mandate. Their 48.7 per cent share of the popular vote, while less than overwhelming, nevertheless stood high in comparison with the Liberals' share in the three previous elections. It was a mandate to govern, a mandate to take the steps necessary to solve the country's economic difficulties. However, the 1930 vote was not a landslide. The Liberals and other parliamentary groups would be present in sufficient numbers to offer a spirited opposition. Furthermore, forty Conservative MPs had carried their seats by a margin of less than 5 per cent of the total vote.[103] Even a small shift of public opinion away from the party would doom these seats at the next election, and plunge the Conservatives back into opposition. As the independent conservative Winnipeg *Tribune* noted,

The Conservative party will be wise ... if it examines carefully the nature of its victory. It has not by its success relieved the country of a grave menace, or defeated a specific measure which in the electors' judgment threatened a national misfortune ... The Conservative party has done little more than present its credentials to the electorate. It has undertaken to accomplish certain things. To that formidable task it must now address itself. On the result of its efforts will depend the length of its tenure of office.[104]

The Canadian electors wanted an end to high unemployment, low farm prices, failing businesses, and tumbling stock prices. They wanted the return of general prosperity. They wanted these things more than any particular program, party, or leader. At Laurier House, Mackenzie King privately predicted the election results would mean 'Bennett for a while then a Liberal party with a long lease of power later on.'[105]

5 The Conservatives in Power, 1930–1933: Action, Reaction, and Reform

In the final days of 1933, the major daily newspapers did their best to paint a bright picture of Canada's prospects. The Montreal *Gazette* featured an upbeat forecast by CPR president E.W. Beatty, predicting rosy times for the company and the country in 1934. The financial pages of the Toronto *Globe* trumpeted good news from the bond market and mining exchange. Recent reports from the Dominion Bureau of Statistics seemed to herald certain recovery. The Winnipeg *Tribune* ran a feature article headed 'Canada Faces 1934 with Assurance of Better Times Ahead.' A casual reader might have concluded that the nation's economy was, if not booming, at least promising.

Other stories, given less space, told a different tale – one of pessimism, frustration, and suffering. The careful *Gazette* reader could find articles about a 'red menace,' a flight from the American dollar, and a record low level of construction in Montreal since 1918. *Globe* subscribers could read stories about world petroleum overproduction, a crushing municipal tax burden, and a mass rally of '2000 communistic sympathizers' at Massey Hall, where the traditional 'God Save the King' was omitted in favour of 'The International.' Hidden among the upbeat stories in the *Tribune* were articles reporting an attack on local relief administration, a call by a clergyman for older people to step aside to give youth a chance, and bad news from the grain exchange.[1]

The prosperity promised by the Conservatives during their successful election campaign of 1930 was nowhere in sight. The Gross National Product, already slipping in 1930 to $5.7 billion, measured a mere $3.5 billion in 1933 in current dollars. Unemployment, scandalously high in mid-1930 at an estimated 370,000 people in a population of around 10 million, was more than double that figure three years later, some 825,000 by one calculation. A bushel of top-grade wheat, which had sold for 92.5 cents in August 1930, now brought only 60 cents on the Winnipeg market. One and a quarter million Canadians depended on government relief for their subsistence. Though the Depression had in fact bottomed out in the first quarter of 1933, the descent was so swift, and the recovery so gradual, that most statistical indicators show 1933 as a whole to have been the very worst year in a dreary decade. The modest signs of recovery evident in December 1933 were of scant comfort to most Canadians.[2]

The prime minister who had confidently guaranteed recovery three years earlier was now an object of public derision, his name used to describe shanty towns (Bennett boroughs), horse-drawn cars (Bennett buggies), abandoned farmsteads (Bennett barnyards), and a boiled grain brew (Bennett coffee). A steady stream of letters from ordinary Canadians kept the prime minister aware of the general misery. 'I have nearly froze in this last week looking for a job with the few clothes I have,' a Saint John resident complained. 'We shall forget what Pears, Grapes, Rasp[berries] and Strawberries taste like soon, 3 or 4 years without even seeing one,' a Saskatchewan farm wife lamented.[3] Though he responded with gifts of his own money to hundreds of such correspondents, Bennett's private generosity could not overcome the failure of his public policies.

One well-publicized action by the Bennett government at year's end seemed to symbolize a wide perceptual gap between the prime minister's state of mind and the public mood. A bold headline – 'Bennett Recommends Titles for Canadians' – faced incredulous newspaper readers across the country amidst all the grim news.[4] Apparently banned by a Canadian parliamentary resolution in 1919, honorary titles were now revived by the same Conservative government that was summarily deporting aliens, including British emigrants, simply because they were destitute. At a time when radical egalitarianism was rapidly gaining adherents, Bennett was moving to enshrine privilege. For a political leader facing an imminent election, the symbolism was quite wrong.

How did the people's saviour in 1930 become the people's enemy in 1933? The standard answer is threefold: severe depression, misguided (if not pig-headed) policies, and administrative ineptitude.[5] This chapter will examine the Conservative party's fall from grace during the first three and one-half years of its mandate, before the significant policy experimentation of 1934–5. The policy record of the Conservative government is a vital consideration, but so, too, is the fate of the marvellous party machine put together by McRae. An assessment of Bennett's leadership style is also instructive. Any government would have had trouble surviving the Depression. The question is: Did the Bennett administration assist in its own downfall?

BENNETT'S PRIME-MINISTERIAL STYLE

On 7 August 1930, the newly installed cabinet issued a minute of council 'regarding certain of the functions of the Prime Minister,' specifically the power to call meetings of cabinet; recommend dissolution and convocation of Parliament; make recommendations in any government department; and recommend a long list of appointments, including cabinet ministers, lieutenant governors, senators, chief justices, and deputy heads of departments.[6] Clearly with these functions confirmed, any prime minister would be more than the clichéd 'first among equals.' Furthermore, Bennett was the first Conservative prime minister to owe his position as party leader not to the caucus, or to cabinet, but to a full party convention. This unique mandate strengthens a prime minister's hand immeasurably. In addition, the style of the victorious campaign just concluded had focused public attention and expectations firmly on Bennett, who could justifiably claim a personal mandate that was almost presidential in scope.

As prime minister, Bennett adopted a vigorous, authoritarian leadership style that soon prompted the charge of one-man government. As the *Ottawa Journal* remarked, six weeks after the Conservatives assumed office, 'there may have been greater men in the office of Prime Minister; there never has been one with a more terrific industry.'[7] Eighteen-hour work days, six days a week, were commonplace for him. Even three years later, the situation had not changed. 'He is still the Government,' observed the *MacLean's* parliamentary correspondent, 'taking upon himself the work of his Ministers or of many of them, trying to be in a dozen places and to do a dozen things at the same time.'[8] Even his Liberal opponents privately respected Bennett's enormous talents. 'He made important decisions rapidly, often based on a knowledge and experience that few Canadians had,' acknowledged Charles 'Chubby' Power, one of his chief parliamentary tormentors. 'There were times when he fairly astonished and entranced the House.' Mackenzie King, too, managed an offhand compliment of sorts when he recorded in his diary, 'Bennett manages to get things done, whether for the best or not – he has great driving power.'[9] The prime minister was largely unperturbed at the charge of excessive domination. 'It may be a one man government,' he retorted on one occasion in the House of Commons, to the delight of his followers, 'but certainly it has more than one man's support.' Bennett was not an ardent democrat, frankly confessing on one public occasion his fear that 'universal franchise without educational test of any kind is a very great danger.' In the same speech, he denounced privilege based on 'position of birth,' opting instead for 'merit' as the true criterion for 'governors of the world.' It was a logical position for the successful son of poor parents to espouse.[10]

The physical pace Bennett set for himself was punishing, made worse by the emotional distress associated with being prime minister in the midst of the Great Depression. Bennett was accustomed to success, but the economic crisis refused to submit to his will. Not surprisingly, Bennett suffered periodic health breakdowns. The first such occasion was in the fall of 1931, just after the onset of a world-wide monetary crisis. The cure was a cruise to Britain, followed by a 'holiday' spent conferring with the new National Government in London. Again, a year later, Bennett suffered visibly from severe fatigue. 'Bennett looked like a man who had been on a drunk the night before,' King noted in his diary in November 1932. He 'was very tired, he was very nervous throughout the day.'[11] By the fall of 1933, Bennett was even beginning to think of retirement. 'The truth is I am very tired,' he wrote to a personal friend, 'and would really like to be relieved of this job.'[12] Bennett's periodic breakdowns were no surprise to Mackenzie King. After watching his opponent's frenetic pace as prime minister for barely a month, Mackenzie King predicted, 'I should not be surprised if his "perish in the attempt" proved a prophecy.'[13]

Bennett demanded much from his personal staff. The key figures were: Arthur Merriam, private secretary, given control of Bennett's appointments; Alice Millar, the office manager; and Andrew MacLean, secretary in charge of correspondence. In addition, there were seventeen other clerical staff: two secretaries, eight stenographers, two in charge of clippings, three assigned to filing, and two messengers. For political advice Bennett relied on his campaign speech-writer and confidant, W.D. Herridge, until the latter's appointment to the Canadian mission in Washington in 1931 made direct communication less frequent. A Winnipeg lawyer, R.K. Finlayson, was then brought in to fill the gap. Finally, there was O.D. Skelton, the under-secretary of state for external affairs. Though initially distrusted by his new boss as a Liberal appointee, Skelton soon became a reliable source of advice in many areas of governmental administration and policy.[14]

Bennett brought ability and a competent staff to the prime minister's office, yet he never achieved the expected results. Immersed in detail, he either would not or could not delegate responsibility. As the Tory MP R.C. Matthews lamented, 'too bad he's such a damn fool.' Colleagues found him to be aloof, domineering, moody, vain, and unforgiving – altogether a difficult person to work with. 'He was not a consensus man' Grattan O'Leary recollected. "He was not above asking the opinions of others, he was only above accepting them.' Staff insiders insisted he was really a shy, sensitive man, but wounded colleagues believed the opposite was true, that he was arrogant and insensitive. As a bitter H.H. Stevens recalled, 'it was typical of him to want to make announcements.' In the Bennett kitchen, there was only one chef.[15]

In August 1930, it might have seemed to an observer that cabinet-making was simply a necessary evil that had to be completed in order that Bennett might be sworn in as prime minister, and empowered to begin solving the country's problems. He received the usual advice, solicited and unsolicited, and endured the usual delegations and representations on behalf of various candidates. Within ten days of the election, the job was complete, the cabinet was sworn in, and the new ministers introduced to the public. Bennett adhered to most of the conventions of cabinet selection, but the result was nevertheless his own creation.[16]

Bennett's cabinet included several prominent Conservatives. His three major opponents at the Winnipeg convention were all selected, though the fourth runner-up, Robert Rogers, was passed over, despite his having won a Commons seat. Hugh Guthrie was given the justice portfolio, R.J. Manion received railways and canals, and C.H. Cahan became secretary of state. Cahan had coveted justice for himself, and was highly offended at the rather junior post offered him. Bennett was adamant, however, and after a day of consultation with his Montreal supporters, Cahan accepted, albeit reluctantly.[17] H.H. Stevens, a key Bennett supporter at Winnipeg, and a prominent front-bencher like the others, also got the nod, even though personally defeated in Vancouver. He took over in trade and commerce, and a seat was soon found for him in Kootenay East. Rounding out his quintet of heavyweights was the Nova Scotian premier, E.N. Rhodes, whom Bennett enticed to Ottawa with the offer of fisheries. Bennett himself retained finance, along with the external affairs portfolio traditionally held by the prime minister.

The Ontario and Quebec caucuses presented Bennett with contradictory problems: the former showing a surplus of experienced and ambitious back-benchers, the latter with no francophone MPs who had sat in the previous Parliament. For the revenue department, Bennett chose the Torontonian E.B. Ryckman, former president of Dunlop Tire and Rubber and a generous financial supporter of the party. In so doing, Bennett passed over two other prime contenders from south-central Ontario with similar business and party backgrounds: J.D. Chaplin of St Catharines and R.C. Matthews of Toronto. Ryckman's previous experiences as minister of public works under Meighen in 1926 tipped the balance in his favour. From western Ontario, Bennett chose Donald Sutherland, the Oxford North physician and distinguished war veteran, to be minister of defence, much to the latter's surprise. The appointment had the approval of Arthur Ford, head of the regional party organization, though some had favoured the bilingual Raymond Morand of Windsor, who had served with Meighen in 1926. The representatives of eastern and northern Ontario were recommended by Howard Ferguson, whose emissary, Home Smith, conferred with Bennett prior to the formation of the new government. From the North, freshman MP Wesley Gordon was elevated to the twin posts of minister of immigration and colonization and minister of mines. A Brockville lawyer, Hugh Stewart, who had represented Leeds since 1921, was given the portfolio of public works.[18] None of the three – Sutherland, Gordon, or Stewart – was very well known, but the final Ontario minister, Senator Gideon Robertson, had a higher profile. He had served both Borden and Meighen as minister of labour, and it was to this post that Bennett again called him.

The prime minister's political problems with the province of Quebec began with his allocation of cabinet posts. There were three traditional cabinet divisions in Quebec: the Montreal district, the Quebec district, and the anglophones. In addition to Cahan, Bennett invited the veteran Sir George Perley to serve without portfolio, thus giving the English-speaking minority two representatives. Cahan's ability and Perley's seniority ensured that their influence would be considerable. Though Ontario had seven ministers, Bennett would not grant Quebec more than five, meaning there were just three for the francophone majority. From the Montreal district, Arthur Sauvé was an automatic selection. The former provincial leader asked for and was given the position of postmaster general. The marine portfolio was conferred upon Alfred Duranleau, a Montreal lawyer and former Quebec MLA who was closely allied to Joseph Rainville, the party's campaign director in the province. Sauvé recommended Armand Lavergne to represent the Quebec district, but Bennett opted instead for Maurice Dupré, a bilingual lawyer recommended by another party faction that included Senators Webster, Chapais, Blondin, and L'Espérance. Dupré was given the very junior portfolio of solicitor general, much to the consternation of Thomas Maher, Rainville's Quebec City counterpart. Lavergne was only partially appeased by his appointment as deputy Speaker of the House of Commons, a position ill-suited to his emotional temperament.[19]

Bennett did as expected in appointing John Macdonald, a veteran of Meighen's cabinet, to represent Prince Edward Island as minister without portfolio. He confounded the experts with his appointment of Murray MacLaren from neighbouring New Brunswick. The Saint John physician, described by Grattan O'Leary as 'shy, reserved, unostentatious' and one who 'spoke but seldom' was much less politically prominent than fellow MPs George Jones, Thomas Bell, and R.B. Hanson. Ironically, the man whom Bennett elevated to minister of pensions and health was not expected to serve long, 'due to failing health.'[20]

As with francophone Quebec, the provinces of Manitoba and Saskatchewan boasted no Conservative MPs who had sat from 1926 to 1930. To the surprise of everyone, including the man himself, Bennett's choice for Manitoba was 'an obscure Neepawa druggist' named Thomas Murphy, whom Bennett had befriended when the latter served briefly as an MP in 1925–6. Murphy was given the traditional western portfolio of interior and Indian affairs. For Saskatchewan, Bennett appointed Robert Weir, a prosperous farmer and stock-breeder born in Ontario, who was the freshman MP from Melfort. Weir was endorsed by the Saskatchewan provincial cabinet, who saw their wish granted when he became minister of agriculture.[21]

The new Conservative ministry contained nineteen members, the same as the previous Liberal cabinet. Of these, sixteen were anglophone and three were francophone; fourteen were Protestant and five were Roman Catholic. There were seven from Ontario, five from Quebec, and one from each of the other provinces. The average age of the ministers was fifty-three. By former occupation, there were nine lawyers, three doctors, two businessmen, one accountant, one druggist, one journalist, one farmer, and one union executive. Four of the lawyers – Bennett, Cahan, Ryckman, and Rhodes – had also made careers in the business world. All nineteen were male. When compared to the general population, then, the cabinet was disproportionately tilted in favour of anglophones, Protestants, business professionals, and males.[22]

Bennett drove his ministers hard, as he did himself and his own staff, and he became frustrated with those who could not keep up. In the first weeks of the new administration, the cabinet met virtually all day, every day, to prepare for the special fall session of Parliament and the imperial conference that would follow. Though the pace slackened somewhat thereafter, still Bennett remained fond of frequent, lengthy meetings. During the 63 months the Conservatives were in office, 1,155 cabinet meetings were held, compared to only 516 during the 46 months the Liberals governed between 1926 and 1930.[23] Though Bennett cited these statistics as evidence of a consultative leadership style, the reverse was actually the case. While the cabinet endlessly debated minor items, Bennett governed, frequently over the heads of his colleagues. Even strong-willed ministers such as Stevens and Cahan endured the indignity of Bennett consulting directly with their departmental officials. Bennett not only made most of the important decisions, but insisted on announcing them as well. His inability to share centre-stage soon sapped the initiative of the other ministers. Manion, in his memoirs, was particularly critical of his chief for 'his almost studied ignoring of his colleagues in public addresses and debates.' Nowhere was this more devastating than with his three French-Canadian colleagues, Sauvé, Duranleau, and Dupré, none of whom enjoyed even a fraction of the confidence King displayed in Ernest Lapointe. Samuel Gobeil was just one of several Quebec back-benchers who complained to Bennett of the 'silly little quarrels' among the three. Nevertheless, Sauvé was right to protest that 'no one ventures to say [we] are not vested with the proper authority.' An outward show of confidence by Bennett in his francophone ministers would have boosted their stature immensely, but none was forthcoming.[24]

The only outstanding minister in the cabinet was Bennett himself, not because there were not half a dozen others of experience, vigour, and ability, but because the prime minister neither wanted nor would permit anyone else to excel. Within his original cabinet (most of whose members served a full five years), there were eight indisputably competent ministers: Cahan, Guthrie, Manion, Perley, Rhodes, Ryckman, Stevens, and Weir. They handled their departments well, stayed out of danger in Parliament, and were strong enough to speak up in cabinet deliberations. Weir, the only parliamentary rookie in the group, was not a partisan sort, but he communicated well with the farm constituency. Unfortunately, four of those in this group – Cahan, Guthrie, Perley, and Ryckman – were getting along in years. A second group of eight ministers were barely adequate in their performance: Dupré, Duranleau, Gordon, Macdonald, Robertson, Sauvé, Stewart, and Sutherland. Some of these were possessed of only average ability, while others, such as Dupré and Gordon, showed much early promise, but were never properly groomed for greatness by their leader, who was more a doer than a motivator. Finally, two ministers – MacLaren and Murphy – can be classified only as inadequate. After their surprising appointments, little was heard from either again.[25]

Despite the indifferent quality of his cabinet as a whole, Bennett made only two shuffles in the first three and one-half years, each occasioned by a grave illness. In February 1932, Bennett brought an old nemesis, Arthur Meighen, in to replace the ailing Gideon Robertson. Meighen was given a Senate appointment, but he did not attend cabinet meetings regularly, nor did he accept a regular portfolio. Robertson's labour portfolio was added to Gordon's load. At the same time, Bennett relinquished the finance portfolio, which was given to Rhodes. Fisheries was passed over to Duranleau. Though the changes met general approval, Bennett had passed up the opportunity to promote anyone from the caucus. As one frustrated back-bencher, R.B. Hanson, complained to a colleague, 'the Government needs a whole shaking up and Bennett has been told this by a multitude of people. He still apparently cannot find time to do it or [if] he has the time he has not the inclination.'[26] In December 1933, the resignation of a gravely ill Ryckman finally forced his hand. The able Toronto MP R.C. Matthews was appointed minister of revenue in his place, but, again, Bennett declined to go farther. The journalist J.A. Stevenson had earlier concluded that Bennett's ministers were 'the more popular with him the more docile they [were].' Bennett's own retrospective assessment of his less glittering colleagues was that 'they were not politicians ... but they really were not unsound administrators.' Evidently they did what they were told.[27]

A leader who treated most of his cabinet colleagues as petty subordinates was not about to elevate mere back-benchers to exalted roles. Preoccupied with his own multitudinous duties, Bennett displayed a characteristic aloofness to the Conservative MPs, and on one occasion even abolished caucus meetings for a time because he suspected information was being leaked to the press. Overawed by Bennett's forceful personality, and conscious that they were elected to support his policies and leadership, the caucus were never genuinely rebellious, though there was considerable grumbling in private. Many rural Tory MPs, for instance, were unhappy with the Ottawa Trade Agreements in 1932, but after a bit of a ruckus in the first subsequent caucus meeting, the back-benchers rallied publicly to support their leader.[28]

One particularly unhappy group was the French-Canadian contingent. Many were not conversant in English, the language of caucus, but even those who were did not feel as if they were equal partners. One such MP, J.A. Barrett, finally went public with a letter published in *Le Devoir*, in which he voiced this regret: 'nous avons perdu en grande partie l'héritage politique que nous avait légué Sir Georges [*sic*] Etienne Cartier, cette égalité dans l'influence politique [we have lost, in large part, the political heritage left us by Sir George Etienne Cartier: equality of political influence].'[29] French-Canadian Conservatives did have some legitimate grievances. Bennett's cabinet of nineteen contained just three francophones, none in a powerful position. One of the Saskatchewan Tory MPs in the caucus, Dr W.D. Cowan, turned out to be a treasurer of the Canadian Ku Klux Klan, notorious for its rabid anti-Catholic and anti-French views. The huge Canadian delegation of ministers and civil servants to the 1932 Ottawa Imperial Conference had contained hardly a francophone above the rank of stenographer until Armand Lavergne publicly complained. The House of Commons staff could not keep up with its French translation requirements because of budget cut-backs. A published list of senior CNR officials showed that none of these handsomely paid executives was of French origin.[30]

A division within the Conservative caucus on language rights crystallized around a private member's resolution introduced by the Quebec Liberal back-bencher Oscar Boulanger in 1933 to alter the Canadian currency from English-only to bilingual. The real issue, of course, was the place of French Canadians in the federal sphere. Boulanger's resolution was talked out during the private member's hour, but the debate revealed a sharp division in Conservative ranks between francophone MPs such as Samuel Gobeil from Compton, Quebec, and anglophone MPs such as Frank Turnbull from Regina, Saskatchewan.[31] This was the same division that had pitted Armand Lavergne against John Wesley Edwards at the 1927 convention. What was to be the true nature of Canada? 'I know the feeling is very widely spread,' Turnbull warned Bennett in the summer of 1933, 'among many of those who voted for us the last time that Quebec governs Canada, no matter who is in office.' In addition to bilingual currency, Turnbull was upset about bilingual forms being utilized by the post office under Sauvé, and French programs being broadcast on the new public radio network.[32]

Working out a partnership in caucus across the gap between two linguistic solitudes was hard enough, but Bennett compounded the difficulty by refusing even to acknowledge the problem, or his part in it. It was not that the prime minister was a bigot. For instance, he had a French Canadian appointed to the Senate from Saskatchewan at a time when Conservatives there were angrily complaining of French domination.[33] It was just that, in a time of economic crisis, he did not attach a high priority to the place of French Canada in Confederation. Quebec was a province like the others. English was the language of convenience for government and business. Traditional constitutional rights should be preserved, but there was little need for radical new departures in linguistic equality. So went R.B. Bennett's thinking on the matter.

The Conservative leader expressed his understanding of the relationship between the government and Parliament in business terminology. In a 1931 debate concerning the delegation of spending powers to cabinet he stated: 'We ask between now and the expiration of the next fiscal year that the board of directors of this country ... shall discharge its duties from a financial standpoint as it best can and take the chances that are incident to so doing by submitting an account of its stewardship.' Manion, too, subscribed to this view. 'The Cabinet is really the Board of Directors of the huge national business,' he wrote, 'and the House of Commons a tediously extended shareholders' meeting.' Mackenzie King put forward a contrary view. 'It is not the cabinet, of which he is Prime Minister, that is the board of directors; it is this House of Commons,' he declared in debate. 'The cabinet is a committee of the House of Commons.' The interesting aspect of Bennett's view is that he did not care to share much of the executive power with his colleagues on the 'board of directors.' Delegating powers to cabinet came to mean delegating powers to himself as prime minister.[34]

As with cabinet and caucus, Bennett knowingly dominated proceedings in the House of Commons. Discussing the merits of Hansard with a journalist, Bennett declared, 'I rather share your view that it is good reading, but I am not a fair judge, for I contribute pretty extensively to what it contains.'[35] Nevertheless, the Commons procedures permitted opposition members to criticize his statements, question his motives, and oppose his policies. The new Parliament had sat for only four days in 1930 before Bennett's frustration at such impudence got the better of him. 'The debate went on tonight,' King wrote in his diary, 'Bennett getting very mad & refusing to answer questions & then lecturing the

House.' 'Chubby' Power best described Bennett's parliamentary demeanour. 'In this house,' Power declared, 'he often exhibits the manners of a Chicago policeman and the temperament of a Hollywood actor.' The opposition aided and abetted such behaviour, for it helped them to portray Bennett as an ill-tempered would-be dictator possessing scant regard for democratic procedures.[36]

Bennett was also unable to control the press, though it was not for lack of trying. He regarded newspaper criticism of the government as irresponsible, even unpatriotic, and lost no opportunity to lecture journalists about their public duty. 'Bennett ... laid it down as a cardinal principle,' Grant Dexter wrote his editor, J.W. Dafoe, 'not only of newspaper ethics but of statutory law, that newspapers must not comment upon public policies in advance of their announcement, nor proffer ignorant and unwelcome advice to those responsible for the government of a country ... Moreover, newspapers should not try and get behind the announcements of public men.' Bennett was particularly distressed at the conduct of Canadian newspapers during the 1932 Ottawa conference. 'Throughout the entire proceedings,' he remarked angrily to Dexter, 'some Canadian journalists did everything in their power, stopped at nothing, to discredit your country's representatives, and your own Prime Minister.' To quell press criticism and speculation, Bennett even made veiled references to sections of the Criminal Code and War Measures Act, which, in his opinion, authorized sanctions against a prying press. It was not just Liberal journalists who clashed with the prime minister. 'I am only one of the numerous victims of the gibes he bandies about very freely,' the London *Times* correspondent informed Dafoe, 'and as his own flock see the most of [him] they get the lion's share.'[37] As with so many of his relationships, Bennett's ongoing feud with the press was ultimately harmful to his own government. Journalists with bruised feelings were apt to pursue the negative aspects of stories emanating from the Conservative regime. Bennett's public image, and that of his party, could only suffer.

The paradox of Bennett's personality was also evident in his dealings on the dominion-provincial and international stages. During the early months of the Conservative regime, Bennett was a model of the consensual federal leadership style. He consulted with the Prairie premiers on the fate of the wheat pools, and listened to provincial objections to the proposed Statute of Westminster. As time went by and conditions worsened, Bennett's patience with provincial premiers lessened noticeably. The voters' replacement of familiar Tory faces with unfamiliar

Grit adversaries around the conference table contributed to the problem. Bennett took more and more to lecturing the premiers as wayward children, rather than to hearing their concerns and considering their ideas.[38] Similarly, Bennett's undoubted ability was widely recognized at the Imperial conferences of 1930 and 1932, but his often abrasive manner turned possible allies into wounded foes. His relations with Presidents Hoover and Roosevelt, both of whom he visited in Washington, while correct, never achieved the close personal warmth attained by King with Roosevelt.

Bennett, who could be witty and charming when the mood struck him, preferred to concentrate on getting things done, alone if necessary. Too often, he failed to consider the negative consequences of his single-mindedness on other people's feelings. In the worlds of law and business, it had not seemed to matter, but a political leader unable to soothe and conciliate was headed for trouble.

IMPLEMENTING A MANDATE

When R.B. Bennett realized on 28 July 1930 that the Conservatives were winning a secure majority, he could hardly wait to take office. It was not just ambition for the prime-ministership, although he was ambitious. Bennett firmly believed that he and his party had put forward the policies that would solve the economic difficulties of 1930, and put Canada back on prosperity road. If he drove his subordinates hard, if he was too brusque with colleagues, if he neglected party obligations – well, that was the cost of getting the job done. Once the arduous task of restoring Canada's economic health was accomplished, there would be time to soothe feelings, stroke egos, and mend fences. In those first heady months in power, the Tory party was eager to follow his lead.

The Conservatives took office believing that Canada did not have to wait passively for the recession to run its course. They had a plan for economic recovery, one rooted in traditional party policy, updated at the Winnipeg convention, and endorsed by the voters in the recent election. 'Canada First' protective tariffs would restore the domestic market for farmers and manufacturers, while creating employment for workers. Step two in the plan would be the negotiation of a new trading system within the British Empire based on the principle of reciprocal preference. At a later date, negotiations that utilized the higher Canadian tariffs as a bargaining chip might secure access to other desirable markets for Canadian products – the prosaic implementation of 'blasting into world markets.' In the meantime, a generous injection of federal funds on a matching-grant basis with provinces and municipalities for job-creating public works and local relief would provide assistance for able-bodied people temporarily unemployed by the recession. As a further part of their economic recovery package, the Conservatives had promised to resume the Canadian tradition of grand transportation projects by launching construction of a St Lawrence seaway and completing the Hudson Bay Railway. Rounding out their plans was the pledge to assume the total cost of old-age pensions.

These proposals were ambitious and expensive. They required energetic federal leadership and an activist governing philosophy. Eventually, their requirements would collide with other policy imperatives, notably the need for fiscal stability to calm the country's creditors and reassure foreign money markets. The dreadful persistence of the Great Depression would call up reform ideas not seriously contemplated at its outset. Nevertheless, in its first phase, the Conservative policy record showed a remarkable adherence to the election platform of 1930.

Bennett had promised the voters action, and action he delivered in the summer and fall of 1930. He drove himself, his ministers, and his staff to the limits of physical endurance preparing for an emergency session of Parliament. MPs were summoned to Ottawa as soon as legally possible. The Throne Speech, normally replete with self-congratulation and long-winded though vague previews, was brief to the point of embarrassment – just twenty-one lines in Hansard.[39] The prime minister was determined to see his promised emergency program in place before sailing for Britain to attend an important imperial conference scheduled for early October.

The first measure introduced by Bennett was the relief bill, a precedent-breaking statute that allocated the princely sum of $20 million for the relief of unemployment. By contrast, in the 1919–21 recession, the Union government had expended just $2 million for relief. The government was careful to state that unemployment was 'primarily a provincial and municipal responsibility,' but acknowledged that the problem had become 'a matter of national concern.' The act envisioned public works sponsored by provinces and municipalities as the primary means through which the federal funds would be disbursed, on a cost-sharing basis. Four million dollars was reserved for direct relief, also on a cost-sharing basis.[40] The new government was willing to enter such a program because it believed the need would prove temporary. The benefits of the new trade policy, combined with a normal upturn in the business cycle, would soon end the emergency situation.

The tariff revision that Bennett introduced, although the sharpest increase in fifty years, was only a preliminary measure, according to its sponsor. He promised 'a general revision of the tariff at the next session.' The 1930 changes, some 130 in number, were frankly selected 'on the basis of the employment that will be given.' The changes were concentrated in such areas as clothing and textiles, iron and steel products, and machinery, and applied largely to goods from countries outside the British Empire. The cabinet itself had decided upon the tariff revisions, aided by submissions from the Canadian Manufacturers' Association. In a parallel move, the revenue minister, E.B. Ryckman, introduced amendments to the Customs Act intended to 'sound the deathknell of dumping.' Bennett believed the combination of tariff increases and anti-dumping measures would create a minimum of 25,000 permanent jobs.[41]

With these initial policies in place, Bennett set sail for Britain, colleagues and advisers in tow, to begin the process of altering Canada's imperial trade policy from the Liberals' unilateral preference to reciprocal preference. 'I offer to the Mother country,' he explained, 'and to all the other parts of Empire, a preference in the Canadian market in exchange for a like preference in theirs, based upon the addition of a ten percentum increase in prevailing general tariffs.' Bennett's proposal was not enthusiastically accepted in the tariff-free mother country. 'There never was such humbug as this proposal,' scoffed J.H. Thomas, secretary of state for the dominions. Bennett was unrepentant. 'Because we gave Great Britain the preferences we did without getting anything back we have been greatly handicapped,' he explained to a Conservative back-bencher, R.B. Hanson, 'and they have concluded that these conditions would continue for ever.' His aggressive manner had provoked some ill-will, but the British government did agree to attend a subsequent economic conference in Ottawa, devoted to increasing empire trade.[42]

Upon his return to Canada, the prime minster faced the first of a series of crises that demonstrated that this economic downturn might be far more serious than he and his colleagues had imagined. The three Prairie wheat pools were on the verge of financial collapse. Caught with a massive carry-over of grain contracted for at prices far in excess of current market value, the pools were unable by December to secure further bank credit. The Prairie premiers, speaking on behalf of western grain farmers, were urging the federal government to guarantee a minimum price of $1.00 per bushel; at the time, December wheat was trading on the Winnipeg Exchange at 57 cents per bushel. This demand was rejected, but Bennett did commit the Canadian government to a guarantee of the pools' financial obligations. The price he extracted was the appointment of John I. McFarland, former president of Alberta Pacific Grain and an old grain-speculating crony of Bennett's, as general manager of the pools' Central Selling Agency. The action was heavy-handed, but it saved the pools from bankruptcy. McFarland proceeded, with advice from Bennett, to manage the marketing of western grain for the next five years.[43]

By the time Parliament met again in March 1931, the government was beginning to change its mind regarding the source of the economic crisis. 'The nations of the world are passing through a period of great economic depression,' the governor general proclaimed in the Throne Speech. 'Canada has not escaped it.' However, the Conservative administration was not yet ready to forsake its master plan for recovery, or to stop blaming Canada's misery on misguided Liberal policies. 'My government,' the governor general continued, 'is firmly of the belief that many of our problems do not arise out of world wide depression, but are antecedent to it.' With this thought in mind, the Conservatives proceeded to implement many of their 1930 campaign promises.[44]

The government introduced a new series of tariff increases in 1931, in essence completing the job begun the previous autumn. The auto industry was a particular target this time. Duties were raised on luxury cars and car parts, while used cars were now to be prohibited entry altogether. Other items subject to increased tariff rates included coal, leather goods, and magazines. Canadian tariffs were now at their highest levels in history. The protectionist lobby had been keeping up the pressure on the government. 'The Conservatives everywhere in Canada promised an upward revision of the Tariff,' the St Catharines manufacturer and Tory MP J.D Chaplin reminded Bennett early in 1931, 'and to lay off doing something now would, in my judgment, absolutely destroy us, especially in this Province of Ontario.' The Canadian Manufacturers' Association persuaded H.H. Stevens to adopt the CMA's 'Produced in Canada' promotional campaign. The Department of Trade and Commerce spent nearly $100,000 to encourage Canadians to buy Canadian products.[45]

The government was already strapped for funds in 1931, and it might well have renounced any more spending commitments. Certainly, the cabinet was cutting back on many existing programs, but, in areas of priority, it was still prepared to move forward, the Depression not-withstanding. For instance, the government increased the transportation subsidy on Canadian coal by twenty-five cents per ton as partial ful-filment of its pledge to promote a 'National Fuel Policy.' The measure was intended to assist Maritime and western coal producers in enter-ing the central Canadian market, now dominated by American coal.[46] The Conservatives also instituted a wheat bonus of five cents per bushel on the 1931 crop, which was selling on the open market for less than forty cents per bushel. Total bonus payments under this one-year pro-gram amounted to more than $12 million.[47]

The election promise to assume the full cost of old-age pensions was redeemed in part, as the federal share was increased from 50 to 75 per cent. At this time, only Ontario and the four western provinces were part of the shared-cost program, which paid $20 per month to Canadi-ans seventy years of age or more whose total annual income, including the pension, did not exceed $365. Prince Edward Island signed on in 1933, and Nova Scotia in 1934, but New Brunswick and Quebec were still not included when the Bennett government left office in 1935.[48] As a social-security program, it was not generous, but it was a start. The Conservatives not only embraced it at their 1927 convention and on the 1930 campaign trail, but strengthened it at the expense of their budget deficit once in office.

A new relief bill continued the policy of allocating funds on a match-ing basis with the provinces and municipalities. The most pressing con-cern was Saskatchewan, where a catastrophic drought had reduced the southern third of the province to a virtual dust bowl. The federal gov-ernment agreed to finance emergency aid, which was administered by a provincially established relief commission. A second emphasis of the 1931 Relief Act was federal assistance to provincial road-building pro-grams. Within months, the Bennett government made an important change to its relief program, necessitated by the rapidly deteriorating economic situation in western Canada. Provincial and municipal gov-ernments there could not afford to pay their share of public-works programs. As a result, for the four western provinces, Ottawa agreed to pay half the cost of approved municipal relief projects, and lend any money needed to make up the difference. In total, more than $28 million was expended under the 1931 Relief Act.[49] Action to assist the unem-ployed was proving costly, but to this point Bennett's government was holding fast to its 1930 pledge.

Conservatives' adherence to their election promise of harmonious relations with the provincial governments was shown in their careful handling of the Statute of Westminster. A series of imperial conferences in the 1920s had prepared the way for a formal recognition of legal independence by the self-governing dominions within the new British Commonwealth. Final discussion of this document constituted one of the main topics at the 1930 imperial conference. Some provincial governments in Canada feared a loss of their autonomy in the process. Prime Minister Bennett heeded a public request made by Premiers Ferguson and Taschereau shortly after the 1930 election not to commit Canada irrecovably to the proposed statute until the provinces had been consulted. A dominion-provincial conference was called for April 1931 to deal with the question. A press statement released at the conclusion of the conference noted that the first ministers had agreed 'that the status quo should be maintained in so far as the question of repealing, altering or amending the British North America Acts was concerned, ' but that, otherwise, 'the Colonial Laws Validity Act should no longer apply' to Canada or the provinces. This action was subsequently ratified by the Canadian Parliament in 'a brief and wholly friendly debate.' By heeding provincial sensibilities, the Conservative government ensured that this penultimate step towards full sovereignty was achieved with a wide national consensus.[50] Working out an acceptable method to amend the constitution without going to Britain, however, would be the task of a future generation.

As 1931 wore on, the thrust of Conservative policy leaned more and more to a desperate defence of the status quo. However, two key items from the original election mandate retained their lustre for the Bennett administration: new trade agreements and the St Lawrence deep-waterway project. The government's major hopes for economic recovery were riding on the outcome of the imperial economic conference slated for July 1932 in Ottawa. Returning from a trip to Britain in December 1931, Bennett gave voice to some of his hopes: 'With the adoption of the Statute of Westminster, the old political Empire disappears, and everywhere I went in the Old Land, I found the people looking forward to the Conference in the belief that we would lay at Ottawa the foundations of a new economic Empire in which Canada is destined to play a part of ever-increasing importance.'[51] The imposition of the first British tariffs in many years by a new national government seemed to bode well for Bennett's plan of reciprocal preference. So, too, did the location of the conference. Part of Bennett's strategy was to surround the Canadian delegation in Ottawa with lobbyists visibly applying pressure against tariff concessions. Prior to the conference, Bennett had sent letters to the provincial premiers, as well as to 'the generally recognized organizations of manufacturers, producers, and exporters,' asking for submissions. The Canadian Manufacturers' Association held its annual convention in Ottawa just prior to the imperial conference, and many of the industrial representatives stayed on to lobby. Within the cabinet, Canadian industry found two stout defenders in C.H. Cahan and E.B. Ryckman. It was time for Bennett to redeem his pledge to use tariffs to 'blast' a way into world markets.[52]

The prime minister spearheaded Canadian negotiations with Britain at the Ottawa conference, while his minister of trade and commerce, H.H. Stevens, handled the bargaining with other Commonwealth countries. For a time it seemed the British negotiators would sail home without any agreement at all, so acrimonious did the closed-door meetings become. In the end, the imperatives of domestic politics forced the British negotiators to concede quite a lot, whereas Bennett conceded very little. Canadian natural products such as wheat, lumber, apples, bacon, fish, and minerals gained a preferred entrance into Britain, while the British secured an advantage for certain metal and textile products, mostly of the sort not produced in Canada. Follow-up statistics showed that, after three years, Canadian exports to Britain had increased dramatically, from $175 million to $274 million, whereas British exports to Canada only edged up, from $106 million to $111 million.[53] At the same conference, agreements were signed with South Africa, Southern Rhodesia, and the Irish Free State, to join ones negotiated by Stevens with New Zealand and Australia prior to the conference. Still, though a new generation of Commonwealth trade agreements was now in place, somehow it did not add up to the new economic order originally envisaged by the Canadian prime minister.[54]

Nevertheless, Bennett and his minister of finance, E.N. Rhodes, took considerable pride from the knowledge that Canada's balance of trade, negative during the last years of Liberal rule, was now positive again. Bargaining down Canadian tariffs in exchange for like concessions by trading partners was continued in 1933. A new trade agreement was negotiated, largely by C.H. Cahan, with France to reduce tariffs on a wide range of products.[55] The one foreign market that would really make a difference, though, was, of course, the United States. Here too, the government showed initiative.

To the shock of many, Bennett announced to the House of Commons in early 1933 his openness to trade negotiations with the Americans. 'If an arrangement can be made for a reasonable time,' he explained to a friend, 'it would be to the advantage of both countries.' W.D. Herridge, the Canadian minister to Washington, arranged an official visit to meet the new American president, F.D. Roosevelt, in April 1933. Privately, the prime minister communicated to the American chargé d'affaires in Ottawa his belief in 'the desirability of an economic agreement with the United States.' At the end of Bennett's Washington visit, the two leaders issued a joint communiqué, stating: 'We have agreed to begin a search for means to increase the exchange of commodities between our two countries.' The search proved a long one, not achieving success until late 1935, after the Conservatives' defeat, but at least it had begun.[56]

The Conservative government had similarly bad luck with another key element of their election platform requiring American cooperation: the St Lawrence deep waterway. Bennett had conducted discussions on the topic with President Hoover at the White House in January 1931. Herridge, once appointed Canadian minister to Washington, drove the negotiations forward. In July 1932, he signed on Canada's behalf a treaty to complete jointly with the United States a navigable deep waterway from the St Lawrence River mouth to the head of the Great Lakes, while permitting the development of associated power projects. The Taschereau government in Quebec was strongly opposed to the project, but Ontario and the Prairie provinces were very supportive. Not only was the seaway a viable long-term transportation improvement that would heighten the competitiveness of Canadian exports, it would also attract badly needed investment into the economy and create thousands of construction jobs. Unfortunately, the American Senate did not seriously consider the treaty until after Hoover's defeat by Roosevelt. The treaty gained the backing of a bare majority of senators in a March 1934 vote, but it needed two-thirds support. The seaway was stillborn. Even Mackenzie King had confessed in his diary that it was 'a fairly good bargain' for Canada, but, alas, the treaty could not be implemented.[57]

The bulk of the Conservative election platform had been converted into policy by the summer of 1932. To the party's chagrin, their program did not bring the expected economic recovery. In fact, the recession of 1930 had turned into the Great Depression. Most indicators showed the economy still hurtling downwards. So severe were the repercussions that Bennett and his colleagues found themselves forced to shift their emphasis from implementing traditional party policies for recovery to a desperate defence of the basic social order. Nothing in their preparation for governmental responsibility had equipped them adequately to meet the series of crises that now befell the country.

HOLDING THE LINE

As the severity of the Depression became ever more apparent, the Conservative government's interpretation of the causes of the economic catastrophe had shifted noticeably. On the hustings in 1930, Bennett had pointed an accusing finger at Liberal mismanagement. Two years later, he was of a different mind. 'What at that time seemed to be a local condition,' he admitted in Parliament late in 1932, 'was a world-wide disease.' It was Bennett, serving as his own finance minster in 1930 and 1931, who first confronted the fiscal consequences of the economic crises. The government's revenues, following the business cycle, were declining rapidly. Expenditures, however, were relatively inelastic. 'Fixed and uncontrollable charges constitute so large a proportion of the expenditures,' he lamented in the House of Commons. 'The interest on the national debt was over $121 millions; war pensions amount to $46 millions.' The implementation of election promises had placed new demands on the treasury. A substantial deficit was inevitable.[58]

Bennett did not like deficits. Neither did his chosen successor as minister of finance, Edgar Rhodes. The March 1931 Throne Speech pledged the government to exercise 'every economy compatible with the proper administration of the state.' In October 1932, the Throne Speech saluted the 'wisdom' of the government's 'steadfast policy of retrenchment.' In his 1933 Budget Speech, Rhodes struck the same note. 'With revenues so reduced,' he asserted, 'it becomes incumbent on the government not only to propose measures which will add substantially to the present income, but also to put into effect every reasonable economy.'[59] Their belief in the need for a balanced budget stemmed from their desire to preserve international confidence in the Canadian dollar, which, in turn, was related to Canada's status as a net debtor country. 'The preservation of our national credit is an indispensable prerequisite to the return of prosperity,' Rhodes declared to Parliament in 1932. The deficit worried Bennett, too. 'Our unbalanced budget affecting our financial reputation here,' he wired Sir George Perley from London, England, in 1933. For this reason, the government would not countenance a lowered interest rate on outstanding government bonds, or an inflated currency. When R.J. Manion ventured to make such a suggestion, Bennett dismissed the idea as 'a lot of damn Communism.'

'Inflation would mean liquidation,' the prime minister told a meeting of the Toronto Board of Trade in January 1933. 'Confidence would be gone. And, with the departure of confidence, credit also. And with credit, the country.' Bennett was aware of the political risk associated with his policies. 'It may be that we will become increasingly unpopular,' he wrote one Tory MP, 'but someone must govern this country or it will fall to pieces.'[60]

On the expenditure side, the estimates for 1931–2 – the first prepared by the Conservative government – contained cuts in nearly every department. In all, a decrease of $37 million was managed out of a total of $241 million of so-called controllable items. Expenditures for relief, capital projects already in progress, and the CNR deficit, none of which were included in this total, more than negated Bennett's cost-cutting, however. Over the next two years, Rhodes slashed the departmental estimates even deeper. 'During the three years we have been in office,' he stated in a 1933 letter, 'we have cut expenditures by $81,000,000.' One major weapon was the Salaries Deduction Act of 1932, which reduced the salaries of public servants by 10 per cent. In addition, vacant positions were abolished, promotions restricted, and temporary positions all but eliminated. A powerful new position, comptroller of the treasury, was established to ensure closer accountability over the disbursement of funds within the government bureaucracy.[61]

Cost-cutting went far beyond trimming civil servants' salaries. Real programs had to be slashed. The wheat bonus was terminated after just one year. A program to financially assist vocational education in the provinces was passed through Parliament in 1931, but not actually implemented because of the projected cost. By 1932, the federal government would have liked to relinquish responsibility for unemployment relief to the provinces, but most provincial governments were even more strapped for funds. A dominion-provincial conference in April 1932 sought to come to grips with the problem of escalating costs. W.A. Gordon, the federal labour minister, reported a 'practically unanimous recommendation ... that public works as relief measures be discontinued in view of their great cost, and that direct relief be adopted instead as the policy.' The dole was more cost-effective than public works because it was less susceptible to patronage abuse, and could be targeted to the most desperately poor.[62]

R.J. Manion sought to apply a tourniquet to the haemorrhaging railway deficit through his bill to force cost-saving cooperation upon the CNR and its privately owned competitor, the CPR. Financial interests centred in Montreal urged a total railway amalgamation under private management, but his plan would have overturned Bennett's categorical campaign pledge: 'Amalgamation? Never! Competition? Ever!' Privately, Herridge warned his brother-in-law of the political consequences. 'A privately-owned monopoly in transportation of such colossal strength,' he predicted, 'would become a power which could successfully control not only industry but Parliament itself.' A royal commission headed by Justice Lyman P. Duff rejected amalgamation but recommended enforced cooperation, thus paving the way for Manion's bill. The actual savings resulting from its passage were rather limited, though, barely making a dent in the CNR's annual operating deficit.[63]

Slashing expenditures was only part of the government's plan to rein in its deficit. Raising taxes was also relentlessly pursued. In 1931, Bennett increased the sales tax from 1 to 4 per cent, raised the corporate tax from 8 to 10 per cent, and imposed a 1 per cent excise tax on all imports. In spite of the increases, the 1931–2 deficit amounted to $114 million, excluding the CNR deficit. In 1932, Rhodes raised the sales tax to 6 per cent, the corporate tax to 11 per cent, and the special excise tax to 3 per cent. Income taxes were raised via a reduced personal exemption, and through a special surtax on net incomes over $5,000. In spite of these increases, the 1932–3 deficit soared to $221 million, which included a $41 million write-off of accumulated CNR deficit. In 1933, the corporate tax was raised yet again, to 12.5 per cent, while income and sales tax exemptions were reduced even more. Still, the deficit for 1933–4 came in at $134 million, on expenditures of $458 million.[64] Balancing the budget in desperately hard times proved impossible. Bennett and Rhodes were determined, though, to demonstrate to Canada's creditors that every effort was being made.

The Conservative government's commitment to a stable currency was clearly shown in September 1931 when Britain abandoned the gold standard, effectively devaluing the pound. The sudden move came as a shock to Prime Minister Bennett. It was as if 'the world's banker, so to speak, had become insolvent,' he later explained. The value of the Canadian dollar rose in relation to sterling, but sank in terms of the American dollar. As Edgar Rhodes later reported to the Commons, 'the low was reached on December 16, when the premium on New York funds was 24 7/8 per cent.' At that time, a Canadian dollar bought just slightly more than eighty U.S. cents. Rather than let the Canadian dollar fall to its own level, however, the Conservatives did what they could to defend its value. Their concern was to preserve the country's credit rating, and minimize the premium required to repay borrowed funds. 'Between October 1, 1931, and March 31, 1932,' Rhodes reported, 'the dominion, provinces, municipalities and semi-public bodies had, it was estimated, $72,000,000 of debt maturing in New York or London, and, in addition, $80,000,000 of external interest charges had to be provided. Added to these, there were the debts of corporations and individuals ... It was imperative that there would be no flight from the Canadian dollar.' The government's defensive moves were sorely handicapped by the absence of a central bank, but Bennett did not hesitate to take action. An order-in-council was issued in October 1931 that 'permitted the export of gold only under license issued by the Minister of Finance.'[65] In practice, the government issued no licences; it bought as much surplus gold as Canadian mines could produce for itself, at the New York price, and used it to prop up the dollar. This bold move saved the dollar from further decline, and even stimulated the gold-mining sector, but the hard-money policy aggravated the problem of declining exports. Preserving investor confidence came at a heavy price.[66]

The most notorious aspect of the Conservative government's record was its strong-armed response to civil dissent. Throngs of unemployed men soon became restive. Manion confided to Bennett his own fear of 'serious riots verging on revolution,' pointing out that 'hungry men can hardly be blamed for refusing to starve quietly.' Bennett attributed the social turmoil not to hard times, but to foreign agitators and communist sympathizers. 'If the government is given reason to believe,' he warned in a 1931 speech to the House of Commons, 'that there is a settled purpose in the minds of a considerable number of people – not large, numerically, but scattered over the various parts of Canada – to take action against the maintenance of law and order ... then we will take such action .... as will free this country from those who have proven themselves unworthy of our Canadian citizenship.' A year later, in a public speech, he invited the citizenry to join in defending the established order. 'We know that throughout Canada this propaganda is being put forward by organizations from foreign lands that seek to destroy our institutions,' he asserted, 'and we ask every man and woman to put the iron heel of ruthlessness against a thing of that kind.' Bennett's 'iron heel' soon became a metaphor widely used to describe his authoritarian approach to public protest.[67]

The Conservative government utilized three legislative provisions to rid the country of many of those it deemed 'unworthy' of Canadian citizenship. Under the Immigration Act, any unnaturalized person guilty of even a minor legal offence, or who became a public charge, could be deported without trial. This provision was utilized more and more as the Depression deepened – even with British emigrants. Section 98 of the Criminal Code, first placed on the statute books in 1919 at the time of the Winnipeg General Strike, made it an offence to attend meetings of, or distribute literature about, any organization whose purpose was to bring about change in Canada through the use, or threat, of force. This section was used, for instance, by the Ontario government with the covert assistance of the federal authorities to arrest, try, and imprison Tim Buck and seven other leaders of the fledgling Canadian Communist Party. Draconian as these measures were, Bennett felt the need for even more discretionary executive power. A section added to the 1931 relief bill permitted the governor-in-council to take appropriate measures 'for the maintenance of peace, order and good government.' This blanket phrase conferred wide and arbitrary authority upon the cabinet and prime minister.[68]

A series of relief camps for single, unemployed males, administered by the Department of National Defence, was established across the country, beginning in the fall of 1932. The idea of federally established camps for itinerant young men had had many sponsors. 'It may be necessary,' R.J. Manion suggested to Bennett in 1931, 'to form camps for those men as in army days.' Charlotte Whitton, an influential social worker, and General A.G.L. McNaughton, chief of the general staff, each urged some version of the plan on the prime minister. Nervous mayors and premiers called on the federal government to take some action to remove potential disturbers from the major cities. The men were housed in a series of work camps, often in remote areas, and engaged in such tasks as restoring fortifications, clearing landing-fields, and building roadways. They received their board, and twenty cents for each day worked. The camps soon became a political liability, though, disliked by the unemployed, organized labour, and much of the general public. Unlike the popular Civilian Conservation Corps in President Roosevelt's 'New Deal' America, the Canadian relief camps smacked more of state control than of community betterment.[69]

Although its approach to the unemployed was heavy-handed, the government seemed unperturbed by the question of civil liberties. 'If ever there was a time in the history of this country when section 98 was justifiable as a part of the criminal law of this country, this is certainly the time,' stated the justice minister, Hugh Guthrie, during a 1933 parliamentary debate. 'Section 98 is not in any sense a hindrance to any right thinking person.' His listeners were left to wonder whether the measure was aimed at those who were guilty of 'wrong thinking,' or simply 'left thinking.' Bennett, himself, seemed to take occasional delight in noisy verbal confrontations with delegations claiming to represent the unemployed. Periodically, he would consent to meet representatives of protesting groups, usually in the Railway Committee Room of the Parliament Buildings. On one occasion, he even had an armoured car parked in plain view on the Hill, with squads of uniformed RCMP on horseback standing by, to intimidate the demonstrators. These well-publicized confrontations heightened the prime minister's reputation, with friend and foe alike, as the chief defender of the established order.[70]

One other government policy has served to stamp Bennett's administration as reactionary in the extreme: the reintroduction of honorary titles bestowed by the monarch. 'I am convinced,' Bennett had once written to Borden, 'that the bestowal of honours has had a very considerable influence in creating and maintaining the almost affectionate relations that now exist between the out-lying Dominions and dependencies of the Empire and the Motherland.' To a correspondent in early 1934, Bennett offered a second rationale: 'I desire to establish merit as worthy of honour by the State.' The ideal of merit and Canada's British heritage were both dear to Bennett's heart. He seems to have cared little that public, and probably party opinion were opposed. 'The Honour List was prepared by me,' he later informed an Ontario Conservative, 'and following the British custom, was not submitted to my colleagues.' Symbolically, of course, honorary titles struck the wrong note at a time of widespread austerity and suffering. Ironically, Bennett had himself recognized this fact in 1932, writing that 'to suggest the restoration of titles would ... be to suggest the destruction of the present Government.' The prime minister should perhaps have heeded his own warning.[71]

As the Great Depression tightened its grip on Canadians, then, the Conservative government was forced to reorder its priorities. Controlling the budget deficit, preserving a sound currency, and defending the social order from internal attack dominated the attention of Prime Minister Bennett and his cabinet colleagues, particularly from mid-1931 through to the end of 1933. Long accustomed to growth and development as the norm for Canada, they found themselves struggling mightily just to hold the line against economic insolvency and social chaos. Hindsight might indicate the wisdom of departing from conventional remedies, but it should not be surprising that, in a crisis, the familiar plans would be tried first. What must be emphasized is that this Conservative government did experiment, did innovate, did try its hand at reform, even in the midst of the worst years of the Great Depression.

TRYING NEW IDEAS

Despite its troubles of both policy and image, the Bennett government was able to make some lasting contributions to the institutional fabric of the nation. One of these was in the new field of radio broadcasting. The Aird Royal Commission had recommended public broadcasting in 1929, but the private broadcasters had objected, as had the Province of Quebec, which launched a court case to determine the legislative jurisdiction of radio. The Privy Council's decision, issued in February 1932, found in favour of the federal government. At that time, Bennett indicated his appreciation of the communication medium's importance. 'Properly employed, the radio can be made a most effective instrument in nation building,' he stated, 'with an educational value difficult to estimate.'[72] As one who had astutely utilized the radio in a successful election campaign only two years earlier, Bennett was personally acquainted with radio's possibilities.

The Prime Minister moved the appointment of a special Commons committee 'to prepare a scheme of radio broadcasting,' without committing himself on the question of public or private ownership. The committee, chaired by Dr Raymond Morand from the Conservative caucus, opted for public control, though individually owned private stations were not precluded. The committee's recommendations were accepted as the basis for the Canadian Radio Broadcasting Act. Bennett gave two reasons for supporting public broadcasting. The first was nationalistic: 'This country must be assured of complete control of broadcasting from Canadian sources, free from foreign interference or influence,' he declared. 'No other system of radio broadcasting can meet these national requirements and empire obligations.' The second reason was surprisingly egalitarian: 'No other scheme than that of public ownership can ensure to the people of this country, without regard to class or place, equal enjoyment of the benefits and pleasures of radio broadcasting.'[73] Many observers were surprised that a Conservative government would opt for public ownership, since the line-up of interests opposed to such a policy was lengthy and influential. The Canadian Association of Broadcasters, the Canadian Manufacturers' Association, the CPR, and several key advertising agencies were among the opponents. Bennett's brother-in-law, Herridge, and his top aide, R.K. Finlayson, both with contacts in the Radio League (an interest group favouring public broadcasting), were influential in persuading Bennett of the merits of a public system. Once convinced of the national urgency of the issue, he was quite prepared to commit the power of the state, and quite capable of overcoming internal party opposition. The new Radio Commission began to function in October 1932.[74]

To the surprise of many, Prime Minister Bennett committed his administration to the introduction of a system of contributory unemployment insurance by the next election in a Commons speech delivered on 29 April 1931. William Irvine, an opposition Farmer MP, congratulated Bennett for 'one of the ablest & most statesmanlike deliverance [sic] that I have ever heard on the subject.' The Conservative leader's promise came as a shock to friend and foe alike, and, just as with public broadcasting, it was opposed by an imposing array of established interests. From within his own party, former Ontario premier Howard Ferguson considered unemployment insurance 'a most vicious and destructive scheme,' on the basis of his observations as high commissioner to London of the British plan. *Canadian Forum*, though impressed by Bennett's speech, noted 'no great enthusiasm for it in most Conservative quarters.'[75] Nevertheless, Bennett set some of his top officials to work in 1932, researching a practicable plan. Among these were Clifford Clark, deputy minister of finance, and his own policy adviser, Rod Finlayson. The matter was raised as a chief topic of discussion at the dominion-provincial conference held in January 1933. The first ministers were unable to agree on a formula by which the Dominion government could introduce legislation in this provincial area of jurisdiction. In spite of the set-back, federal officials continued to work on a draft plan, behind the scenes.[76]

In yet another swipe at powerful interests, the Conservatives laid the groundwork for a central bank. Rhodes's 1933 budget had contained a proposal to establish a royal commission on banking. His deputy minister, Clifford Clark, strongly supported the establishment of a central bank, and Bennett's own experience with credit and currency matters had brought him to the same conclusion. The commission, headed by Lord Macmillan of Britain, was formally established in July 1933.

'Bennett knew the background of the men named on the Commission,' his aide, Rod Finlayson, noted later. 'There were thus a majority of the Committee [sic] that would, in all probability, recommend the establishment of a central bank in Canada.' The Macmillan Commission proceeded at nearly breakneck speed to conduct hearings and then prepare its report, which was in the government's hands by the end of September. By a three-to-two margin, the commissioners recommended a central bank. Bennett and Clark had the verdict they wanted.[77]

Though it championed many traditional policies, the Conservative government was not a devotee of *laissez-faire*. It was far too activist by nature. When the conclusion became inescapable that the international economic crisis was not abating of its own accord, or retreating in the face of trade agreements and retrenchment, a search began for new solutions. One that appealed to the Conservative leadership was supply management. Eliminating surpluses was seen as the key to raising commodity prices, not just in Canada but in 'New Deal' Washington and elsewhere around the world. The first concrete step in this direction was taken at the World Monetary and Economic Conference in London during the summer of 1933. An agreement signed in July between five major silver-producing countries (Canada, Australia, Mexico, Peru, and the United States) and three major holders of silver (China, India, and Spain) committed the signatories to collectively withhold 35 million ounces per year from the world market for four years, beginning in January 1934. The Conservative government ensured Canada's adherence to its export quota by buying up the country's surplus silver production. Though the international cartel eventually broke down, its immediate effect was to increase the price of silver.[78]

Prime Minister Bennett presided at the World Wheat Conference, a meeting of major importing and exporting countries held in England in August 1933. For several months prior to the conference, the four main wheat exporters – Canada, the United States, Australia, and Argentina – had been discussing various export-reduction schemes. In fact, a discussion of possible ways to restrict the world production of wheat (and silver) had been one of the key items on the agenda for Bennett's meeting with President Roosevelt in April.[79] At London, the four main exporting countries reached agreement on export quotas, based on a 15 per cent reduction in foreign sales for the 1933–4 and 1934–5 crop years. Canada's share was 200 million bushels. In order to institute an acreage-reduction plan, the Dominion Parliament and the legislatures of the three Prairie provinces introduced concurrent legislation to create an emergency wheat control board. Many of his own cabinet colleagues were opposed to this blatant interference in free markets, but Bennett acted in London with the firm support of the leaders of the three Prairie wheat pools, and of the Prairie premiers. Their justification was simple. 'The purpose of the agreement is to raise the price of wheat,' declared Bennett in Parliament, 'which can only be done when the surplus carryovers have been removed from the market.' As it turned out, the onslaught of drought and rust in the Canadian West removed the necessity for any significant acreage reduction in Canada. The international cartel arrangement eventually broke down when Argentina exceeded its quota.[80]

The innovative economic ideas of J.M. Keynes were beginning to filter out from Cambridge University in Britain, but neither Bennett nor Rhodes became a convert. Preserving investor confidence through a balanced budget and a sound currency was an article of faith for both men. Nevertheless, there were some expansionary elements to their overall economic policy, elements often overlooked by critics of the Conservative administration. For example, despite all their rhetoric, the Conservatives, in fact, ran up huge budgetary deficits each year. These deficits amounted to $114 million in 1931–2, $221 million in 1932–3, and $134 million in 1933–4. Total government expenditures during this three-year period averaged only $480 million so that the actual annual deficit ranged between 25 and 40 per cent. Furthermore, despite a morbid fear of inflation, the government did act to increase the money supply in the fall of 1932 by adding $35 million to the bank reserves, thus raising the lending capacity of the chartered banks. This action was quietly approved by order-in-council, under authority of the Finance Act.[81]

A number of prominent Conservatives had come up with innovative recovery plans of their own. R.J. Manion, for instance, suggested to the prime minister a proposed 'Bennett Recovery Programme.' His main proposals were two: a massive public-works program, financed by a peacetime version of the Victory bonds, and a conversion loan to reduce interest payments on the national debt. H.H. Stevens submitted ideas for a 'New National Policy.' He wished to use government pressure to induce manufacturers to raise wages, banks to loosen credit, and business to begin a large reconstruction program in the major cities. Raymond Morand urged currency inflation, manufacturing subsidies, public works, a minimum-wage law, maximum-hours-of-work standards, and unemployment insurance. Bennett's chief aide, R.K. Finlayson, prepared a memorandum for him in September 1933 summarizing 'the content and purpose of the Roosevelt legislation.' Herridge, writing from Washington, was advocating public works as a means to 'prime the engine.' Robert Weir, the minister of agriculture, was 'working on a marketing measure, making some compulsion possible.' The prime minister himself promised in a November radio broadcast that the government's program in 1934 would include the creation of a central bank and a new series of public works.[82]

As 1933 drew to a close, then, the Conservative administration could point to a number of major reforms launched, in preparation, or under active consideration. They were not prisoners of either tradition or reactionary forces. What they could not point to was much evidence of economic recovery. This factor alone caused their political fortunes to nosedive. More than ever, they would need a strong party organization to carry them through the next election.

PARTY DISORGANIZATION

R.B. Bennett's attitude towards the Conservative party organization, once he became prime minister, may be summed up in a single word: neglect. He, himself, later agreed with this assessment. 'I gave too much time to the problems of government,' he confessed to a correspondent in 1938, 'and too little to the interests of my Party.' It was as if, having ridden the party machine to power, he no longer saw the need for it. Indeed, one close observer, Harold Daly, concluded that 'after the election of 1930 he took the attitude that he had won it himself and refused to support the organization.'[83]

The superb organizational machine that A.D. McRae had built up over a two-year period was abruptly dismantled, beginning just one day after the smashing victory of 28 July 1930. On McRae's instruction, Redmond Code had written to each provincial headquarters, informing them that the central party office would 'cease to function on the 29th of July,' thus terminating all subsidies to the provincial party offices. 'My responsibility here,' McRae informed Premier Rhodes, 'under my original arrangement with the Chief and Caucus, was to cease the day after the election, win, lose or draw.' Rhodes, McRae, and Sir George Perley, all urged that steps be taken to put the central party office on a permanent basis, but to no avail. 'The question,' McRae noted to Rhodes, 'is one of finances and that is something which is up to the Chief.'[84] Bennett's priorities now lay elsewhere.

Shortly after the election, Code and Lipsett submitted detailed plans to Bennett for keeping the Ottawa headquarters functioning, albeit with a skeleton staff and budget. For only $3,425 a month, they estimated that a general secretary, a director of publicity, and five supporting staff could keep the main features of the party headquarters intact, including the news services and mailing list. Code pointed out the advisability of keeping the mailing list constantly updated, and advocated expanding it from 250,000 to 500,000 names by the next election. He also cited the need 'to maintain a direct contact with and direction over the activities of these various provincial organization headquarters as they constitute our direct contact with the individual constituency organizations.'[85] Regarding the Standard News Service, Lipsett pointed out, 'If it is dropped, even for a brief space, or if the publishers develop any suspicion of it as a propaganda medium, it will be impossible to re-institute it while this generation of weekly editors live.' Lipsett already had mapped out plans to cover major events such as the economic conference in Britain. 'The most cogent reason for continuing this office,' he stressed to the prime minister, 'is to develop through this service a state of mind which will not expect that economic conditions throughout the country will be overturned in a day.'[86]

Somehow, funds were scraped together for one final issue of *The Canadian*, which was released in October 1930. Its contents give a fair indication of what might have been produced throughout the 1930–5 period. A 32-page, 6-by-9-inch booklet entitled *Canada First Is a Fact*, vol. 1, no. 10, of *The Canadian*, carried photos of R.B. and Mildred Bennett, biographies of each minister in the new cabinet, riding-by-riding results of the election, highlight of the special parliamentary session (with legislation specifically related back to Conservative campaign promises), and the text of Bennett's speech to the Imperial Conference.[87] Had such publicity material been circulated throughout the next five years, the party's image with the public would have fared much better.

Such was not to be the case, however. Code left the party office in December to resume his law practice, and Lipsett followed him a few months later, eventually finding a press-gallery job with the *Mail and Empire*. McRae was given a Senate appointment in 1931, but this reward was insufficient to mollify a proud man who had seen his two preferred appointments, high commissioner to Britain and minister to Washington, bestowed upon Howard Ferguson and W.D. Herridge, respectively. Bennett's neglect broke up the team that had installed his party in office.[88]

The prime minister received no end of advice about the need to restart the organization. As early as December 1930, the Conservative advertising proprietor, J.J. Gibbons, advised him to appoint 'someone to take charge of our finances,' and 'someone to function as your Dominion organizer.' Many in his own cabinet, including Stevens, Manion, and Sauvé, offered the same advice repeatedly over the next three years.[89] Bennett was aware of the problem. 'As a matter of fact,' he confessed to Stevens in 1932, 'we have no organization.' His stock answer was that, as he was too busy 'dealing with the urgent problems that confront this country,' others should take on the job, specifically 'the Ministers and the organization as it exists.' In other words, he would do the governing; his ministers should do the politicking. That this arrangement did not work out was a source of endless frustration to him. At one point near the end of 1933, he lashed out at Manion: 'Why don't these people do something? Why turn to R.B. for everything?'[90]

Bennett failed to realize that would-be party organizers could not act without receiving his authorization. Several MPs and senators did meet in November 1932 and formed a temporary committee on party organization, passed resolutions to form an executive committee representing all the provinces, appoint a national director, and set up a publicity bureau. The resolutions came to naught, however, because the party leader would neither act on them nor empower anyone else to do so. After much cabinet badgering, Bennett finally appointed Stevens, Manion, and Wesley Gordon in June 1933 to a special committee to draw up plans for party organization. Gordon dropped out, but the other two drew up a detailed plan requiring a budget of just $25,000 for the first year. It envisioned a finance committee, an organizational headquarters in Ottawa supervised by Harold Daly, and appointment of a field organizer such as Dr Hodgson of Manitoba, or Earl Rowe, the Ontario MP.[91]

Before he had even received the Stevens-Manion report, Bennett proceeded on his own to ask Earl Lawson, MP, to accept the position of party organizer. Lawson, who had chaired the party's 1933 Summer School for Ontario Young Conservatives, was prepared to take on the job, but he had one important condition. 'I must be assured of an income of $25,000 a year,' the Toronto lawyer informed his party leader! Lawson recommended the job be given to a member of cabinet. 'Bob Manion could do this job,' he assured Bennett. 'He is keen and exceedingly popular with the Members of the House of Commons.'[92] Manion, of course, was recommending Hodgson or Rowe. Around and around it went. As of January 1934, only a few months before a possible election campaign, there still was no organization, no central office, no national director. Bennett seemed to be repeating the mistake King made prior to 1930, forgetting the responsibility of the prime minster to act as a party leader.

A central problem, of course, was the lack of funds. With the Depression in full swing, raising money was difficult. Bennett did designate Ryckman, and then Chaplin, to oversee this task. However, their efforts were devoted to paying off debts accumulated in the 1930 campaign. Chaplin was forced to respond negatively to a query from Manion in mid-1933 as to the availability of money to launch a new organizational headquarters: 'As you know, General McRae and I were busy for several months raising funds to pay off a lot of old debts that had accumulated. We did hope at one time to try and raise enough money to carry on some propaganda, but the amounts that were owing seemed to grow as we went along, and we never got any surplus. For your information, I might say that we collected over $250,000.00, but every cent of it has been paid out, and there are still some amounts yet unpaid.'[93] Ward Pitfield, the Montreal stockbroker, had suggested a traditional means of raising party funds. 'Having in mind financial necessities for the future,' he wrote Bennett in October 1930, 'some arrangement must be made to obtain control of at least a portion of patronage in Montreal and Quebec. One method would be to have such patronage paid into our present common fund.' Contractor kickbacks and the like seem not to have appealed to Bennett. Neither was he prepared, however, to finance the party organization himself. 'This question of providing finances for the Committee,' Stevens pointedly reminded his leader in December 1933, 'was on several occasions brought to your attention.' Still, no money was forthcoming. Stevens and Manion 'did not have a single dollar with which to carry on.'[94]

The Conservative organization in Quebec was in a similarly dismal state. As his reward for a job well done, Joseph Rainville, the chief organizer, was appointed to the Montreal Harbour Board only weeks after the 1930 election. His colleague in the Quebec district, Thomas Maher, remained at his post until 1932, when he was elevated to the new Canadian Radio Broadcasting Commission. In October 1932, Georges Laurin, MP, was selected by the Quebec caucus to serve as chief organizer for the Montreal district, but his effectiveness was hampered by two things. First, he was perceived to be Sauvé's man, meaning that the Duranleau and Cahan factions would have little to do with his organizational efforts. Second, he had few funds with which to work.

A significant portion of the money raised by Chaplin had to be allocated to Quebec, where the Montreal district owed $36,000 for 'past expenses' and the Quebec district was $26,000 in debt.[95] Nothing more clearly indicated the problems of the Quebec organization than the press situation. By the end of 1933, *La Patrie* had been sold by Conservative senator Lorne Webster, to the Liberal *La Presse*, leaving only three lukewarm Blue dailies, *L'Illustration* (Montreal), *L'Evénement* (Quebec City), and *La Nouvelliste* (Three Rivers), none of which Laurin felt could be 'trusted.' Of fifty-five weeklies, only seven were pro-Conservative.[96]

The federal organization in Ontario completely disappeared. Home Smith managed to clear up the election debts within two years, but, at that point, the joint committee reverted to a provincial one. 'The members of the Committee who may be said to represent the Ottawa element in the Party cannot even be brought to a Meeting,' Smith complained to Premier Henry. This complaint was echoed by the permanent secretary of the Ontario party, W.G. Clysdale, who informed Manion in April 1931, 'For the last eight months, I have not received $1.00 from the Federal Organization.' A year later, Arthur Ford lamented that he was forced to finance the preliminary work in the South Huron by-election himself, with 'so far no signs of any help from Ottawa.' The Ontario party made repeated requests to Bennett, through Home Smith, Attorney General W.H. Price, and Earl Lawson, to appoint a federal liaison with the provincial party, all to no avail. 'The only reason you have not heard from the Federal Organization,' Harold Daly informed Clysdale in March 1933, 'is that there isn't any.'[97]

The story was the same across Canada. Funds from the federal wing of the party were non-existent, as was interest by the federal leader, with the exception of his own province, Alberta. Ministers such as Manion, Stevens, and Weir did what they could, but to little effect. The result was the almost complete atrophy of the fearsome election machine of 1930. Yet, by the summer of 1933, Conservative operatives such as H.R. Drummond-Hay of Winnipeg were beginning to notice the vigour of the opposition parties: 'For Heaven's sake can't we get started? We are dawdling around while Mackenzie-King [sic] is getting out a lot of propaganda, the C.C.F. are getting out their propaganda and if we don't get out some propaganda and get busy it won't be worth our while in the West to put any Candidates [sic] in the field.' Still, the Conservative organization slept.[98]

Among other failings, the Bennett government largely mishandled what patronage was available to it for rewarding party supporters. Although the Civil Service Act of 1918 had largely removed one aspect of traditional party patronage, namely the appointment of the faithful to civil-service jobs, there still remained public works, advertising, legal work, and a host of special appointments not covered by the regular hiring procedure. Some ministers, such as Manion and Stevens, were very adept at handling this aspect of their jobs, carefully consulting the local party executives before reaching decisions. Others, such as E.B. Ryckman, seemed to make enemies out of friends. 'The Federal Government ... begrudgingly gave me a $12,000 advertising contract for the Department of Inland [sic] Revenue,' R.A. Stapells of the J.J. Gibbons agency (which had handled the Conservatives' advertising in the 1930 election) complained to Howard Ferguson in April 1931. 'We had it last year through the Mackenzie King Government, and it amounted to $35,000. E.B. Ryckman was almost offensive in his attitude.'[99]

Government retrenchment naturally caused a sharp reduction in the amount of government money available for patronage, as did the switch in emphasis from public works to direct relief. The change in policy was resented by many Conservatives, who rightly saw the connection between patronage and re-election. Nowhere was the political effect of the government's ineffectiveness in patronage more telling than in Quebec. Thomas Maher sought to explain to Bennett the impatience of the party workers there: 'Our people fail to grasp how and why their cherished ideal of responsible government fails to work adequately with our party in office. To put it grossly, they asked us everywhere that same question: 'Why do we elect members to Parliament? Is it only to make speeches?' Discontent within the party was not confined to Quebec, however. A complaint from the Kingston MP General A.E. Ross was typical of many. 'Our Executive is almost a unit in its desire to throw up [its hands] and retire from the field,' he thundered in exasperation. 'Most appointments here have been made from Liberals.'[100]

One of Bennett's failings was the long delay he incurred before deciding upon the appointments that were within his prerogative. The lieutenant-governorship of Ontario was vacant for a year before Dr H.A. Bruce was appointed. Both Stevens and MacLaren had to remind Bennett repeatedly over a period of several months of the need to appoint new deputy ministers for their departments, before the posts were filled. Bennett's preoccupation with the complexities of governing seems to have blinded him to the political importance of patronage, and the manipulative control over a party that the powers of appointment, shrewdly used, give to a prime minister.[101] Ironically, his use of appointments removed from the provincial spheres three of the five premiers who had been so helpful during the 1930 campaign. Rhodes of Nova Scotia came to Ottawa to join his cabinet, Baxter of New Brunswick was elevated to the bench, and Ferguson of Ontario was dispatched to Britain as high commissioner. In each case, the replacement was a leader of less political acumen.

In a pre-polling era, provincial elections and federal by-elections offered rare glimpses of the relative popularity of the various parties. The 1931 results were mixed. A provincial victory in Prince Edward Island was encouraging for the Conservatives, but the sound trimming they took in Quebec was equally discouraging. There were two federal by-elections that year. In Hamilton East, a working-class riding, the Conservatives lost the seat to a Labour candidate, but in Three Rivers–St Maurice, they picked one up at the expense of the Liberals. The year 1932 began auspiciously enough, with a victory in the Athabasca, Alberta, by-election, where the Liberals lost another seat. The Grits were suffering for their involvement in the Beauharnois scandal. In two other by-elections that summer, the Conservatives held Royal, New Brunswick, while the Liberals defended Montreal-Maisonneuve successfully. In the only provincial election of the year, the Farmer-Liberal coalition in Manitoba won re-election, leaving the Conservatives as the largest opposition group. The most decisive contest was the October 1932 by-election in South Huron, Ontario. The Conservatives chose to elevate this contest, in a riding narrowly held by the Liberals in 1930, to a near-referendum on the Ottawa Trade Agreements. Five cabinet ministers, including Stevens and Manion, were sent into the riding. The result was a crushing defeat, by 2,000 votes. The inability of the federal Conservatives to organize properly was a major contributing factor in the loss.[102] By 1933, the election news was all bad for the Conservatives. They lost both provincial elections, in Nova Scotia and British Columbia, and all three federal by-elections: in Restigouche-Madawaska, New Brunswick, where the party had won in 1930; in Yamaska, Quebec, where they had hoped to capitalize on growing discontent with the provincial Liberals; and in Mackenzie, Saskatchewan, where the Conservative challenger finished a distant third, behind the victorious Liberal, and a runner-up from the fledgling CCF.[103] The political omens for Tories were bad indeed. It was no wonder that a discouraged R.B. Bennett talked openly of retirement in the fall of 1933.

STANDING ON THE PORTAL

In the normal course of events, 1934 would have been an election year for the Dominion. Even the customary New Year's optimism, however, could not mask the fact that the Conservative government was in deep political trouble. In the 1930 election, Bennett had promised action to end unemployment, abolish the dole, and find markets for Canadian products. He had certainly delivered action. Under his leadership, the government had provided emergency relief funds; jacked up tariffs; hosted an imperial conference; negotiated trade treaties; established control of the wheat export trade; nationalized radio broadcasting; forced the two great railways into cooperation; slapped export controls on gold; negotiated a treaty with the United States to construct a St Lawrence deep waterway; increased coal subsidies; provided a temporary wheat bonus; increased the federal share of old age pensions; helped set up international wheat and silver cartels; launched a system of relief camps; raised personal, corporate, sales, and excise taxes; rolled back civil servants' salaries; and deported thousands of aliens.

All this action ultimately failed to deliver on Bennett's real promises. As Mackenzie King delighted in pointing out, 'the promises were that he would end unemployment, and that he would find markets; these other things, the tariffs and the expenditures, were the means to that end.'[104] Unemployment was not banished; it was much worse. The dole was not abolished; it was far more widespread. Markets were found, but they did not begin to replace those that were lost. Despite all this action, the problems of 1930 were worse, not better, in 1933. That the causes of a good many of Canada's economic difficulties were beyond the control of any domestic government did not matter, for Bennett in 1930 had brushed aside such objections, guaranteeing a return to prosperity if he were elected. So far, he had failed to deliver, and the government's mandate was running out.

Within his own party, Bennett's leadership had failed miserably. The vaunted electoral machine of 1930 was gone, neglected by the man it had put in power. The provincial supports for the national organization had begun tumbling to defeat. The leader who had so generously underwritten party expenditures in the three years prior to the victory of 1930 now closed his pocket-book. Perhaps he felt the poor of Canada who wrote to him requesting money were more deserving of his assistance than the party, and indeed, perhaps they were. However, the party had grown accustomed to his financial support. Bennett would

neither undertake party organization and finance himself, nor authorize others, in cabinet or out, to do the job for him. He appears to have
decided that the party's re-election depended wholly on his own ability,
and that of a few close advisers, to solve the Depression.

Implementation of the election promises of 1930 had not accomplished this objective. Application of the conventional wisdom for com-
bating hard times – balancing the budget, stabilizing the dollar – had
not worked either. New ideas there were aplenty in the swirling vortex
of public discussion. Which ones held the key to ending the Depression?
The prime minister and his colleagues would have to choose soon.
Already, they had shown some willingness to try reforms. The remaining months of their mandate would test the mettle of the Conservative
party under Bennett. Was it a reactionary party? A party of reform?
Perhaps both?

6 Reform and Disunity:
January 1934 to July 1935

Harry Stevens's Sunday-afternoon press conference caught the Ottawa press gallery by surprise. As they assembled on 7 July 1935, speculation centred on the former minister's political future. His acute unhappiness with the current direction of the Conservative party was well known. It was also widely accepted that he was not the sort of person to turn his back on active politics just when his popularity was at an all-time high. What did the veteran BC politician have on his mind? Stevens did not keep them wondering long. He announced his decision to head a new political party. 'On Saturday last a delegation representing many thousands of citizens resident in all parts of Canada waited upon me,' he explained, 'and presented a petition asking that I accept leadership of a party having for its object a reconstruction and reform program similar to that which I have been advocating during the past eighteen months.' After a day of discussion and reflection, Stevens had agreed to take the plunge.[1]

The delegation meeting with Stevens had consisted of three moderately successful businessmen. Warren Cook of Toronto was president of the Garment Manufacturers' Association. Thomas Bell headed a Montreal stationery company. Thomas Lisson was a partner in a Hamilton printing firm. Together, they had journeyed to Ottawa as delegates from a Hamilton meeting of Stevens supporters representing many parts of the country. That gathering had passed a resolution urging the former minister to head a new national party. Stevens also cited thousands of supportive letters he had received from the general public in recent months as further evidence of wide popular approval for his bold step. 'There is a great body of public opinion that is disgusted with the two old parties,' he declared to reporters, 'largely because it is now clear that both are unduly influenced by the policies and will of the large corporations and those who control them.' His party would be based on 'the average citizen, worker, farmer, smaller businessman, or the professional man.' Though it had no platform, no organization, no funds, not even a name as yet, the new Stevens party set out on its quixotic quest to challenge the established Conservatives and Liberals for the right to govern Canada.[2]

Conservatives across Canada hardly knew how to react. Harry Stevens had been a Conservative MP since 1911. Three times he had served as a minister of the Crown, first under Meighen and then under Bennett. Stevens had renounced his own leadership ambitions in 1927 to work for the selection of R.B. Bennett. In 1930, Bennett had returned the favour by bringing Stevens into his cabinet, in spite of the latter's personal defeat at the polls. The Montreal *Gazette*, representing a big-business wing of the party, dismissed Stevens as an ill-informed agitator. 'The former Minister has appealed, and still appeals, to the prejudices of ignorant people,' it declared in an editorial. Stevens's hometown *Vancouver Province*, by contrast, voiced regret along with its disapproval. 'We have had more than a little sympathy with his policies,' it stated, 'but we can not approve of his latest departure.' Party members mirrored the party press in their ambivalence.[3]

The Depression produced several new parties in federal and provincial politics. The Reconstruction Party is unique in that it grew out of a conflict within the ruling Conservative party. Stevens believed there was no room for real reformers in his former party. Prime Minister Bennett, however, claimed for himself the mantle of true reformer, and sought to paint the Liberals as the reactionary party of the past. Other Conservatives, including the editors of the Montreal *Gazette*, believed by 1935 that both Bennett and Stevens were dangerous radicals who had somehow hijacked the Tory party from its traditional moorings. C.H. Cahan best represented their views in cabinet. Why did the Conservative party, seemingly united at the beginning of 1934, break up so publicly eighteen months later? Was it a split based primarily on policy, or personality? Answers to these questions will go a long way to explaining the fate of the party in the 1935 election, and in the two bleak decades that followed.

THE CONFLICTING VIEWS OF THREE CONSERVATIVES

The turmoil in the Tory party at this time revolved around these three men: H.H. Stevens, C.H. Cahan, and R.B. Bennett. Their differences arose from the following three factors: the ambitions they harboured, the interests they represented, and the philosophies they followed. All were possessed of a generous dose of personal ambition; each could see himself as the ablest leader of the party. Stevens came from a small-business background in Vancouver; Bennett was a lawyer-tycoon from Calgary; Cahan had been legal counsel for some of the most influential Montreal companies. Nevertheless, each considered himself a good Conservative in the Macdonald tradition, and each had stoutly upheld tariffs and the value of the British connection for years. The issue that best illustrated their philosophical differences was government involvement in business, though, even here, they agreed that communism was evil, socialism abhorrent, and private property a fundamental right.

For Harry Stevens, the ideal capitalist was the small, independent businessman. Whether involved in merchandising, manufacturing, farming, or fishing, the simple entrepreneur represented the virtues of self-reliance, diligence, integrity, thrift, and compassion. Not all devotees of capitalism would include compassion, but Stevens believed in what he called 'Christian economics.' Much to Stevens's regret, this old-time free enterprise did not seem to be working anymore in Depression-ridden Canada. He had little trouble in designating a villain. It was big business, 'the so-called "great leaders of industry and business" whose main object is to crush the competition of the smaller businessman.' The old laws of economics no longer worked because selfish corporate interests, 'that little coterie at the top,' were playing the game unfairly. While the masses of the people suffered, 'the unscrupulous and cold-blooded' minority prospered.[4]

Stevens's faith in capitalism was too deep to reject it out of hand, despite the rampant injustice. 'Capitalism,' he stated in 1933, 'is a natural outgrowth of a democratic social system.' The evils, he believed, were 'capable of correction.' If corporate Canada were powerful, one institution stood mightier yet – the Parliament of Canada. Stevens saw in the democratic state the means by which the chaos in the marketplace could be righted. 'Let parliament,' he admonished, 'hold the balance in such a way that genius and enterprise may receive a just reward, but not at the cost of the happiness and well-being of our people.'[5] This was people's capitalism, one might say, and when combined with Stevens's outspoken condemnation of the big interests, it marked his views as a form of populist conservatism.

The world looked very different to C.H. Cahan. A self-confessed

'Conservative of the old school,' he wanted no part of new forms of direct government intervention in the realm of business. His was the faith of rugged individualism, tempered by an appreciation of the value to Canadian industry of tariffs. 'Life is work,' he maintained. 'Mere existence does not postulate nor imply the right to exist at the expense of the community. The sick, the infirm and the feeble-minded must ever be the concern and care of the whole community, but those of us who have health and strength must each personally assume the responsibility of acquiring, by careful training and preparation, individual efficiency in whatever work is available, if society is to be maintained on the basis of individual liberty and individual responsibility.' As Cahan saw it, there were 'two general classes in the community, those who, of their own initiative and by their own trained efficiency, can provide employment for themselves and others, and those who depend on others to find employment for them.' Such being the case, it was the part of wisdom to ensure that 'those most enterprising, efficient and thrifty receive the largest rewards,' and the part of folly to shackle them with restrictive regulations and punitive taxes. In Cahan's view, the Depression was a cyclical phenomenon only, capitalism needed no drastic reforms, and the best thing the government could do was to leave business alone. All the interventionists would accomplish, he was sure, would be to delay the inevitable recovery, impair capitalism's long-term health, and encourage the common people to embrace communism.[6] Cahan's philosophy may best be described as *laissez-faire* conservatism.[7]

Where Stevens embraced the federal government as the one national institution powerful enough to tackle corporate power, Cahan stood resolutely for provincial rights. It is true that the provincial governments seemed less able and, in Quebec at least, less willing to impose the regulations upon business that Cahan abhorred. Two other points must be made, however. As a lawyer, Cahan found it exceedingly difficult to ignore several decades of entrenched judicial precedent. Furthermore, as one of the few anglophone politicians with a feel for French Quebec's sensitivities, he understood the importance of safeguarding the protections granted to religious minorities by the division of powers in the constitution.[8]

R.B. Bennett did not share Stevens's faith in the average citizen. He saw a danger in 'universal franchise without educational test.' He welcomed certain aspects of privilege, though privilege based on merit rather than birth, and, as prime minister, he made a gesture in that direction by restoring honorary titles to Canada. Furthermore, Bennett became increasingly annoyed with Stevens's methods, which to him reeked of muck-raking attacks and rabble-rousing oratory, whose net effect was to inflame the masses unnecessarily. 'The first step towards dictatorship,' he warned at one point, 'was a prejudicial appeal to the little man .... Then followed the inevitable utter disregard of constitutional limitations.' Social order was a crucial aspect of Bennett's ideal system.[9]

On the other hand, though much wealthier than Cahan, Bennett did not share the latter's unshakeable faith in an unchanging capitalism. He quoted with approval Tennyson's aphorism: 'That man is the true conservative, that lops the mouldered branch away.' He had no fear of an activist national government. 'There must be the collective power of the state, as indicated by its laws,' he asserted, 'to curtail the power of capital, which, unbridled and unrestrained, means ruin absolutely to the community in which it flourishes.'[10] Nevertheless, his beliefs constituted a paternalist form of conservatism. As Bennett's own aide, Andrew MacLean, observed in a 1935 biography, 'He believes in government by the ablest and best.' It was the duty of those in the ruling class, having achieved their prominence on the basis of their own merit, to direct the community's affairs wisely and with compassion for those less fortunate and less gifted. As he declared to the Winnipeg convention in 1927, 'no man may serve you as he should if he has over his shoulder always the shadow of pecuniary obligations and liabilities.' The wealthy new leader had then added, meaningfully, 'Such as I have I consecrate with myself to the service in which I am.' Conscious of his success in law and business, Bennett felt himself both fitted for, and called to, public service at the highest level. His views remained consistent throughout his eleven years as party leader. In 1938, addressing a Conservative banquet, Bennett reiterated his beliefs about the proper motivation for public officials: 'It is a philosophy of service, not of opportunism. Not of power, except to serve. Not of place, except as a means of service, not of the party, but of mankind, for the high and low, for the poor and rich, for equality under the law.' Just as Stevens's did, the prime minister's values bore a strong imprint of Christian responsibility.[11]

These three men – Stevens, Cahan, and Bennett – embodied three important strains of Canadian Conservatism: populist, *laissez-faire*, and paternalist. Normally, these elements coexist within the party; at best, they complement one another.[12]During 1934 and 1935 they emerged as warring factions within the bosom of a fractured Tory party.

CONSERVATIVE POLICY IN 1934: TWO STEPS FORWARD ...

In 1934, the Depression was as intractable as ever. True, the economic indicators had shown a slow, but steady improvement since the first quarter of 1933. Still, the cumulative effects of four years of hard times were demoralizing for the nation as a whole, and particularly so for those on relief. An estimated two million Canadians received public relief at some time during 1934.[13] The crisis posed a difficult economic problem for the Conservative government. It also represented a serious political challenge. Normally, the ruling party went to the country for a renewed mandate after four years in office. That would mean an election in 1934. However, provincial governments were finding it difficult to be re-elected in the midst of the Depression. If the federal Conservatives were to be successful, they would need to produce more than a slow improvement of business conditions. This political imperative helped persuade many Conservatives of the need for reform. It also exacerbated the growing divisions in the cabinet between those, like Cahan, who felt the best policy was to wait out the Depression, and others, like Stevens, who urged some fundamental restructuring of the economy. Presiding over the debate was Prime Minister Bennett, a man unaccustomed to seeking a consensus among his colleagues at the best of times.

The corner-stone of the government's economic policy continued to be the effort to bring expenditures in line with revenues. To Bennett, the chief effect of a Keynesian-style counter-cyclical approach was that political leaders would find it too difficult to cut back popular spending programs in order to produce the required budgetary surpluses during boom periods. Nevertheless, with penny-pinching retrenchment and a new tax on the gold-mining industry, Rhodes was still unable to eliminate the deficit. Revenues in the 1934 fiscal year would amount to only $362 million when expenditures were $478 million. The balance had to be covered by government borrowing. To the finance minister and his boss, a deficit representing one-quarter of the total federal budget might be a fiscal embarrassment, but their orthodox economic instincts were tempered by the practical realization that a balanced budget would be a political disaster.[14]

One target of retrenchment was the federal contribution to unemployment relief. At a dominion-provincial conference in January, Bennett sought to reduce Ottawa's contribution, but was rebuffed. In July, the federal government reopened the case. Referring to 'the question of direct relief,' Sir George Perley informed the premiers by letter of Ottawa's attitude. 'The necessity for it,' he stated, 'is greatly lessened on account of the improved conditions.' At an ensuing conference, the provinces complained, but to no avail. Federal aid for direct relief was cut by 20 per cent, and took the form of negotiated grants-in-aid, rather than matching funds. 'Ottawa calls it a relief agreement,' Premier Taschereau of Quebec snapped, 'when in reality it is an ultimatum.' The federal treasury was somewhat relieved, but at the cost of heightened provincial animosity, and increased hardship for the country's poor people.[15]

The Conservatives did take one hesitant step towards reflating the economy, while at the same time creating jobs for some of the unemployed. Ministers such as Manion and Stevens had long been advocating a major public-works program, along the lines of the one begun by the Roosevelt administration in the United States. Just how well the Tory cabinet understood the intricacies of pump-priming is unclear, but it certainly understood pork-barrelling. Public-works projects created jobs, even if only temporarily, and, with an election expected, jobs were more vital than ever. Rhodes and Bennett had fought off such demands in the past, on the grounds of fiscal stringency, but in 1934 the government adopted a new plan to finance them painlessly. It printed $40 million of new money, and used these funds to pay for the construction of new federal buildings, post offices, wharves, and so on, throughout the country. Bennett found justification for the new policy in 'the action of the world in placing a new value upon gold.' Since the recent rise in the international value of gold had increased the worth of the government's bullion, more money could be safely circulated. 'This is not inflation,' he insisted to fellow MPs, 'in the sense in which that term is used in this chamber.' To an Alberta MLA, he explained further: 'The pubic works programme was primarily for the purpose of dealing with unemployment.'[16]

The government broke new ground by setting up a central bank to regulate credit, issue currency, manage foreign exchange, and offer financial advice. Bennett had paved the way for the Bank of Canada earlier by appointing the Macmillan Commission, a majority of whose members favoured such an institution. Speaking in Parliament, Bennett related how he had become convinced of its need when he 'realized for the first time that this Dominion of Canada could not carry on direct exchange operations with London for any substantial amounts except through Wall Street.' The government was adamant, however, that the central bank would be kept isolated from partisan politics and patronage appointments. 'The Bank of Canada, though privately-owned, will operate as a public trust,' explained Rhodes. Its ownership was placed in dispersed, privately held shares, 'to preserve the unchallenged independence of this bank.'[17] Opposition Liberals and the CCF portrayed the private-ownership feature of the bank as evidence that the Tory government intended it to kowtow to private interests. Bennett stoutly denied the charge that his administration was so intimidated. 'You must realize,' he exclaimed to W.M. and H.S. Southam, 'that the reason we have had no central bank in Canada is because the chartered banks were powerful enough to prevent it, and they are accepting it now under protest.' Indeed, the chartered banks were required to surrender their gold holdings to the new Bank of Canada, and to accept its direction in the areas of currency, credit, and exchange. As with radio broadcasting, once Bennett became convinced of the need for a reform, he was not one to be dissuaded by powerful interest groups. Privately, even Mackenzie King conceded, 'I think the act is an exceedingly good one.' Within the bureaucracy, the deputy minister of finance, W.C. Clark, rejoiced that the central bank's creation would at last 'repair this major defect in our financial set-up.' Graham Towers, a senior manager with the Royal Bank, was appointed the first governor of the new Bank of Canada on 10 September 1934.[18]

The year's most controversial legislation was Weir's Natural Products Marketing Act. It was widely recognized that low commodity prices were at the root of Canada's economic difficulties. In an attempt to increase the return to the country's primary producers, the agriculture minister introduced a bill, not dissimilar to the National Recovery Administration experiment launched in the United States, by which domestic marketing boards could be set up for all natural products. The purpose, he stated, was 'to give the producers, to the extent indicated by their organizing powers, the control, regulation and marketing of their own products.' A marketing board, once set up by majority vote of the growers or producers of a given product, could set prices, impose production quotas, and install quality standards. There was some question concerning the constitutional validity of the act, but the government felt this problem was met by a provision for concurrent legislation to establish local boards within participating provinces, as well as a Dominion board to regulate interprovincial trade. The hope, of course, was to control supply and thereby raise prices. The bill had the support of several provincial governments, most farmers' groups, and the CCF, but the Liberals decided to fight it as an invasion of individual rights, a drain on the public treasury, and a violation of the constitution. In this opposition, they were joined by most of the country's business community, which objected to the government's proposed intervention in the market-place. Harry Stevens was one cabinet minister who strongly supported Weir's proposed law in Parliament. 'The bill,' he stated, 'is designed to give some opportunity to the producers of agricultural and other products to get a fair chance in the markets instead of placing them under the control of the great marketing institutions.' Weir sought to portray the marketing legislation, which he conceded at one point was 'to a large extent ... an experiment,' as a moderate measure with broad-based support among producers. 'Regulation with a minimum of interference with trade practices is the keynote of this legislation,' he emphasized in the House of Commons. *Canadian Forum*, though, saw the bill as another indication 'that Mr. Bennett has decided to continue his policy of stealing thunder from the left.'[19]

A major problem, both for the government itself and for businesses and individuals, was the crushing debt burden, mostly incurred at high pre-Depression interest rates. Many voices urged the government to unilaterally lower these rates, but on the question of principle Bennett was adamant. 'We cannot repudiate without destroying our credit,' he maintained. In practice, however, the government did put through legislation to ease the debt load on farmers. Under the Farmers' Creditors' Arrangement Act, official receivers were appointed to facilitate compromises between farmers and their creditors that would avoid bankruptcy but assure repayment under more flexible terms. A board of review in each province was empowered to impose settlements where compromise failed. Complementary amendments to the Canadian Farm Loan Act allowed the existing Farm Loan Board to advance more money to credit-worthy farmers at lower rates through mortgages. Both bills were ably piloted through Parliament by Bennett himself, without significant opposition. 'The object,' the prime minister explained, 'is to keep the farmer on the farm.'[20]

M.A. MacPherson, formerly the attorney general of Saskatchewan, came to Ottawa to set up the administrative machinery for the Farmers' Creditors' Arrangement Act. The required officials were in place on the Prairies by 1 September 1934, and in all other provinces two months later. A statement issued by E.N. Rhodes in July 1935 stated that the

7,600 debt settlements reported to date had resulted in an annual reduction in interest payments of $1.8 million. Total debt reduction averaged 30 per cent, according to an internal memo sent to the prime minister. Meanwhile, the number and total amount of mortgage loans authorized by the Canadian Farm Loan Board shot up nearly 1,000 per cent over the next three years. So successful were the credit arrangements under these two measures that a senior official in the Department of Finance informed Rhodes of 'the large number of small home owners' who approached government officials, inquiring whether 'they might be entitled to secure protection similar to that afforded to farmers.'[21]

As a matter of fact, the Companies' Creditors' Arrangement Act had been passed by Parliament in 1933, with an apparently similar intent – to authorize credit compromises between debtor companies and unsecured creditors. However, this law sat on the shelf and had little real impact. 'The provisions of that legislation,' H.F. Gordon of the Department of Finance apprised Rhodes in September 1935, 'are little known throughout Canada, and while the measure has been in effect for more than two years, regulations thereunder have only now been drafted.' The problem seemed to be that the legislation was the responsibility of 'the Department of the Secretary of State.' C.H. Cahan was not one to encourage citizens to take lightly their obligations for debt repayment – Depression or not. The bill he had steered through the Commons in 1933 was narrow in scope and given little administrative support.[22] Similar charges were laid against another of the government's reform measures, this one introduced by Cahan in 1934.

In the aftermath of the stock-market crash of 1929, evidence of shady stock-promotion practices had come to light. To rebuild public confidence, the government undertook to reform the Companies Act. The Dominion had invited submissions from the provinces, as jurisdiction in this matter was divided. Receiving no replies, Cahan proceeded alone. He introduced amendments to the federal law designed 'to afford greater security to investors, shareholders and creditors.' The changes placed restrictions on share promotion and underwriting, while requiring more stringent auditing by publicly traded companies. Most observers were unimpressed, however, and one academic observed that it was difficult 'to resist a temptation to regard it, in part, as a deliberate attempt to perpetuate the practices of predatory finance while taking credit for their elimination.'[23]

Another supposed reform of Cahan's landed the government in trouble with French Canadians, normally a constituency well understood by the crusty Montrealer. The tempest arose from a bill introduced by Cahan to centralize all government translation services in his own Department of the Secretary of State. The proposed Bureau of Translations, he claimed, would increase the efficiency of English-French translation and, at the same time, save money. In his speech to the Commons on second reading, Cahan acknowledged that his bill had been 'the subject of rather violent criticism in certain sections of the public press.' Quebec Liberals took up the cause in Parliament, accusing the government of trying to save a few dollars by laying off translators, most of whom were French Canadians. Prime Minister Bennett received a letter signed by eleven members of his caucus, expressing 'the strong opposition of the Quebec Conservative members of the House to Bill No. 4, introduced on January 29th by Hon. Mr. Cahan, to centralize the translation services.' Bennett, who had been kept informed of the bill's progress since the earliest drafting stage by Cahan, did not relent. Duranleau and Dupré were prevailed upon to speak in favour of the bill, and with the whips on, the bill carried by a comfortable margin. Nevertheless, an impression of diminished francophone status within the Conservative government lingered, particularly in view of a simultaneous controversy over another aspect of bilingualism.[24]

This second issue concerned the language of the currency to be issued by the new central bank. Many Conservative MPs from Quebec were on record as favouring a bilingual currency. Bennett also had to contend with outspoken anglophone MPs such as F.W. Turnbull of Regina, who baldly stated, 'We do object to being made to use the French language.' Rhodes produced a compromise whereby bills in French would be issued in francophone areas, and bills in English elsewhere. The government was outmanoeuvred when Lapointe and King managed to swing the entire Liberal party behind Lapointe's proposal for a bilingual currency. The Liberal amendment failed, but four Quebec Conservatives broke ranks, and many more were embarrassed. It was a Pyrrhic victory for the Tories. In the midst of heated debate, Bennett had shouted across the Commons, 'Since when has it become the law of Canada that the will of a minority shall prevail over that of the majority?' As Deputy Speaker Armand Lavergne informed Senator Meighen, 'l'attitude prise par le Gouvernement ... serait exploité ... par les libéraux' [the attitude taken by the Government ... will be exploited ... by the Liberals].[25]

As the parliamentary session of 1934 wound down, the government's public image was a decidedly mixed one. On the side of reform, they could list the Bank of Canada, the Natural Products Marketing Act, the

Farmers' Creditors' Arrangement Act, and the public-works program. Balanced against these measures were reactionary efforts like the continuing struggle to balance the budget and the 20 per cent cut-back in unemployment-relief grants. Some policies intended as reforms, such as the Companies Act, the Translations Bureau, and French-language currency, were so maladroitly handled that they came out looking like backward steps. For a considerable period, the reforming initiative passed from Prime Minister Bennett to his cabinet colleague H.H. Stevens.

THE RISE OF HARRY STEVENS

For much of 1933, Stevens had been troubled by the mounting evidence of small Canadian businesses being driven into bankruptcy or forced into sweatshop labour conditions by the market power of a few large corporations whose profits seemed hardly to be affected by the Depression. As minister of trade and commerce, he received submissions from interest groups such as the Canadian Manufacturers' Association and the Canadian Association of Garment Manufacturers, begging the government to do something to save their members from ruin. An investigative report prepared for the latter group by two academics associated with the League for Social Reconstruction, H.M. Cassidy and F.R. Scott, provided particularly damning evidence. Stevens sent the prime minister a long memo, suggesting reforms, but in follow-up discussion Bennett rejected the possibility of federal action on constitutional grounds. Stevens dropped the matter, but continued to brood over it.[26]

Early in January 1934, Bennett asked Stevens to fulfil a speaking engagement for him in Toronto, at a convention of the boot and shoe industry. Having received more requests for help from millers, livestock dealers, and clothiers, Stevens launched an aggressive attack on 'big business' for abusing its power to the detriment of small business, labour, and farmers. In particular, he hit out at 'the practice of mass-buying by huge department stores.' No companies were specifically mentioned, but Eaton's, for one, felt the sting of his attack. R.Y. Eaton publicly denied his company was guilty of malpractice, and privately approached both Stevens and Bennett, demanding either proof of wrongdoing or a retraction.[27]

Bennett was appalled. He sternly upbraided Stevens, both for being unfair to Eaton's and for breaking cabinet solidarity by committing the government to a policy that had never been discussed. Stevens thereupon submitted his written resignation. Attached to his letter was a copy of his Toronto speech, samples of the evidence on which it had been based, and a detailed justification of his behaviour. The temperamental Bennett, who quarrelled often with his more capable aides and ministers, was taken aback by the resignation, and surprised also by the support aroused by Stevens's charges within the party, the Tory press, and the public. Once again he summoned Stevens, the resignation was quietly set aside, and Bennett thrust the direction of a special Commons inquiry into the surprised minister's hands.[28]

Stevens had wanted a royal commission presided over by a judge, but Bennett insisted on a parliamentary committee to investigate business abuses, and assigned Stevens to draft the terms of reference. It was Bennett who moved the resolution in the Commons, however. The all-party committee, with Stevens as chairman, was empowered to investigate the causes of large price spreads, the effects of mass buying, and the resultant labour conditions.[29]

There were sound reasons for doubting Stevens's impartiality as chairman. His Toronto speech had revealed clearly his bias against the large packers and department stores. His Commons speech supporting the committee resolution attacked the practice 'of selling goods at less than cost of production.' Loss leaders were, of course, a common technique of the large retail businesses. Soon after, an opposition MP tabled a letter from Stevens that further indicated his biases. 'Thank you very much for the illustrations attached to show the evil influence of the department and chain store system,' it read. 'We are now continuing the investigation and hope to build up a pretty strong case.' It should have been apparent to Bennett at the outset that Stevens was proceeding more as a prosecutor than as a judge.[30]

The Stevens Committee attracted country-wide publicity. The hearings drew press, politicians, and the public, and the revelations that poured forth shocked the nation. As the evidence of wilful exploitation, collusion, manipulation, and evasion mounted, Stevens became the people's hero. The 'little guys' who testified before the committee were treated sympathetically, but the 'big shots' who appeared were put peremptorily in their places, with none of the deference normally accorded businessmen of their stature. The common folk of Canada loved it.[31]

Stevens's cabinet colleagues were perplexed. Their own mail, and feedback from party back-benchers, indicated that the price-spreads inquiry was by far the most popular initiative undertaken by the government. Yet, Stevens's attacks on the pillars of business were alienating the usual sources of election funds. Furthermore, those with ties to big business themselves – Bennett, Cahan, Rhodes, Perley, Matthews – were scandalized at the reckless way in which Stevens and the committee counsel, Norman Sommerville, pursued the corporate witnesses. 'Auditors are asked question and give answers,' Matthews complained to the prime minister, 'without being able to explain, giving the public very wrong impressions.' Stevens's popularity shielded him from public attacks, but, in the sanctity of cabinet, these colleagues began to snipe at him. Stevens was not impartial, they said, his inquiry was costing too much, and anyway, nothing could be done about the alleged abuses because the power to deal with them was provincial.[32]

Stevens ignored his carping colleagues and pressed forward. So juicy were the revelations that the committee had not even exhausted its list of witnesses, let alone considered recommendations, when the parliamentary session ended. Much as he might have liked, Bennett could not close down the popular inquiry that he had launched himself. In case he wavered, the Retail Merchants' Association engineered a telegram campaign by its members in support of the inquiry. An order-in-council on 7 July transformed the committee into a royal commission, chaired by Stevens.[33]

Stevens's crusade was popular with the Tory back-benchers. For many of them, re-election seemed to rest on his shoulders. On 26 June, he accepted an invitation to address the Conservative Study Club, an informal luncheon group of Tory members. His was an impassioned speech, delivered totally off the cuff. Intended to be a summary of the inquiry's work to date, it became a blistering attack on both the country's economic structure and many of the major corporate leaders. Stevens named names, and cited cases. The sixty-five back-benchers rewarded him with resounding applause.[34]

The tale might have ended there. But, so popular was Stevens's speech with the Tory members that many requested written copies. Muskoka MP Peter McGibbon wanted 3,000, just for his own constituency. It was the custom for Study Club speeches to be transcribed, and one copy given to each member present. Stevens took this verbatim report and had it edited by an employee of his department, James Muir. Stevens proof-read the edited version, then ordered 3,000 copies printed. No attempt was made to verify the facts he had expounded from memory. Only the stylistic irregularities were corrected. Muir, a former press-gallery reporter, proceeded on his own initiative to send copies to a number of his newspaper friends. One found its way, via the *Toronto*

Daily Star, to C.L. Burton of Simpson's, one of the companies attacked in the pamphlet. Another made its way into the hands of Grant Dexter, who wired its contents to his boss, J.W. Dafoe, of the *Winnipeg Free Press*.[35]

Burton immediately wired the prime minister, threatening to sue for libel if the pamphlet was not withdrawn. Bennett, unaware of its existence to this point, scoured the civil service for a copy, read it, and was outraged. Muir was instructed to recall every copy he had sent out. Stevens, on his way to Vancouver, was tracked down in Winnipeg, and asked for an explanation. The trade minister denied any intention of publicly issuing his speech. Meanwhile, rumours of the controversial pamphlet were circulating on the front pages of several newspapers. On 7 August, the *Winnipeg Free Press* published the pamphlet in its entirety, despite veiled warnings by Cahan that to do so would be to invite a libel suit.[36]

The political effects were twofold. On the popular level, Stevens's support grew from the incident. The pamphlet seemed to offer proof of Stevens's sincerity, and its attempted suppression appeared to confirm the determination of the establishment to hide the truth from the public. Many Tory back-benchers agreed with J.S. Bowman, a Manitoba MP, who wrote to Manion: 'The ordinary man ... believes that Stevens is one hundred percent right in attacking conditions which allow frame ups like Simpsons.' Stevens's cabinet colleagues felt differently. Manion thought Stevens had committed 'a bad faux pas.' Rhodes considered that he had put the government 'in a most embarrassing position.' Cahan believed he had shown 'his total unfitness to be Chairman of the Royal Commission.' Bennett, too, was perturbed. 'The difficulty,' he stated privately, 'is that the statements in the document are incorrect, and when they are corrected it places the Minister in a very difficult position and the Government in a worse one.' It was bad enough that Stevens was discussing a case before all the evidence was in, but he did not even have his facts straight. Bennett left for Europe shortly on government business, still brooding over his colleague's indiscretion. Stevens, undaunted, continued his public speech-making.[37]

The first full cabinet meeting following the pamphlet's publication was on 25 October. Stevens was emotionally distraught. His daughter Sylvia, aged twenty-three, was terminally ill, suffering from colitis. Bennett, too, was upset. The commission hearings were to resume shortly, and so he confronted Stevens about his conduct as chairman of the inquiry, pointing out the factual errors in his pamphlet, and the impropriety of taking sides before the evidence was all in. Other ministers joined the round of denunciations, particularly Matthews and Cahan. Rhodes suggested that Stevens issue a statement prior to the first hearing, making amends for any damage resulting from publication of the pamphlet. Stevens stoutly defended his actions, and the meeting broke up without a decision.[38]

Word of the division was leaked to a reporter by Cahan. Stevens spent the night considering his political future. When he learned the afternoon papers would carry the story that he had been asked to recant, his mind was made up. He sent his resignation to the prime minister, and declined to attend the day's cabinet meeting. Stevens did not go public yet, and, in fact, denied to a reporter that he had resigned. He hoped the shock of his threatened resignation would cause Bennett and his colleagues to reconsider. The ploy had worked in January. This time, Bennett's office leaked Stevens's resignation to the press. The following morning, Stevens called a press conference to confirm his resignation. Later that day, Bennett made public his own letter accepting Stevens's resignation.[39]

Where Stevens's letter had been short and somewhat conciliatory, though accompanied by a copy of his January resignation, Bennett's reply was condescending, even insulting. He chided Stevens for failure to follow 'the principles of British justice and fair play,' then poured acid on his sores with this statement: 'As much has been said about business ethics, I cannot but think it is the duty of any member of a Government who is responsible for the publication and circulation of a pamphlet containing inaccurate statements, to take the earliest opportunity to correct or withdraw such statements, with an appropriate expression of regret.' Privately, Bennett confessed to Howard Ferguson: 'I understand he did not expect his resignation to be accepted but what else could we do when he had resigned twice in the same year.'[40]

Stevens struck back bitterly. 'I deeply resent your thinly veiled insinuation that I have been deliberately untruthful,' he retorted in a hostile letter of reply, also released to the press. All the frustration he had felt at the indifference and opposition of his colleagues came out in a torrent of anger directed at the prime minister: 'When you refer in your closing words to "British justice and fair play" I cannot but bring to my mind the countless thousands of citizens of Canada who are patiently suffering while others whom you champion in such eloquent terms have been reaping rewards far beyond that which any citizen might reasonably expect to win.' The intended insult found its mark. Bennett was infuriated.[41]

The political fall-out was not what Bennett had hoped. Far from un-masking Stevens as an unprincipled charlatan, the incident had made him a martyr. Worse, it seemed to confirm Bennett's cartoon image as the consummate capitalist. Even Tories who supported Bennett's position reported that it had hurt the party's standing. 'For the present,' Earl Lawson informed his chief,' the Government are [sic] on the short end of this situation politically.' While some Conservative newspapers, particularly the Montreal *Gazette*, Toronto *Mail and Empire*, and Toronto *Telegram*, applauded Stevens's departure, others disapproved. The *London Free Press* spoke for many when it stated, 'politically Mr. Bennett has made a big blunder.'[42]

THE BENNETT-HERRIDGE NEW DEAL BROADCASTS

After the Stevens resignation, Conservative prospects fell to a new low. With a moribund organization, dispirited caucus, and divided leadership, the party's chances for re-election seemed non-existent. Bennett had no desire to lead his party to electoral oblivion. Furthermore, he was jealous of the popularity of Stevens, a man he considered a traitor. 'The government which I have the honour to lead is responsible for the Price Spreads Commission,' he curtly informed one correspondent. 'I moved the Resolution providing for its appointment. I named the members of the Commission sitting on our side of the House. I arranged for the necessary financial assistance.' In Bennett's mind, he was the true reformer. Stevens was a usurper.[43]

Into the breach strode W.D. Herridge. As Canadian minister to Washington, he had had a ringside seat as the Roosevelt New Deal unfolded. He had concluded that 'the idea itself was what was best in the New Deal.' The specific measures adopted by president and Congress met indifferent success as recovery schemes, but, taken as a whole, the New Deal program was a resounding political success. It worked, Herridge reasoned, because the American public believed it was working. Bold government action, combined with Roosevelt's masterful rhetoric, had sparked a recovery of national confidence. Herridge, who dined with members of the president's brain trust, was eager to cast aside old dogmas. 'I do believe that the days of *laissez-faire* are over,' he informed Bennett in one of the wordy memos he periodically dashed off for his brother-in-law's edification. 'I do believe that the capitalist or profit system can never work again as it once worked. I believe that government is in business to stay.' Herridge urged Bennett to transform Canadian Conservatism into 'the new Tory party ... the party which ... put government into business,' and to do it with a big public-relations splash.[44]

Bennett was not easily convinced. According to his personal aide, Finlayson, he considered most of Herridge's reform ideas to be based on 'the works of fanatics and crackpots.' Nevertheless, in the autumn of 1934, while Bennett was in Europe, Herridge and Finlayson together drafted a rough Canadianized version of the New Deal. After the negative public reaction to the Stevens resignation, Bennett was more disposed to listen. The Herridge plan offered him a chance to reclaim centre-stage in his own party, and a plausible hope for re-election. Herridge and Finlayson were duly set to work preparing a series of speeches embodying the new reform program.[45]

A carefully orchestrated strategy was devised to obtain maximum publicity for the Canadian New Deal. Bennett set the stage for it in a series of five speeches in December, delivered at Brockville, Halifax, Toronto, Montreal, and Ottawa. Taken together, they previewed his January broadcasts. In particular, he promised to curb business abuses by implementing the recommendations of the Price Spreads Commission, and to introduce unemployment insurance. Meanwhile, Herridge accepted an invitation to address the Ottawa Canadian Club, where he tried out some of his radical rhetoric. Many, including Sir Robert Borden, and even Bennett himself, were scandalized to hear the Canadian minister to Washington openly attacking capitalism: 'In the beginning, capitalism established the open marketplace. It was founded upon free competition. Profit was the hub of the system. Profit remains. The open marketplace and free competition are no more. Concentrations of business and combines have destroyed the open marketplace.' Herridge's real target was neither Bennett nor Borden, but another politician in attendance, Mackenzie King. He hoped to lure the cautious Liberal leader into an open defence of the status quo. 'If we hang on to this idea,' he informed Manion, 'he will be forced back into *laissez-faire*.'[46]

Late in December, the prime minister's office released a press statement announcing that Bennett would be making a series of radio broadcasts to the nation early in January. Bennett personally rented air time on a network of forty stations for five half-hour broadcasts, at a total cost of $11,000. Finlayson arranged with the press gallery to prerelease the text of the speeches, which ensured maximum morning-after coverage. As for the speeches themselves, Herridge and Finlayson collaborated on their preparation. The dramatic phraseology of the first one was almost purely Herridge's work. Finlayson's influence was more pronounced in the next three, which dealt more in policy specifics. The concluding address, which sought to paint the Liberals into a *laissez-faire* corner, repeated a theme Herridge had first developed in a summer memo to the prime minister.[47]

Herridge's radical rhetoric, combined with Bennett's booming voice, had the desired effect on the public. Listeners could hardly believe their ears when, on 2 January 1935, the prime minister launched his radio attack on the status quo. 'The old order is gone,' he declared. 'If you believe that things should be left as they are, you and I hold contrary and irreconcilable views. I am for reform. And, in my mind, reform means Government intervention. It means Government control and regulation. It means the end of *laissez-faire*.' This was not J.S. Woodsworth talking, this was R.B Bennett. In one half-hour, the prime minster regained the initiative from Woodsworth, Stevens, King, and the rest. For at least a few months yet, the country's political agenda would be his to set.[48]

The next three speeches were less dramatic, but with more content. Bennett proposed federal legislation to set minimum-wage and maximum-hours-of-work standards; establish an insurance plan for unemployment, sickness, and accidents; increase taxation on the idle rich; strengthen the Farm Loan Board; broaden the Natural Products Marketing Act; implement the Price Spreads recommendations; and amend the Companies Act to protect investors. The program contained something for each of labour, agriculture, and small business. The promised reforms were far from revolutionary, but, in the context of the times, they represented a radical departure for the Conservative party. By contrast, the fifth address sought to convince voters that the Liberal party stood for '*laissez-faire* and the unrestricted operation of the profit system and the complete freedom of capitalism,' while Bennett captained the party of reform.[49]

The Bennett broadcasts injected a transfusion of hope into the Conservative party. Organizers such as Arthur Ford observed 'an entirely different spirit' among the rank and file. From the West, John Diefenbaker reported that the broadcasts were being 'enthusiastically received' in Saskatchewan. Although the cabinet had been kept in the dark like any private citizen, many ministers were enthusiastic – Guthrie urged an immediate election call to capitalize on the popularity of the reform program. Manion professed himself 'entirely in accord' with the new policy.[50] Some ministers were not so disposed. Meighen thought the speeches a mistake, and told Bennett so. Cahan prepared to resign, and was dissuaded only by the pleas of his Montreal supporters, who urged him to stay and 'fight it.' The Montreal *Gazette* lost no time in asserting that Bennett's new policies did 'violence to every Conservative principle.' The complainers were in the minority, however. Most Tories agreed with Sir Robert Borden, who concluded privately that, as a result of the Bennett broadcasts, the Conservative party was 'animated with new-born hope of success.'[51]

Response outside the Conservative party was mixed as well. Predictably, some businessmen opposed his verbal assault on *laissez-faire*, but many others were ready to accept state intervention to stabilize the market-place. 'As far as this city is concerned,' Senator Ballantyne wrote from Montreal on 8 January, 'your addresses so far delivered have met with universal appeal from all classes, with the exception of a few industrialists and financiers ... Such prominent men as Mr. J.D. Johnson, President of the Canada Cement Company Limited, Mr. J.W. McConnell, and many others thoroughly endorse all of your policies.'[52] Mackenzie King found the broadcasts 'sickening and disgusting. If the people will "fall for" that kind of thing,' he declared in his diary, 'there is no saving them.' Nevertheless, the Liberal journalist Grant Dexter reported to his editor that Ottawa observers believed Bennett had 'gained much ground with his broadcasts.' From a socialist point of view, Frank Underhill, writing in *Canadian Forum*, contrasted Bennett's 'present solicitude for the forgotten man' with his 'past sneers.' 'Mr Bennett's reforms,' he continued, 'will not touch the root of our troubles, which is the ownership and control of the instruments of production by private profit-seeking interests.' Both Liberal and CCF insiders viewed the Bennett broadcasts strictly as a pre-election gambit.[53]

The New Deal broadcasts did represent a bold gamble for the Conservatives.[54] Despite the many worthwhile reforms already accomplished during his prime-ministership, Bennett's public image had remained that of the strong and decisive, but essentially small-c conservative business tycoon turned politician. Would the public accept Bennett in his new guise as the great reformer? Would his own party go along? For every Tory like Manion strongly in favour, there was another like Cahan obstinately opposed. How would Stevens fit in, if at all? In Herridge's mind, a key part of the strategy was to trap the Liberals into a stout defence of *laissez-faire*, a role they had willingly assumed in 1934 when opposing the marketing board legislation tooth and nail. Would the wily Mackenzie King acquiesce? Bennett had scored a major public-relations coup for his party, but, as any marketing manager knows, once you have the customer's attention, you still have to make the sale.

THE PRICE-SPREADS REPORT

The prime minister did not have a clear field in his quest for recognition as the leading Conservative reformer. Harry Stevens had not abandoned the world of politics upon his resignation from cabinet in October 1934. He continued his public speech-making, and his association with the Price Spreads Commission, albeit as an ordinary member. He was amused by the reformist tone creeping into Bennett's speeches. 'You seem to have at last impregnated his mind with some really sound economic truths,' he wrote Herridge in mid-December, 'and he is trotting out to the front in great shape.' As for himself, Stevens was adamant. 'I am going to plow the furrow I have started as straight as I can,' he insisted.[55]

During the summer and autumn of 1934, a number of investigative studies had been carried out under the auspices of the Price Spreads Commission. Lester Pearson, seconded from external affairs, served as secretary to the inquiry, and coordinated the research and analysis. The commission resumed its public hearings on 30 October, and heard 157 witnesses over the next three months, at 65 sessions. The new chairman was W.W. Kennedy, a Conservative MP from Manitoba. Kennedy's style was less combative than Stevens's. Witnesses were allowed to bring counsel with them. Bennett, at least, was pleased with the change, claiming the inquiry was receiving 'less hearsay and more real evidence.'[56]

The Bennett radio broadcasts initially drove the commission hearings out of the headlines. Before long, however, firsthand evidence of deplorable labour conditions in the textile industry landed the probe back in the centre of public attention. Once the commission went *in camera* to prepare its report, Stevens did his best to feed the press enough information to maintain the level of public awareness. Aided by Robert Lipsett, now parliamentary reporter for the *Toronto Daily Star*, Stevens regularly 'leaked' his own recommendations on the various topics before the commission. In April, fearful the government might try to bury the commission's work, he leaked the entire draft report. The practice annoyed his commission colleagues, and infuriated the government, but it was an effective publicity tactic. The Retail Merchants' Association conducted a parallel campaign. They turned Stevens's leaked recommendations into a pamphlet and used it as a means of orchestrating public pressure on the government.[57]

The final report echoed Stevens's own views on the evils of business concentration.

The evidence before us ... has shown that a few great corporations are predominant in the industries that have been investigated; also that this power, all the more dangerous because it is impersonal, can be wielded in such a way that competition within the industry is blocked, the welfare of the producer disregarded, and the interests of the investor ignored ... The corporate form of business not only gives freedom from legal liability, but also facilitates the evasion of moral responsibility for inequitable and uneconomic practices.

Further, the report declared it 'a tragic delusion' to assume that the economic abuses associated with quasi monopolies would be corrected by 'automatic forces.' The principles of simple competition, so dear to the hearts of 'the laissez-faire economists,' no longer applied. In the face of powerful corporations, only one institution possessed the power and legitimacy to redress the inequities: the federal government.[58]

The key recommendation, from a list of several dozen, was the establishment of a federal trade and industry commission to regulate competition. The royal commissioners concluded that a flexible regulatory approach was required. In an industry such as public utilities, monopoly appeared inevitable. In other industries, classic simple competition continued to thrive. Between these two extremes were several gradations of imperfect competition. Only a federally established independent commission would possess the flexibility and strength needed to regulate this patchwork of competitive situations. The goal of the new commission would be to encourage just as much competition as was conducive to the general welfare, with emphasis on the needs of farmers, small businesses, and labourers.[59]

There were numerous other recommendations in the report. The commission advocated government action to prevent stock-watering, augment the rights of labour, protect consumers from false advertising and inaccurate measurement, and assist farmers and fishermen in marketing their products. The report recognized the problem of provincial jurisdiction in some of these areas, but suggested a vigorous Dominion exercise of all its legitimate powers, combined with constitutional amendments and joint dominion-provincial programs. The problems were too serious, it argued, to continually sweep under the BNA Act's division of powers.[60]

The majority report carried the signatures of all six Conservatives on the commission, three of the four Liberals (who added supplementary remarks stressing the importance of international trade), and the representative of the United Farmers of Alberta. Notwithstanding this multipartisan support, Stevens's attitude towards the report was almost parental. 'I may say, with deep humility, that the Report is virtually mine,' he stated. It would be his monument, his contribution to solving Canada's economic problems. Now his goal became the enactment of the report's recommendations. Stevens was still ploughing the same straight furrow.[61]

IMPLEMENTING THE 'NEW DEAL'

While Stevens busied himself with the price-spreads inquiry, the government prepared to meet Parliament. According to Herridge's master plan, the election should be held in April. Parliament would sit for only a month or so. The purpose of the session would not be to pass reform legislation, but 'to evangelize the country,' as Herridge instructed Bennett in a mid-January letter. The ambassador was equally pointed in his directions to Finlayson. 'You must talk reform, and preach reform, and offer reform, and show that King is against reform,' he said. 'Your next plan is to relate your Government measures to your theory of reform. Dress each one of them up as a reform prodigy.' Herridge's daring scheme just might have worked. It was not given a fair chance, however, for he was abruptly banished from Bennett's inner circle of advisers. As Finlayson recalled the blow-up, Herridge 'questioned Bennett's ability to draft a Throne Speech. The result was dramatic. The lead horse took over. He figuratively kicked Herridge out of the office.' Bennett resolved to be his own chief political adviser, and Herridge's role shrunk to sending occasional plaintive messages from Washington.[62]

The Throne Speech proved to be a toned-down synopsis of the radio speeches. It cited the existence of 'grave defects and abuses in the capitalist system' that required government action by way of 'reform measures' in order to ensure 'a greater degree of equality in the distribution of the benefits of the capitalist system.' There was little shock value left in these tame phrases. The Conservatives needed to push the Liberals into a corner, but the Throne Speech did not accomplish that objective. King was able to endorse the broad goal of reform, while attacking the government for its insincerity, inconsistency, and ineptitude. Sensing the Tory trap, he shrewdly declined to launch an all-out assault on the government program. Instead, the Liberals shunned a continuation of the Throne debate, and invited the government to introduce its promised reforms.[63]

Bennett was caught flat-footed. One flaw in Herridge's strategy had been that it overestimated the degree of ideological commitment among Liberals to the philosophy of *laissez-faire*. The Liberal party was, in fact, a pragmatic, centrist conglomeration, primarily motivated by the lure of office. True, it had traditional policies, but few that could not be modified to suit the needs of the moment. The tariff provisions of the Dunning budget ought to have been proof enough of the Grits' flexibility. Furthermore, most of the reform bills were not ready for introduction to the Commons. And, without Herridge to advise him, Bennett was no match for King in political tactics or strategy.[64]

The first phase of the 1935 legislation consisted of a handful of bills promised in the radio broadcasts, and largely piloted through Parliament by Bennett himself. The most important piece was the unemployment insurance bill. First promised by Bennett in 1931, it had been drafted by 1934, but held over, pending constitutional talks with the provinces. Although a welcome reform, the bill was a disappointment to many because it did nothing for those already unemployed. Seasonal workers, and those earning over $2,000 per year, were also excluded. The plan was a contributory one, to be funded largely by employers and employees, with the government contributing one-fifth of the total cost. It was intended to enforce working-class savings, not redistribute income on a large scale. Furthermore, many doubted the bill's constitutionality. Bennett based its validity on the recent court decisions in the radio and aviation cases, as well as 'interprovincial and international trade, peace, order and good government, and the power of taxation.' Hoping for a split in Liberal ranks, the prime minister insisted on a recorded vote on second reading. King was one step ahead. The vote was 101 to 0 in favour of the principle of the bill.[65]

The government based the validity of three other reform bills – minimum wage, maximum hours of work, and weekly day of rest – on the federal treaty-making power. Most experts had hitherto assumed these matters were in provincial jurisdiction, under the property and civil-rights clause. The three acts were modelled on the international labour conventions associated with the 1919 Treaty of Versailles. To buttress the Dominion's case in the expected court challenge, Parliament was requested to approve the labour conventions before the reform bills were introduced. The minimum-wage law empowered the federal government to fix a minimum rate for wages, but provincially set rates would prevail if higher. The second bill established the eight-hour day and forty-eight hour week as legal maximums. The third measure decreed one day off from work per week, wherever possible on Sunday. The three bills applied to full-time wage-earners and lower-paid salaried workers only.[66]

These few bills represent the New Deal in legislative form, at the time of Bennett's major illness in late February. While directed to worthy objectives, they did not begin to fulfil his New Deal rhetoric of a 'new order,' nor did they represent much of a platform from which to seek re-election. Meanwhile the Liberals were professing sympathy for the government's objectives, and encouraging it to present the full reform program. This Liberal failure to follow Herridge's script prevented the Conservatives from reaping any significant harvest of popular approval. Furthermore, many observers suspected the labour and unemployment-insurance bills were unconstitutional, a view later sustained by the courts. 'Things have sagged a good deal since his broadcasts,' Manion admitted.[67]

In devising his scheme for the Conservatives' re-election, Herridge was aware of the extraordinary physical effort it required from Bennett and his staff. 'How you are going to get through the work which must be tackled in the next few months,' he wrote Finlayson, 'the Lord only knows.' Naturally, the lion's share fell upon Bennett, who had to evangelize the public, and help to draw up the reform bills, while continuing his usual duties as head of the government and party. It was a killing pace. Bennett's health had failed him in 1934, when he had a physical breakdown while in Geneva in the fall. Throughout that year, he had made the usual noises about retiring. In February 1935, at a crucial point in Herridge's schedule, when Bennett should have been preparing to have Parliament dissolved and the re-election campaign launched, he suffered the most serious breakdown yet.[68]

It began as laryngitis, escalated to a cold, then to a serious respiratory infection. After several days of bedrest, Bennett prepared to resume his duties when he was stricken by a serious fainting spell. His condition was complicated by a marginal diabetic condition and some fluctuations in his heart rhythm. Subsequent examinations in Canada and Britain revealed there had been no real heart attack, but it was close enough to alarm his doctors. Bennett was overweight and overworked; he exercised little, and was subject to extreme stress. In short, he was a prime candidate for heart disease. The prescription was four weeks of complete rest, followed by a life of more leisure and no strain – not a lifestyle to which prime ministers are accustomed. Bennett was mentally as well as physically shaken by his experience, and he prepared to follow his doctors' orders. For three months, from mid-February to mid-May, he was essentially out of the political arena.[69]

Bennett's illness left the government in an embarrassing position. 'As was his custom,' Rhodes explained to Sir Robert Borden, 'he had kept both the contents of the Bills and the material to be used with them entirely to himself, with the result that we are now in the position of having different Ministers coached by his Secretary.' This difficulty was exacerbated by the Liberal strategy of hurrying the bills through the Commons with no obstruction and very little debate. Phase two of the legislative session was marked by confusion in the government ranks, as the cabinet strove to maintain the reform momentum while Bennett recovered. Sir George Perley assumed his customary position as acting prime minister, but it was Rod Finlayson, the executive aide, who assumed the major burden of coordination in Bennett's absence.[70]

Rhodes was pressed into service to take up the slack with an early budget. 'The last paragraph of the first draft was only completed at twenty minutes to six the day before the Budget was delivered,' he informed a journalist. Rhodes did his best to dress it up as a reform measure. In pursuit of his goal of a balanced budget, taxes were raised, but this time the bite was aimed at the rich and powerful. The corporation tax was raised by 1 per cent. New graduated surtaxes were imposed on investment incomes over $5,000, and gifts over $1,000. A number of reductions were introduced in the tariff as well. The projected deficit was $117 million, a figure that proved optimistic in view of subsequent spending commitments.[71]

Other ministers did their best to carry on. Perley introduced the economic council bill, to set up an advisory body to apprise the prime minister and cabinet of major trends in economic and social conditions. This measure had been promised in the third New Deal broadcast. As the Liberal 'Chubby' Power had noted to a friend earlier, however, 'the mention of an Economic Council to give Bennett advice cannot be made without raising a laugh from those who know him.'[72] Weir brought in the Prairie Farm Rehabilitation Act, a measure vaguely previewed in the Throne Speech. Under this law, a special advisory committee was to be appointed for the purpose of investigating and recommending action to restore the soil-blown, drought-stricken areas of the southern prairies. For the first year, $750,000 was appropriated, with provision for up to $1 million of expenditure in each of the next four years. A notice of motion for a potentially divisive grain-board bill was also placed on the Commons order paper.[73]

Other measures introduced during this period when Bennett was absent did not display the same progressive hues. Gordon's relief bill merely repeated the niggardly grant-in-aid policy of 1934. The unpopular relief camps remained in place. Stewart presented a public-works bill for $18 million to be spent on new projects, a sum that was less than half of the 1934 figure. A divided cabinet had initially recommended $45 million for 1935, but 'R.B. in [his] sick-bed' had opposed the proposal 'in practically every detail.' A row erupted in cabinet, with Cahan and Perley leading those on Bennett's side, while Manion, Gordon, Guthrie, and R.B. Hanson (the replacement for Stevens at trade and commerce) forcibly argued for the original figure. Eventually a compromise figure of $30 million was agreed to, but the prime minister subsequently insisted on slicing even that amount nearly in half. The radical-sounding Bennett of the winter months seemed to be reverting to more typical attitudes while recovering from illness.[74]

The third phase of the legislative program encompassed the final two months of the 1935 session. Parliament had recessed for over a month, but, when it reconvened on 20 May, Bennett was again at the Tory helm. There were essentially two classes of bills during this period: those recommended by the Price Spreads Commission and those originating elsewhere within the government or Parliament. Prominent among the latter was the wheat-board bill.

Originally introduced by Bennett on 10 June as a measure to introduce compulsory marketing of all grain through a government-appointed board, the bill was referred to an investigative Commons committee chaired by the prime minister himself. In moving second reading, Bennett maintained the bill merely created 'a wheat board in name – because we have had one in reality during the last two years.' He was referring, in part, to the continuing efforts of his man John McFarland to market Canadian wheat, but also to the cooperative effort of Dominion and Prairie governments to limit wheat production in order to meet Canada's export quota, as agreed upon at London in 1933. Entrenched opposition to the bill soon became apparent. The Canadian Chamber of Commerce sent the prime minister an urgent letter stating it viewed 'with the gravest concern the introduction of Bill No. 98, to provide for the Constitution and Powers of the Canadian Grain Board.' While the bill was generally favoured by representatives of the western wheat pools, testimony before the committee revealed that the Winnipeg Grain Exchange and the Vancouver business community were ardently opposed. In the light of such opposition, the bill that the committee reported back to the Commons was considerably watered down. Most of the compulsory features were gone, and the new board would deal only with the buying, selling, storing, and transporting of wheat. In this more moderate guise, the bill was not opposed by the Liberals.[75]

A further initiative was the Dominion Housing Act, which allocated federal funds to assist mortgage loans to home-buyers. The lieutenant-governor of Ontario, Dr Herbert Bruce, had been privately urging some such program upon Bennett for some time, but with little apparent success. At the time that the 1934 public-works bill was being discussed, Bruce had suggested 'the first public work to be undertaken should be the improvement of housing conditions of the poor,' but his suggestion, similar to one made by J.S. Woodsworth in Parliament, was ignored. Lieutenant-Governor Bruce, who was the moving force behind an investigation of substandard housing in Toronto, continued to pester the prime minister. 'Please do not project a provincial or even civic problem into the realm of federal issues,' a harried Bennett had ordered in November. After the New Deal broadcasts, he did agree to the establishment of a special Commons committee to investigate the matter. Bennett still had serious misgivings, which he shared by letter with Bruce. 'I am interested in the housing problem. The only difficulty is the financial one. Unfortunately, everyone is now turning to Governments for help. If we assist agriculture with low-priced money, I am afraid we will have to leave the cities to the private lenders. However, the matter is to be studied by a Committee and we will see what develops as a result of the investigations.'[76] The committee report recommended federal intervention, and the Dominion Housing Act was the result. Under this measure, $10 million was set aside to assist prospective home-builders who were able to raise 20 per cent of the cost of a new house on their own. The government would match this amount, with the remaining 60 per cent to come from approved private lending institutions. The rate of interest charged to the home-builder was not to exceed 5 per cent. The act had its shortcomings. It applied only to new housing, it was not directly helpful to lower-income Canadians unable to come up with the required down payment of 20 per cent, and some lending institutions refused to take part. Nevertheless, its passage did stimulate the construction of some 5,000 housing units over the next few years – none of them before the 1935 election, however. The administrative machinery took several months to set in place.[77]

Robert Weir brought in some administrative amendments to the Natural Products Marketing Act, along with one substantive change. Its mandate was now broadened to include forest products.[78] Along with the wheat-board bill and the housing act, these three measures represented the last major measures of reform introduced by the Bennett government that had not been included in the report of the Royal Commission on Price Spreads.

The major recommendation of the Price Spreads report had been the creation of a new federal commission to regulate competition and internal trade. R.B. Hanson duly introduced a bill to create such a body. It was controversial. In the government's view, as expressed by Bennett, the powers given to the proposed Dominion Trade and Industry Commission were the maximum 'within the legal competence of ... parliament.' In the view of Stevens, however, 'it was drafted and confined to the narrowest interpretation of constitutional law.' Stevens was also incensed that the existing Tariff Board would become the new regulatory body, in addition to retaining its existing duties. This was 'the chief weakness' of the bill, in his view, and to expect any results from an anaemic bill administered by an overworked tribunal was 'an impossibility.' Some other Conservatives shared Stevens's opinion. Onésime Gagnon, MP, privately expressed himself 'very much dissatisfied with the handling of the federal Trade Commission by the Tariff Board.' W.W. Kennedy, Stevens's successor as chairman of the inquiry, also complained vigorously to Bennett about the bill's ineffectiveness.[79]

The complementary legislation to implement other recommendations of the royal commission was similarly muted. Hugh Guthrie introduced Criminal Code amendments to enforce prohibitions against false advertising, evasion of minimum-wage laws, predatory selling, and other abuses pointed out by the Price Spreads report. Incredibly, Guthrie admitted in the Commons his own 'doubt about the right of parliament constitutionally' to enact the very amendments he was proposing. Similarly, Cahan went out of his way to disown the minor amendments he introduced to the Companies Act. Cahan had already produced all the changes to the law that he felt were necessary the year before.

Citing the government's desire 'to bring before the house the recommendations of this commission' as the bill's only rationale, Cahan virtually invited opposition. 'We leave it entirely to the judgment of the house on second reading and in committee,' he stated, despite the fact he had already weeded out most of the commission's stiffer recommendations. Bennett, who had promised reform of the Companies Act in his fourth radio broadcast, had insisted that some reform bill be passed, but he did not force Cahan to meet the commission's standards. Some minor amendments to the Livestock Act, the Weights and Measures Act, and the Combines Investigation Act rounded out the list of Conservative legislation related to the Price Spreads report.[80]

Both Kennedy and Stevens were angry. Kennedy, in a letter to Bennett, described the proposed legislation to implement the report as 'practically useless.' Stevens voiced his objections publicly. The amendments to the Companies Act and Criminal Code were 'ill-considered bills that were damned when they were introduced by those who introduced them.' The proposed changes to the Livestock Act were 'little more than worthless.' It did seem strange to impartial observers that the government would stretch constitutional principles to the limit for the unemployment-insurance and labour-convention bills, then revert to the traditionally narrow interpretation of federal powers to justify its failure to fully implement the recommendations of its own commission.[81] Bennett, in his own mind, was being consistent. The previous December, he had warned a fellow Conservative that 'a situation is being created which is going to be very hard for Mr. Stevens, because people are being led to believe that something can be done, which is not true.' In June, he was lecturing a Maritime member of the Retail Merchants' Association on the same point. 'Apparently,' he wrote in angry frustration, 'you and your friends do not realize that the Parliament of Canada has a very limited jurisdiction with respect to the business abuses you mention.' The lack of enthusiasm felt by R.B. Bennett for the reforms proposed by the Price Spreads Commission was only partly related to the constitution, however. The Conservative leader's attitude clearly was also related to the ongoing feud between himself and the self-proclaimed father of that report – Harry Stevens.[82]

A QUESTION OF LEADERSHIP

Behind the scenes, a struggle for control of the Conservative party had been set in motion by Stevens's resignation in October 1934. The three major players were Bennett, Stevens, and Cahan. The prime minister, it seemed, could accommodate one of the other two men, but not both. The dispute was partly ideological, but partly personal as well. In the end, loyalty weighed more heavily with Bennett than commitment to reform.

Bennett's image as a pro-business, anti-reform Tory had seemed confirmed by the Stevens resignation. By January 1935, however, his public swing to the left via the dramatic radio broadcasts nearly caused the resignation of Cahan. The secretary of state had been doing some speech-making of his own in the fall of 1934, criticizing irresponsible politicians who advocated undue meddling in business. On 27 November, he offered this assessment: 'Political and social propagandists, blind leaders of the blind, were persistent in efforts to induce Parliament to exercise illegal powers inseparably vested in the provinces. No purpose could be served by an illegal attempt by either parliament or the provinces to exercise powers vested in one or the other.' Mackenzie King gleefully hurled this quotation back in the government's face in the 1935 Parliament. Did Bennett agree with Stevens, who felt the Dominion could proceed constitutionally to reform business, or with Cahan, who believed it could not? If the former, as the radio broadcasts seemed to indicate, why was Cahan still in the cabinet, and Stevens out?[83]

Cahan did come close to resigning from cabinet twice during this period. On the first occasion, early in December, the issue in dispute had nothing to do with business reform. Cahan was incensed that Bennett had removed responsibility for a proposed nationality bill from the secretary of state. 'If ... you have lost confidence in my administration of this Department,' Cahan wrote to Bennett, 'my resignation is available at any time.' Bennett ignored the letter for over two months. Again, Cahan was shaken by the radical rhetoric of the January broadcasts, about which he had not been consulted. He decided to resign, but was talked out of it by some influential Montreal supporters who urged him to resist the changes from within cabinet. Bennett was well aware of Cahan's disaffection, telling King in mid-February that the secretary of state had been 'at the point of resigning ... a dozen times or more.' It would have been quite easy for the prime minister to nudge Cahan out, had he wanted to do so. He did not. When he finally replied to Cahan's written offer of resignation, in a letter dated 4 December but sent 5 February, Bennett combined a defence of his action with a plea that Cahan not take offence. 'I would deeply regret that you should interpret my action as an intimation of lack of confidence,' he wrote soothingly.[84]

As for Stevens, he would not re-enter any cabinet that contained Cahan, the ex-colleague he most blamed for his departure. He was hardly less charitable towards the prime minister. 'The Old Book says "Ye shall not hitch an ox and an ass together,"' he informed one correspondent who urged a reconciliation. For his part, Bennett could not speak of the former trade minister without launching into a violent rage. 'That man has done me irreparable harm,' he exclaimed to a former MP, Leon Ladner. Bennett's temper was not improved by the reports he was receiving from around the country attesting to Stevens's continuing popularity, despite the 'New Deal' broadcasts. 'Stevens is still the man most talked of with regard to Reform in the West,' H.C. Hodgson, the Manitoba organizer, reported. 'Something with regard to a reprochement [sic] between Mr. Stevens and yourself is necessary before we can take full advantage of your policies.'[85]

Several attempts were made by Tories such as Meighen, Herridge, Hanson, and Manion to reconcile the two men. Ladner succeeded in getting Bennett early in 1935 to agree that Stevens should be invited to caucus, and in persuading Stevens that he should go. But when caucus met, neither man would make the first move to greet the other, and after a short stand-off, Stevens walked out. The public exchange of cutting letters in October had deeply wounded each man. Bennett's stiffly formal telegram of sympathy at the time of Sylvia Stevens's death in December did not heal the schism. Nor did a short letter Bennett sent him on 21 February. Stevens's reply was insulting and aggressive: 'I do believe that ten per cent of the people, who govern the other ninety per cent, is mostly composed of crooks or ignoramuses ... I express my views and beliefs to you as though I were writing them to a close and fast friend, and for that reason I know that you will consider them in the light of staunch amity. Otherwise, you and I shall fight on the hustings of our Country against each other, John L. Sullivan style.' After this exchange, the two men neither spoke nor wrote to each other again.[86]

As the gravity of Bennett's illness in the spring of 1935 became apparent, rumours began to circulate about a successor. The most popular choice among the Conservative back-benchers was Stevens. Manion was ambitious himself, but he conceded that 'if R.B. dropped out there would be a majority demand that Stevens be put in as leader.' Stevens's friend Warren Cook, along with George Hougham, secretary of the National Retail Trade Confederation, worked to firm up this feeling by having 'some pressure brought to bear from the outside on the members.' Retail merchants in each Conservative-held constituency were urged to 'wire their member, suggesting that as it was apparent a new leader would be chosen for the Party, they insisted on their member demanding [Stevens's] leadership.' The covert lobbying had Stevens's quiet approval.[87]

Even Cahan was approached to support Stevens, but the secretary of state indignantly rebuffed the conspirators. He informed King he 'would quit public life before he would do anything of the kind.' With Bennett away from Parliament in convalescence, Stevens and Cahan crossed swords twice in Commons debate. On the first occasion, the issue was the constitutionality of the minimum-wage bill. Stevens questioned Cahan's right to remain in the cabinet when he obviously doubted the government's ability to legislate on a matter that formed a key part of the government's reform program. Attacking Cahan was akin to attacking St James Street, at least symbolically, and Stevens's popularity shot up again. This was obvious a month later when he again lashed into Cahan, to the noisy approval of the Tory back-benchers. This time Mackenzie King provoked the confrontation. He questioned the propriety of Stevens's behaviour in speaking publicly of matters still before the Price Spreads Commission. Stevens's rebuttal induced Cahan to quote from Bennett's October letter to Stevens, whereupon Stevens rehashed the whole resignation episode, with very critical references to Bennett as well as Cahan. As Manion observed, 'Stevens' action was a little like tearing open R.B.'s wounds and pouring in acid.' Cahan later revealed to King that he had 'deliberately read in the House from the correspondence between Stevens and Bennett out of loyalty to the Prime Minister.' Cahan preferred to see his former colleague out of the party. 'Stevens' "Spiritual Home" is with the C.C.F.,' he declared to King.[88]

When Bennett returned from England in May, after attending the King's Silver Jubilee, he was determined to do two things: find an able successor, and retire. His first choice was Rhodes. The Nova Scotian had other ideas. Rhodes's wife had died in 1934, his mother was an invalid, and his own health was impaired. In March, he had secretly informed his riding association of his impending reitrement from active politics. Bennett sought to persuade him otherwise, but Rhodes, who was bedridden himself for the month of May, was adamant. Next, Bennett approached Meighen. The senator considered the matter briefly, then rejected it. He had no more desire than Rhodes to disrupt his own plans for an apparently hopeless cause. Manion was willing, but Bennett did not consider him leadership material. In fact, the two men carried out an indiscreetly loud quarrel right on the benches of the House of Commons, after Manion had denied the substance of an independent report tabled by the minister of pensions, Donald Sutherland, critical of the number of ex-servicemen employed in Manion's department. The *Globe* reproduced the argument on its front page, including Manion's threatened resignation.[89]

The dilemma for Bennett was a simple one. If he retired, a majority in caucus would insist that Stevens replace him. If he remained, a demand would be raised that Stevens be taken back into the cabinet. Neither alternative appealed to the prime minister. 'While I was in England, he [Stevens] was intriguing against me,' Bennett later recounted, 'and had the effrontery to say that seventy-six Members of the last House of Commons desired to oust me to make way for him.' Stevens was as bitter as Bennett, but he avoided picking a fight until he saw the government's proposed price-spreads legislation. These bills, when introduced, seemed so inadequate to him that he could no longer keep silent.[90]

The showdown occurred in the Commons chamber on 19 June. Neither man pulled his punches. Stevens quoted liberally from Bennett's January radio speeches, then contrasted them sharply with the reality of the legislation. 'These are noble words,' he concluded, 'but I fail to find in the measures so far submitted to parliament that degree of remedy which was indicated in these words of the Prime Minister.' He sat down to scattered applause. Bennett rose to the challenge. Privately he had declared 'that if that skunk had to be skinned, he supposed he'd have to do the job.' He accused Stevens of seeking to lead the country to dictatorship. 'If the people of the country have been led into the belief that this parliament can pass any kind of legislation it likes regardless of the constitution,' he asserted, 'the age of lawlessness is upon us.' He belittled the recommendations of the Price Spreads Commission, and defended Guthrie and Cahan for their lukewarm defence of the reform bills. As he sat down, the Tory benches erupted in thunderous applause. The 'skunk' had been 'skinned.'[91]

That evening, at a dinner tendered him by the party caucus, Bennett announced his intention to lead the Conservatives into the next election. Stevens was formally excluded from subsequent caucus meetings, by instruction of the prime minister. Two days later, in supporting a committee recommendation to reduce mortgage interest rates, Stevens voted against the government for the first time. There was now no question of him re-entering the government. For Bennett, however, the lesson was clear. 'Ignorance can be forgiven. Stubbornness one understands, but treachery can neither be forgotten nor forgiven.'[92]

WHITHER CONSERVATISM?

A further blemish on what lustre may have remained of the government's reform image was inflicted by the Regina riot of Dominion Day, 1935. Over a thousand young men, 'on strike' to protest relief-camp conditions, had begun a well-publicized trek from Vancouver east to Ottawa to present their demands for change to the Conservative government. Travelling largely on empty railway boxcars, the trekkers attracted more recruits for their army of unemployed at each stop along the way. The federal cabinet, fearing insurrection, ordered the RCMP to halt their advance at Regina. While the strikers asked for work and wages, Guthrie and Bennett spoke in Parliament of 'communistic elements' and plots 'to effect the overthrow of constituted authority.' On 1 July 1935, the inevitable happened. A bloody battle between strikers and police erupted when the civil authorities sought to arrest the leaders of the 'On-to-Ottawa Trek.' In the ensuing riot, one police officer was beaten to death; dozens of strikers, policemen, and spectators were seriously injured; and more than one hundred people were arrested. The incident was one more nail in the coffin of Conservative hopes.[93]

By the time the parliamentary session closed on 5 July, the Conservative party could justly claim to have piloted through a number of important new laws, but nowhere did it have a compelling issue on which to fight the upcoming election. In that sense, Herridge's New Deal strategy, as implemented by Bennett and his Tory colleagues, had failed. What was clear by 7 July, with Stevens's announcement of his decision to lead a new party of reconstruction, was that the Conservative party was still very much the Bennett party. Furthermore, the prime minster had opted to retain Cahan, who was loyal through not reform-minded, over Stevens, who was reform-minded though not loyal. Bennett's New Deal program had more in common with Stevens's populist conservatism that with Cahan's *laissez-faire* conservatism, but a deep personality conflict proved more influential than ideological compatibility. Admittedly, Bennett had stretched his paternalist conservatism to the limit to accommodate Herridge's radical rhetoric. With the latter's relegation to the background by early 1935, Bennett's views began to drift rightward, back to the party centre, where most of the cabinet had always been. As an election cry, ministers such as Rhodes and Guthrie were prepared to support the New Deal, but as actual legislation, they were noticeably more reticent in their enthusiasm. Bennett seemed to follow the same metamorphosis. As for Stevens, when it became clear that the Conservative party would neither adopt his reform policies whole-heartedly nor draft him as its leader, he left the fold to establish a new party that would do both those things.

Nevertheless, Bennett's inability to retain Stevens and his popular appeal within the Conservative ranks represented a failure of leadership. So, too, did the alienation of customary business support, crucial to the party in an upcoming election, first by Stevens's abrasive conduct of the Price Spreads inquiry, and then by the rhetorical excesses of Bennett's own New Deal broadcasts. A leader skilled in the arts of conciliation and compromise would have squared these circles somehow, but the task was beyond Bennett, who alienated nearly everyone. Nor could he claim as his excuse that he had too much to do. The prime minister's leadership style inevitably placed all the reins in his own hands.

It was in the area of policy that the Bennett-led Conservative government did achieve its most noteworthy successes. True, the Depression continued to checkmate its recovery plans. True also, the courts eventually rejected a major chunk of the reform legislation: unemployment insurance; the minimum-wage, maximum-hours, and weekly-day-of-rest laws; and the marketing-board legislation. To the credit of the Conservative ministry, though, it pursued an activist policy, utilizing many levers of state in a vigorous attempt to lift the country out of the Depression. The government's willingness to incur deficits; its modest attempts at currency expansion and easier credit; its ventures into supply management; its pioneering efforts with nationalized radio broadcasting, a central bank, government-assisted grain marketing, and unemployment insurance – all were laudatory. In fact, the Canadian Radio Broadcasting Commission, the Bank of Canada, and the Canadian Wheat Board, though altered in certain particulars by the Liberals after 1935, became institutional pillars of the Canadian landscape. Although the Unemployment Insurance Act was ruled *ultra vires* in 1937, its initial passage by a Conservative government helped to ensure its political acceptability once the constitutional hurdles could be cleared. Progressive legislation such as the Farmers' Creditors' Arrangement Act, the Prairie Farm Rehabilitation Act, and the Dominion Housing Act made its contribution to recovery from the economic crisis.

Balanced against these enlightened policies are others of a more reactionary nature. To the very end, the Conservatives confronted popular dissent with a very heavy hand. Personal pique and jealousy towards Stevens prevented Bennett from rendering the reform proposals recommended by the Price Spreads Commission anything but token support. A continuing morbid fear of runaway deficits and ballooning inflation held back the prime minster, and those in the cabinet such as Rhodes, Cahan, and Perley, who thought as he did, from really getting serious about reversing the deflationary trend. Within Bennett, as within the party he led, the impulse to reform coexisted with the instinct to preserve. Progressivism and conservatism in this political party certainly predated 1942, when the two names were formally linked. Macdonald's moniker for the historic coalition of 1854 and after – Liberal-Conservative – had expressed much the same paradox. Unfortunately for the Conservatives, Bennett alienated a key spokesman for the left wing of his party, right on the eve of the 1935 election.

Was there a Bennett New Deal? Only in a public-relations sense, if by New Deal is meant a distinctive policy of radical reform, originating in the New Year's broadcasts of 1935, and translated into legislation over the next six months. Bennett's public image was, indeed, radically transformed, from the corpulent, prosperous tycoon with friends in high places to the fire-breathing prophet of a new economic and social order, with justice for all. Neither caricature of the prime minister was particularly accurate, though there were elements of the truth in each. The expectations raised in early January simply could not be met, if Bennett were to remain true to his own beliefs. He did not fear reform, but he was not for it either, unless convinced that it would result in some improvement. A largely self-made man, Bennett believed in the traditional values and institutions that gave structure to the world in which he had risen to prominence. His efforts at reform were always designed to preserve the essentials of the existing system, by enabling it to adapt to changing times and circumstances.

As a matter of fact, there is a great deal of continuity between the Conservative policies of 1935 and Conservative actions in the preceding years. Unemployment insurance was promised in 1931, and the legislation drafted by 1934. Bennett and McFarland took the first step to a wheat board in December 1930, when the wheat pools were rescued. The housing legislation traced part of its lineage to a Toronto slum investigation instigated by a Bennett appointee, the Conservative lieutenant-governor of Ontario, Dr Herbert Bruce. The Price Spreads report, which led to certain reform measures, originated with a Commons committee set up by Bennett in 1934, a year before the broadcasts.

The labour-convention bills were foreshadowed in the Conservative platform approved at the 1927 leadership convention. Bennett, himself, in later years dropped the pretence of a sudden dramatic shift to reform at the time of the radio broadcasts. 'All the so-called reform legislation was embodied in the Resolutions passed at Winnipeg,' he stated in 1938.[94] While not true in every particular, Bennett's claim is certainly accurate in its wider sense. A pragmatic desire to appeal to western farmers and urban workers led the Conservative party at that time to give its new leader a broad mandate to adopt the very kind of moderately reformist policies that Bennett and his colleagues eventually put into place. If his government's undoubted departure from the largely *laissez-faire* policies and assumptions of Canadian public life in the 1920s constitutes a 'New Deal,' then so be it. We must date this New Deal to 1930, however, and thank the Great Depression for it.

7 The 1935 Election:
Going Down with the Ship

'The Bennett Government Has Made Good.' Thousands of Conservatives across Canada yearned to see some such headline gracing the front page of their daily newspaper on Tuesday, 15 October. Alas, it was not to be. That particular phrase did dominate a full-page party ad in the Winnipeg *Tribune* on Saturday, 12 October. And, at national headquarters in Ottawa, the party predicted it would retain its parliamentary majority by capturing 137 of the 245 available seats. Other parties offered other prognostications, however. The Liberals who, like the Conservatives, were fielding a candidate in virtually every riding, prophesied 140 Grit MPs when all the votes were counted. A newsletter issued from Harry Stevens's party headquarters foresaw 126 Reconstruction candidates elected. The CCF and Social Credit parties, each running standard-bearers in nearly half the constituencies, also confidently expected the voters to elect a sizeable contingent of MPs from their ranks. Clearly, a lot of fond hopes would be dashed once the votes were actually counted. R.B. Bennett, Conservative leader since 1927 and prime minister for the last five years, chose to await the results at his office in the East Block of Parliament Hill. With him was his sister, Mildred Herridge, up from Washington. A few blocks away, Mackenzie King listened to the returns at his residence, Laurier House, accompanied by two personal aides.[1]

The polls closed at 6:00 p.m., local time. Voter turn-out was about equal to 1930, with 4,452,675 Canadians casting ballots, representing 75 per cent of the total electorate. The Maritime results, reported first, were stunning. Only one Conservative riding, Royal in New Brunswick, survived the Liberal tide, and that by fewer than 200 votes. In Quebec, the francophone ridings went almost en bloc to the Liberals, leaving the Conservatives just five seats there. The Grit sweep was only some-what slowed by the loyalty of Tory strongholds in rural eastern and urban south-central Ontario. The final tally there showed a virtual re-versal of the 1930 results, with Liberals holding fifty-six of the province's eighty-two seats to twenty-five for the Conservatives. With a parlia-mentary majority before they reached the Manitoba border, the Liber-als added thirty seats in Manitoba and Saskatchewan before their steamroller slowed down, picking up just seven victories in the two westernmost provinces. The Tories fared poorly on the Prairies, picking up only a single seat in each province. Coastal voters awarded them five British Columbia seats, as well as the Yukon, to bring their meagre national total to forty. The CCF managed to elect seven members from the West: two from north Winnipeg, two from rural Saskatchewan, and three from labour ridings in British Columbia. Social Credit virtually duplicated its provincial sweep of Alberta, and added a couple of Saskatchewan seats, for a total of seventeen. The lone Reconstruction victory was won by Stevens himself, in the interior of British Columbia. In addition, seven independent candidates were elected, five of these in Quebec.[2]

The dimensions of the government's defeat were staggering. A dozen ministers had been toppled. The party's embarrassing loss in 1921, when only fifty Conservatives were returned, now looked respectable by comparison. Though hurt and angry on the inside, Bennett neverthe-less conceded gracefully. 'The result is decisive. The Liberal party has been entrusted with the responsibility of governing Canada. I wish them well.' Mackenzie King was less gracious. 'The results,' he crowed, 'afford the strongest condemnation of the attempts made by the Bennett government to debauch the people with expenditures from the public treasury.' Privately he wrote, 'I waited five years to do that.'[3]

The raw statistics of seats won and lost told a story of a parliamentary landslide unparalleled to that point in Canadian history. The name of R.B. Bennett was fated to be forever associated with the débâcle of 1935, and not the victory of 1930. In hindsight a Liberal cakewalk, the 1935 election was, for contemporaries, fraught with uncertainties. No one knew how the vote would break in an election where most ridings had four candidates or more. The most common prediction from im-partial observers was for a minority government, probably but not nec-essarily headed by the Liberal leader, Mackenzie King. The very best that Bennett could have hoped for was that his party would constitute the largest group in a House of minorities. At worst, the historic Conservative party might have been reduced to permanent third-party status, eclipsed by one of the new reform parties. The great British Liberal party, split between Lloyd George and Herbert Asquith at a time of national crisis in the 1920s, had suffered this very fate. As Bennett viewed his former seatmate and cabinet colleague, Harry Stevens, ripping into the Tories with the same, or even more, gusto as when he was denouncing the Grits, the prime minister must have wondered if Canadian politics would imitate the mother country he so much admired. If talent, effort, and money still counted, then Bennett determined he would save his party from oblivion. This chapter will examine that Olympian quest, made all the more tragic because he, himself, was largely responsible for the party's inescapable weaknesses.

THE RIVAL STRATEGIES

The setting for the 1935 campaign was Depression grey. Wheat prices had risen somewhat, but an attack of rust plagued western grain crops. The employment picture had improved over 1933, but hundreds of thousands still lacked jobs. Thousands of single men languished in relief camps, or engaged in fruitless treks to Ottawa or the provincial capitals. A million Canadians remained dependent on government relief payments. Average real income per capita was still 25 per cent lower than the peak year of 1929.[4] The international scene was bleak, too. Relations between Italy and Ethiopia threatened war, which might well involve the other European powers, including Britain. Tales of ethnic persecution in Nazi Germany and Japanese aggression in the Far East were beginning to invade the public consciousness.

The political omens for the government were not propitious. The last provincial government to survive an election was that of the Manitoba Progressive party, and even they had prudently negotiated an arrangement with the provincial Liberals before the vote. Between January 1934 and June 1935, there had been three provincial elections and six federal by-elections. The Conservatives lost each provincial contest – in Saskatchewan, Ontario, and New Brunswick – by a decisive margin, and salvaged just one of the by-elections, in Toronto East. The swing in popular vote away from the Conservatives was remarkable. For example, in Frontenac-Addington, long considered a bastion of Tory support in Orange eastern Ontario, the swing away from the party in the September 1934 by-election amounted to an astounding 6,000 votes, out of some 16,000 cast. Two more provincial elections during the summer preceding federal balloting in October 1935 confirmed the trend. Neither the Conservative administration of Prince Edward Island on 23 July, nor the United Farmers of Alberta regime on 22 August, succeeded in electing a single member. The only minor consolation for the Tories was that, although the Liberals swept Prince Edward Island, both old parties were knocked flat by the new Social Credit juggernaut in Alberta.[5]

The Conservatives controlled the timing of the federal election. Bennett opted to delay the vote as long as legally possible, for several reasons. He, the party organization, and the national economy, all needed the maximum time for recovery. Furthermore, delaying the election beyond the expected September date upset the Liberal tactics. King, with a series of broadcasts and speeches scheduled for mid-summer, was forced to disrupt the planned momentum of the Liberal campaign.[6]

Herridge, more or less back in the prime minister's good graces, advised Bennett to wage an energetic reform campaign, reminiscent of the successful 1930 effort, but couched in the rhetoric of the January broadcasts. 'The dominant political force in Canada today should naturally be a new sort of Toryism ... Our reform programme of January was part of it ... Tariffs and economic planning are two of its essential instruments. The blast is its battle cry. "Canada First" is its guiding genius.' For Herridge, 'action by strong government' was the solution both to the Depression and to the election. He was adamant that the Conservatives should leave the defence of traditional policies to the Liberals. 'The conventional exposition of orthodox remedies simply puts you in parallel with Mr. King,' he explained. 'He has the start of you.' Herridge, stuck in Washington, did not have Bennett's ear the way he had in 1930 while riding along in Bennett's private railway car. The Conservative reform cry was muted, combined with more traditional appeals to imperial sentiment, sound currency, and law and order. Herridge did not approve. 'For God's sake, forget the Ottawa agreements,' he implored Finlayson, three weeks before the vote. 'King is on the defensive. Don't join him on the defensive.' Herridge saw the need to reach out for the large protest vote. Bennett felt a stronger need to retain the traditional Tory vote.[7]

The Liberals entered the campaign brimming with confidence, yet fearful that some chance happening might rob them of victory. As Dafoe explained to Dexter in July, 'the battle is won right now by a wide margin and the trick is to see that conditions stay that way until polling day.' Ultimate strategy was left to King, who was determined to wage a cautious campaign, concentrating on the flaws in the government's record. He drilled this philosophy into the Liberal caucus just prior to dissolution: 'I stressed the importance of the Liberal party not making a target for its enemies to fire at ... The main thing from now on is to realize that the people vote against, rather than for something and to keep their mind focussed on Bennett and his mismanagement of things.' King relied on traditional party loyalty, buttressed by provincial Grit machines and the promise of victory, to hold the Liberal vote. With so many parties competing for votes in a first-past-the-post electoral system, King knew that holding the traditional Grit vote would ensure a substantial victory.[8]

None of the remaining three parties of significance – Reconstruction, CCF, and Social Credit – was really aiming to form the next government. Each hoped to elect a sizeable number of members to a House of minorities, where the fluid nature of the resulting parliament would assure them of influence and bargaining power. Moreover, for the CCF and Social Credit movements, the election campaign provided a golden opportunity for proselytizing, for spreading the word of their programs and making new converts. The Reconstruction Party, in part a breakaway fragment of the Conservative party, but to some degree also a movement based on the Retail Merchants' Association, shared some of the Messianic fervour of the other two, but for it the election of MPs was a higher priority. Furthermore, while the CCF campaign emphasized the replacement of capitalism by the cooperative commonwealth, and Social Credit stressed the mystique of the social dividend, Reconstruction focused on the personality of its leader. 'Your best campaign material is Honourable H.H. Stevens,' a campaign letter instructed the Reconstruction candidates.[9]

With so many parties running, Conservative hopes rested on a divided opposition vote. 'I imagine that Stevens has strengthened our chances,' Manion concluded hopefully in mid-July, 'in as much as he will ... cut much more into the anti-Government vote than into ours.' What Manion's analysis failed to consider sufficiently was, first, the disruptive effect of five years of grim depression on traditional voting patterns, and, second, the weakness of the Conservative election machinery.[10]

PLATFORMS AND ISSUES

There was a schizophrenic quality to the Conservatives' campaign platform. Under Herridge's influence, Bennett launched the party's formal drive for re-election with a four-broadcast exposition of the new Toryism in early September. He declared for controlled inflation, debt conversion to lower rates, mandatory retirement at age sixty, improved civil aviation, beefed-up national broadcasting, extension of the Companies' Creditors' Arrangement Act to home-owners, neutrality in foreign wars, freer trade with the United States, and an amendment of the constitution to increase the scope for federal intervention in the economy. Yet, at the same time, he defended capitalism, upheld tariffs, and hinted that something would have to be done about the money-losing, publicly owned CNR. From Washington, Herridge sent his strong disapproval of these compromises with 'the old type of fat-headed, unthinking, big-business Conservatism.' As the campaign developed, however, Bennett leaned more and more to the traditional Conservative policies. Doubtless he was not unaware of the need for campaign funds from the business sector. This process reached a climax at a large rally in Toronto's Maple Leaf Gardens on 9 October, only days before the vote. The prime minister laid out his prescription for economic recovery: rigid government economy, a balanced budget, no repudiation of contracts, a solution to the railway-debt problem, and vigorous prosecution of communist agitators. It was a program to gladden the heart of any capitalist. Over six weeks Bennett had marched the party from left to right, and seemingly repudiated some of his own reforms.[11]

By contrast, Mackenzie King kept his party firmly on the course of moderate, safe reform. The Liberal platform was simply a repetition of the principles of Liberalism that King had enunciated in the House of Commons in 1933. Freer trade, a balanced budget, the integrity of the CNR, the repeal of Section 98, support for peace, and the end of government by order-in-council were all good partisan Liberal fare, and they were reassuringly within the boundaries of traditional ideology. Even the reforms supported by the Grits – unemployment insurance, a central bank – were already legislation by the time of the campaign. To this 1933 statement King added very little: a pledge to consult Parliament in the event of war and a plea for a majority mandate. The most important component of this platform was the oft-repeated reminder that the Liberals had no part in the sorry Tory record.[12]

Both the CCF and Reconstruction parties issued lengthy election manifestos in mid-July. The keynote of the CCF platform was 'establishment of a planned and socialized economic order' that would be free from 'the monopolistic concentration of economic power in the hands of a small group.' As immediate steps in that direction, it advocated more generous relief, vast public-works projects, comprehensive social insurance, the socialization of banking, and steeply graded income and inheritance taxes.[13] The Reconstruction platform posed two major goals: the elimination of unemployment and a more equitable distribution of economic wealth and power. To further these ends, Stevens advocated public works, housing assistance, easier credit, profit restriction, increased taxes on the rich, equal pay to women for work of equal value, and full implementation of the Price Spreads report. This last item was the core of the Reconstruction program. Stevens promised to translate the commission's recommendations for controlling business abuses into 'virile, vital, living legislation.'[14] When the Alberta Social Credit League decided in late August to enter the campaign, it simply transferred its attacks on the 'Fifty Big Shots of Canada,' and its promise of a basic monthly dividend of twenty-five dollars for every citizen, to the federal arena.[15]

Two issues dominated the campaign. The first of these was the Conservative government's record. A central feature of the Liberal strategy was to hold the Conservatives accountable for the economic depression. 'You have had five years of the Bennett Government,' King told a Port Arthur audience. 'I wonder if any of you are as well off now as when it started.' Bennett was too proud to resist defending what was, to him, a very personal record of achievement in the face of grim adversity. 'The record of our Government is a proud one,' he stoutly admonished fellow Tories in a campaign letter. Bennett marshalled statistics to show the improved trade balance since 1930, the drop in unemployment since 1933, and the establishment of new branch plants. Furthermore, he boasted, 'the Conservative government that it has been my privilege to lead has placed on the statute books more legislation designed to forward the social welfare of the Canadian people than all other governments since Confederation.' It was to no avail. With such a marvellous record, voters wondered, why were living conditions so appalling? As King repeated, over and over, 'Mr. Bennett has had five years ... to fulfill his promises. He has failed.'[16]

The second overriding issue was the question of majority government. Did voters want it or not? The Liberals believed they did. They were delighted to hear a leader like Woodsworth predict a parliament of minorities and a follow-up election long before the end of five years. In their view, the largest number of voters desired political stability, and feared a situation where radical fringe parties might extract major policy concessions from a minority government. The unpopularity of incum-

bent governments, the split in Conservative ranks, and the prolifera-
tion of third parties seeking the protest vote, all pointed to a Liberal
plurality. The Grits asked the voters to make it a clear majority. 'Stability
and an unmistakable majority are more essential than ever,' King declared in a *MacLean's* article. In an attempt to undercut this appeal and
secure the support of certain groups around the country who were
urging a national government, Bennett pledged to invite the cooperation,
regardless of party, of all elected MPs in the new parliament for a non-
partisan government dedicated to economic recovery. King deftly ridiculed the notion as 'the strangest bedfull of fellows ever seen,' and
announced that Liberals would not take part in such a regime. Bennett
would be left with the likes of his well-known friend Stevens, the Socialist Woodsworth, and the Social Credit fanatics of Alberta, none of
whom seemed anxious to cooperate with him. Clearly, the idea was
ludicrous. If the voters wanted a stable majority, it seemed they must
opt for a Liberal one.[17]

King attempted to make mileage out of the alleged dictatorship of
Bennett. Throughout the previous five years, he had hammered away
at an apparent one-man government, decrying the increasing use of
orders-in-council, the blank-cheque relief legislation, the resort to a
peace-order-and-good-government clause to deal with social agitators,
and the long delay before calling an election. The issue of Bennett's
authoritarian leadership style was dear to King's heart, and it had presented the Liberals with a rallying cry around which they could all
unite, but it does not seem to have carried much weight with voters.
Bennett may even have gotten the better of King on this issue by ex-
ploiting its reverse, namely, the law-and-order cry. Bennett made no
bones about where he stood on this one. For five years his government
had waged a public battle against radical political dissent. 'Section 98
will never be repealed so long as this Government is in power,' he
declared in Hamilton. Whatever appeal there lay in Commie-bashing
certainly accrued to the Conservatives.[18]

The minor parties sought to elevate the question of capitalist reform
to primacy in the campaign. Woodsworth declared the key issue was
'reform versus the abolition of capitalism.' For Stevens, the crux of the
matter was a yes-no question: 'are we to reassert the democratic principle
of directing our affairs in the interests of the people as a whole?' For
Social Credit, the focus of the campaign was whether the currency and
credit system would serve the 'Fifty Big Shots' or all the people. Al-

though, upon examination, these three parties stood upon quite different principles, to a lot of voters their appeals sounded quite similar. Furthermore, if one were to believe the campaign rhetoric, there were five reform parties. Both Conservatives and Liberals included reform planks prominently in their platforms, and the Conservatives had already translated several reform policies into legislation. Consequently, the reform issue was never a clear-cut one. Every party tried to accommodate reform-minded people within its ranks.[19]

The two major parties resurrected an old standby issue, the tariff question. This issue presented Bennett with some difficulties, for protective tariffs were as important as ever to the traditional Tory strongholds in urban Ontario and anglo Montreal. However, Herridge and he desperately wanted a tariff-reduction agreement with the United States before election day to open up markets for Canadian products, and incidentally boost their political chances. Though active negotiations with the American government, begun in earnest in August 1935, proceeded throughout the campaign, an agreement was not forthcoming. In desperation, Bennett fell back on the Ottawa agreements of 1932. 'If you defeat the Conservative Government, then you will be striking a blow at the Empire agreement,' he announced in Hamilton: 'that is the issue.' The Ottawa treaties had not helped much in the earlier by-elections and their appeal was no greater in October 1935.[20]

One issue that might have been very controversial was kept on the back burner. Italian forces invaded Ethiopia in the midst of the election campaign. The armed conflict had long been rumoured. Both Bennett and King feared the political repercussions of a war scare in Canada. King resorted to the tried and true 'Parliament will decide' subterfuge to avoid taking a position. Privately, he feared 'another Nationalist party in Quebec going over to Stevens.' Bennett made Canada's non-involvement 'in any foreign quarrel where the rights of Canadians are not involved' an important part of his party's policy. From the campaign trail, he wired Perley, 'Am greatly disturbed over European situation ... I fear repercussions in Quebec.' Despite the similarity in the two leaders' positions, it seems probable that the Liberals benefited from this unwanted issue. Bennett's soothing words could not erase the memories of 1917. Furthermore, he authorized a strong stand against Italy's actions by the Canadian delegation at the League of Nations, just before the election. However, neither leader raised the matter when it could be avoided.[21]

LEADERSHIP STYLES

R.B. Bennett was the dominant figure in the Conservative national campaign. The 'curtain-raiser' for his personal tour of the country was a series of four half-hour radio broadcasts delivered between 6 and 14 September. For the next four weeks he stumped the country, addressing forty meetings in all nine provinces. Audiences were large: 8,000 at the Sherbrooke Armoury, 12,000 at the Montreal Forum, 15,000 at Maple Leaf Gardens in Toronto. No Bennett rally was complete without several noisy hecklers, often obligingly supplied by the communists, whom Bennett delighted in shouting down. As his aide Finlayson recalled it, the prime minster 'was somewhat perturbed if [he was] not occasionally interrupted by a communist.'[22]

Bennett's energetic campaign breathed life back into the Tory corpse. Manion was so enthused by his leader's 'splendid' broadcasts and 'great receptions throughout the West' that he allowed himself to dream again of the Conservatives winning 'perhaps a majority over all.' R.B. Hanson also felt that things were 'perking up since the P.M. went on the air.' To the voters, Bennett projected force, ability, and courage. The questionable state of his own health, and the Tories' dismal re-election chances, had been well known. Bennett's determined, energetic pursuit of the impossible even evoked a bit of the sympathy customarily reserved for the underdog. This was tempered, of course, by the public's ongoing perception of him as a rich bachelor, a friend of big business, and an iron-heeled autocrat. Bennett's overall election image can perhaps best be described as that of the vigorous man of action.[23]

The Tory leader did not have much of a supporting cast. R.J. Manion spent several weeks on the road in August and September, and campaigned in seven provinces. Aside from him, few ministers ventured out of their own ridings. As Hanson stated, in turning down a request to address an out-of-province rally, 'Don't count on me. I regret this, but we are all fighting with our backs to the wall.' By this time, there were no Tory provincial premiers left. Bennett asked Meighen to help out by addressing some meetings in the West, but the latter refused outright, maintaining, 'as Senate Leader I should not take active part [sic] in political contest.' Meighen no doubt remembered 1930, when he was anxious to help out but was never asked, allegedly because of the influence of Howard Ferguson.[24]

Many of the Conservative ministers had retired from politics on the eve of the campaign. The aging MacLaren had departed in November

1934, replaced by Grote Stirling of British Columbia, and Bennett soon appointed the New Brunswicker to the post of lieutenant-governor of his native province. The other retirements did not come till after the prorogation of Parliament in July. Rhodes, Sauvé, and Macdonald had gone to the Senate, Duranleau to the Bench, and Guthrie to the Railway Board. Matthews had simply retired to private life. Manion, for one, resented these eleventh-hour appointments, likening them in one stormy cabinet session to 'a lot of rats running away from a sinking ship.' Bennett apparently felt their loyalty should be recognized. A number of Tory back-benchers were similarly rewarded. Unfortunately, the new recruits brought into the ministry in the summer arrived too late to establish their credentials in the public mind. Furthermore, the cabinet shuffle was badly mishandled.[25]

Cahan expected to be made justice minister, but this portfolio was handed to one of the newcomers, G.R. Geary, a Toronto MP and lawyer. Gustave Monette, a prominent member of the Montreal bar, actually went to the swearing-in ceremony under the impression he was to be made justice minister. When he discovered he was being sworn in as postmaster general, he abruptly stalked out. Samuel Gobeil, a rural MP and dairy farmer, was hastily summoned to fill the gap. Eventually, another prominent Montreal lawyer, L.H. Gendron, was persuaded to enter the cabinet as minister of marine. This enraged Maurice Dupré, who had languished in the minor portfolio of solicitor general as the only representative of the Quebec district, since 1930. To mollify Dupré and his supporters, Bennett appointed his law partner, Onésime Gagnon, the defeated rival of Duplessis in 1933, as minister without portfolio. The confusion illustrated without doubt that Bennett was no closer to understanding the internal workings of the Quebec wing of his party in 1935 than when he first became leader. The other appointments, W.G. Ernst from Nova Scotia to fisheries, J.E. Lawson to national revenue, and Earl Rowe as minister without portfolio, were made with the election in mind. Ernst had threatened to join the long list of retiring Nova Scotia MPs if he were not promoted, while Lawson was the Dominion Organizer, and Rowe figured prominently in the Ontario organization. All three were young but experienced MPs. However, the prestige of cabinet status was balanced by the claims that departmental duties would place upon their time – time perhaps better spent on the hustings. In the public mind, Bennett fought the election as he had headed the government: alone, with all the responsibility on his own shoulders.[26]

King could be as single-minded and despotic as Bennett in private, but he kept this side of himself away from public view. In 1935, the Liberal campaign portrayed him as the great conciliator, the one who could persuade Canadians to work together again. Sharply contrasting with the lone-wolf crusades of Bennett and Stevens was King's practice of appearing everywhere with prominent Liberals in tow. He shared platforms with Premier T.D. Pattullo in Victoria, Ian MacKenzie in Vancouver, T.L. Crerar and Premier John Bracken in Winnipeg, Premier Mitchell Hepburn in Woodstock, Ontario, Senator A.C. Hardy in Brockville, Fernand Rinfret in Montreal, Ernest Lapointe and Premier L.A. Taschereau in Quebec City, Premier A.A. Dysart in Fredericton, and Premier Angus L. Macdonald in Halifax. The climax of the Liberal campaign came on 8 October, when King addressed an overflow crowd of 17,500 at Maple Leaf Gardens. His speech to the massed throng was preceded by brief live addresses from the eight Liberal premiers via radio hook-up from their respective provincial capitals. The point was well made. King might be overly partisan, and even a bit smug, but he was a team leader. Furthermore, he was cautious and safe, not one to plunge into new adventures on a whim. The Liberal image of reliability was further strengthened by two broadcasts delivered by Charles Dunning, the former finance minister who had entered the business world in 1931. Behind King's attacks on the follies and dangers of the Bennett regime, the opposition leader sold himself as the proven conciliator so desperately needed in Ottawa.[27]

In Stevens's own mind, he was a committed reformer, and sincere advocate for the disadvantaged merchants, farmers, workers, and unemployed young people. Over the course of a four-month campaign, however, Stevens assumed the public role of chief rabble-rouser. He attacked R.B. Bennett, Mackenzie King, big business, the chartered banks, St James Street, Bay Street, Canada Packers, the large department stores, Herbert Holt of Montreal Light, Heat and Power, and any other big-shot politicians or businessmen who stood in his way. Over time, he began to appear shrill, negative, and repetitive. Later, Stevens explained his predicament: 'As I addressed the meetings I found that my very clearest and best founded arguments based on statistics, etc. were usually received with respect but little understanding. Whereas, the moment I touched the human side of the story, such as economic slavery, sweatshops, etc. or condemned the banks' I would get the audience on their toes at once.' Stevens was the show. If he was dull, the crowds would dwindle away. The skeletal organization being thrown together by Warren Cook and the Retail Merchants' Association could not deliver captive audiences on demand. Furthermore, Stevens needed constantly to parade new revelations and accusations before the public, in order to stay on page one of the nation's newspaper. Although any exposure seemed better than none, this need for publicity trapped Stevens in an image that failed to reveal the whole man. As the chief rabble-rouser in the campaign, Stevens drew applause and headlines, but, in the end, comparatively few votes.[28]

J.S. Woodsworth toured the West and Ontario on behalf of CCF candidates much as the other party leaders were doing, though he avoided Quebec and the Maritimes, where the new movement was not yet well established. His hope was to see a modestly sized group of MPs elected to further the socialist message from Ottawa. Meanwhile, the campaign was an excellent avenue for public education. Many who knew him only by reputation considered Woodsworth a dangerous utopian demagogue, but those who heard him speak saw a sincerely committed humanist doggedly evangelizing for his cause.[29] The invisible man in the campaign was William Aberhart, guiding light of the Alberta Social Credit League. Preoccupied with setting up the new provincial Social Credit administration, of which he was premier, Aberhart contented himself with supporting the federal candidates by a few radio addresses broadcast from the Prophetic Bible Institute.[30]

ORGANIZATION, PUBLICITY, AND FUNDS

The Conservative organization was hampered by a late start, inexperience, inadequate funds, and lack of coordination. Preoccupied with policy and administration, Bennett had not got around to revitalizing the party machinery by the time of Stevens's resignation in October 1934. With the development of Herridge's New Deal strategy for re-election, the need for organization became imperative. Finally, in December, the Toronto MP J. Earl Lawson stepped forward to take on the job of chief party organizer. 'I am terribly "fed up" with the way the poor old Tory Party is being kicked around for lack of organized publicity and organization. If you are still of opinion that I can do a job for the Party as organizer, I am willing to try it. I will arrange my business affairs and be prepared to start on the job on January 3rd, 1935.' Bennett quickly accepted his offer. Lawson, however, did not have a lot of back-room political experience. He had chaired the party's summer conference at Newmarket in 1933, and helped the Ontario Conservatives in their unsuccessful 1934 campaign. At age forty-three, he had been an MP for six years, representing York South. His appointment was welcomed in Ontario party circles, but elsewhere in the country he was an unknown quantity, with little time to become acquainted with the key personalities and problems.[31]

Lawson wasted little time setting up the headquarters in Ottawa. He was 'a "no-nonsense" man,' according to an associate, Richard Bell, 'quick, decisive, the fastest man to clear his desk that I have ever worked with.' Downtown office space was found, and clerical staff were hired. Lou Golden, who had assisted Lawson at Newmarket as registrar on behalf of the Federation of Young Canada Conservative Clubs, was taken on as general secretary. An effort was made to bring Robert Lipsett back on board to head the publicity bureau, as he had in 1930. Lipsett was tempted, but a substantial salary increase from his new employer, the Liberal *Toronto Daily Star*, dissuaded him. Lawson thereupon hired Frederick Edwards, another journalist, as his director of publicity.[32]

Edwards and Lawson did their best to re-create the publicity machine directed in 1930 by Lipsett and McRae. Unfortunately, they had to begin from scratch to create a mailing list, from names submitted by the Conservative MPs. Copies of Bennett's New Deal addresses were mailed to those on the new list, as well as propaganda articles on such topics as the Farmers' Creditors' Arrangement Act and the Empire Trade Agreements. *The Canadian* was revived, and three editions were published during the 1935 parliamentary session. The common slogan for each issue was 'Reform for Security,' an attempt to relate Bennett's new program to the conservative instincts of the party stalwarts. Lawson also launched a project to produce two-minute newsreels by several of the ministers, including Bennett, for circulation to the moving-picture theatres.[33]

The publicity effort suffered from two major drawbacks. Because the party headquarters was not even set up until January 1935, there was an inevitable loss of momentum after the New Deal broadcasts. It took time to accumulate names for the mailing list and generate propaganda pamphlets. As H.R. Milner of Alberta informed Herridge, 'there is too much lag between the radio talks and the follow-up publicity. The effect is being largely lost.' Second, there was a crippling shortage of funds. 'The third issue of "The Canadian" should have gone on the press on April 25th and been distributed on May 1st,' Lawson complained to Manion. 'I have been compelled to hold it up owing to financial stringency.' The third issue was not mailed out until 1 June. The late start and lack of money were handicaps difficult to overcome.[34]

The shortage of funds was a long-standing problem. 'The Prime Minister has not and apparently will not name anybody to collect funds for the party for organizational purposes,' Stevens had lamented to a party supporter in June 1934. 'There is not a cent in the exchequer.' Bennett did not rouse himself to tackle the problem until January 1935, when rumours began to circulate that he was 'digging down again for the campaign fund.' Mackenzie King's sources told him that Bennett had contributed $100,000 to launch the organization, as part of the New Deal strategy for re-election. When illness made it doubtful he would continue to lead the party, his purse-strings were closed, hence Lawson's lack of funds. 'No one has any heart,' W.H. Price of Toronto wrote Manion in early June.[35]

The problems of the national organization were mirrored in Quebec. Georges Laurin had managed to keep an organizational skeleton alive in the Montreal district, but he was not widely respected, and in March 1935, he requested 'that someone else be appointed to take charge.' With the support of Duranleau, Senator Rainville was persuaded in April to reassume the role of chief organizer. His appointment was controversial, provoking opposition from the younger Montreal Conservatives, as well as from the Quebec district. With such a late start, French-language propaganda could not be produced until the final parliamentary session was nearly over. There was virtually no money to fund it, anyway. This lack was entirely Bennett's fault, as Ward Pitfield had volunteered to spearhead the financial side of things. 'Eric McCuaig ... and I are ready to work with anyone you nominate,' he had informed Bennett in a November 1934 letter, 'or if you wish, to work along ourselves.' Bennett did not authorize either course of action.[36]

The situation was nearly as grim outside of Quebec. In Ontario, where the Conservatives were out of office for only the second time since Borden's days in opposition, the party machine was underfinanced and demoralized. Lawson appointed Denton Massey, another youthful Conservative, as Ontario campaign director. W.H. Price, the former attorney general and political fixer, summarized the Ontario situation for Bennett in June: there were 'well-laid and developed plans in Ontario, but no progress.' The problems for the organizers were twofold: the leadership question and an absence of funds. No funds meant no publicity, which meant an apathetic party, which, in turn, meant no funds.[37] There were no bright spots elsewhere in Canada, either. British Columbia's Conservative party was still rent by the dissensions arising from the collapse of the provincial party into three factions in 1933, and the campaign fund was 'at zero.' For lack of funds, the Saskatchewan organizational office had to be closed after the disastrous provincial campaign of 1934. 'I have been paying for everything since the provincial election out of my own pocket,' the provincial organizer confessed to John Diefenbaker in February 1935. That same month Dr H.C. Hodgson, the former Manitoba organizer, made a tour of the West. 'I could not find any signs of real organization in any of the Western provinces,' he reported to Bennett. 'On the other hand, the Liberal Party are well organized, and are working overtime.' Lawson, himself, toured the Maritimes in January. His report to Bennett was pessimistic. New Brunswick did not have anything 'in the nature of a provincial or central organization,' while the Conservative forces in Nova Scotia were 'divided into four cliques.' From one coast to the other, there was no end of organizational work to be done.[38]

Despite the late start, Lawson managed to pull together a functioning party headquarters with links to the provincial wings by the end of June 1935. Bennett's decision to fight the coming election as party leader removed one debilitating source of uncertainty. Unfortunately, by the fall, Lawson had to split his own time between ministerial duties, running for personal re-election, and directing the Tories' national organization. In his absence, management of party headquarters was left in the hands of the general secretary. Unfortunately, Lawson's original choice for this post, Lou Golden, developed osteomyelitis, an infectious bone disease, and had to resign in August. Richard Bell, his replacement, was a recent graduate from the University of Toronto who had been working in the office of R.C. Matthews, minister of national revenue. Bell was a more than adequate replacement, but the disruption in personnel came at an awkward time. Moreover, Bennett had tabbed Bell to replace the ailing A.W. Merriam in his own office, but had to forgo Bell's services in the interests of the party headquarters. The central office in Ottawa was responsible for planning the leader's national tour, as well as speaking engagements by other party notables, in consultation with the provincial party offices. It was responsible for churning out campaign propaganda, and placing advertisements with the media. In addition it was to cooperate with, coordinate, and motivate the provincial Conservative branches, which saw to the endorsement, and occasionally the selection, of candidates for each riding.[39]

Lawson and Bennett appointed campaign directors in each province, specifically for the election of 1935. There was no particular pattern to the appointments. The provincial directors for the West were: in British Columbia, Frank Patterson, president of the BC Conservative Association; in Saskatchewan, F.W. Turnbull, Regina MP; and in Manitoba, Ralph Webb, provincial MLA. Bennett's long-time secretary, Alice Millar, seems to have directed the party effort in Alberta, with her boss's advice. The two key figures in the Maritimes were R.B. Hanson, Fredericton MP, and Leonard Fraser, former private secretary to then-Premier Rhodes of Nova Scotia. The campaign director for Ontario was the youthful Toronto MP Denton Massey, described by Richard Bell as gifted with 'great public relations flare ... but somewhat less administrative talent.' Senator Rainville was again at the helm in the Montreal district. The need for campaign directors separate from the provincial parties was heightened by the complete absence of Tory provincial governments. The advantages of local patronage would be in other hands – Grit hands – except in Alberta.[40]

Bennett was accompanied on his nation-wide tour by a small group from the prime minister's office. Rod Finlayson wrote most of his speeches, sometimes reworking drafts submitted from Washington by Herridge. Bennett's brother-in-law was in and out of the prime minister's good graces throughout the year, but he could still turn a colourful phrase. Alice Millar also travelled with Bennett, ensuring that his personal, constituency, and prime-ministerial business was attended to with her usual efficiency.[41]

'The organization to-day is but a shadow of the fighting machine of 1930,' complained John R. MacNicol to Bennett in mid-July. He was right in his assessment, and this situation did not change much between July and October, despite the best efforts of Lawson and Bell. The dominion headquarters did assemble a mailing list of 300,000 Conservative supporters in English Canada, and another 100,000 in French Canada. However, the patchwork organization seemed to lurch from one foul-up to another. 'When I take a matter up with Toronto,' an annoyed S.C. Robinson, MP from Windsor, wrote sharply to Bell, 'I am referred to Ottawa, who in turn, refer me back to Toronto.' The confusion also existed in Quebec. On 24 September, John Hackett, MP for Stanstead, received explicit instructions from Ottawa: 'Our method of distribution is to distribute campaign material from here to the Campaign Directors ... who then distribute it to the candidates.' Three days later his office received the following instruction from the Quebec campaign director's office: 'The Honourable J. Earle Rowe [sic] has asked our office not to look in any way after the propaganda in English.' The upshot of this little snafu was that Hackett was 'unable to get anything' from Montreal or Ottawa suitable for use in his largely anglophone riding. On-the-job training was no substitute for back-room experience, as the Tory head-quarters staff discovered.[42]

The overriding theme of the Conservatives' publicity campaign was best depicted in a cartoon by A. Racey that appeared in the fourth and final issue of the party's in-house publication, *The Canadian*, released in August 1935. Bennett was shown alone on the deck of the good ship *Canada*, firmly grasping the wheel, bravely steering a path through stormy seas. 'Stand by Canada,' the caption commanded, 'and the Pilot Who Has Weathered the Storm.' Variations of the patriotic slogan appeared in newspaper and magazine ads, billboards, leaflets, and posters. A second prominent slogan was featured in the 'speakers' handbook.' It urged Tory candidates to emphasize 'Bennett, our Man of Action.' In Quebec, the same theme was translated to become 'Bennett, L'homme d'action.' The Conservative strategists decided Bennett's leadership was their strong suit, and they orchestrated their publicity campaign to contrast his firm decisive leadership with what they conceived to be the *laissez-faire* stance of King, the opportunistic demagoguery of Stevens, and the utopian idealism of Woodsworth.[43]

The man in charge of publicity at Conservative headquarters was Frederick Edwards. As a propagandist, he was 'tip top,' creative and imaginative, but 'his addiction to booze' drove Lawson to distraction. As the campaign reached its later stages, Lawson instructed young Richard Bell 'to supervise all his work.' The Conservatives' national advertising account was handled by the J.J. Gibbons agency out of Toronto. The key figure was R.A. Stapells, 'a glib, fast talking salesman.' For Quebec, however, advertising was handled by the McKim agency.[44] One of the promotional innovations dreamed up by the Gibbons company for the Conservative campaign was a series of six dramatized radio programs using professional actors called the 'Mr. Sage' broadcasts. These programs were carried over the Canadian Radio Broadcasting Commission network without any acknowledgment of their sponsorship by the Tory party. 'Mr. Sage' was a small-town philosopher who debated with and converted lifelong Liberals to the support of the Conservative cause with homespun but apparently irrefutable logic. The programs, broadcast between 7 September and 11 October enraged Mackenzie King, who charged the public network was being debased for partisan purposes.[45]

The radio featured prominently in the Conservative publicity campaign. Bennett's speeches, some from studios, others at campaign rallies, were broadcast to a national audience nine times, and to regional audiences on eleven other occasions. National broadcasts were usually half an hour in length, while regional ones could last up to two hours. The Liberals, too, used radio broadcasts frequently, to reach larger numbers of voters at once. Whereas the Conservatives featured Bennett almost exclusively, major Liberal broadcasts included such prominent speakers as Charles Dunning, Mitchell Hepburn, J.L. Ralston, and Norman Rogers, in addition to the leader, King. The symbolism was intended by both parties. King was the conciliatory team leader, while Bennett was the vigorous man of action.[46]

The Liberal publicity department churned out scores of themes for pamphlets, posters, windshield stickers, billboards, newspapers, and magazines. Prominent among these were the 'forgotten consumer,' the markets 'lost' by Bennett and Stevens, and Bennett's 'broken promises' of 1930. In the end, the most telling theme was probably the billboard slogan 'Only King Can Win: Give Him a Working Majority,' which was shortened in most ads to four catchy words: 'It's King or Chaos.' To the average voter, 'Stand by Canada: Vote Bennett' just did not convey the same compelling sense of urgency. In most other organizational aspects as well, the Liberals were superior to their opponents. With a head start over the Tories in setting up their dominion headquarters, and eight kindred provincial governments, the Grit party machine was far superior to its 1930 predecessor.[47]

Viewed from another perspective, the Reconstruction organization made the Tory machine look positively professional by comparison. While Stevens's tour was organized from his office in Ottawa, Warren Cook, who operated out of Toronto, acted as the chairman, Dominion organizer, and treasurer. Meanwhile, the publicity department was headed by Thomas Lisson, who worked out of Hamilton. As chief Quebec organizer, Stevens lured Jacques Cartier from the Canadian Radio Broadcasting Commission. Cartier had served as Rainville's right-hand man in the Montreal district in 1930, but his more recent political associates tended to be the francophone ultra-nationalists. Second in command in Quebec was Thomas Bell, a 'John Bullish' anglophone, who had trouble working with Cartier. The other provincial organizers, such as Tom Learie in Ontario and P.B. Scott for Manitoba, tended to come from either the Retail Merchants' Association or its affiliated bodies. From this motley assortment, Stevens hoped to conjure up an organized party in only four months. The basic unit for nomination purposes was the Stevens Club, of which many dozens were formed in the summer and fall of 1935. In ridings where two or more aspirants were nominated by rival clubs, Cook was to be the final arbiter. The wonder was not that the Reconstruction organization, staffed by volunteers, worked so poorly, but that it worked at all.[48] The CCF was set up as a federated body, and was dependent on the efforts of a number of affiliated entities for its campaign organization in 1935. As yet, there was no firm coordinating office at the national level. The Social Credit candidates could depend on a vibrant grass-roots movement in Alberta, but little elsewhere.[49] The three minor parties were unable to compete in publicity with the Grits and Tories. They simply could not afford advertising space and broadcast time, nor could they buy the promotional expertise of a J.J. Gibbons or Cockfield Brown agency.

Contrary to most scholarly analysis,[50] lack of finances was not a major cause of the Conservatives' decisive defeat in 1935. It must be remembered that Canada was experiencing a severe depression. Wealthy individuals and companies were less numerous than in headier times, and also less willing to part with their cash. This factor affected both parties. Even into September, the Liberals were experiencing difficulty in acquiring adequate finances. 'Massey & Lambert are much in a funk over the absence of funds,' King recorded in his diary on 11 September after conversations with key Liberal organizers. Over the final four weeks of the campaign, substantial funds did flow into the Liberal coffers,[51] but the same thing was happening with the Conservatives. D.M. Hogarth of Toronto reported the dramatic upturn to R.J. Manion on 10 October, four days before polling: 'Elements which only a few weeks ago refused to take the strap off the roll, have within the last two weeks been coming forward in a comparatively liberal [sic] way. So much so, in fact, that the acute financial problem no longer exists ... Our crowd ... are reasonably financed and in that respect are at least as well off as our chief opponents.' This analysis was confirmed the day after the election by W.H. Price, the chief Tory fund-raiser for Ontario. 'We were reasonably well financed,' he informed Bennett. 'I do not think there can be many complaints in the Ridings. More money would not have stemmed the tide.' Lord Atholstan relayed a similar story about Montreal fund-raising. 'We exceeded what you asked by [$]45[000],' he reported to the prime minister.[52]

It appears that the Liberals, on the whole, were somewhat better financed than the Conservatives, but the margin was far narrower than has generally been assumed. Taking Montreal as an example: the Tory fund-raising committee set up by Lord Atholstan collected $458,360,[53] compared to $626,000 raised by Senator Raymond for the Grits. In the case of both parties, funds originating in Montreal were distributed to ridings throughout Quebec and the Maritime provinces. Consequently, the Liberals in eastern Canada had a bit of an advantage over the Conservatives, but only by a ratio of four to three. Exact figures are unavailable for Conservative fund-raising in Toronto, but from the statements by Hogarth and Price, quoted above, it may be assumed that they were at least able to approach the same 75 per cent proportion of Liberal collections, which amounted to $558,478 in 1935. However, the National Liberal Federation spent a total of only $45,000 for radio time, whereas the J.J. Gibbons Agency had already disbursed $47,000 on behalf of the Conservative headquarters by the end of September, with another seven regional and three national broadcasts scheduled for the first two weeks of October. The Maple Leaf Gardens broadcast alone cost over $2,000. In radio broadcasting, at least, the Conservatives spent more than their rivals. It is quite likely that Bennett's own money accounted for the difference. In addition, his generosity to his own province meant that Alberta Tory candidates received more outside funds than did their Grit counterparts.[54]

Although the Conservative campaigns financed from Montreal and Toronto appear to have been adequately funded, the Dominion headquarters in Ottawa was the poor relation in the Tory party. Not just during the months leading up to the election call, but even during the campaign itself, the national office faced a constant cash shortfall. To alleviate the problem, Lawson attempted to do some fund-raising himself, to the great annoyance of Hogarth in Toronto and Atholstan in Montreal.[55] Lawson, though able, did not command the respect accorded his formidable predecessor, General McRae. The result was that party headquarters had to cut back on its press advertisements, even cancelling the whole weekly newspaper advertising program, while the Montreal campaign treasurer, George B. Foster, would report a surplus to Bennett in March 1936. Three years later the national party office still owed over $40,000 to its landlord, the Runge Press, for printing costs incurred in the 1935 election campaign.[56]

While the two major parties complained that finances were not as plentiful as in 1930, the minor parties had next to none at all. Jacques Cartier, Quebec organizer for the Reconstruction Party, had initially promised his candidates $5,000 for their campaigns. Later, he scaled his estimate down to $2,000. In the end, Stevens's standard-bearers in Que-

TABLE 7
Federal election results, 1935

Province	Conserv-tive		Liberal		Recon-struction		CCF		Social Credit		Other	
	S	%	S	%	S	%	S	%	S	%	S	%
Prince Edward Island	0	38.4	4	58.2	0	3.4	0	0.0	0	0.0	0	0.0
Nova Scotia	0	32.1	12	52.0	0	13.9	0	0.0	0	0.0	0	2.0
New Brunswick	1	31.9	9	57.2	0	10.5	0	0.0	0	0.0	0	0.4
Quebec	5	28.2	55	54.4	0	8.7	0	0.6	0	0.0	5	8.1
Ontario	25	35.3	56	42.7	0	11.5	0	8.0	0	0.0	1	2.5
Manitoba	1	26.9	14	40.5	0	5.9	2	19.4	0	2.0	0	5.3
Saskatchewan	1	18.8	16	40.8	0	1.3	2	21.3	2	17.8	0	0.0
Alberta	1	16.9	1	21.2	0	0.7	0	13.0	15	46.6	0	1.6
British Columbia & Territories	6	24.7	6	31.8	1	6.6	3	33.4	0	0.6	1	2.9
Canada	40	29.6	173	44.9	1	8.7	7	8.9	17	4.1	7	3.8

SOURCES: Howard A. Scarrow, *Canada Votes* (New Orleans 1962), 90–1; M.C. Urquhart and K.A.H. Buckley, eds., *Historical Statistics of Canada* (Toronto 1965), 619–20
NOTE: S = seat totals; % = percentage of vote

bec counted themselves lucky to get $250 from the provincial office. Where Bennett and King toured the country in private cars, Stevens travelled by motor car, or took a simple train berth. His party could afford just one national broadcast, on Saturday, 12 October, between 11:00 p.m. and midnight, Eastern time. As one candidate noted to Stevens, 'by that time the old parties had lined up their people most effectively.'[57] The lack of funds was similarly apparent in the CCF campaign. Social Credit, confining itself to a limited geographical area, was less handicapped by the shortage of finances.

ACCOUNTING FOR THE RESULT

Analysis of the riding results (see table 7) reveals that the Conservatives' elected candidates came almost exclusively from three geographic regions of the country: Montreal, southern Ontario, and British Columbia. They were without representation in two provinces – Prince Edward Island and Nova Scotia – and held just one seat in four others: New

TABLE 8
Conservative results in three elections: 1921, 1930, 1935

Province	1921		1930		1935	
	Seats	% of vote	Seats	% of vote	Seats	% of vote
Prince Edward Island	0	37.2	3	50.0	0	38.4
Nova Scotica	0	32.3	10	52.5	0	32.1
New Brunswick	5	39.4	10	59.4	1	31.9
Quebec	0	18.4	24	44.7	5	28.2
Ontario	37	39.2	59	54.4	25	35.3
Manitoba	0	24.4	11	47.7	1	26.9
Saskatchewan	0	16.7	8	37.6	1	18.8
Alberta	0	20.3	4	33.9	1	16.9
British Columbia & Territories	8	47.9	8	49.3	6	24.7
Canada	50	30.3	137	48.7	40	29.6

SOURCE: Scarrow, *Canada Votes*, 34–5, 76–7, 90–1

Brunswick, Manitoba, Saskatchewan, and Alberta. They trailed the victorious Liberals in the popular vote in every single province, and actually came third in the three westernmost provinces. While the Liberals nearly maintained their 45 per cent share of the national popular vote from 1930, in spite of the presence of three new parties, the Conservatives slipped badly, from nearly 49 per cent to less than 30 per cent. In fact, the Conservative showing was reminiscent of the débâcle of 1921 (see table 8). In that election as well, Ontario and British Columbia had ensured the Tories' survival, providing most of the party's fifty seats. The only major change was that Loyalist southern New Brunswick had been replaced by anglophone Montreal as the other leg in the tripod.[58]

Conservative mythology for several years after the 1935 election attributed the party's disastrous defeat in large part to the split in the Conservative vote occasioned by the existence of the Reconstruction Party. Howard Ferguson, for one, claimed in a letter to Lord Beaverbrook that the Stevens party accounted for the loss of 75 to 100 ridings. 'I think Bennett, but for Stevens, would have been leading this Government today,' he declared. Bennett himself maintained, in 1938, that 'Stevens and his candidates ... were responsible for the loss of 50 seats.[59]

It is true that, if all the Conservative and Reconstruction votes were combined, the party would have carried an additional forty-two seats. Nevertheless, the Liberals would still have won an absolute majority in the new Parliament. Furthermore, it is fallacious to assume that every Reconstruction vote would have gone to the Conservatives, had the Stevens party never existed. Among the Reconstruction candidates in southwestern Ontario with known party affiliations, for instance, there were three ex-Liberals, two ex-Conservatives, and one ex-Progressive, according to Tory organizer Arthur Ford. In Nova Scotia, the same party recruited two Conservatives, one Liberal, one Labourite, and one Farmer to be among its candidates.[60] Still, it cannot be denied that Stevens had been a very popular Conservative prior to his split with the party, or that the membership of the Retail Merchants' Association had been largely sympathetic to the Tories prior to 1935. A more realistic breakdown might be to assign three-quarters of the Reconstruction vote to the Conservatives, and one-quarter to the Liberals, in three-cornered contests. In ridings where the CCF was also involved a better ratio would be three-fifths to the Conservatives, one-fifth to the Liberals, and one-fifth to the CCF. When such analysis is done, only fifteen seats would pass from the Liberal to the Conservative column: three in Nova Scotia, one in New Brunswick, three in Quebec, seven in Ontario, and one in Manitoba. The result would still have been a Liberal landslide, at least in terms of seats.[61]

The Conservatives did relatively better in urban ridings (at least half the population inhabiting a community of 20,000 or more) than in non-urban ones, in terms of seats won (see table 9). Over half their caucus, twenty-two of forty, would represent urban constituencies. In terms of the total national vote, however, the party's popularity was slightly lower in urban than non-urban areas for the first time in decades. The contrast with the situation in both 1930 and 1921 is shown in table 10. Although detailed polling data are not available for substantiation, it is tempting to conclude that the long-time Tory popularity with urban Canadian voters suffered from the combined assaults of the CCF appeal to workers and the Reconstruction appeal to the lower middle class.[62] Certainly, any significant decline in urban support was ominous for the party's long-range future, since the proportion of Canadians living in cities would continue to grow rapidly.

In an analysis of French, bilingual, and English ridings, Escott Reid

TABLE 9
Conservative seats by urban and non-urban classification: 1921, 1930, 1935
(percentage of seats in parentheses)

Category	1921			1930			1935		
	Total	Won by Conservatives		Total	Won by Conservatives		Total	Won by Conservatives	
Urban	52	21	(40.4)	67	42	(62.7)	74	22	(29.7)
Non-urban	183	29	(15.8)	178	95	(53.4)	171	18	(10.5)
Canada	235	50	(21.3)	245	137	(55.9)	245	40	(16.3)

NOTE: The complete list of 'urban' constituencies in these years is available in the author's unpublished paper, 'Party Development in Canada: A Case Study of the Conservative Party, 1921–1949.'

noted that the Conservatives had lost in every one of the country's French ridings, thus wiping out the beachhead of 1930.[63] Further analysis of the popular vote reveals that the downward swing in Conservative share of the total vote cast was in the range of 20 per cent right across the country (see table 8 page 197). When experiencing a swing of that magnitude, only the safest seats, with previous victory margins of several thousand votes, could resist the tide. None of the majority-French ridings won by the party in 1930 fitted into this category. The Conservative party did manage to retain a considerably higher share of the Quebec popular vote than it had in 1921, but this was in part attributable to its strength in anglophone Montreal. Here again, a serious problem for the party's future viability was revealed: a weak and vulnerable base among French Canadians.

Useful as post-election statistical analysis can be, it should not be forgotten that a Conservative defeat was virtually assured, even as the election writs were being issued. The Liberal sweep of all thirty seats in the Prince Edward Island vote of 23 July had merely confirmed the anti-Conservative trend evident in provincial elections and federal by-elections since 1933. The stunning Social Credit upset in Alberta on 15 August may have struck fear in the hearts of some Canadian Liberals, but it was absolutely no consolation for the Conservatives. Fundamentally, the reasons for the Conservatives' unpopularity in 1935 originated in their great victory of 1930. Bennett had confidently promised in that

TABLE 10
Conservative percentage of popular vote in urban
and non-urban ridings: 1921, 1930, 1935

	1921	1930	1935
Urban	34.8	51.7	29.5
Non-urban	28.0	46.7	29.6
Canada	30.3	48.7	29.6

SOURCES: Scarrow, *Canada Votes; Report of the Chief
Electoral Officer; Census of Canada*

campaign to end unemployment, or go out of office. Unemployment
had not been ended. It was far worse. The majority of voters stood
ready to hold Bennett to his promise. For most of them, Mackenzie
King and the Liberals were the chosen instrument of retribution. If the
Liberals did not bring better times, they could be dealt with at the next
election.

The Conservatives' re-election problems were compounded by Bennett's neglect of his cabinet and party during five years of office. One
of his strongest ministers, Stevens, had become so alienated by the
prime minister's domineering attitude and style that he was now leading
a new party. The undignified scramble by half a dozen others for ap-
pointive offices just prior to the election campaign did nothing to raise
the government's credibility. Bennett's consistent refusal to shake up
the cabinet until his hand was forced by resignations had made for a
mediocre supporting cast behind him. The party organization had
completely atrophied by the time Bennett awoke in 1935 to its need for
re-election purposes. With limited funds, a late start, inexperienced
personnel, and no provincial governments upon which to rely, the organization was only a shadow of the fighting machine of 1930.

Bennett's flirtation with radical reforms of the economic system in
January 1935 had initially seemed a brilliant political manoeuvre.
Guided by Herridge's advice, and mouthing his colourful rhetoric,
Bennett had regained the initiative. A combination of Bennett's own
hesitation, his quarrel with Herridge, his continuing feud with Stevens,
King's masterful tactics, the reluctance of some influential Conservatives
to accept the new Toryism, and then Bennett's illness, all conspired to
reverse the Conservative advantage. Although a number of important

bills were eventually passed, Bennett's image as a sincere reformer was tarnished, while his very attempt to become one shook the allegiance of many traditional party loyalists. Instead of the best of both worlds, he had the worst.

Discouraging though the results were, some Conservatives had feared even worse. In September, the *Round Table* observer noted the party was waging 'a desperate rearguard action,' hoping to 'claim the right to be the official opposition in the new Parliament.' One saving factor was party loyalty. As John Cripps observed in a pre-election analysis in the British journal *The Political Quarterly*, 'Party allegiances are strong in Canada.' Funds expended on publicity helped to rekindle the old ties. As one Reconstruction candidate explained to Stevens: 'At first it seemed as if we were going to get a good vote, but during the closing days of the campaign, due partly to the absence of newspaper advertising and radio talks, the support seemed to drift back to the old parties.' The promise of funds to help the local campaign was also a potent force in persuading erstwhile Stevens supporters in the Tory caucus to run as straight Conservatives. Finally, it was conceded by one and all that Bennett ran a magnificent personal campaign in the face of heavy odds. As the *Globe* remarked on the election morrow, 'Mr. Bennett put up a strong campaign, and undoubtedly rescued his party from the grave position it was in two months ago.' Tories agreed. D.B. Plunkett, one of the victorious forty, offered this appreciation to his leader: 'Had you not toured the country and spoken as often as you did our Party would have been almost completely obliterated.' Bennett, who had skippered the Tory ship to the verge of destruction, managed through a supreme effort at the last moment to salvage at least the basic structure of the craft.[64]

There were, of course, regional elements that altered the basic national pattern. A key factor in the Maritimes was the popularity and power of the three Liberal premiers – Angus L. Macdonald, A.A. Dysart, and the newly elected Walter M. Lea – and the potent forces of patronage and organization that they wielded on behalf of the federal Liberals. A similar situation prevailed in Ontario, where Premier Mitchell Hepburn instructed his ministers to 'go the limit in Ontario ... to assure a Liberal Government at Ottawa.' In the West, Premiers John Bracken, Duff Pattullo, and Jimmy Gardiner similarly threw their provincial forces into the fray. The tariff issue still played havoc with Tory hopes on the Prairies, where desperate farmers remembered bitterly Bennett's promise to make higher tariffs fight for them. Some Conservative members also complained that the Farmers' Creditors' Arrangement Act and the Farm Loan Board amendments had cruelly raised expectations that were not being met.[65]

In Quebec, the Conservatives reaped the reward of five years characterized by weak French-Canadian ministers, mishandled patronage, and an overall government misunderstanding of the province typified by the damaging bilingual currency issue. Bennett did his best to defuse the war scare prompted by events in faraway Ethiopia, but this was the type of emotional issue that did not need banner headlines to have an impact. The memories of 1917 were still fresh in Quebec. The wild card in Alberta was the Social Credit phenomenon. One defeated Conservative candidate analyzed the new movement as 'a mixture of religious fanaticism, a mythical monthly dividend and some high class political organizing.' A major factor in British Columbia was the growing strength of the CCF, and the effect this had on non-socialist voters. Although the CCF outpolled every other party in this province, it was held to three seats. One Tory candidate speculated that 'many conservatives voted liberal [sic] so as to not lose their vote and by so voting they were sure of defeating the CCF Party.'[66]

Bennett's initial post-election assessment of the Conservatives' defeat emphasized the Depression's effects. 'The resentment of the people had to find expression,' he wrote the Ontario lieutenant-governor, 'and the easiest way they could vent their resentment against conditions was by voting against the Government.' A month later, in a campaign follow-up letter to party stalwarts, he conceded that the Conservatives had 'failed to give to party organization the attention that it deserved,' though he did not admit that this was his own fault. In private correspondence he expressed the view, based on conversations with and letters from most of the Tory candidates, that 'the railway vote' and the vote of 'our Roman Catholic friends' went solidly Liberal. Still, he was not under any illusion. 'I will be held responsible for the disaster that has overtaken our Party,' he predicted shortly after the election. Outwardly, at least, he was prepared for his fate, writing to Sir Robert Borden, 'I went down with the ship and did not seek to evade punishment.'[67]

DEFEATED, DIVIDED, DEMORALIZED

The election of 1935 was an election of realignment. Unlike the situation after 1921 when Tory fortunes outside of Quebec quickly revived, the

1935 vote marked the beginning of a long period of Liberal dominance that would extend for twenty-two years. The Conservative party would have to content itself during that period with an opposition role, at times even in danger of relegation to minor-party status. Others would assume the responsibilities and privileges of governing the country. All this was not apparent to party observers the day after the election. What was apparent was that the party needed rebuilding. The parliamentary caucus was small, and unrepresentative of the country. The leader was old and tired, though still fearsome when aroused. The organization needed a permanent secretariat and regularized fund-raising. The party's policies, for eight years largely the prerogative of the party leader, were no longer clear in Conservative minds, let alone in the mind of the general public. Serious internal splits, over policy and personality, needed healing.

Party disunity was a serious problem. There seemed little prospect of mending the breach with the Reconstruction leader. 'As a result of Mr. Stevens' treachery, the Liberals are in power,' Bennett declared hotly, a month after the election. For his part, Stevens was 'even now considering ways and means of carrying on,' to build a permanent base for his new party. Meanwhile, Cahan, outwardly loyal to Bennett, confessed privately to King that he was 'not unhappy with the result of the elections,' despite the Tory rout. 'The people of Canada,' he concluded, 'are not disposed to espouse the economic fallacies of Karl Marx, as expressed in the Radio addresses of the late Prime Minister in January last.' So much for party solidarity.[68]

What Cahan refused to acknowledge was that Canada was a changed and changing country. The harsh depression conditions of the 1930s merely emphasized a transformation that had been in process for some time, a change from a rural-agricultural society to an urban-industrial one. New problems had arisen, new interest groups had surfaced, and new demands were being placed upon the political system. True enough, the Conservatives had found themselves in power during the worst years of the Great Depression, and for this as much as anything they were punished at the polls in 1935. However, the challenge facing them on the morrow of that election was to regroup, reorient themselves to this new Canada, and prepare themselves to govern it when their next opportunity arose.

One priority would be to rebuild the party organization, and another to recruit a new generation of party activists. But, above all, Canada's Conservatives needed to confront anew the question posed in 1927 by

Arthur Meighen: 'What manner of party' did the Tories wish to be? A party of reform, whether of Stevens's populist or Bennett's paternalist variety, or a party of tradition and *laissez-faire*, in the Cahan mould? In its most successful periods, the Conservative party had creatively combined elements from each of those ideological strains. Perhaps the greatest need was for a leader able to harmonize the divergent strands of opinion within Canadian Conservatism, and then inspire its followers to battle Grits and Socialists, rather than each other.

8 The Search for Redemption: November 1935 to July 1938

As the minutes ticked on towards four o'clock, the tension in the air at the Coliseum in Ottawa's Lansdowne Park mounted steadily. Many of the more than 1,500 delegates to the Conservative national convention fanned themselves with programmes against the oppressive heat. Occasionally they rose as one body to support yet another policy resolution. In the galleries above, draped with Union Jacks, another 2,000 spectators looked on. The date was Thursday, 7 July 1938. Under the stands, party officials were busy counting ballots. Five candidates – Joseph Harris, Earl Lawson, Murdoch MacPherson, Robert Manion, and Denton Massey – had offered themselves for the party leadership. Each was seeking to replace R.B. Bennett, the retiring chieftain, who had been selected at a similar gathering in Winnipeg, nearly eleven years earlier.[1]

Senator John Haig, chief returning officer at the convention, came to the platform to read the results. They were: Manion, 726; MacPherson, 475; Harris, 131; Massey, 128; and Lawson, 105 (see table 11). Lawson was automatically dropped from the second ballot, but Harris and Massey opted to remain with the two front-runners.[2] Manion was only sixty votes from a clear majority, but rumours of a movement to 'stop' him by uniting behind MacPherson had circulated along the corridors of the Château Laurier throughout the previous night. However, since the delegates were seated by province, rather than by candidate allegiance, it was impossible to tell who might be moving to support whom. Candidates, delegates, journalists, spectators – all would have to wait for the results of a second ballot.

Voting proceeded briskly and before too many more resolutions had been heard, Senator Haig was returning to the podium. To the hushed

TABLE 11
Leadership voting results at 1938 convention

Candidate	First ballot	Second ballot
R.J. Manion	726	830
M.A. MacPerson	475	648
Joseph Harris	131	49
Denton Massey	128	39
J.E. Lawson	105	
Totals	1,565	1,566

SOURCE: P.C. Party Papers, vol. 417, Proceedings of the Convention of the National Conservative Party of Canada, 5–7 July; John C. Courtney, *The Selection of National Party Leaders in Canada* (Toronto 1973), 149

crowd he simply announced that as a result of the second ballot, the Honourable R.J. Manion had been elected leader of the National Conservative Party. Vote totals subsequently released told the story: Manion, 830; MacPherson, 648; Harris, 49; and Massey, 39.[3] The Fort William doctor's first-ballot lead had been more than sufficient to withstand a second-ballot surge to his chief rival. With difficulty the candidates made their way through the crowd to the front of the hall, mounted the platform, and congratulated their new leader. MacPherson, as runner-up, moved that the selection of Manion be made unanimous. His words were greeted with a roar of approval.

'I am your chosen leader, not your commander,' 'Fighting Bob' Manion announced to cheering partisans. He pledged to 'start up a real organization' that would drive 'the Do-Nothing Government' of Mackenzie King out of office. The Conservative party he led would be 'the servant of no group or class or interest, big or little.'[4] The pugnacious spirit of the new leader was admirable, but many delegates sensed something important was missing in all the hoopla. R.B. Bennett was nowhere to be seen. He had not even attended the final day of the convention. There would be no laying on of hands, no ritual passing of the torch from retiring chieftain to anointed successor. Manion had captured Bennett's job, but not his blessing. Across town, at Laurier House, an old foe aptly summarized the event. 'The House of Bennett has fallen,' Prime Minister King noted in his diary.[5]

Since his own elevation to the party leadership in 1927, R.B. Bennett had dominated the life of the Conservative Party of Canada, in office and out. Once the dismal results of the 1935 election were disgested, party members began to confront two crucial, but nevertheless unsettling, questions. How could the shattered party be rebuilt, and who should lead them through this trying time? Linked to these concerns was the question of the incumbent leader's role. Where did R.B. Bennett fit in? He had often proceeded as if the Conservative party were 'his' party. This chapter will focus on the direction of the party during the final three years of his leadership. One of the sad ironies of this era was that, though few Tories outside of the leader's own office felt the party could win, or even meaningfully rebuild, with him at the helm, Bennett continued to demonstrate more ability, drive, and experience than any pretender to his throne.

THE PARLIAMENTARY PARTY

The Tory caucus had been decimated by the 1935 election, in terms of quantity, quality, and regional balance. It numbered only forty, and over half came from southern Ontario. Gone were Hanson and Manion, two of the best parliamentary in-fighters, along with ten of their cabinet colleagues, all defeated. Stevens, of course, had burned his bridges, and, though re-elected, would toil in obscurity as leader and sole member of the Reconstruction Party. Besides Bennett, only six Conservative privy councillors remained to occupy the front benches. Two of these, Sir George Perley and C.H. Cahan, were in their seventies, while two others, H.A. Stewart and Grote Stirling, were, like Bennett, in their sixties. Only Earl Rowe and Earl Lawson, last-minute additions to the cabinet from Ontario in the summer of 1935, were younger men, each in his early forties. The number of freshman MPs in the caucus was small, and although much would be heard from Gordon Graydon and Howard Green in years to come, only Denton Massey made much of a mark in the Eighteenth Parliament.

Bennett completely overshadowed his caucus. At one point in April 1936, it was calculated that his words in Commons debate represented over 40 per cent of the total pages of Hansard. Even Mackenzie King was impressed, noting that Bennett had 'remained with remarkable steadfastness to [sic] his seat throughout the whole session.' Bennett took the role of opposition leader seriously. 'Democracy,' he stressed to one correspondent, 'is only possible if in Parliament there is an Opposition with some knowledge of public questions, and even though small in numbers, with courage to criticise measures that may be submitted.' As a one-man opposition, Bennett really was quite effective. Ironically, by keeping the ministers on their toes, he may have been helping the Liberal party more than his own. Furthermore, with their own leader on his feet so often, other Conservatives had little chance to practise their parliamentary skills or develop a public profile. Moreover, his preoccupation with affairs on Parliament Hill prevented Bennett from fulfilling other critical tasks expected of the leader of a party in opposition. 'He would be contributing considerably more to the good of the Conservative Party,' the vice-president of the Manitoba Conservative Association wrote to Rod Finlayson, 'by getting away from Ottawa occasionally and rubbing shoulders with the rank and file of the Party.' Bennett, however, persisted in sticking to his seat for as long as the Commons was sitting. 'As our numbers are limited in the House,' he stated in 1937, 'I am constantly in attendance from three to six o'clock and from eight to eleven.' The old bruin still actively patrolled his lair.[6]

Bennett did not approach the role of opposition with any grand strategy in mind. Much of his effort during the 1936 session was spent defending the record of the Conservative administration he had led, jealously denying the Liberals credit for policies initiated by the Tories, and angrily denouncing any efforts to dismantle legislation introduced by himself and his colleagues. In 1937, this situation seemed to change somewhat. 'There were a good many occasions during the past Session,' an incredulous Thomas A. Crerar informed J.W. Dafoe, 'when his criticism of legislation was pertinent and helpful.' A year later, he was as combative as ever, raising serious allegations of corruption against the scholarly labour minister, Norman Rogers, and generally attacking the government from all directions. Even though he finally conceded the honour of chief budget critic to Earl Lawson, Bennett was still playing a lone hand. After two and a half years, the overall result of all his efforts, when measured in terms of by-election results, was a net loss of one seat in some twenty contests, despite the fact the economy had fallen into a serious recession in mid-1937.[7]

Bennett and the Conservatives were unable to find a marketable winning issue. They criticized the Liberal budgets for their failure to reduce taxes, but the fact was that Dunning came much closer to balancing the books than Rhodes ever had, despite the Conservatives' dogmatic insistence on this point while in office. The Liberals' success in completing the negotiations begun by himself concerning a trade treaty with the United States enraged Bennett, who jealously opposed it in Parliament. 'This treaty is disastrous to Canada,' he maintained, reinforcing his party's reactionary protectionist image in the process. And, no matter how much he might harp on unemployment, Bennett always faced the rebuttal that it had been worse under his government.[8]

Bennett resented the Liberals tampering with any of the Conservative policies, regardless of their unpopularity. When Section 98 of the Criminal Code was repealed, he asked, 'Is there anything in Section 98 which reasonable citizens should desire to have removed?' He defended the relief camps, when Rogers announced plans to close them. He denounced the nationalization of the Bank of Canada, done cautiously in two stages, in 1936 and 1938. 'This bank now becomes a political bank,' he declared. When the Canadian Radio Broadcasting Commission was transformed into the Canadian Broadcasting Corporation, he again voiced disapproval. 'We had hoped that broadcasting in Canada might be out of the hands of governments,' he contended. When the Liberals referred the heart of his New Deal program of reform to the courts, Bennett was again enraged. Such reactions were altogether human and consistent with his character, but, taken together, they did not constitute a fresh policy image for a rebuilding opposition party. Bennett insisted on carrying all his old baggage, no matter how burdensome.[9]

Bennett continued to alienate the French-Canadian support that had contributed so significantly to the 1930 electoral victory. He stoutly opposed a bilingual currency when the issue came up again in 1936. In part, he was merely following his own pattern of knee-jerk opposition to all Liberal tampering with Conservative policies. More important, however, he revealed a fundamental lack of appreciation for the French fact in Canada by asking if 'in a community that is overwhelmingly British the circulation of notes of that kind is not fraught with the gravest danger to harmony between races.' A disappointed former colleague, Maurice Dupré, tried to explain to his leader how Quebec was changing: 'French Canada has the impression that it is not well treated; that it has not its share of public offices; that its existence and cooperation is only tolerated; that the tendency is to have it limited to the Quebec reserve; and that, for this attitude among some of our Anglo-Saxon friends, the conservative party is more responsible than the liberal party.' For most of the 1935–8 period, the Tory caucus contained just one French Canadian, a fact that served to reinforce the mutual misunderstanding.[10]

Just before stepping down as leader, Bennett elevated the question of empire defence to the forefront of public debate. He either did not know, or perhaps did not care, how French Canadians would feel about the issue. Bennett, through Senator Meighen, had learned that the King government was reluctant to grant permission to the British to set up an air training school in Canada. King denied that such a request had actually been made, but went on to paint the issue in nationalistic terms. 'Long ago,' he declared, 'Canadian governments finally settled the constitutional principle that in Canadian territory there could be no military establishments unless they were owned, maintained and controlled by the Canadian government.' 'When Britain goes we go,' Bennett shot back. 'If it was the last word I ever uttered in this house or with the last breath in my body I would say that no Canadian is worthy of his great heritage and his great traditions and his magnificent hope of the future who would deny to the old partner who established us the right in this country to create those centres which she may not have at home to preserve her life and the life of every man who enjoys freedom and liberty under the protecting aegis of that flag.' The issue was a pertinent one in an increasingly unsafe world, but the jingoistic phrases in which he couched his appeal ensured Bennett a deaf ear from French Canadians.[11]

Overall it seemed that Bennett and the Conservatives he led had lost interest in new reforms, though they would stoutly defend those introduced previously by his own government. The party's opposition to the Liberals lacked focus, and, while it may have helped ensure more effective government legislation, it did not produce fresh policies on which to campaign in the next election. Furthermore, with a caucus weak in representation from non-WASP areas of the country, party stands taken on issues such as bilingual currency or imperial defence tended to reflect a British-Canadian outlook.

THE PARTY ORGANIZATION

Unlike the situation in 1930, when the Dominion Conservative Headquarters was locked up the day after the election, the central office was kept open five years later, albeit with a skeleton staff. Jane Denison, who had worked at Conservative headquarters in the 1920s when S.F. Tolmie was the party organizer, was hired to keep the national party office alive, and, in so doing, she performed the executive as well as stenographic duties. Later, a second full-time staffer was added. Her office was expected to maintain contact with the provincial associations, federal constituencies, and parliamentary caucus. She kept the party's mailing lists up to date, and performed policy research for the MPs. With what time and funds were available, the central office produced and distributed publicity as well. Two issues of *The Canadian* were produced in 1936. The first was mailed to 60,000 'key' supporters on the English-language mailing list, while the second, because of budgetary restraints, could be mailed to only 25,000 of these party loyalists. The party office mailed a thank-you letter from Bennett to the full mailing list in November 1935, and arranged through Rainville's Montreal office to have a French translation sent to 100,000 French-Canadian Conservatives. In 1937, a copy of Bennett's budget address was mailed to the full English-language mailing list. In addition, the headquarters produced a weekly political letter that was distributed to 97 Conservative weekly newspapers with a combined circulation of 400,000. Finally, the central office responded to requests from constituencies and clubs for general party publicity material. Denison managed to perform all these tasks on a total annual budget of only $4,000, which included her own salary.[12]

The scarcity of funds was a continuing crisis for the party organization. Bennett, faced with a debt of $170,000 arising from the unpaid bills of the 1935 campaign, refused to grant more than a pittance to keep the central office open. Yet, when party members such as John MacNicol or Earl Lawson suggested a Toronto fund-raising dinner to put the party back on its feet, he would not go along. By comparison, Norman Lambert at the National Liberal Federation had ample funds. 'Altogether,' Lambert informed Mackenzie King in December 1938, '$150,000 has been collected and spent through this office on straight Federation work, and on outside party activities in three years.'[13]

Indeed, Bennett's attitude was a major roadblock to effective reorganization. As he told the veteran Manitoba organizer Ralph Webb, 'the general view is that I can continue to finance the Party, which of course I cannot do.' In addition to viewing himself as the milch cow of the Tory party, Bennett saw little point in the federal party exerting itself organizationally until the provincial wings were healthy again. 'I do not think it is intended at the present time to undertake any ambitious programme of organization but rather to maintain an office here, with the hope that we may be able to assist Provincial organization in such a manner as to get it fairly under way before any effort is made to coordinate the various Provincial activities, for the Provincial elections will be held before the next Federal election.' After a quarter-century of political experience, Bennett still did not understand the organizational side of politics. He continued to blame the 1935 defeat on, first, 'the treachery of Mr. Stevens,' and, second, the failure of 'each Member organizing and winning his own seat.' Frank Turnbull, Saskatchewan organizer and defeated MP, had attempted to set his chief straight on the relative importance of a national headquarters: ' The Western provinces and the Maritimes rather look to a central office for leadership and guidance ... The Conservatives of Saskatchewan feel pretty much like a child lost at the Exhibition, who does not know where to go or what to do, and feels very sad and lonely.' The plea fell on deaf ears.[14]

Province by province, the Conservative party was in sad shape. As of December 1935, it counted no elected legislative members in three provinces – Prince Edward Island, Saskatchewan, and British Columbia – while, in another – Alberta – the party was in third place. Even in the five provinces where it formed the official opposition, the party was far behind the government in numbers, except in Quebec, where an alliance with dissident Liberals placed the Conservative leader, Maurice Duplessis, in a strong position. Over the next two and one-half years, the picture did not improve much. Provincial elections in Ontario, Manitoba, and British Columbia did result in a somewhat improved showing by provincial Tories, but, in each case, the party remained in opposition. A Saskatchewan election left the party seatless again in that province. Only in Quebec did provincial Conservatives gain office, but the circumstances were such that the federal party did not gain much from the breakthrough. Duplessis had formed a new provincial party, based on the Conservative alliance with reform Liberals, called the Union Nationale. He accentuated even more the traditional arm's-length relationship to federal Conservatives practised by the former leaders, Arthur Sauvé and Camillien Houde. With their hands on the provincial government at last, Quebec Conservatives were not eager to lose power because of the damaging image of their anglophone cousins. 'We have the local government,' said one to H.H. Stevens in 1938, 'and we are not prepared to hurt our cause in the Provincial field just for the sake of a party whose chances are still problematical.'[15]

The organizational difficulties of the national Conservative party were mirrored in the provincial field. 'Our organization has disintegrated and must be entirely rebuilt,' George Nowlan, the new president of the Nova Scotia Conservative Association, wrote to Bennett in 1936. 'Party finances in this Province do not exist,' reported the new provincial leader in Saskatchewan, John Diefenbaker, in 1937. 'We have no money. We have no organizer, and therefore I have to continue to be both leader and organizer,' Errick Willis, Manitoba Tory leader, informed the party convention in 1938. What funds the Conservatives could scrounge up were expended in the Ontario election of October 1937. 'A demonstration has to be made that we are still alive, and this is the place that it is intended to make it,' Arthur Meighen explained to a British Columbia Conservative begging fruitlessly for funds for the provincial election there. At a crucial moment, however, the Ontario Conservatives were split, when party organizer George Drew publicly differed with his leader, Earl Rowe, on the twin issues of coalition with the Liberals and attitude towards labour unions. Subsequently, both Drew and Rowe were defeated, and the Conservatives increased their meagre numbers in the Ontario legislature by only a handful. The national party's fortunes were so low that, on 1 July 1938, barely 10 per cent of the provincial legislators in the entire country called themselves Conservatives.[16]

THE CONVENTION QUESTION

Conservatives were divided on the advisability of Bennett continuing his leadership of the national party. His parliamentary followers well realized his capacity in the Commons, and on the hustings, and they generally favoured his retention of the post. Outside Parliament, party supporters were less enthusiastic, particularly in view of the lack of progress in organization and provincial strength. Bennett, himself, was of two minds on the subject. To anyone who inquired, he professed a great desire to be released from his responsibilities. 'I am only carrying on in a sense of duty,' he informed an Ontario Tory, 'and with the very earnest hope that a condition will arise that will make it possible for me to gracefully retire.' Most of the time Bennett did not act like a leader eager to retire, however, only like one weary of criticism and unwanted suggestions. As Hanson wrote to Manion, both of them banned from political centre court by the voters, 'I, too, rather agree on what you say about R.B. not wishing to drop out. He loves it.' Bennett's rival, Mackenzie King, also doubted Bennett's oft-rumoured intention to retire, usually accompanied by a hint of heart trouble. 'My own impression is that he has no intention of giving up public life,' King noted in his diary, 'but is simply anxious to put the Party in a position where his continuing on will be at their request.'[17]

Bennett summoned the caucus to Ottawa in August 1937, upon his return from an overseas trip that included consultations with British medical specialists. Behind closed doors, Bennett submitted his resignation to the assembled members in the morning, only to allow himself to be talked into staying by the end of the afternoon. 'Frankly, I had no desire to remain at a thankless task,' Bennett informed Dr Bruce, 'but I could not leave without being regarded as a "quitter."' Robert Manion heard a different story: 'R.B. stayed – as I expected. On conditions I understand, such as that he is to spend no more money on organization etc. Had I been present I fear I should have said things that needed saying. Nothing was said by anyone. One fellow told me they were all afraid he would quit!' With the leadership question apparently settled, Bennett and the caucus proceeded with plans to reorganize the party. To that end, a conference was scheduled in Ottawa for March 1938. In addition to MPs and senators, former ministers still supporting the Conservative party, as well as representatives of the provincial associations, received invitations. In all, some 150 Tories assembled to discuss organization, finance, and policy.[18]

At the March gathering, the finance committee recommended the appointment of joint treasurers and a permanent finance committee, to put party funding on a sustainable basis. The organization committee recommended the immediate appointment of a national organizer by the leader, the formation of a national Conservative council to coordinate the activities of the national and provincial parties, the establishment of permanent headquarters in each province, a greater role for women and youth in the party, and much more frequent publicity in both English and French. The committee was named the 'Policy and Convention Committee.' Many delegates to the conference had agreed with the Montreal *Gazette*, which stated just before the March meeting that 'a definition or redefintion of Conservative policy ... cannot be accomplished except through a convention that will be more representative of the rank and file.' Manion's Fort William riding association, in a preconference letter widely circulated in the weeks prior to the meeting, had requested a national convention 'at the earliest possible date.' Part way through the conference, Bennett stated his intention to retire as leader. This time there was no stampede to persuade him to change his mind. The caucus, many of them still favourable to his continued leadership, was in a considerable minority. Most other delegates were prepared to see the old chief depart. In the absence of a unanimous demand that he stay on, Bennett issued a press statement: 'The action of my heart is impaired and ... this condition necessarily involves drastic limitations upon my activities.' Taking him at his word, the Policy and

Convention Committee thus proceeded to plan a policy and leadership convention.[19]

The committee recommended early July 1938 as the best date for the convention, subsequently set for 5–7 July. It further recommended either Ottawa or Winnipeg as the site. The conference opted for Ottawa by a vote of forty-nine to thirty-three. The committee also advocated a name change for the party, dropping the seldom-used modifier 'Liberal' and replacing it with 'National' – thus 'National Conservative Party.' The change was adopted by the conference. The influence of the Quebec delegation was evident in both decisions. Ottawa as a site was much closer for prospective Quebec delegates than Winnipeg, and 'National Conservative Party' sounded akin to the provincial Union Nationale party. The significance of Duplessis's support had been driven home to Conservatives in the Argenteuil by-election just days before the March conference. Assistance from the Union Nationale organization had elected the Conservative, Georges Héon, by a handsome margin in a seat, narrowly held by Sir George Perley in 1935, that the Liberals had confidently expected to win.[20]

'This convention is a success,' co-chairman John R. MacNicol announced to the assembled Tory delegates on 5 July 1938, 'because we have followed almost totally the splendid plan laid out by General A.D. McRae.' Organizationally, the 1938 gathering did resemble the 1927 convention in most respects. An umbrella committee, the National Convention Committee, with representatives from all provinces, was set up to oversee the planning. Ongoing executive leadership was provided by the organization committee, consisting of the joint national chairmen, J.R. MacNicol and Maurice Dupré; the joint secretaries, Gordon Graydon and Georges Héon; and the executive secretary, Jane Denison. Pre-convention subcommittees, again with country-wide representation, were established to handle local arrangements, transportation, and finance. Once assembled, five standing convention committees – credentials, nominations, resolutions, party organization, and publicity – were struck, with the membership chosen by each provincial association.[21]

Although an auditor's report showed convention expenses of $10,176.67, and contributions of $10,303.61, in actual fact the finance committee chaired by H.A. Stewart raised a good deal more than that. R.K. Finlayson and the Montrealer J.C.H. Dussault served as joint treasurers. The actual collection was spearheaded by George B. Foster in Montreal and J.M. Macdonnell in Toronto. Foster coaxed $8,000 from thirteen corporate donors in Montreal, while Toronto contributed nearly as much. In all, $14,900.70 was raised, none of it from Bennett. Of course the bulk of the expenses, for rail fare, accommodation, and time off work, was borne by the delegates themselves[22]

The breakdown of delegates was substantially similar in 1938 to that of the previous national convention. Each federal constituency was eligible to select four official delegates. Four alternate delegates could be chosen as well, though they could vote only in place of an official delegate. The following categories of ex-officio delegates were accredited: Conservative MPs, defeated candidates from the 1935 election, senators, privy councillors, former lieutenant-governors, MLAs, and provincial leaders. In addition, all members of the National Convention Committee not otherwise eligible were given ex-officio status. A third type of representation was provided: the delegate at large. Each provincial association was allowed to select delegates equal to the number of federal ridings in that province. As well, youth delegates at large were allotted according to the following formula: nine males and nine females from each of Ontario and Quebec, and three males and three females from each of the other provinces and from the Yukon. Proportionally, the convention consisted of 54.0 per cent riding delegates, 27.5 per cent ex-officio delegates, and 18.5 per cent delegates at large. In all, 1,814 delegates were eligible to attend the July convention. A total of 1,597 ballot books were issued, indicating most spots were filled.[23]

The Saskatchewan and Alberta associations had the most difficulty in completing their delegations. Typical was this report from an Alberta Tory, H.R. Milner, to Arthur Meighen: 'Unless some financial assistance can be given, I am doubtful if there will be many delegates from Alberta. People are hard-up.' 'It is going to be a problem to secure even a partial representation,' John Diefenbaker lamented from Saskatchewan. Such a situation prevailed for a time even in Quebec. 'Nobody is in control,' former MP John Hackett informed Hanson in May, 'and the delegates, in such circumstances, may be chosen and voted by any interest that will take the trouble to see that they are selected and shipped to Ottawa f.o.b.' Into the breach stepped Maurice Dupré. 'I took charge of the organization throughout the province,' he informed MacNicol in 1939. 'I decided that I would advance all the monies necessary to carry the work to a successful conclusion.'[24]

Some 1,600 delegates descended on Ottawa the week of 4–8 July 1938, from every corner of the Dominion. By comparison with 1927, there were a few more women and youth delegates, and the geography of location favoured eastern over western delegates this time. More than ever, the high cost of attendance in a depression period ensured a preponderance of affluent Conservatives among the delegates. Once the welcoming festivities were attended to, they set to work crafting a statement of policy and choosing a new leader.

BUILDING A PLATFORM

'The new leader should not find the platform a severe restraint,' lamented the independent-conservative Winnipeg *Tribune*, 'for it represents just about the least common factor of Conservative opinion.' The degree of its blandness may be inferred from Mackenzie King's reaction upon reading the policy resolutions. 'The Convention's programme with an exception or two might have been that of our own,' he recorded. 'If anything, it is milder.' Many Conservatives would have preferred a more eloquent, more substantive document than the collection of vague resolutions produced by the convention. The problem was that, whenever the wording of a proposal became too specific, the party's internal divisions rose quickly to the surface. The end result was a document that favoured caution over boldness, platitudes over specifics.[25]

Many of the party's old guard were leery of handing over outright the job of constructing a platform to a national convention dominated by the rank and file. Sir Thomas White spoke for this element when he warned Bennett, 'To entrust such a task wholly to committees of delegates to a Convention, arguing and disputing throughout long hours of the night (as has been the practice in the past) in an atmosphere (physical and mental) prohibitive of real deliberation or finished expression of ideas, is the height of absurdity.' White's view was certainly élitist; he felt that the convention's resolutions committee should be presented with 'well-drafted declarations of policy in accord with the traditions of the party and the needs of the time as its leaders see them.' Bennett and the party hierarchy agreed. A pre-convention Resolutions Committee, chaired by Joseph Harris and consisting of seven MPs and seven senators, sifted through the resolutions submitted from Conservative riding associations, then prepared a draft platform. This document was screened by C.H. Cahan and Arthur Meighen, then submitted to Bennett for further revisions. The old chieftain was determined to hold his party to the sound course he felt he had set for it.

When the Resolutions Committee of the convention finally met at 5:00 p.m. on Tuesday, 5 July, it was handed a ready-made program prepared for and agreeable to the outgoing leader.[26]

Under the chairmanship of R.B. Hanson, the committee divided into ten subcommittees based on policy topics. Each subcommittee met separately Tuesday evening, deliberated on the draft resolutions before it, then prepared statements for adoption by the committee, meeting as a whole, on Wednesday. Once passed in committee, the resolutions were ready for presentation to the full convention on Thursday. With a leadership race proceeding simultaneously, the attention of the delegates was not wholly upon policy matters. Indeed, convention organizers hoped that any contentious issues would be ironed out in committee, behind closed doors. The wording of many resolutions was kept deliberately vague, to avoid a divisive floor fight. For the most part, the strategy succeeded. Many resolutions sailed right through the convention, without amendment or even discussion. Nevertheless, three issues did provoke open controversy. They coincided with three of the most significant cleavages in the party itself, cleavages that might be labelled English-French, heartland-hinterland, and reform-reaction.[27]

The English-French cleavage crystallized over the issue of Commonwealth defence, and specifically the British air training scheme that Meighen and Bennett had raised in Parliament only days before the convention. Meighen, at Bennett's invitation, delivered a stirring address on the subject at the opening of the convention, reminiscent of his 1927 speech in both its emotional eloquence and its divisive effect. 'Have we come to the pass in this country,' he demanded rhetorically, 'when the Old Land asks for permission to establish at her own expense, and train in her own way, her own citizens for their defence and ours?' His call to arms brought most of the English-speaking delegates to their feet in tumultuous applause. In the Quebec section, the French Canadians sat on their hands. The next morning, Georges Héon, newly elected MP from Argenteuil, delivered a pointed rebuke to Meighen from the podium for 'certaines praroles inappropriées.' To the Quebec delegation he pleaded: 'Je demande à mes amis de Québec encore une fois d'être patients.' Switching to English to make his meaning very clear, he stated, 'Let us tell the Dominion at large that the Conservative party is a party of the people, that no clique can dictate to us.' It was clear from his words that most of the Quebec delegation were vigorously opposed to active Canadian participation in any joint defence program with Britain.[28]

In his farewell address to the convention on Wednesday, Bennett picked up the topic again: 'My friends from Quebec, you and I are British subjects together, not English or French, but British subjects, and in that proud name I ask you to join with other British subjects not only in Canada but in every part of this great world, to ensure the prosperity of Canada and the safety of the Commonwealth.'

'Today, as yesterday,' reported the *Globe and Mail's* correspondent later, 'the English-speaking delegates thundered their approval. Today, as yesterday, the Quebec delegates stood silent.' When, at the climax of his long, powerful, and, at times, emotional address, Bennett demanded the convention rise as a body and pledge anew their partnership in the British Commonwealth, some in the Quebec delegation did not stand up. The serious division in party ranks was now out in the open.[29]

In an attempt to paper over the split, the Resolutions Committee, after much internal debate, proposed an innocuous resolution that pledged 'abiding loyalty to the Crown' and affirmed that 'the defence of Canada and the preservation of our liberties can best be promoted by consultation and co-operation between all the members of the British Commonwealth of Nations.' The statement was a far cry from the vigorously pro-British position recommended to the committee in the Harris-Cahan-Meighen draft. The watered-down version was still unsatisfactory to some Quebec delegates, who moved an amendment requiring a national referendum before Canadian troops could be sent overseas. The amendment was eventually defeated, but not before an acrimonious exchange on the convention floor. In Laurier House, Mackenzie King chuckled at the effect of the 'monkey wrench' he had thrown into the workings of the Tory convention by taking a nationalist stand on the air training scheme.[30]

The heartland-hinterland cleavage surfaced during debate on the transportation issue. For years, eminent denizens of the Montreal business community, most notably Sir Edward Beatty, president of the Canadian Pacific Railway, had been clamouring for a forced amalgamation of the two transcontinental railways as a means of ending the perennial deficits incurred by the government-owned Canadian National Railway. Both Bennett and the former minister of railways and canals, R.J. Manion, were on public record as opposing unification. Still, the deficits mounted. Some Conservatives, principally from Montreal and Toronto, hoped the convention would reverse the old policy and come out for amalgamation as a cost-cutting measure. The pre-convention draft had skirted the issue, avoiding the use of either inflammatory word, 'unification' or 'amalgamation,' but pledging to seek a solution that would lessen 'the annual cost of the national railways to the taxpayers.' The Resolutions Committee would not stand for such ambiguity. As one reporter learned, 'the Western delegates declared that unification was the one thing they had been instructed to oppose.' As the chairman, R.B. Hanson, later recalled, 'Not 5% of the delegates on the Convention Committee, and they numbered 85 and were representative of every Province in Canada, were in favour of unification.' When a revised resolution declaring 'opposition to any plan of unification or amalgamation for the great railways of Canada' reached the convention floor, it encountered opposition from some Ontario delegates. One of them, Kelso Roberts, contended that 'unification may be a solution,' but his amendment was voted down. Again, Mackenzie King smiled. 'A real surprise was the resolution from the Convention denouncing amalgamation,' he wrote. 'Bennett and Manion can be thanked for losing the Party the support of the CPR, another of their main supports.'[31]

Bennett, whose on-again, off-again support for social and economic reform had done so much to cloud the party's image on this front, raised the reform-versus-reaction issue himself in his valedictory address.

Three years ago, consistently with the mandate received from Winnipeg, we endeavoured to give the capitalistic system some needed help to carry out the necessary changes by which the system might effectively serve the people. Reactionary forces opposed us ... not men like these sitting on the platform who realize that progress means change and that change must come when the outworn system has shown its uselessness ... But reactionary forces prevailed ... They were not going to have these measures. Bennett must be defeated in 1935, and he was.

Bennett was cheered when he delivered these lines, but, when his brother-in-law, W.D. Herridge, picked up on them the next day during policy debate, he was roundly booed. What had provoked Herridge was a resolution on public finance and taxation that pledged the party to 'a sane monetary policy' and measures 'to reduce the intolerable burden of taxation.' Labelling the platform approved thus far as 'a lot of junk,' an 'insult to the intelligence of this Convention,' and 'a treachery to the people of this country,' he proceeded to move a lengthy amendment. The meat of his resolution was a pledge 'to undertake whatever economic and monetary reforms may be required to stabilize production upon its maximum level, and to raise purchasing power to that level.' Ironically, the resolution that had provoked his wrath was substantially similar to the preliminary draft proposed by the Harris pre-convention committee, vetted by Cahan and Meighen, and apparently approved by Bennett, himself. At any event, Herridge's amendment was voted down decisively, with only scattered support from some western delegates. Again, King was amazed by the Conservatives' behaviour. 'Herridge's speech was unbelievable but gave the Convention what they were entitled to for suffering him and Bennett so long,' he noted in his diary, a bit smugly.[32]

The balance of the platform was composed of ritualistic banalities common to many such documents. The party reaffirmed a 'continued adherence to its traditional policy of ... fiscal protection.' It pledged to help farmers, fishermen, miners, labourers, tourist operators, and, by implication, anyone else who worked for a living. For those who could not find work, the party promised unemployment insurance and public works. The ghost of Maritime Rights was recognized yet again with promises to implement the Duncan Report of the 1920s and develop a national fuel policy. The party declared for the 'selected migration of British families,' with, of course, 'similar advantages ... extended to France,' all this without in any way affecting unemployment. Orientals, however, were to be excluded. The party's name-change, to National Conservative, was endorsed unanimously. Resolutions on organization and publicity, based largely on the suggestions proposed at the March conference, but with added emphasis on the involvement of women and youth, were proposed, passed, and seldom heard of again.[33]

'I think we have a good sound platform,' R.B. Hanson declared shortly after the convention, 'a balanced platform intended to appeal both to the East and West.' Of his own role as chairman of the Resolutions Committee, he stated, 'I had no idea what I was letting myself in for ... but I kept the peace.' R.B. Bennett was less sanguine. 'The platform is wholly inadequate,' he asserted. 'The Resolutions Committee did not fully discharge its duties.'[34] Bennett's criticism missed the point. It is true that some resolutions were too specific, and others were so blurred as to be incomprehensible. Indeed, some issues, such as Quebec's restrictive padlock law, were ignored altogether. However, in a democratic convention, the platform cannot be stronger than the party that passes it. The Conservative party was a divided party, struggling to come to grips with the critical issues and cleavages of a troubled society. Furthermore, the Resolutions Committee was no more to blame for the uninspiring platform than the leader himself, who had established the process by which the preliminary draft was created. But Bennett was much better at apportioning blame than accepting it.

THE LEADERSHIP RACE

There was no heir apparent when Bennett notified the March 1938 Conservative conference of his intention to resign as party leader. Most of the Conservative ministers who had served with him either were defeated in the 1935 election or had retired from politics. Of the handful still in Parliament, most were too old for a position that promised to require several years of party rebuilding before power could be regained. Since the Conservatives did not form the government in any province, there were no powerful provincial premiers akin to Ferguson and Rhodes in 1927. In the absence of an obvious choice, a host of names were suggested.

Perhaps the most 'available' man was R.J. Manion. Though defeated in 1935, he was still immensely popular with the party rank and file right across the country. Rare was the riding in English-speaking Canada that 'Fighting Bob' had not visited during the campaigns of 1930 and 1935. A genial companion, spirited debater, and fiery stump orator, he had paid his dues to the party faithful. His parliamentary experience included eighteen years as an MP, and three stints in cabinet. At age fifty-six, he was still young and vigorous enough to take on the demanding post. As a former Liberal Unionist, he might have been suspect in Quebec, but his being a Roman Catholic with a French-Canadian wife was thought to offset that weakness. As a Catholic, his appeal to the Protestant majority was a question mark, but it early became apparent that some of his staunchest supporters were the Orangemen of eastern Ontario. He had, after all, served overseas with valour in the Great War, defending king and country. A consensus quickly developed among political observers that Manion was, in H.H. Stevens's words, 'by long odds, the favourite in the running.'[35]

Manion was not without his detractors, however. Arthur Meighen was one of these. 'On the score of loyalty, courage and long service he is the best entitled,' noted the former leader. 'At the same time I have very serious question whether he can win, and have still graver question as to how he could handle the job after he did win.' R.B. Hanson was another who damned him with faint praise. After citing his 'wonderfully pleasant personality,' the former trade minister concluded, 'of course ... he does not measure up to the standard of Meighen or Bennett, but what can you do?' Manion was anything but Bennett's chosen successor, too, particularly in view of some of the cutting remarks the doctor had inserted in his recently published memoirs about the former prime minister. 'At times his apparent contempt for the opinions of others whom he deems less able than himself stirs up antagonisms against him,' Manion had written. While perfectly true, and a quite accurate reflection of the relationship between Bennett and Manion, such a statement was not likely to gain the approval of so vain and sensitive a man as R.B. Bennett. 'R.B. has not yet forgiven me my remarks regarding himself,' Manion informed his son in August 1937. 'I was really too kind.' Manion was also suspect with the Montreal business community, on account of his outspoken opposition, while minister of railways and canals and since, to their pet proposal of railway unification. While the residents of Plutoria Avenue had few votes, they traditionally provided much of the wherewithal that allowed the Tories to wage campaigns in all the Mariposas across the land.[36]

Three members of the Tory caucus, all from the Toronto region, saw themselves as leadership material. J. Earl Lawson, alone among them, had cabinet experience, though his was a brief three-month sojourn ended by the 1935 election. An MP since 1928, his political experience included assisting with the organization of the losing Ontario campaign of 1934, and directing the losing national campaign of 1935. His status received a boost when Bennett selected him to lead off the opposition criticism of the 1938 budget. Some, including Lawson, took that gesture to mean that he had Bennett's personal support to succeed him. The second Torontonian making a bid was Joseph Harris, the MP for East York since 1921. Harris was a no-nonsense businessman whose chief political accomplishment had been to chair the Commons Committee on railways, canals, and telegraph lines from 1930 to 1935. The third member of the Toronto triumvirate was the youthful Denton Massey, of the Massey-Harris Masseys. An MP only since 1935, he had served as Ontario campaign director under Lawson during that election. Perhaps Massey's proudest achievement was his leadership of the York Bible Class, a mass gathering of 2,000 young men held every Sunday in Toronto. The candidacies of all three of these men suffered a common deficiency, one noted by the Alberta Tory H.R. Milner: 'A Toronto man would not be very acceptable to the other parts of Canada.' Even without that problem, none of the three was considered a political dynamo.[37]

'I am convinced we have a good chance of winning the next election only if Arthur Meighen is at the helm,' wrote Mark Senn, the veteran

Ontario MP, to Arthur Meighen. Many in the party agreed. Even Manion was prepared to step aside if the former party leader decided to let his name stand. 'Not because I think he can win elections (that has been disproven three times, and I am told the feeling in Quebec has not changed),' Manion confided to his son, 'but because he is somewhat of an idol of the party because of his great debating ability, and would likely win the convention anyway.' Meighen, however, was definite. 'I am not in the field at all,' he wrote to some of the friends who were urging him to enter.[38]

For a time, W.D. Herridge was considered a possible candidate. The former minister to Washington had returned to his Ottawa law practice after the 1935 defeat, but he kept his profile high with a series of provocative speeches around the country, urging reform in the guise of state intervention. Some Conservatives, among them Hanson and Manion, thought Bennett would like to pass the mantle of leadership to his brother-in-law, if he could. Such an event was highly unlikely. Herridge, a former Liberal, was not popular in the party, both for his outspoken ways and for his privileged access to Bennett. 'Herridge is hopeless,' said Milner to Meighen, and most Conservatives agreed.[39]

Another outsider considering a run at the leadership was H.H. Stevens. By 1938, the Reconstruction Party he had led was little more than a mailing list in his parliamentary office. Many of his key advisers, men such as Warren Cook, Tom Lisson, Jacques Cartier, and Harold Daly, urged him to seize the opportunity occasioned by Bennett's retirement to make a bid for the leadership that had eluded him in the early months of 1935. 'The Conservative Party would be the proper medium for you to carry out your plans,' Cook assured him. Stevens was initially sceptical. Bennett, he knew, was still bitterly opposed to him, and would do everything possible to block his chances. Other prominent Conservatives felt the same way. Furthermore, Stevens had his own pride: 'I cannot and indeed will not go to the door seeking admission.' Nevertheless, Stevens could not help but be interested, particularly when Cook arranged a meeting for him with Sir Edward Beatty to discuss the leadership situation. Lisson cranked up his publicity machine one more time, to distribute copies of a speech Stevens was to deliver on 22 June at the Royal York Hotel in Toronto. 'We want to build up interest immediately to a point where the newspapers take note of every word you utter until the big convention is over,' he informed Stevens. Meanwhile, Jacques Cartier was utilizing his organizational talents in Quebec. On 29 June, Stevens received a telegram: 'Les conservateurs de la division électorale fédérale Rosemount-Maisonneuve réunis en assemblée pour choisir leurs délégués à la convention nationale conservatrice ... vous ont choisi unanimement délégué [The Conservatives in the federal riding of Rosemount-Maisonneuve, meeting to choose their delegates for the national Conservative convention, have unanimously elected you].' The odds were still long that the Conservatives would select as their leader the very man blamed by many for their recent electoral disaster, but at least Stevens had a ticket to get into the convention.[40]

For those, like Meighen, who were unhappy with all the likely candidates from Ottawa, a search of the rest of the country turned up only two real prospects. The first of these was Murdoch MacPherson, the Saskatchewan Tory who had come to Ottawa in 1935 to set up the machinery to administer the Farmers' Creditors' Arrangement Act. From 1929 to 1934 he had served as attorney-general in the Anderson government, adding the duties of provincial treasurer in 1931. As a lawyer, a well-decorated war veteran, and a westerner with Cape Breton roots, MacPherson possessed many of the symbolic traits desirable in a candidate. Westerners at the March 1938 conference had touted him as a very viable candidate. However, his association with the Anderson government's restrictive school legislation limited his appeal in Quebec. Furthermore, he was not in good health, either physically or financially. Finally, he was angry at the lack of support by wealthy eastern Tories for the Saskatchewan Conservatives, and accused them, in a bitter letter to Bennett, of funding the provincial Liberals instead.[41]

Believing that MacPherson's 'health would never stand the murderous experience' of Conservative leadership, Meighen turned his eyes on Sidney Smith, the youthful president of the University of Manitoba. Smith was another westerner with Nova Scotia roots. Meighen believed that, in addition to his proven talents as administrator, speaker, and debater, he would possess 'a tremendous advantage in coming from the outside, uncontaminated (as viewed by the public) with previous political programmes and affiliations.' Meighen's co-conspirators in the attempt to start a boom for Smith were Senator McRae, the journalist Grattan O'Leary, and Henry Borden. Manion was actually approached to go west and persuade Smith to consider the leadership, an honour that Manion declined. He typified the plot as 'a great running around by some in search for another white hope ... some entirely unknown man (professor preferred!) [who] would not smell of past associations.' Meighen eventually dropped the idea, when it became clear that Smith would not even carry much support from Manitoba itself.[42]

Inevitably, a number of Conservatives tried to persuade Bennett to succeed himself. Some observers were convinced that was the very thing he planned to do. 'I got the idea in Ottawa,' J.W. Dafoe wrote to a colleague on 9 June, 'that the drive for R.B. to succeed himself is now on with his connivance and assistance.' Even Meighen was not sure Bennett would keep to his retirement plans, prefacing a letter to a party insider with the phrase 'if Mr. Bennett does not contest.' Bennett continued to deny such aspirations, citing doctor's orders. Yet, in the House of Commons, he was a virtual whirlwind of activity. Many prominent Conservatives urged him to reconsider, among them R.B. Hanson and Senator Dennis, publisher of the Halifax *Herald*.[43]

As the delegates headed to Ottawa, then, there were really eight possible candidates. Manion, Lawson, Harris, and Massey were openly available. MacPherson, Stevens, Meighen, and Bennett were publicly denying any intention to run, though each had a noisy group of supporters, eager to draft him for service to the party. Of the declared candidates, Manion was the odds-on favourite. Of the undeclared candidates, only Meighen and Bennett were thought to possess sufficient appeal with the delegates to threaten Manion's commanding lead.[44]

The negative reaction by the Quebec delegation to Meighen's keynote address on Commonwealth defence ended any hopes the Meighen backers had of persuading their idol to stand. Meighen, who really did not want the job, was certainly not about to take on the leadership of a party divided by his very presence as its head. As an Acadian delegate put it, 'he is a "red flag to a bull" to the French Canadians.' Stevens, too, declined to run, even though he had earlier stated to one supporter, 'my being at the convention will probably result in my standing for leader.' It became clear that his candidacy would not attract many votes. Hanson's reaction was typical of many delegates. 'I was glad to see Mr. Stevens return to the Party,' he wrote after the convention, 'but he will not be able to dominate things, because those of us who suffered from his activities in 1935 are not apt to accept him soon.'[45]

A major effort was made to persuade Bennett to offer himself for the leadership again. Howard Ferguson was a prominent figure in the draft-Bennett movement. Herridge, too, favoured such a move, though he had little sway in the party. The retiring leader was apparently ready to consider standing again, but only if the other candidates would bow out in his favour, making the selection unanimous. Lawson, Harris, and Massey were reported ready to comply, but the front runner,

Manion, was understandably opposed to a move designed to block his own accession. Bennett's banquet address on the first evening, and powerful farewell speech the next afternoon, drew a strong response from English-Canadian delegates, but, like Meighen, Bennett was given the cold shoulder by francophone Quebec delegates. After the latter speech many of the Québécois, who had sat on their hands during Bennett's dramatic appeal for a show of support, ostentatiously removed bilingual Manion buttons from their pockets and pinned them on. Bennett's name was not placed in nomination that evening. On the following day, his supporters, spearheaded by Ferguson, made one last attempt to get the other candidates to retire in Bennett's favour. Less than an hour before voting was to begin, Meighen was called to Bennett's room. The retiring leader was on the verge of entering the race! Meighen persuaded him such a move would be unwise, unfair, and, perhaps most important, unsuccessful. 'You took the proper course on Thursday,' Meighen informed Bennett a few days later. 'Things had gone too far.'[46]

MacPherson was aware of his potential favourite-son support from western delegates, but he came to the convention apparently prepared to nominate Earl Lawson for the leadership. If either Meighen or Bennett had a change of mind and ran, he would support that man, as doubtless Lawson would have, too. MacPherson had no organization, not even a picture of himself for the press. His wife was home in Saskatchewan. He was much impressed by Meighen's Tuesday speech on the defence issue, and dismayed at the attempts by the other candidates to evade the question. 'From what I could learn,' he later recollected, 'there was an inclination on the part of all to expect certain support from Quebec which had to be catered to. At midnight I agreed definitely to stand.' His last-minute candidacy did not really take hold, other than with a few westerners, until Wednesday evening, when the nominees made their speeches.[47]

'I was thrilled yesterday by the speech of a former Prime Minister of this Dominion,' MacPherson told the perspiring delegates at the end of a long, hot evening of speeches, 'and I say to you to-night – because you are entitled to know – where he stood yesterday I stand now.' With that simple declaration, MacPherson threw down the gauntlet to the party. There would be no mistaking his views on defence or any other important issue. He endorsed wholeheartedly the Bennett reform program, specifically citing unemployment insurance, a contributory pension plan, and labour legislation. He supported the amending of the constitution to enable the national government to deal effectively with nation-wide problems. He called for 'some re-writing of the National Policy' to benefit primary producers as well as labour and industry. He ended his speech with an eloquent plea for action by the Conservative party: 'It is all very well for us to pass resolutions; it is all very well for us to elect a leader; but unless we proceed on a crusade throughout the length and breadth of this country we shall be defeated at the next election - and we shall deserve to be defeated.' It was the speech of the evening, and it sparked a strong movement of delegates to the MacPherson camp.[48]

Despite his protestations to the contrary, Manion's campaign was well organized. A headquarters for Manion supporters had been established in the Château Laurier. The three men jointly in charge were Georges Héon, dominant figure in the Quebec delegation; Errick Willis, Conservative leader in Manitoba; and W.J.P. MacMillan, former premier of Price Edward Island. Representing Quebec, the West, and the Maritimes, respectively, they neatly balanced Manion's own Ontario roots. Supporters were urged to wear the bilingual Manion buttons, complete with his picture. 'Manion is the man,' they read. 'C'est Manion qu'il nous faut.' The weakness in the Manion campaign was supposed to be his reliance on Orange Ontario and the Quebec bloc, two elements thought to be mutually antagonistic. Manion was aware of his vulnerability, and he interpreted Meighen's opening-day speech as a direct attempt to drive a wedge into his support. 'Much ill feeling was stirred up re Imperial relations,' he stated later, 'all with the object of either driving the Ontario vote away from me or driving out the Fr. [sic] vote.' In his own speech, Manion stressed the need for party harmony and national unity, of following 'the example of Macdonald and Cartier.' He combined this with a call for economic reform, an attack on unemployment, a forthright rejection of railway unification, and a declaration of independence from the big interests. It was not the best speech of his career, but it held his coalition of supporters together.[49]

Not so fortunate were the threesome from Toronto. Neither Harris, Massey, nor Lawson ignited a fire in his audience. After the close of the evening session, with the words of MacPherson ringing in their ears, supporters of the three Toronto candidates began to reconsider their position. Those who were interested in stopping Manion concluded that MacPherson offered the most likely opportunity. Lawson was particularly hard hit by defections, for he had attracted much of the latent Bennett and Meighen support that was opposed to Manion.[50]

In the end, Manion's Ontario Orangemen stuck with him. Combined with what *Le Devoir* estimated as a 90 per cent–solid Quebec delegation, these two blocks gave Manion a commanding lead on the first ballot. Willis in Manitoba and MacMillan in Prince Edward Island brought some support with them. MacPherson believed he carried Alberta and Saskatchewan almost unanimously, and won a majority of support in the other two western provinces. His campaign also drew considerable support in Ontario and the Maritimes, but precious little from Quebec, whose delegates had received his speech coolly. The support for Harris, Massey, and Lawson doubtless came largely from Ontario, particularly the Toronto region, where they were best known. Aggregate totals indicate most of their support switched to MacPherson on the second ballot, but Manion was so close to a majority that, by gaining just one-third of the freed-up votes, he received more than enough to be elected the new party leader.[51]

The key ingredients in Manion's victory had been his popularity with the English-speaking rank and file, his symbolic appeal to Quebec, and his campaign organization, which was the best at the convention. MacPherson's drive, while dramatic, began too late to surmount Manion's lead, a lead largely accumulated before the convention had even begun. The value of Manion's organization, with its buttons and hospitality suites and regional coordinators, was that it helped to cement together his coalition of delegates in the face of divisive appeals from others. Not even the opposition of his two illustrious predecessors, Bennett and Meighen, sufficed to deny him the prize.

PROGNOSIS FOR THE FUTURE

'Unless the Party is united and a leader is chosen who is not reactionary in outlook, fortified by a policy in keeping with present day conditions,' John Diefenbaker had warned Denton Massey in June 1938, 'the Conservative party will pass out of existence.' In reality, the Conservative party, on the day after the 1938 convention, was not much further ahead than on the day after the disastrous 1935 election. True, it had a new leader, but the circumstances of his selection ensured his tenure would be a troubled one. Many of the most respected party elders, including two former prime ministers, had sought by every legitimate means available to deprive him of his victory. They were not likely to be reconciled easily to his leadership. True, Stevens was back in the party fold with his diminished following, but Herridge had departed in anger, soon to start up a new reform movement. True, the party had developed a new platform, but at the cost of divisive battles on the critical issues of defence, railway unification, and economic reform. Most of the policy statements were tired clichés and empty platitudes. True, the party had developed elaborate plans for organization and publicity, but, as Manion well knew, 'the money bags [were] largely behind Beatty and [railway] unification.' Without funds to implement them, the new plans would amount to very little.[52]

Robert J. Manion was an able field commander in the ongoing partisan battles of Parliament Hill and the campaign hustings. He was not a commander-in-chief to measure up to Macdonald or Borden – or even to Meighen or Bennett. The misgivings of the latter two regarding his candidacy were not based simply on petty jealousy. The good doctor from Fort William never backed away from a political scrap. 'Fighting Bob' he certainly was. But, in terms of vision, drive, talent – the capacity to seize the reins and inspire a team to rise above itself – he was not of the first rank. His victory was attributable largely to the absence of any other candidate acceptable to an assertive Quebec delegation weary of several decades of impotence and neglect by the federal Conservative party. In terms of ideology, Manion was on the reform side of the party, much like Stevens, though without the moral idealism. Dr Manion was a practical politician, however, and likely to agree that everyone in politics had his price. On the very day he accepted the party leadership, this would-be prime minister backtracked on one of his fundamental campaign themes. 'Last night,' he began, 'I said it was time the Conservative party should take off the label that one heard put on it – that the Conservative party was the servant of big interests.' So far so good, but then came the punch line: 'By that I did not mean big business.'[53] Poor Manion was destined to spend much of his short time as party leader trying to convince Canada's business community that he was their true ally, while simultaneously attempting to persuade farmers, workers, and the unemployed that he was really their champion. The task was beyond him.

One sage, though biased, observer of the Canadian political scene neatly summed up the overall partisan significance of the National Conservative Convention. On the night of 7 July 1938, after mulling over the events of the last four days, Mackenzie King confided prophetically to his diary: 'Liberalism should be able to retain power in Canada for some years to come.'[54]

9 'We Have Made Mistakes': The Legacy of the Bennett Years

'This dinner is by way of tribute to Mr. Bennett,' said Arthur Meighen as he began a testimonial speech at the Royal York Hotel in Toronto, 'a demonstration of esteem to a very eminent Canadian who has already done a life's work and is leaving to reside abroad.' The date was 16 January 1939. As the storm clouds of war gathered over Europe, several hundred of Canada's most prominent citizens assembled in the Ontario capital to honour a former prime minister who was about to leave his native land for permanent residence – or was it exile? – in Great Britain. Meighen, himself a former prime minister and leader of the Conservative party, had crossed swords with Bennett several times in the past, but, on this occasion, he was happy to mimic Mark Antony and praise the fallen Caesar.

We sometimes hear it said: 'Oh, Mr. Bennett was defeated. His party was crushed. Its members in the House of Commons are few. He failed as a leader of Canada.' This reasoning I dispute ... I think R.B. Bennett did a splendid job as Prime Minster, and I do not think it argues in the least to the contrary that he met defeat at the hands of the voters of Canada. I go further and say this: that in our Dominion where sections abound, a Dominion of races, of classes and of creeds, of many languages and many origins, there are times when no Prime Minister can be true to the nation he has sworn to serve, save at the temporary sacrifice of the party he is appointed to lead. Without a question there never was a Prime Minister who could have done so in the years when Mr. Bennett was in office ... If anyone tells me that fidelity to party and fidelity to country are always compatible, or that the wisdom of mere numbers is the wisdom of heaven, then I tell him that he loves applause far more than he loves truth. Loyalty to the ballot box is not necessarily loyalty to the nation; it is not even loyalty to the multitude.

'Take that, Mr Mackenzie King!' he might have added, on behalf of both Bennett and himself.

Meighen even saluted his Conservative successor for the radical-sounding reform policies that had upset many Canadians, himself included, when first broadcast as a dramatic new Conservative program:

There are many excellent citizens who have still something of a horror of what is called the New Deal programme of 1935. I am a long way from being a visionary radical, but I know something about that legislation, and make the statement that in all its important features it was sound and timely. Our guest will not be offended when I say that what a lot of people have still in their minds like a nightmare is not the legislation, which was enlightened, but the speeches, which frightened. The Statutes, indeed, received almost unanimous approval from both Houses of Parliament.

Few political leaders of the 1930s were able to hold the affection of their people. R.B. Bennett, who had been swept into power in 1930 on a tide of discontent, was swept out in 1935 on a stronger tide. Meighen, for one, felt the public verdict would again be reversed: 'The guest of tonight must not leave our shores with any consciousness in his heart of failure as directing head of this country. There was no failure in that capacity. He certainly cannot leave our shores without knowing that he has the admiration of many, the gratitude of some, and the respect of all.' Meighen agreed with Grattan O'Leary, the prominent Conservative journalist who had written a year earlier, 'History will be more kind to Bennett than his times.'[1]

History's verdict has not yet been reversed. The prevailing notion is still that of J.W. Dafoe, editor of the liberal *Winnipeg Free Press*, and arch-opponent of all that R.B. Bennett suggested or stood for. He summed up his assessment of the Conservative leader in this acrid note to his parliamentary reporter, Grant Dexter, in 1932: 'Mr. Bennett is not a great man. I think Laski hit him off very neatly when he said he was a little man with a big manner. It is perhaps fortunate that his talents are limited because with his delusions of grandeur and his various obsessions he would certainly wreck this country if his abilities matched his ambitions.' Bennett's overbearing, authoritarian manner was masterfully captured in an editorial cartoon by Arch Dale, also of the *Winnipeg Free*

Press, that first appeared in 1931. Entitled 'My Government,' it depicts a balding, pince-nezed, imperious-looking R.B. Bennett playing the roles of every single person at a cabinet session, from chairman of the meeting to assembled ministers, to waiting servants, to portraits on the wall.[2] A starring role in a one-man band – this is the sort of image that prevails when the Right Honourable Richard Bedford Bennett's name comes up.

A few contemporary observers felt differently. Robert Borden, Conservative leader when Bennett first won election to the House of Commons in 1911, had on numerous occasions endured the prickly side of the Calgary MP's personality. Nevertheless, Borden had also seen evidence of immense talents in this blustery talkative westerner. At the time of Bennett's crushing defeat in 1935, Borden set down his impressions: 'His splendid ability, his keen grasp of general conditions, both national and international, his complete devotion to public duty and to the welfare of our country, the admirable resourcefulness and fine courage with which he has faced the overwhelming difficulties of the past five years, entitle him to the respect, admiration and gratitude of all right-thinking Canadians.' Even this sincere tribute from one who knew personally the pressures of high elective office was balanced by an admission that Bennett's character flaws were fully as leonine as his strengths.

Bennett might be described as a man of unbalanced and erratic brilliancy; arbitrary, but lacking decision in important incidents of public affairs; impulsive, vacillating, unable to work with colleagues, capricious. His faults have been those of the qualities with which nature has endowed him. In the use of time, he has been utterly lacking in system and in any sense of proportion. His manner towards his colleagues and towards the press has been, on occasion, abrupt and even insulting. On other occasions, perhaps within a few days, he greets the same persons with utmost graciousness.[3]

What Bennett perceived as verbal jousting often came across as crushing put-downs by the recipients of his sarcastic quips. His inability to appreciate the importance in politics of glad-handing and back-slapping, even when he was not in a good mood – which was often during his time as leader – was, at once, both a petty and a profound failing. Petty, because when viewed individually, each incident paled in significance compared to the awesome problems facing the country. Profound, because they seemed to denote a lack of caring by the prime minister for the human side of public affairs. 'The sun never sets on the day on which the Prime Minister hasn't insulted some good and loyal Conservative,' C.H. Cahan complained.[4] Mackenzie King flattered the vanity of Liberals with whom he was in profound disagreement. R.B. Bennett sorely wounded the feelings of Conservatives whose views he shared.

Bennett combined arrogance and insensitivity towards others with an extreme vulnerability to apprehended slights or criticism from those around him. Andrew Maclean, secretary to the prime minister for four years, observed that 'he would rather do almost anything than admit he was wrong.' It was completely in character for him to declare, as he did in his farewell address to the Conservative party at the 1938 convention, that he would not change anything about his time as leader. 'My friends,' he proclaimed, 'I have nothing to regret and nothing to retract – not a thing.'[5] Occasionally, in private, with long-time acquaintances, Bennett would let down this guard – even admit to a bit of human fallibility. Shortly before his retirement, Bennett managed to combine humility, hurt, and defiance in this comment to Brigadier-General A.E. Ross, the former Conservative MP from Kingston: 'I am not unaware of my own limitations. I have made many mistakes, but I served this country as disinterestedly as any man who ever occupied public office, and I have never expected more than loyalty from those with whom I was associated. That I did not receive it may perhaps be a criticism of myself.'[6] Introspection did not come easily to Bennett. He preferred to be active, busily engaged in doing things, whether dictating replies to all his correspondence; speaking to minor civil servants personally on the telephone; mastering complex details of technical amendments to existing legislation; or dominating proceedings in caucus, cabinet, and Commons. He was by nature a commander, not a coordinator.

Shortly after Bennett's death, his personal secretary, Alice Millar, began assembling his private papers from England and Ottawa, to be deposited at the University of New Brunswick. 'She is not satisfied with the judgment of current history regarding Bennett,' a former cabinet colleague, R.B. Hanson, noted to Grote Stirling, another Tory veteran of the Bennett era. Subsequent history has not been particularly kind in its assessment of Bennett's leadership. In a 1956 study of the Conservative party, for instance, John R. Williams declared that Bennett 'was more responsible than any other individual for the decline of the Conservative party.' Among his many alleged sins he had split the party, ignored the organization, quarrelled with everyone, and stamped Conservatism for a generation with his own wealthy, reactionary image.[7] While these accusations did contain considerable truth, still, such criticism is just too one-sided. From 1927 to 1930, Bennett was virtually a model party leader. He tended the organization, motivated the caucus, and stumped the country with energy and flair. As a campaigner, Bennett far outshone King in 1930. It was after attaining power that Bennett seriously neglected his party. In this failing, however, he was merely duplicating the complacent attitude of King following the 1926 election.

'History,' Donald Creighton observed, 'is the record of an encounter between character and circumstance.'[8] The devastating effects of the Great Depression on the fate of Bennett and the Conservative party cannot be overlooked in assessing his performance as leader. The unemployment crisis during the winter of 1929–30 helped defeat the Liberals. Five years later, with conditions immeasurably worse, the electorate understandably turned again on the government of the day, this time even more decisively. The same pattern was repeated at the provincial level across Canada. In fairness, also, Bennett cannot be blamed for the countless blunders committed by the Conservative party after his retirement, which contributed to such a long stretch in opposition. It is true that the party he turned over to Manion was sorely divided on several issues, but such had also been the case when Meighen laid down the leadership mantel in 1926. It is true, too, that Bennett had not understood Quebec, but who among his predecessors after Macdonald and Cartier had? The tragedy in this case was that Bennett had been given by the unusual economic circumstances in 1930 a rare opportunity to overcome the party's isolation from Quebec, and he was unable to exploit the opening beyond one election.

If his stewardship of the party has attracted widespread criticism, Bennett's tenure as prime minister had fared scarcely better. 'It has been said of Richard Bedford Bennett that he destroyed his party while saving his country,' H. Blair Neatby wrote in 1972. 'Certainly he left the Conservative party shattered. It is less certain that he had saved his country.'[9] Measured against the standards Bennett had recklessly laid out in the victorious 1930 campaign, his years in office were an abject failure. The Depression he had promised to solve was far worse in 1935. It should be noted, though, that the Depression stymied the best efforts of most of the world's leaders. It is no disgrace that Bennett could not do better. He was not Canada's greatest prime minster, but his record certainly has its strong points. Among these are such lasting Canadian institutions as the Bank of Canada, the Canadian Broadcasting Corporation, and the Wheat Board. Although they are often taken for granted today, their initiation by Bennett in the 1930s represented significant innovations in three key areas of the government-business relationship. To that list of reforms might be added the Natural Products Marketing Act, the Farmers' Creditors' Arrangement Act, unemployment insurance, the labour-protection bills, the Dominion Housing Act, the Prairie Farm Rehabilitation Act, and the Economic Council. Not all of them survived intact the transition to Mackenzie King's Liberal administration, but all were directed to solve key problems evident in the 1930s. Furthermore, the Bennett government's willingness to incur budget deficits, its modest attempts at currency expansion, and its pioneering ventures into supply management were all laudatory efforts at promoting economic recovery, particularly in view of the conventional wisdom favouring balanced budgets, sound money, and *laissez-faire*. Was Bennett a serious reformer? Yes, if his record is considered in the context of his party and his times. Was he a radical? No, he was not. His goal throughout was to preserve the essentials of the established capitalist order, an order that rewarded talent and effort but also cared for the helpless. Was he a reactionary? Yes, that too, when judged in terms of his 'iron heel' suppression of extraparliamentary political dissent.

Bennett summarized his own understanding of the purpose of government in a speech delivered at the Ottawa convention's opening banquet in July 1938. 'One purpose, and one purpose only, can make this party an instrument for the good of Canada,' he proclaimed. 'That purpose is to use the collective power for the general good.' In that sense, Bennett's repressive measures against the relief camp strikers and his sponsorship of unemployment insurance and a minimum wage were consistent. In each case, the power of the state was being actively utilized to combat a perceived evil. Out of the limelight, Bennett dipped into his own resources time and time again to aid ordinary Canadians whose misfortunes became known to him. 'During the last year,' he informed a correspondent in March 1936, 'my Secretary and I have sent small sums to one thousand people, scattered over every Province in Canada, to try to help them battle with conditions over which they have no control.' Even as he directed the government's battle against the Great Depression, Bennett took time to assist individual victims financially. He had done so from his earliest days as prime minister. This compassionate impulse was a side of Bennett that he generally kept well hidden from public scrutiny. While helpful in any assessment of the man's worth, it does not constitute the grounds upon which the prime minister would wish to be judged. He wrote his own epitaph, unknowingly, in a letter hastily dictated in mid-July 1935, just prior to the federal election campaign of that year: 'I have given my best to the country during the last five years, and I believe there is written a record of which no one need be ashamed, although it is quite probable that we have made mistakes as all poor human creatures must.' In a rare moment of personal introspection, Bennett accurately summarized five years in the prime minster's office.[10]

In his memoirs the prominent Liberal, 'Chubby' Power, recollected that, in the late 1920s and 1930s, 'Bennett *was* the Conservative party.'[11] For over a decade this did often seem to be the case. However, the Conservative party was greater than any single person, even one so domineering as R.B. Bennett. The party had chosen him to be its leader at the 1927 Winnipeg convention, and it nudged him into retirement at the Ottawa conference of March 1938, selecting his successor at a full convention several months later. The sinking realization that, despite all the money, time, and effort he had expended on its behalf, the party was not truly his, and could take away as well as give a position of responsibility, left him embittered at the end. But, just as Bennett was not, in himself, the whole party, so an analysis of Bennett's leadership does not constitute a complete assessment of the Conservative party in this era.

Measured in terms of voter support, the Conservative party in 1938 was considerably weaker than it had been in 1926. At the time of Meighen's resignation, the Conservatives were strong in the Maritimes, Ontario, and British Columbia, but weak in Quebec and the Prairies. Twelve years later, the party was weak everywhere but anglophone Montreal, central and eastern Ontario, and the interior of British Columbia. The ninety-one seats won by Meighen in 1926 compared to only forty by Bennett in 1935. Provincially, the Tories had ruled three provinces in 1926: Nova Scotia, New Brunswick, and Ontario. At the time of Bennett's retirement in 1938, they did not govern a single province, unless Maurice Duplessis's Union Nationale administration in Quebec could be considered a loose affiliate of Canada Conservatism. At their peak in 1931, the Tories had ruled in Ottawa and five out of nine provinces. How the mighty had fallen!

The frank advice offered by party elder Sir Joseph Flavelle to his party in 1927 was just as appropriate a decade later. 'I can see no reason why the Conservative party would expect to return to power for two or three parliaments, unless through blunders of their opponents,' he had written to Senator Rufus Pope in January of that year. 'Conservatives have now to prove they have the needed courage and resource [*sic*] to rebuild, and the patience to wait.' Flavelle had advised the party then to rediscover its principles, clarify its ideas, and broaden its base of support. Above all, he urged Conservatives to accept and understand the new Canada of pulp mills, mines, and automobiles, being built upon the old Canada of prairie wheat, transcontinental railways, and sheltered eastern industry. 'A declaration of faith which expresses sincere conviction must precede organization,' he had recommended. 'Without it, organization is merely a mechanical activity.'[12]

Flavelle and a few others of his day had recognized that Canada was in the midst of a great transformation, from a primarily rural and agricultural society to one that was ever more urban and industrialized. This complex process is often referred to as 'modernization,' involving, as it does, other significant changes such as mass education, secularization, and rising consumer expectations.[13] In Canada's case, two other factors acted to magnify the impact of change. Canadian society was absorbing a large number of immigrants from other cultures. Furthermore the economy was being reoriented from a primarily East-West basis with strong links to Great Britain, to a North-South axis more and more dominated by the United States. These immense changes brought new benefits, but also new stresses to Canada. A politics still based upon the National Policy paradigm of 1878 and 1891 was an obsolescent politics, less and less able to meet the problems generated by the political environment. The Conservative party must adapt or die.

Canada during the 1930s, then, was a modernizing country undergoing a severe economic and social crisis – largely a crisis of distribution, since the system was capable of producing goods and services in relative abundance. The Conservative party found itself in power, forced to cope with problems it barely understood. Its record of adaptation to the reality of Canadian modernization during the twelve years under study was decidedly mixed. One key analytical benchmark, in terms of policy, is the degree of acceptance by a party in a modernizing society of the concepts of 'managed economy' and 'welfare state.' In each case, *laissez-faire* is renounced in favour of an activist state that attempts to create, or at least enhance, economic growth while redistributing sufficient of the national income to ensure an acceptable standard of living for every citizen.[14] Under Bennett's leadership, the Conservative party advanced

along this road a considerable distance, though not without great trepi-
dation. The 1927 convention platform contained a lengthy social-welfare resolution, much of which the party turned into legislation as part
of the New Deal. More federal funds for unemployment relief and old-
age pensions, while perhaps given grudgingly at a time of fiscal stringency, nevertheless indicated acceptance by the Conservatives of a social-welfare role for Ottawa. Furthermore, the Conservative government
went considerably beyond tariff protection and railway subsidies in its
attempts to foster economic recovery. The aforementioned Bank of
Canada, Wheat Board, and Canadian Radio Broadcasting Commission,
for instance, were all tangible proofs of a modernizing state. Nevertheless, in the two key areas of fiscal and monetary policy, most Conservatives, including Prime Minister Bennett and the minister of finance,
Edgar Rhodes, remained committed in principle to the ideals of a balanced budget and a sound currency. The most influential advocate of
the deliberate manipulation of fiscal and monetary policy to sustain
and enhance economic growth was John Maynard Keynes of Great
Britain. He did not publish his General Theory until 1936, however, so
his ideas had not had time to penetrate the consciousness of many
professors in Canada, let alone practising politicians.

A second indicator of adaptation is the party's electoral appeal to
urban voters, the fastest-growing segment of a modernizing population.
The Conservative party, which had traditionally gained its strongest
support from the major urban areas, saw its share of the popular vote
in Canadian cities plummet from around 50 per cent, in 1925, 1926, and
1930, to less than 30 per cent, in 1935. Their share of the non-urban vote
declined also, but not as drastically. This discouraging weakness with
urban voters would continue for several more elections.[15] In 1935, the
competition from the new CCF and Reconstruction parties was obviously
a contributing factor, as they offered competing programs for urban
labour and small business voters.

Finally, in terms of organizational capability, the Conservative party
had seemed in 1930 to be adapting well to a technological age. The innovative and effective use of the radio, the Addressograph mailing
system, and the phonograph was a significant contributing factor in
the Tory victory. Just as important, General A.D. McRae had put together
for the first time a viable national organization that was far more than
the sum of its provincial parts. This Conservative advantage was thrown
away, shortly after the 1930 election, just when the Liberals were form-
ing the National Liberal Federation to provide themselves with the sort

of effective national organization the Conservatives were discarding.[16] It would be many years before the Conservatives equalled the innovative efficiency of their 1930 organizational machine.

In the face of bewildering changes, then, the Conservative party did moderately well in adapting itself to modernization during the Bennett years. The process of reorienting its policies was begun, though accompanied by much internal disagreement and some backsliding at the end. Similarly, modernizing the party organization was begun, and well begun, but then largely abandoned for lack of money and the absence of support from the leader, until the eleventh hour. In appealing to voters, the Conservatives in 1935 lost even more of their urban strength than rural, a bad omen when urbanization is a key aspect of modernization. Furthermore, the presence of vigorous new third parties competing with the two traditional ones for the right to govern was a direct challenge to the Conservatives' very survival in the long run.

It is all very well to criticize Canadian Conservatives for being slow to recognize and adapt to the transforming changes of urbanization and industrialization. However, it is hardly fair to criticize a Conservative party for being conservative. By habit, by preference, by their very nature, we would expect members of a Conservative party to be cautious about change, hesitant about reform, sceptical about progress. While party lines in Canada have never been so clearly demarcated as to include all liberals in the Liberal party, and all conservatives in the Conservative party, still the tendency has been for the two parties to lean in the direction their names would indicate. Consequently, a Conservative party would include as one of its guiding principles a spirited, though discriminating, defence of the established social order. While the reformer can see many things that need changing, the traditionalist can cite just as many things that ought to be preserved. Not all new ideas are good; not all old ideas are valuable. The continuing dialectic struggle between the proponents of change and the champions of stability, at its best, ensures a creative adaptation to an evolving future, while preserving a valuable heritage from the past.[17]

Successful Canadian parties since the days of John A. Macdonald in pre-Confederation Canada have been very broad-based coalitions. The very name chosen by Macdonald for his party, 'Liberal-Conservative,' unites these two basic tendencies in a hyphenated title. This same name was utilized by the party during the Bennett era. Not surprisingly, the party duplicated within its own ranks the ideological debate between right and left that has just been described. In the vernacular of the interwar years, it was a struggle between reaction and reform.

While always present to some degree, this battle came to the fore in the three-way struggle for control of the party acted out in 1934–5. Bennett, as a prime beneficiary of the old capitalist order, was not inclined to experiment with new ideas when a proper application of the old ones seemed likely to restore prosperity. But he was unafraid of the state, and quite prepared to use its power actively in the areas of economics, culture, or social welfare whenever the need was evident, whether it was to aid wheat farmers, protect Canada's independent nationality, or provide relief to the destitute. His paternalist conservatism contrasted with C.H. Cahan's *laissez-faire* conservatism. Intervention for business in the form of tariffs Cahan accepted readily – this was the traditional National Policy. Beyond that he was not disposed to go. In Bennett's New Deal he professed to see dangerous Marxist principles. Different again was Stevens's brand of populist conservatism. As defender of and spokesman for small, independent entrepreneurs, he sought to tame the large corporations that both Bennett and Cahan had served. Stevens best exemplified the reform wing, while Cahan represented the forces of reaction in the party. And Bennett – he stood for both, a progressive conservative before that apparent oxymoron was coined to describe the party to which they all belonged.[18]

The Conservative party, if it is to be successful in Canadian electoral politics, must weave all three strands of conservatism into the fabric of a unified public appeal, for each strand is historically legitimate and capable of generating large numbers of supporters. Bennett succeeded at this task in 1930, but failed abysmally in 1935. He did not create these contrasting ideological approaches within the party, but then his authoritarian leadership style was not suited to conciliating them either. In the decisive election battle of 1935, Stevens were leading a breakaway Reconstruction Party, while Cahan restricted his efforts to holding his own riding, possibly even hoping for a decisive Liberal victory to repudiate the reform programs of both Stevens and Bennett.

Certainly the harsh circumstances of the Great Depression contributed to the unravelling of the Conservative consensus. It had less to do with the Conservatives' inability to bridge the two solitudes of English-speaking and French-speaking Canada. The bridgehead of 1930, with 24 of 65 Quebec seats, and 45 per cent of the popular vote, was not defended, let alone expanded upon. In part the fault was Bennett's. He never really understood the politics of national unity in Canada. Minority groups and dissenting interests must be placated, not bullied into place. However, he inherited a party with a long history of indifference, even hostility, to French-Canadian interests. Furthermore, Bennett and the Conservatives were up against the political master himself in William Lyon Mackenzie King. As Frank Underhill grudgingly conceded, King was 'the only man in his day who could hold French and English together inside one party.'[19]

The most telling indictment against the Conservative party and government led by R.B. Bennett is that they lost touch with the people they meant to serve. Grattan O'Leary, veteran journalist with the pro-Conservative *Ottawa Journal*, and a perceptive observer of Canadian politics for several decades, penned this sad epitaph for the Bennett-led Tory administration in 1938:

Between 1930 and 1935 the Conservative Party, to the extent that it existed at all, was out of touch with its leader, and its leader out of touch with the people. Mr. Bennett, living between his office in the Parliament Buildings and his rooms in the Château Laurier, was remote from realities. He could be magnificent in Parliament. He could know what to do when England went off the gold standard ... He did not know what the people were saying, what they were thinking, what many of them were enduring. It was not that he was indifferent or callous. He was simply without facilities for knowing. Yet no leader of a national party in our day may live the life of a monastic, no matter what his integrity or his talents.[20]

The breakdown in understanding was partly Bennett's fault. It was also the fault of his cabinet, the caucus, and the extraparliamentary party. There was blame enough for all. In the end, the shareholders of Canada no longer had confidence in this board of directors. Bennett, who often used business analogies, surely understood.

Epilogue

To make the single meaning doubly clear
He ends the journey – as a British peer.[1]

Throughout his lengthy bachelor's life, R.B. Bennett had been truly devoted to two women: his mother, Henrietta, and his sister, Mildred.
The latter's marriage to William Herridge had not diminished the
genuine affection that passed between sister and brother. The untimely
death of Mildred in May 1938, coming on the heels of the party conference at which Bennett had announced his retirement from the Conservative leadership, had precipitated a personal crisis for him. What was
he to do with the remaining years of his life? The decision of the subsequent Conservative convention to choose his former cabinet colleague
Robert Manion as leader when Bennett had let it be known that he was
still available further embittered a proud, sensitive man. Rejection by
his party in Ottawa, coming on the heels of rejection by the voters in
1935, was more than he could take. Though he tried to cover his feelings,
they would seep out at odd moments. 'I have worked very hard,' he
had noted to a correspondent in February 1936, 'although I received no
thanks from the electorate.' A year later he wrote, almost pathetically,
'The results of the last election indicate that my services are no longer
required.' Though he said these things, the party leader really wanted
to be assured that his services were still required, his presence still
desired. It was a great blow to learn most of the party wanted him to
step down.[2]

On a trip to Britain in September 1938, Bennett arranged through his
long-time friend and fellow New Brunswick native Max Aitken, now
Lord Beaverbrook, to acquire a country estate there. He had made the

decision to retire to the mother country, turning his back in his final years on the country of his birth. To a Canadian journalist, he gave as his reason the belief that 'his activities of the past militate against his usefulness to Canada as a private citizen.' Most people at the time assumed the former prime minister went to Britain so he might accept an appointment to the House of Lords. In due course, Beaverbrook was able to arrange this matter for him, and R.B. Bennett became Viscount Bennett of Mickleham, Surrey. Although removed to Britain, Bennett retained his bitterness concerning the apparent ingratitude of Canadians, in general, and his own party, in particular. A query from Charlotte Whitton in 1939 as to whether he might return to Canada brought this sharp response:

Don't you think I was given a furlough by the Canadian people in 1935? They rejected me and all my plans and ideas and hopes. Hadn't I right to accept the views of doctors? I think I had. And for one with your intellect do you not think that you are already wrong in even suggesting that I will ever be missed to the extent of being thought of a few months from now? As for wanting me back that is sheer nonsense, Charlotte, and you must know it. They gave me a great 'send off' for many reasons. Some for 'conscience sake'; some for real regard; some glad to be rid of me. But it just became a bit of mob manifestation; Hosanna in the highest and 'Crucify Him Crucify Him' a week later.

The former Canadian prime minister lived out his remaining years in lonely comfort on his British estate, until death came on 27 June 1947.[3]

At the time of Bennett's passing, few of his Conservative contemporaries were still active in Canadian politics. His successor, R.J. Manion, had a short and inglorious career as party leader, much as Bennett had expected. After a decisive electoral defeat in 1940, in which Manion lost his own seat, the Conservative party let him know his leadership was no longer required. Bennett's predecessor, Arthur Meighen, attempted a political comeback in 1942, but a stunning by-election defeat rudely ended his leadership plans. C.H. Cahan and H.H. Stevens, the principals with Bennett in the struggle for control of the party's future direction in 1934–5, each sought re-election in 1940, but the voters rejected them both. By 1947, Cahan and Manion were deceased, while Meighen and Stevens were in retirement.

The national party was by this time led by John Bracken, the one provincial premier in Canada to survive the political devastation wrought by the Great Depression. The Manitoban had been heading a coalition of Progressives and Liberals, so, in deference to his wishes, the formal party name was altered to 'Progressive Conservative' in 1942. Three years later, the party again went down to defeat. Not long after Bennett's death, Bracken too was out of the leadership. His replacement was George Drew, Earl Rowe's successor as the Ontario party leader, and premier of that province for five years. Drew was no more successful than his predecessor, despite two election tries against a triumphant Liberal party now led by Mackenzie King's successor, Louis St Laurent. The Conservatives did not regain power in Ottawa until 1957, led this time by John Diefenbaker, the youthful leader of the Saskatchewan provincial party when Bennett retired in 1938. Significantly, this Prairie populist developed a great admiration for the Calgary Conservative, though initially he had misgivings. 'I felt that Mr. Bennett with his reputed millions could not hope to get the support of the average Canadian,' he stated in his memoirs. 'I was wrong.' Diefenbaker further declared that, over the years, he 'came to develop a profound appreciation of his courage and political vision.' Upon his selection as Saskatchewan provincial leader in 1936, Diefenbaker had promised the party a 'radical' program, radical 'in the sense that the reform programme of the Right Honourable R.B. Bennett was radical.'[4]

Diefenbaker, too, came and went. The party changed leaders so frequently, and with such acrimony, in the four decades following Bennett's retirement that it acquired its own academic diagnosis: The Tory Syndrome.[5] By the time Brian Mulroney seized the leadership prize in 1983, the old struggle between reaction and reform had taken an interesting twist. Under the imported titles of Thatcherism and Reaganomics, the laissez-faire principles of C.H. Cahan acquired a whole new respectability, though it is doubtful that many in the party had ever heard of him. State intervention of the sort advocated by H.H. Stevens and R.B. Bennett in the 1930s, and adopted as fundamental party policy in the intervening years, began to lose favour. It remained to be seen whether the party had learned it must not choose reaction or reform. To be successful, the Conservative party in Canada must be a party of reaction and reform.

Notes

PROLOGUE

1 Public Archives of Canada (PAC), MG 28 IV 2, Progressive Conservative (PC) Party Papers, vol. 239, Proceedings of the Convention of the National Conservative Party of Canada, 5–7 July 1938 (Convention Proceedings), 277–9; *Winnipeg Free Press*, Toronto *Globe and Mail*, *Vancouver Sun*, *Calgary Herald*, Montreal *Gazette*, and *Toronto Daily Star*, all 6–9 July 1938

CHAPTER 1

1 Election background is derived from three daily newspapers: Montreal *Gazette*, 13–15 Sept. 1926; Toronto *Globe*, 10–16 Sept. 1926; *Winnipeg Free Press*, 13–15 Sept. 1926.
2 Roger Graham, *Arthur Meighen, II: And Fortune Fled* (Toronto 1963), 452–77, describes the election and its result from Meighen's viewpoint. See also H. Blair Neatby, *William Lyon Mackenzie King, II: 1924–1932, The Lonely Heights* (Toronto 1963), 158–71.
3 Arthur Meighen, *Unrevised and Unrepented: Debating Speeches and Others* (Toronto 1949), 206
4 Frank H. Underhill, 'The Development of National Political Parties in Canada,' *In Search of Canadian Liberalism* (Toronto 1960), 24–30
5 Ibid., 33–7
6 Bernard Ostry, 'Conservatives, Liberals and Labour in the 1870s,' *Canadian Historical Review* 41 (June 1960): 93–127
7 H.G.J. Aitken, 'Defensive Expansion: The State and Economic Growth in Canada,' in W.T. Easterbrook and M.H. Watkins, eds., *Approaches to Canadian Economic History* (Toronto 1967), 203–10

8 Alastair Sweeny, *George-Etienne Cartier: A Biography* (Toronto 1976), stresses Cartier's equal, and at times overriding, role alongside Macdonald.
9 'The Loyalist in Canada ... creates a myth that helps him survive – he insists that he is British.' David V.J. Bell, 'The Loyalist Tradition in Canada,' in J.M Bumsted, ed., *Canadian History before Confederation: Essays and Interpretations* (Georgetown, ON, 1972), 210–29
10 M.C. Urquhart and K.A.H. Buckley, eds., *Historical Statistics of Canada* (Toronto 1965), 620
11 'Since the death of its first leader, Sir John A. Macdonald, in 1891, the Progressive Conservative party has been subject to recurring crises of internal conflict focused on its leadership': George C. Perlin, *The Tory Syndrome: Leadership Politics in the Progressive Conservative Party* (Montreal 1980), 1.
12 Robert Craig Brown, *Robert Laird Borden*, I: *1854–1914* (Toronto 1975), 129–35
13 Robert Craig Brown and Ramsay Cook, *Canada, 1896–1921: A Nation Transformed* (Toronto 1974), 328–9
14 John English, *The Decline of Politics: The Conservatives and the Party System, 1901–20* (Toronto 1977), 176
15 Roger Graham, *Arthur Meighen*, Canadian Historical Association (CHA) Booklet No. 16 (Ottawa 1968)
16 Graham, *Arthur Meighen*, II, 452–79

CHAPTER 2

1 The description of the convention is based on these sources: a / Public Archives of Canada (PAC), MG 28 IV 2, Progressive Conservative (PC) Party Papers, vol. 239, Verbatim Report: National Liberal-Conservative Association Convention (Verbatim Report), 10–12 Oct. 1927; b / John R. MacNicol, *The National Liberal-Conservative Convention* (Toronto 1930); c / Toronto *Globe*, 10–13 Oct. 1927; d / *Winnipeg Free Press*, 10–13 Oct. 1927; e / Winnipeg *Tribune*, 10–13 Oct. 1927.
2 Verbatim Report, 271
3 PAC, MG 27 III B 22, R.B. Hanson Papers, vol. 1, Hanson to Hon. I.R. Todd, 27 Sept. 1926
4 Cited in Roger Graham, *Arthur Meighen*, II: *And Fortune Fled* (Toronto 1963), 478
5 Public Archives of Nova Scotia (PANS), MG 2, E.N. Rhodes Papers, vol. 613, Rhodes to Hon. R.H. Pope, 14 Jan. 1927
6 PAC, MG 27 III F 9, H.M. Daly Papers, vol. 3, Daly to R.B. Bennett, 15 Sept. 1925
7 Queen's University Archives (QUA), Sir Joseph Flavelle Papers, Flavelle to Hon. R.H. Pope, 12 Jan. 1927

8 University of New Brunswick Archives (UNBA), R.B. Bennett Papers, reel 13, extract from Resolutions Passed at Ottawa Conference, 11 Oct. 1926

9 Archives of Ontario (AO), G. Howard Ferguson Papers, vol. 15, F.D.L. Smith to Ferguson, 20 June 1927

10 PAC, MG 26 I, Arthur Meighen Papers, vol. 108, Sir Thomas White to Meighen, 7 Oct. 1926

11 Ibid., vol. 67, John R. MacNicol Meighen, 29 Sept. 1926

12 MacNicol, *National Liberal-Conservative Convention*, 15

13 *Le Devoir*, 23 Feb. 1927, cited in Thomas C. Nesmith, 'R.B.Bennett and the Conservative Party in Quebec, 1927–1930,' MA thesis, Queen's University, 1975, 6. Guthrie, the interim party leader, stressed the symbolic importance of Winnipeg as the convention site in an interview with the Winnipeg *Tribune*, 6 Oct. 1927.

14 Bennett Papers, reel 13, List of Members of Special Committee, n.d.; ibid., Minutes of National Convention Committee (NCC), 22 Mar. and 7–8 Oct. 1927

15 M. Grattan O'Leary, 'The Rival Chiefs of Staff,' *MacLean's* 43 (1 July 1930): 8. Note that the contemporary spelling of *MacLean's* (with capital 'L') is used, rather than the post-1945, modern, usage (*Maclean's*). See also Ruth M. Bell, 'Conservative Party National Conventions, 1927–1956: Organization and Procedure,' MA thesis, Carleton University, 1965, 25–6.

16 Bennett Papers, reel 13, Minutes of NCC, 22 Feb. 1927 and 4 July 1927; vol. 10, Harold Daly to Hugh Guthrie, 2 July 1927

17 Ibid., reel 13, Minutes of NCC, 1 Sept. 1927. Significantly, the Dominion delegates-at-large were to be selected by McRae's organization committee, and not by MacNicol's Dominion Association. Later correspondence between MacNicol and Bennett revealed a continuing rift between MacNicol and members of the parliamentary caucus regarding convention arrangements. See ibid., vol. 957, MacNicol to Bennett, 17 Aug. 1935, and Bennett to MacNicol, 26 Aug. 1935.

18 Rhodes Papers, vol. 613, Liberal-Conservative Association of Ontario Circular, signed by John R. MacNicol, President, n.d.

19 Ibid., T.H. Blacklock to Rhodes, 5 May 1927

20 Bennett Papers, reel 13, Minutes of NCC, 4 July 1927; PC Party Papers, vol. 239, Chart: 'Women Delegates to 1927 Convention,' n.d.

21 Bennett Papers, reel 13, Minutes of NCC, 1 Sept. 1927

22 William Marchington, Toronto *Globe*, 11 Oct. 1927. A very good wage in 1930 was $30 a week. See Lita-Rose Betcherman, *The Little Band: The Clashes between the Communists and the Political and Legal Establishment in Canada, 1928–1932* (Ottawa 1982), 97.

23 Verbatim Report, 147

24 Bennett Papers, reel 13, Minutes of NCC, 22 Mar. 1927

25 Montreal *Star*, 12 Oct. 1927, cited in R. MacGregor Dawson, *The Government of Canada*, 5th ed., revised by Norman Ward (Toronto 1970), 489–90
26 Ferguson Papers, vol. 15, Ferguson to Smeaton White, 19 July 1927
27 Verbatim Report, 24
28 Bennett Papers, reel 13, Minutes of NCC, 7–8 Oct. 1927. McRae had recommended a committee of eighty-two, divided strictly in accordance with each province's representation in the House of Commons: PC Party Papers, vol. 239, McRae letter to each delegate, 21 Sept. 1927.
29 O'Leary, 'The Rival Chiefs of Staff,' 8
30 *Ottawa Journal*, 12 Oct. 1927, in Ferguson Papers, vol. 15
31 Verbatim Report, 93; Winnipeg *Tribune*, 12 Oct. 1927
32 Except where otherwise indicated, the source for convention resolutions is PC Party Papers, vol. 239, Resolutions Passed at the National Liberal–Conservative Convention, 1927.
33 Several respected sources cite the following pro–western Canada convention resolution: 'the Conservative Party pledges itself to maintain the Canadian National Railways as a publicly owned and operated utility.' Among these are C.P. Stacey, ed., *Historical Documents of Canada*, V: *The Arts of War and Peace, 1914–1945* (Toronto 1972), 46; J.H. Stewart Reid, Kenneth McNaught, and Harry S. Crowe, *A Source–Book of Canadian History* (Toronto 1964), 414; and *The Canadian Annual Review of Public Affairs, 1927–28* (Toronto 1928), 51–2. Some contemporary newspapers also listed such a resolution, such as the Toronto *Globe*, 13 Oct. 1927; Montreal *Gazette*, 12 Oct. 1927; and *Ottawa Citizen*, 13 Oct. 1927. This resolution was not included in the list of convention resolutions preserved by the Conservative party (PC Party Papers, vol. 239); it was not mentioned anywhere in the Verbatim Report; it does not appear in the list of resolutions outlined by MacNicol in *The National Liberal-Conservative Convention*, 36–53. Apparently, such a resolution was passed by the Resolutions Committee, printed, and circulated on the convention floor, but it was never brought before the full convention for debate and formal adoption. See the Winnipeg *Tribune*, 12–13 Oct. 1927. Nevertheless, the Canadian Press included the bogus CNR resolution in a list it sent to its affiliates, and newspapers across the country treated it as if it had the convention's approval.
34 Ernest R. Forbes, *The Maritime Rights Movement, 1919–1927: A Study in Canadian Regionalism* (Montreal 1979), 158–81
35 Verbatim Report, 222, 247
36 Ibid., 124–8, 238–9
37 Bennett Papers, vol. 543, Platform of the Liberal Party as adopted at the National Liberal Convention of August 1919
38 Verbatim Report, 102–5

39 Flavelle Papers, vol. 15, J.M. Macdonnell to Flavelle, 15 Oct. 1927
40 Ferguson Papers, vol. 15, George Nicholson to Ferguson, 22 Oct. 1927
41 Verbatim Report, 223–48
42 Ibid., 273–5
43 Peter Oliver, *G. Howard Ferguson: Ontario Tory* (Toronto 1977), 269–76, 280–6
44 Ferguson Papers, vol. 15, Ferguson to Senator R.H. Pope, 13 May 1927
45 Ibid., F.D.L. Smith to Ferguson, 20 June 1927
46 Ibid., James G. Ross et al. to Ferguson, 3 Oct. 1927
47 Ibid., Ferguson to Lord Atholstan, 3 Oct. 1927
48 Ibid., George Lynch-Staunton to Ferguson, 5 Oct. 1927
49 William Marchington, Toronto *Globe*, 7 Oct. 1927
50 'Current Politics,' in *Round Table*, Dec. 1926, 155
51 Meighen Papers, vol. 89, Arthur R. Ford to Meighen, 18 Oct. 1926
52 Ibid., vol. 244, Donald Sutherland to Meighen, 11 Sept. 1927; Meighen to Sutherland, 13 Sept. 1927
53 Ibid., vol. 231, Meighen to Armand Lavergne, 27 Sept. 1927
54 Verbatim Report, 26–44
55 P.D. Ross, *Ottawa Journal*, 11 Oct. 1927, in Ferguson Papers, vol. 15
56 Marchington, Toronto *Globe*, 11 Oct. 1927
57 *Winnipeg Free Press*, 11 Oct. 1927
58 Verbatim Report, 45–9
59 That Meighen could have won easily was the judgment of observers and participants alike: E. George Smith, Toronto *Globe*, 11 Oct. 1927; PAC, MG 30 D 45, John W. Dafoe Papers, vol. 4, Dafoe to Sir Clifford Sifton, 15 Oct. 1927; Meighen Papers, vol. 226A, Manuscript Notes for use of Roger Graham, 42; John G. Diefenbaker, *One Canada*, I: *The Crusading Years, 1895–1956* (Toronto 1975), 155.
60 Winnipeg *Tribune*, 11 Oct. 1927
61 Rhodes Papers, vol. 613, Rhodes to H.R.C. Breuls, 16 May 1927
62 In addition to Meighen, Ferguson, Rhodes, Baxter, Stevens, and Perley, one other man was nominated but did not run: Col. John A. Currie, a little-known Ontario MLA: PC Party Papers, Verbatim Report, 150.
63 Richard Wilbur, *H.H. Stevens, 1878-1973* (Toronto 1977), 81–2; PAC, MG 27 III B 9, H.H. Stevens Papers, vol. 3, Stevens to R.B. Bennett, 7 Nov. 1929. Bennett talked Stevens out of retirement in 1930.
64 Throughout this work, the contemporary usage of the 1920s and 1930s will be utilized when citing electoral ridings (e.g., West York, not the more familiar – to modern readers –York West).
65 Meighen Papers, vol. 226A, Meighen to W.R. Graham, 5 Jan. 1954
66 Marchington, Toronto *Globe*, 10 Oct. 1927

67 Flavelle Papers, vol. 15, J.M. Macdonnell to Flavelle, 15 Oct. 1927; PC Party Papers, Verbatim Report, 187–91

68 Graham, *Meighen*, II: 241–8

69 Hector Charlesworth, *I'm Telling You: Further Candid Chronicles* (Toronto 1937), 22–3

70 Ferguson Papers, vol. 15, F.D.L. Smith to Ferguson, 20 June 1927

71 Verbatim Report, 177–81

72 PAC, MG 27 III B 7, R.J. Manion Papers, vol. 105, Diary: 1925–30, 10 Oct. 1927

73 Toronto *Globe*, 13 Oct. 1926

74 Verbatim Report, 204–10; C.B. Pyper, Winnipeg *Tribune*, 12 Oct. 1927

75 Manion Papers, vol. 105, Diary, 10 Oct. 1927

76 Verbatim Report, 164–71; Marchington and Smith, Toronto *Globe*, 12 Oct. 1927

77 M. Grattan O'Leary, 'Cabinet Portraits: Cahan,' *MacLean's* 43 (1 Nov. 1930): 36

78 A Politician with a Notebook, 'Inside stuff,' *MacLean's* 43 (1 May 1930): 16

79 A Political Correspondent, 'Cross Currents at Ottawa,' *Canadian Forum* 6 (Feb. 1926): 140

80 Bennett Papers, vol. 10, C.C. Ballantyne to Hugh Guthrie, 16 Nov. 1926; *Montreal Star*, 14 Nov. 1927, cited in Nesmith, 'Bennett and the Conservative Party in Quebec,' 8–9

81 PAC, MG 30 E 143, R.K. Finlayson Papers, Memoir (Finlayson Memoir), 120

82 Ferguson Papers, vol. 15, Cahan to Ferguson, 26 Aug. 1927; Cahan to William Marchington, 12 Sept. 1927

83 Marc La Terreur, *Les tribulations des conservateurs au Québec de Bennett à Diefenbaker* (Quebec 1973), 9

84 Flavelle Papers, vol. 15, Macdonnell to Flavelle, 15 Oct. 1927

85 A Political Warrior-Retired 'Who's the Tory Moses?' *MacLean's* 40 (15 Aug. 1927), 3

86 Marchington, Toronto *Globe*, 7 Oct. 1927

87 *Winnipeg Free Press*, 11 Oct. 1927

88 Verbatim Report, 156–61

89 Montreal *Gazette*, 24 June 1927, cited in Nesmith, 'Bennett and the Conservative Party in Quebec,' 20; *Le Devoir*, Jan. 1927, cited in ibid., 11

90 PAC, MG 27 II E 1, Henri Bourassa Papers, reel M–721, C.H. Cahan to Georges Pelletier, 23 May 1927

91 Ferguson Papers, vol. 15, Ferguson to Senator Smeaton White, 28 Dec. 1927; Meighen Papers, vol. 227, Guthrie to Meighen, 8 Jan. 1928; *Sydney Post*, 19 Oct. 1927, in Rhodes Papers, vol. 636

92 M. Grattan O'Leary, 'Cabinet Portraits: Guthrie,' in *MacLean's* 43 (1 Oct. 1930): 48

93 There is to date no definitive biography of R.B. Bennett. In order of publication, the three attempts have been: Andrew D. MacLean, *R.B. Bennett: Prime Minister of Canada* (Toronto 1935); Lord Beaverbrook, *Friends: Sixty Years of Intimate Personal Relations with Richard Bennett* (London 1959); and Ernest Watkins, *R.B. Bennett: A Biography* (London 1963).

94 Dafoe Papers, vol. 3, Grant Dexter to Dafoe, 15 Sept. 1926; Alvin Finkel, 'Origins of the Welfare State in Canada,' in Leo Panitch, ed., *The Canadian State: Political Economy and Political Power* (Toronto 1977), 347–8

95 Toronto *Globe*, 12 Oct. 1926; 'Canada: The New Parliament at Work,' *Round Table*, June 1927, 595

96 Ferguson Papers, vol. 15, F.D.L. Smith to Ferguson, 20 June 1927

97 PAC, MG 27 II G 1, Lord Beaverbrook Papers, vol. 1, R.B. Bennett to Beaverbrook, 10 Nov. 1927; Stevens Papers, vol. 162A, Munro interview no. 9, 25; Meighen Papers, vol. 226A, Manuscript Notes, 40; Finlayson Memoir, 58–9

98 Arthur R. Ford, *As the World Wags On* (Toronto 1950), 108; M. Grattan O'Leary, 'The Rival Chiefs of Staff,' *MacLean's* 43 (1 July 1930): 8; *Winnipeg Free Press*, 10 Oct. 1927; Stevens Papers, vol. 162A, Munro interview no. 9, 24–5

99 Verbatim Report, 191–200

100 *Montreal Star*, 17 Oct. 1927, cited in Nesmith, 'Bennett and the Conservative Party in Quebec,' 47

101 Toronto *Globe*, 13 Oct. 1927; *Ottawa Journal*, n.d., in PAC, MG 27 II D 7, Sir George E. Foster Papers, vol. 95. Prime Minister Mackenzie King wired Bennett his 'very hearty congratulations,' but privately he was less sanguine. 'I should have preferred any of the others on personal grounds. Bennett's manner is against him, his money is an asset & he has ability. He will be a difficult opponent, apt to be very unpleasant, and give a nasty tone to public affairs': PAC, MG 26 J, William Lyon Mackenzie King Papers, Series J13, Diaries (King Diary), 12 Oct. 1927.

CHAPTER 3

1 Background information for this section is taken from these newspapers: Toronto *Globe*, Montreal *Gazette*, Ottawa *Citizen*, and Winnipeg *Tribune*, all 1–7 May 1930.

2 House of Commons *Debates*, 1 May 1930, 1614–31

3 Ibid., 1678–80

4 Ibid., 6 May 1930, 1834–5

5 Ferguson Papers, vol. 15, Ferguson to Senator Smeaton White, 28 Dec. 1927

6 PC Party papers, vol. 310, Memorandum for Dr Robb, 15 Nov. 1938

7 Public Archives of New Brunswick (PANB), R.B. Hanson Papers, vol. 7, J.E. Denison to Hanson, 6 May 1927
8 Bennett Papers, reel 15, Bennett to Howard Ferguson, 4 Feb. 1928
9 Ibid., reel 16, J.R. Long to Bennett, 28 Dec. 1927
10 Ibid., vol. 954, Bennett to Stevens, 22 May 1928
11 Toronto *Globe*, 26 Jan. 1928
12 Douglas MacKay, 'The Session in Review,' *MacLean's* 41 (1 July 1930): 17
13 Beaverbrook Papers, vol. 1, Borden to Beaverbrook, 16 Apr. 1928. The caucus was so happy with Bennett's leadership by 1930 that they presented him with 'a very handsome gold cup': Flavelle Papers, vol. 16, Flavelle to Lord Byng, 28 May 1930.
14 Public Archives of Canada (PAC), Hanson Papers, vol. 1, Hanson to Bennett, 14 Nov. 1928
15 Bennett Papers, vol. 950, McRae to Bennett, 23 Dec. 1929
16 R.J. Manion, *Life Is an Adventure* (Toronto 1939), 275
17 Stevens Papers, vol. 3, Bennett to Stevens, 3 May 1928
18 H.H.Stevens was one who particularly resented the patronizing attitude of some of the party's wealthy members: ibid., Stevens to Bennett, Nov. 7, 1929; Stevens to R.J. Manion, 6 Dec. 1929. Stevens eventually decided to resign, because of financial losses suffered by his private business, in late 1929. Bennett was able to talk him into remaining at least until the end of the 1930 session: ibid., Stevens to Bennett, 31 Oct. 1929; Bennett to Stevens, 27 Dec. 1929.
19 Bennett Papers, vol. 472, Report of the General Secretary, Conservative Federal Headquarters, 23 Aug. 1930
20 Ferguson Papers, vol. 15, Ferguson to Senator White, 28 Dec. 1927
21 Bennett Papers, vol 950, McRae to Bennett, 23 Dec. 1929
22 House of Commons *Debates*, 30 Jan. 1928, 13–30; 20 Feb. 1928, 617–30; 7-11 Feb. 1929, especially 17–29 for Bennett's speech; 1 Mar.–11 Apr. 1929, especially 740–58 for Guthrie, and 1295–9 for Cahan
23 The Dominion Bureau of Statistics employment index registered 119.0 for 1929 and slipped to 113.4 for 1930: *The Canadian Annual Review, 1935–36*, 485.
24 House of Commons *Debates*, 24 Feb. 1930, 18 and 28. At this point, Prime Minister King interpreted the Conservative strategy as an attempt to outbid the government. 'The Tory Party intend to make a demand for expenditure from the Federal Treasury, in as many directions as may be possible. They know that we will have to refuse these demands and they will seek to capitalize them in every appeal to different classes of the electorate.' King Papers, Series J1, King to J.G. Gardiner, 30 Jan. 1930
25 House of Commons *Debates*, 3 Apr. 1930, 1227–8
26 Ibid., 1 May 1930, 1678–80; 5 May 1930, 1811–35

27 Ibid., 8 May 1930, 1875; 13 May 1930, 2016; 14 May 1930, 2085; 15 May 1930, 2138–9

28 Rhodes Papers, vol. 631, MacNicol to Rhodes, 8 Nov. 1927; 4 Apr. 1928

29 Bennett Papers, reel 18, Bennett to Errick Willis, 10 Apr. 1928

30 Toronto *Globe*, 23 Apr. 1928; *The Canadian Annual Review, 1927–28*, 44

31 Sydney *Post*, 22 Oct. 1927, in Rhodes Papers, vol. 636; Bennett Papers, reel 15, George Beardsley to McRae's constituents, 16 Apr. 1928

32 Ibid., reel 18, Arthur R. Ford to Bennett, 11 Aug. 1928

33 Ibid., reel 19, Bennett memo, n.d.

34 Ibid., reel 15, McRae to A.W. Merriam and Redmond Code, 9 July 1929; PC Party Papers, vol. 314, Conservative Federal Headquarters Statement of Receipts and Disbursements, February 1930. Lipsett was 'a brilliant newspaperman' who had served in the Press Gallery before assuming the job of city editor at the Montreal *Star*: Arthur R. Ford, *As the World Wags On* (Toronto 1950), 146.

35 Bennett Papers, vol. 472, Report of the General Secretary, 23 Aug. 1930; M. Grattan O'Leary, 'The Rival Chiefs of Staff,' *MacLean's* 43 (1 July 1930): 46

36 Ibid., reel 15, Redmond Code to J.D. Stewart, 11 Oct. 1929

37 Ibid., McRae to Code, 10 Dec. 1929

38 McRae faulted the Quebec district organizer, Thomas Maher, for 'scattering his efforts entirely too much': ibid., McRae to Bennett, 20 Dec. 1929; McRae to L.W. Williamson, 7 Apr. 1930.

39 Ibid., reel 16, Code to all Conservative MPs, 30 May 1929

40 Ibid., reel 15, Code to all Conservative MPs, n.d.

41 Ibid., Code to W.A. Grimsdale, 31 Dec. 1929

42 Ibid., vol. 950, McRae to Bennett, 21 Dec. 1929

43 Ibid., vol. 475, Post-election memo from Robert Lipsett to R.B. Bennett, n.d.

44 Ibid.

45 Ibid.

46 Ibid., reel 15, McRae to Lipsett, 24 Feb. 1930

47 Ibid., Lipsett to Bennett, 31 Jan. 1930

48 Ibid., McRae to Bell, 7 Mar. 1930; McRae to H.C. Hodgson, 7 Apr. 1930; reel 16, McRae to Bennett, 12 Feb. 1930; vol. 472, Code to Bennett, 23 Aug. 1930

49 AO, G.S. Henry Papers, vol. 17, McRae Letter to Stalwarts and McRae Letter to General List, Apr. 1930

50 Bennett Papers, McRae to Conservative MPs, 6 Mar. 1930

51 Ibid., vol. 472, Code to Bennett, 23 Aug. 1930

52 Ibid., reel 15, Pamphlets: *Why I Am a Conservative; Election in Sight*

53 Ibid., McRae to Lipsett, 24 Feb. 1930

54 Ibid., vol. 475, Lipsett to Bennett, n.d.

55 Ibid.; also reel 15, Lipsett to A.W. Merriam, 16 Apr. 1930
56 Ibid., reel 417, Conservative Party Headquarters Budget, 1930, approved by A.D. McRae
57 Ibid., reel 14, Bennett to Sir George Perley, 22 Feb., 14 Mar., 11 Apr., 17 May, 5 June, 29 June, 3 Sept., 3 Oct., and 5 Nov. 1929
58 Rhodes Papers, vol. 653, McRae to Rhodes, 4 Dec. 1929
59 Bennett Papers, vol. 951, Sir George Perley to Bennett and McRae, 6 Jan. 1930
60 Rhodes Papers, vol. 653, McRae to Rhodes, 4 Dec. 1929
61 Bennett Papers, vol. 951, Bennett to Bank of Nova Scotia, 5 Feb. 1930; reel 16, McRae to Bennett, 12 Feb. 1930; reel 21, Bennett to George Lynch-Staunton, 13 May 1930; vol. 880, Bennett to T.A. McAuley, 7 June 1930
62 Ibid., reel 19, L.J. Gauthier to Bennett, 10 June 1928; Antoine Cimone to Bennett, 28 June 1928; Arthur Brossard to Bennett, 27 Oct. 1928
63 Robert Rumilly, *Maurice Duplessis et Son Temps,* I (Montreal 1978), 77; Marc La Terreur, *Les tribulations des conservateurs au Québec de Bennett à Diefenbaker* (Quebec 1973), 16–18; Ferguson Papers, vol. 15, Senator Smeaton White to Ferguson, 20 Oct. 1927; Roger Graham, *Arthur Meighen,* II: *And Fortune Fled* (Toronto 1963), 455
64 Bennett Papers, reel 19, Bennett to J.M. Macdonnell, 25 May 1928
65 Ibid., Bennett to Arthur Brossard, 1 Nov. 1928; PAC, Hanson Papers, vol. 1, Bennett to Hanson, 16 Nov. 1928; Queen's University Archives (QUA), John T. Hackett Papers, vol. 5, Bennett to Montreal Conservative Club, 23 Sept. 1928; *Montreal Star*, 26 Oct. 1928, in ibid.
66 Bennett Papers, reel 19, N. Garceau to Bennett, 12 Oct. 1928; Arthur Sauvé to Bennett, 15 Nov. 1928
67 Ibid., A.D. McRae to G.E. McCuaig, 16 Apr. 1929
68 Ibid., vol. 951, George Perley to Bennett, 18 May 1929
69 Ibid., reel 19, R.J. Manion to Bennett, 10 May 1929; ibid., Ward Pitfield to Bennett, 9 May 1929; Hackett Papers, vol. 5, private memo, 16 May 1929
70 Bennett Papers, vol. 951, Perley to Bennett, 18 May 1929
71 Ibid. (PAC), reel M-3173, Lord Atholstan to Bennett, n.d.
72 Ibid. (UNBA), reel 19, Arthur Sauvé to P.E. Blondin, 9 Apr. 1929; Armand Lavergne to Bennett, 11 Apr. 1929
73 Hackett Papers, vol. 5, private memo, 10 June 1929
74 Bennett Papers, reel 19, Procès Verbal de la Conférence Conservatrice, 15 May 1929
75 Ibid., Bennett to Mrs Charles Fremont, 20 Mar. 1930; reel 15, A.D. McRae to Bennett, 20 Dec. 1929; reel 21, Joseph Rainville to Bennett, 20 Mar. 1930; vol. 950, McRae to Bennett, 21 Dec. 1929
76 Ibid., reel 20, Thomas Maher to Bennett, 12 Dec. 1929, 18 Mar. and 23 May

1930; reel 15, McRae to Bennett, 20 Dec. 1929; reel 20, Bennett to Maher, 11 Apr. 1930

77 Lita-Rose Betcherman, *The Swastika and the Maple Leaf* (Toronto 1975), 6–10; *Le Bulletin des Agriculteurs*, 24 Apr. 1930, in PAC, MG 27 III B 16, Maurice Dupré Papers, vol. 10

78 Bennett Papers, reel 19, P.E. Blondin to Bennett, 7 June 1929; John H. Price to Bennett, n.d.; Bennett to Dr Edouard Montpetit [*sic*], 13 June 1929; Edouard Montpetit to Bennett, 17 June 1929

79 Ibid., vol. 192, J.H. Rainville to Redmond Code, 5 May 1930

80 Henry Papers, vol. 15, G.S. Henry to J.R. MacNicol, 4 Nov. 1929

81 Oliver, *Howard Ferguson*, 357–63

82 Bennett Papers, vol. 950, A.D. McRae to Bennett, 21 Dec. 1929; vol. 951, A.W. Merriam to Bennett, 15 July 1929

83 Ibid., vol. 446, D.M. Hogarth to Bennett, 7 Apr. 1930

84 Ibid., vol. 543, G.C. Nowlan to Bennett, 15 Apr. 1929; reel 18, E.N. Rhodes to Bennett, 19 Mar. 1929

85 Ibid., reel 14, Party Expenditure Statement, 28 Feb. 1930; vol. 951, A.W. Merriam to Bennett, 15 July 1929

86 Ibid., reel 14, E.N. Rhodes to Bennett, 24 Jan. 1930; Thomas Cantley to Bennett, 25 Jan. 1930

87 Ibid., vol. 951, A.W. Merriam to Bennett, 15 July 1929; vol. 950, A.D. McRae to Bennett, 21 Dec. 1929; Party Expenditure Statement, 28 Feb. 1930

88 Ibid., reel 16, Bennett to S.F. Tolmie, 29 Aug. 1929

89 Ibid., reel 16, H.H. Stevens to A.D. McRae, 24 Apr. 1929; vol. 950, McRae to Bennett, 21 Dec. 1929; reel 15, Bennett to J.A. Clark, 14 May 1930

90 David E. Smith, *Prairie Liberalism: The Liberal Party in Saskatchewan*, 1905–71 (Toronto 1975), 193–4

91 William Calderwood, 'Pulpit, Press, and Political Reactions to the Ku Klux Klan in Saskatchewan,' in Samuel D. Clark, J. Paul Grayson, and Linda M. Grayson, eds., *Prophecy and Protest: Social Movements in Twentieth-Century Canada* (Toronto 1975), 164–72

92 Bennett Papers, vol. 67, Charles E. Campbell to Thomas H. Blacklock, 20 June 1928; Bennett to P.H. Gordon, 2 Oct. 1928; P.H. Gordon to Bennett, 5 Oct. 1928; S.G. Dobson to Bennett, 19 Feb. 1929; Bennett to P.H. Gordon, 18 May 1929; Declaration of Trust (Somerville and Gordon for Bennett), 10 Apr. 1929; Declaration of Trust, 15 Oct. 1929; also, A Correspondent, 'The Elections in Saskatchewan,' *Canadian Forum* 9 (Aug. 1929); 375

93 *Regina Daily Star*, 8 June 1929, in Bennett Papers, reel 14

94 Ibid., Bennett to F.R. MacMillan, 14 May 1928; Bennett to A.G. MacKinnon, 5 Feb. 1930, cited in Calderwood, 'Ku Klux Klan,' 169

95 Keith A. McLeod, 'Politics, Schools and the French Language, 1881–1931,' in Norman Ward and Duff Spafford, eds., *Politics in Saskatchewan* (Toronto 1968), 143–6
96 Bennett Papers, vol. 472, Redmond Code to Bennett, 23 Aug. 1930
97 Ibid., vol. 950, A.D. McRae to Bennett, 21 Dec. 1929; 23 Dec. 1929
98 A Politician with a Notebook, 'Inside Stuff,' *MacLean's* 43 (1 May 1930): 16; QUA, H.A. Bruce Papers, vol. 1, Bruce to Lord Beaverbrook, 26 May 1930
99 'Attended a Liberal caucus which I had called to discuss matters of organization. I spoke of what the Tories were doing, their office & staff of 15, the weekly paper they are about to issue, the franking of campaign material, the amounts of it being sent out, the organization in the ridings, etc. etc. I said we had none of these': King Diary, 2 Apr. 1930.

CHAPTER 4

1 Canada, House of Commons, *Report of the Committee on Election Expenses* (Ottawa 1966), 498
2 Montreal *Gazette*, 29 July 1930
3 Election-day details were taken from the Toronto *Globe* and the *Winnipeg Tribune*, as well as the *Gazette*.
4 The Gross National Product, $6.134 billion in 1929, declined to $5.728 billion in 1930: M.C. Urquhart and K.A.H. Buckley, eds., *Historical Statistics of Canada* (Toronto 1965), 130. Unemployment, averaging 116,000 in 1929, shot up to 371,000 in 1930: ibid., 61. The price of wheat, which reached $1.78 a bushel in July 1929, dropped to less than $1.00 by June 1930, for the first time in fifteen years: Vernon C. Fowke, *The National Policy and the Wheat Economy* (Toronto 1957), 247–8.
5 James H. Gray, *The Winter Years* (Toronto 1966), 14
6 King Diary, 22 July 1929
7 King Papers, Series J4, vol. 72, Andrew Haydon to King, 18 Mar. 1929
8 King Diary, 9 Feb., 9 Apr. 1930
9 Bennett Papers, vol. 192, Bennett to A.D. McRae, 8 July 1930
10 Dafoe Papers, vol. 5, Dafoe to B.C. Nicholas, 6 Aug. 1930
11 Ibid.; M. Grattan O'Leary, 'The Political Scene,' *Queen's Quarterly* 37 (Winter 1930): 206; A Politician with a Notebook, 'Now It Can Be Told,' *MacLean's* 43 (1 Aug. 1930): 48
12 See Harold D. Clarke, Jane Jenson, Lawrence LeDuc, and Jon H. Pammett, 'Images of Political Parties' and 'Issues in Canadian Politics,' *Political Choice in Canada* (Toronto 1980), 113–34, 157–79; also Murray Edelman, 'Mass Responses to Political Symbols,' *The Symbolic Uses of Politics* (Chicago 1967), 172–87

13 Montreal *Gazette*, 10 June 1930, cited in C.P. Stacey, ed., *Historical Documents of Canada*, V: *The Arts of War and Peace, 1914–1945* (Toronto 1972), 100–1
14 Ibid.
15 Dennis Guest, *The Emergence of Social Security in Canada* (Vancouver 1980), 76
16 Montreal *Gazette*, 17 June 1930, cited in Stacey, *Historical Documents*, V: 103
17 King Diary, 14 June 1930
18 *Canadian Press* report, 10 July 1930, read by Mackenzie King into House of Commons *Debates*, 9 Sept. 1930, 25
19 King Diary, 25 May 1930
20 Ottawa *Journal*, 11 July 1930, read by King into House of Commons *Debates*, 9 Sept. 1930, 26
21 Toronto *Globe*, 12 July 1930
22 Public Archives of New Brunswick (PANB), Hanson Papers, vol. 8, A.D. McRae to Hanson, 12 July 1930; King Diary, 25 Aug. 1930
23 Bruce Papers, vol. 1, H.A. Bruce to Lord Beaverbrook, 29 July 1930
24 Official text of Bennett's Winnipeg speech, read by King into House of Commons *Debates*, 9 Sept. 1930, 29
25 Rhodes Papers, vol. 653, R.B. Bennett form letter, 7 July 1930
26 Dominion Bureau of Statistics, *Trade of Canada* (Ottawa 1935), cited in Alfred E. Morrison, 'R.B. Bennett and the Imperial Preferential Trade Agreements, 1932,' MA thesis, University of New Brunswick 1966, 48
27 Bennett Papers, vol. 191, undated memo
28 *Canadian Annual Review*, 1929–30, 97. In the Conservatives' printed propaganda to English Canadians, the slogan became 'Canada first, and Canada in the British Empire,' a subtle but significant change, aimed at soothing the party's imperialist supporters: Bennett Papers, vol. 193, Bennett to Conservative 'stalwart' list, n.d.
29 Marc La Terreur, *Les tribulations des conservateurs au Québec de Bennett à Diefenbaker* (Quebec 1973), 23
30 King Diary, 25 Aug. 1930. Two days later, King wrote, 'I confess when I see the way he stressed Canada first as opposed to Britain I marvel [th]at the Conservative Party stood for it as they did': ibid., 27 Aug. 1930.
31 J.L. Granatstein and J.M. Hitsman, *Broken Promises: A History of Conscription in Canada* (Toronto 1977), 122; *Canadian Annual Review*, 1929–30, 84
32 F.C. Engelmann and M.A. Schwartz, *Canadian Political Parties: Origin, Character, Impact* (Scarborough 1975), 276. Recent empirical research indicates that, in terms of impact upon voter choice, 'party leader effects are greatest for flexible low-interest voters, while issue effects are strongest among flexible high-interest voters': Clarke et al., 'Voting Behaviour,' *Political Choice in Canada*, 234.
33 Rhodes Papers, vol. 653, A.D. McRae to Rhodes, 9 June 1930

34 George C. Perlin, *The Tory Syndrome: Leadership Politics in the Progressive Conservative Party* (Montreal 1980), 14

35 Bruce Hutchison, *Mr. Prime Minister, 1867–1964* (Toronto 1964), 242

36 Ottawa *Citizen*, 16 July 1930, read by King into House of Commons *Debates*, 9 Sept. 1930, 24; *Montreal Star*, 27 June 1930, cited in *Canadian Annual Review*, 1929–30, 98; Toronto *Globe*, 16 July 1930; 'He seems to have had but the one speech everywhere,' King remarked in amazement after studying reports of Bennett's campaign speeches: King Diary, 27 Aug. 1930

37 Bennett Papers, reel 15, 'Itinerary, Hon. R.B. Bennett, K.C., MP,' n.d.; also, Toronto *Globe*, Montreal *Gazette*, Winnipeg *Tribune*, and *Canadian Annual Review*, 1929–30

38 Rhodes Papers, vol. 653, John R. Haig to Rhodes, 25 June 1930; ibid., Rhodes to Haig, 5 July 1930; Bennett Papers, vol. 192, Bennett to A.D. McRae, 8 July 1930

39 Montreal *Gazette*, 28 July 1930

40 Public Archives of Canada (PAC), MG 31 D 19, J.R.H. Wilbur Papers, R.K. Finlayson to Wilbur, 29 June 1967; Arthur R. Ford, 'As the World Wags On,' *London Free Press*, 30 Sept. 1961, in W.D. Herridge Papers (Private), File: U.S. Convention; Charles Vining, 'Mr Herridge,' *Bigwigs* (Toronto 1935), 70–3

41 Bennett Papers, vol. 192, McRae to Miss Mildred Bennett, 10 June 1930

42 Arthur R. Ford, *As the World Wags On* (Toronto 1950), 144

43 King Diary, 17 May 1930, 19–26 July 1930; King Papers, Series J1, vol. 178, James Malcolm to King, 8 July 1930; Montreal *Gazette*, 28 July 1930; Christopher Armstrong, *The Politics of Federalism: Ontario's Relations with the Federal Government, 1867–1942* (Toronto 1981), 175

44 Bennett papers, vol. 950, Bennett to A.D. McRae, 10 June 1930

45 Sir Robert L. Borden, *Letters to Limbo*, ed. by Henry Borden (Toronto 1971), 17; A Politician with a Notebook, 'Now It Can Be Told,' *MacLean's* 43 (1 Aug. 1930): 42; Roger Graham, *Arthur Meighen*, III: *No Surrender* (Toronto 1965), 26

46 Marc La Terreur, 'R.B. Bennett et le Québec: un cas d'incompréhension réciproque,' in Canadian Historical Association, *Historical Papers* (CHAP) (1969), 94; Robert Rumilly, *Maurice Duplessis et Son Temps*, I: 1890–1944 (Montreal 1978), 84; Finlayson Memoir, 120

47 PC Party Papers, vol. 356, *The Canadian*, 8 and 16 July 1930

48 Bennett Papers, vol. 950, A.D. McRae to Key List, n.d.

49 Ibid., A.D. McRae to Bennett, 7 June 1930

50 PAC, MG III G 5, Escott Reid Papers, vol. 1, interviews with W.F. Kerr, 7 Aug. 1931, and Mr Stewart, 13 Oct. 1931; see also Escott M. Reid, 'The Saskatchewan Liberal Machine before 1929,' in Hugh G. Thorburn, ed., *Party Politics in Canada*, 3rd ed. (Scarborough 1972), 32.

51 Bennett Papers, vol. 472, Redmond Code to Bennett, 23 Aug. 1930; ibid., vol. 88, Thomas Maher to Bennett, 25 June 1930; Hector Charlesworth, *I'm Telling You: Further Candid Chronicles* (Toronto 1937), 183; Robert Rumilly, *Maurice Duplessis*, 84

52 Bennett Papers, vol. 192, Bennett to Alice Millar, 16 July 1930

53 Queen's University Archives (QUA), T.A. Crerar Papers, vol. 87, A.K. Cameron to Crerar, 19 July 1930

54 King Diary, 29 June 1930

55 Reginald Whitaker, *The Government Party: Organizing and Financing the Liberal Party of Canada, 1930–58* (Toronto 1977), 9–12; H. Blair Neatby, *William Lyon Mackenzie King, II: 1924–1932, The Lonely Heights* (Toronto 1963), 327–32

56 Bennett Papers, vol. 950, A.D. McRae to A.W. Merriam, 4 June 1930

57 Ibid., vol. 475, Robert Lipsett to Bennett, n.d.

58 Ibid., vol. 193, A.D. McRae to Bennett, 5 July 1930

59 Ibid., Redmond Code to Bennett, 28 June 1930, and vol. 472, Code to Bennett, 23 Aug. 1930

60 Ibid., vol 475, Lipsett to Bennett, n.d.

61 PANB, Hanson Papers, vol. 8, A.D. McRae to Hanson, 16 June 1930

62 Bennett Papers, vol. 475, Lipsett to Bennett, n.d.

63 Ford, *As the World Wags On*, 146; Bennett Papers, vol. 475, Lipsett to Bennett, n.d.

64 Bennett Papers, vol. 193, Memo – R.A. Stapells, In Trust, 16 Aug. 1930

65 A Politician with a Notebook, 'Now It Can Be Told,' 9

66 King Diary, 4 and 25 June 1930; King Papers, Series J1, vol. 175, Norman Rogers to Andrew Haydon, 9 July 1930, and vol. 179, King to P.J. Veniot, 16 June 1930

67 Cited in Robert A. MacKay, 'After Beauharnois – What?' *MacLean's* 44 (15 Oct. 1931): 8

68 House of Commons *Debates*, 31 July 1931, 4394

69 Reid Papers, vol. 1, Interviews, 1930–2. C.H. Cahan estimated campaign expenses of 'about $25,000' in his Montreal riding: House of Commons *Debates*, 11 Feb. 1932, 146.

70 Bennett Papers, reel 417, Estimated Monthly Requirements, June and July, by A.D. McRae; vol 472, Redmond Code to Bennett, 23 Aug. 1930; vol 193, R.A. Stapells, In Trust, 16 Aug. 1930

71 Ibid., vol. 473, A.D. McRae to E.B. Ryckman, 30 May 1930

72 J.L. Granatstein, 'Conservative Party Finance,' in *Studies in Canadian Party Finance* (Ottawa 1966), 257–61

73 Bennett Papers, vol. 191, A.D. McRae to Bennett, 5 July 1930

74 Hackett Papers, vol. 1, George B. Foster to Hackett, 9 July 1930

75 Rhodes Papers, vol. 652, Ward Pitfield to Rhodes, 19 June and 9 July 1930

76 Bennett Papers, vol. 191, J.H. Rainville to A.D. McRae, 25 July 1930
77 King Diary, 22 July 1930
78 Bennett Papers, vol. 191, A.D. McRae to Bennett, 5 July 1930
79 Ibid., vol. 880, Untitled list of campaign donors, 2 Sept. 1930. This original list coincides with a copy contained in the Manion Papers, vol. 73, except that the latter shows Canada Cement's donation as $17,500, rather than $7,500.
80 Daly Papers, vol. 3, Untitled list of campaign fund expenditures, n.d.
81 Bennett Papers, vol. 485, J.J Gibbons to Bennett, 22 Dec. 1930
82 Manion Papers, vol. 11, Manion to Thomas G. Murphy, 19 July 1933
83 Reid Papers, vol. 1, Interviews, 1930–2
84 Bennett Papers, vol. 192, Bennett to Miss A.E. Millar, 16 July 1930
85 Reid Papers, vol. 1, Interview with Mr Craig, 15 Aug. 1931; Daly Papers, vol. 3, Untitled list of Saskatchewan campaign expenditures by constituency, n.d.
86 Turnbull quotation cited in K.Z. Paltiel, *Political Party Financing in Canada* (Toronto 1970), 43; Bennett Papers, vol. 493, Bennett to F.W. Turnbull, 14 Oct. 1932; vol. 880, Bennett to T.A. McAuley, 7 July 1930
87 A Politician with a Notebook, 'Now It Can Be Told,' 42
88 Bennett Papers, vol. 192, W.T.R. Preston to Bennett, 6 July 1930; Daly Papers, vol. 1, Mr Regan to General McRae, 1 July 1930
89 House of Commons *Debates*, 28 July 1931, 4259–60; 31 July 1931, 4399
90 King Diary, 28 and 29 July 1930
91 Although the Canadian census has traditionally used 1,000 as the threshold number that defines an urban community, the UNESCO definition of 20,000 seems a more realistic number for an industrialized age: Leroy C. Stone, *Urban Development in Canada* (Ottawa 1967), 15.
92 Reid defined the ridings on the basis of party vote, rather than winning candidate. This results in a slightly modified allocation of ridings by party, owing to the existence of several Independent Liberal candidates in 1930. Escott M. Reid, 'Canadian Political Parties: A Study of the Economic and Racial Bases of Conservatism and Liberalism in 1930,' in John C. Courtney, ed., *Voting in Canada* (Scarborough 1967), 73–5
93 Dafoe Papers, vol. 5, Dafoe to R.J. Deachman, 6 Aug. 1930
94 F.H.U., 'O Canada,' *Canadian Forum* 10 (Aug. 1930): 400
95 Bennett Papers, vol. 192, Bennett to A.D. McRae, 8 July 1930; vol. 951, E.E. Perley to Sir George Perley, 9 Jan 1931; vol. 362, F.W. Turnbull to Bennett, 27 Feb. 1934; vol. 472, A.D. McRae to E.N. Rhodes, 5 Aug. 1930
96 J.A. Stevenson, 'The Canadian Election,' *Queen's Quarterly* 37 (Summer 1930): 578; 'Canada – The General Election,' *Round Table* (Dec. 1930): 168; Richard DesBrisay, 'Nationalism Wins,' *Canadian Forum* 10 (Sept. 1930): 431; Frederic

H. Soward, 'The Canadian Elections of 1930,' *The American Political Science Review* 24 (Nov. 1930): 1000; Bennett Papers, vol. 191, A.O. Dawson to Bennett, 23 June 1930

97 La Terreur, *Les tribulations*, 23

98 George Henry, one of Ferguson's cabinet colleagues, observed; 'We were not as successful in Ontario as we had anticipated. Doubtless the gesture with regard to Imperial trade got some of our people': Henry Papers, vol. 18, Henry to C.F. Bailey, 31 July 1930.

99 Part of Bennett's Moncton speech, 10 July 1930, read by King into House of Commons *Debates*, 9 Sept. 1930, 25

100 Part of Bennett's speech in North Vancouver, 17 June 1930, read by King into ibid., 27

101 Beaverbrook Papers, vol. 1, R.L. Borden to Beaverbrook, 31 July 1930

102 Dafoe Papers, vol. 5, Dafoe to Charles Craig, 14 Aug. 1930; Bennett's Regina speech, 10 June 1930, read by King into House of Commons *Debates*, 9 Sept. 1930, 20; Arthur Meighen to T.R. Meighen, 18 July 1930, cited in Graham, Arthur *Meighen*, III: 26

103 Howard A. Scarrow, *Canada Votes* (New Orleans 1962), 79

104 Winnipeg *Tribune*, 29 July 1930

105 King Diary, 29 July 1930

CHAPTER 5

1 Montreal *Gazette*, Toronto *Globe*, and Winnipeg *Tribune*, 27–30 Dec. 1933

2 M.C. Urquhart and K.A.H. Buckley, eds., *Historical Statistics of Canada* (Toronto 1965), 130, 61; Vernon C. Fowke, *The National Policy and the Wheat Economy* (Toronto 1957), 248; James Struthers, *No Fault of Their Own: Unemployment and the Canadian Welfare State, 1914–1941* (Toronto 1983), 103; A.E. Safarian, *The Canadian Economy in the Great Depression* (Toronto 1970), 109–10-; Michiel Horn, *The Great Depression of the 1930s in Canada*, CHA Booklet No. 39 (Ottawa 1984)

3 Excerpts are from Michiel Horn, ed., *The Dirty Thirties: Canadians in the Great Depression* (Canada 1972), 232; and L.M. Grayson and Michael Bliss, eds., *The Wretched of Canada: Letters to R.B. Bennett, 1930–1935* (Toronto 1971), 61.

4 The Toronto *Globe*, 30 Dec. 1933, used this particular headline. The story was front-page news in all the major newspapers.

5 See, for example, J.L. Granatstein, Irving M. Abella, David J. Bercuson, R. Craig Brown, and H. Blair Neatby, *Twentieth Century Canada* (Toronto 1983), 215–16; also Robert Bothwell, Ian Drummond, and John English, *Canada: 1900–1945* (Toronto 1987), 261–2.

6 Stevens Papers, vol. 29, Privy Council Minute, 7 Aug. 1930

7 Ottawa *Journal*, 24 Sept. 1930, in Public Archives of Canada (PAC), Maurice Dupré Papers, vol. 9

8 A Politician with a Notebook, 'Backstage at Ottawa,' *MacLean's* 45 (15 Apr. 1933): 50. See also Finlayson Memoir, 125.

9 Norman Ward, ed., *A Party Politician: The Memoirs of Chubby Power* (Toronto 1966), 281; King Diary, 16 July 1932

10 House of Commons *Debates*, 17 Mar. 1931, 57; R.B. Bennett, 'Democracy on Trial,' *Canadian Problems as Seen by Twenty Outstanding Men of Canada* (Toronto n.d.), 18

11 Bennett Papers, vol. 496, Sir George Perley to H.J. Barber, 8 Dec. 1931; Queen's University Archives (QUA), Charles A. Dunning Papers, vol. 10, Dunning to E.M. Macdonald, 5 Nov. 1931; King Diary, 25 Nov. 1932

12 Bennett Papers, vol. 952, Bennett to George S. Robinson, 18 Sept 1933; ibid., vol. 470, Dr H.A. Bruce to Bennett, 7 Oct. 1933; Manion Papers, vol. 4, Bennett to Manion, 22 Nov. 1933; PAC, Hanson Papers, vol. 1, Hanson to George B. Jones, 10 Nov. 1933

13 King Diary, 16 Sept. 1930

14 Bennett Papers, vol. 497, memo: 'Office Routine,' n.d.; see also J.L. Granatstein, *A Man of Influence: Norman A. Robertson and Canadian Statecraft, 1929–68* (Toronto 1981), 33

15 Finlayson Memoir, 117; Grattan O'Leary, *Recollections of People, Press, and Politics* (Toronto 1977), 69; Stevens Papers, vol. 162A, Interview No. 10, 5

16 Montreal *Gazette*, Toronto *Globe*, and Winnipeg *Tribune*, all 29 July–8 Aug. 1930

17 Finlayson Memoir, 121; PAC, MG 27 III B 1, C.H. Cahan Papers, vol. 1, Bennett to Cahan, n.d.; Bennett Papers, vol 101, Cahan to Bennett, 7 Aug. 1930

18 Bennett Papers, vol. 102, Ford to Bennett, Aug. 1930; ibid., Sauvé to Bennett, 6 Aug. 1930; QUA, D.M. Sutherland Papers, 7 Aug. 1930; William Marchington, Toronto *Globe*, 5 Aug. 1930, 1

19 Bennett Papers, vol. 101, Lorne C. Webster to Bennett, 1 Aug. 1930; vol. 484, Armand Lavergne to Bennett, 29 July 1932; vol. 481, Bennett to Arthur Sauvé, Maurice Dupré, and Alfred Duranleau, 18 Apr. 1933; vol. 102, Thomas Maher to Bennett, 5 Nov. 1934

20 Grattan O'Leary, 'Cabinet Portraits,' *MacLean's* 43 (15 Dec. 1930): 35; F.C. Mears, Montreal *Gazette*, 7 Aug. 1930, 1

21 C.B. Pyper, Winnipeg *Tribune*, 9 Aug. 1930, 2; Bennett Papers, vol. 101, W.C. Buckle to Bennett, 1 Aug. 1930; ibid., vol. 102, James F. Bryant to Bennett, 29 July 1930

22 F.C. Engelman and M.A. Schwartz, *Canadian Political Parties: Origin, Character, Impact* (Scarborough 1975), 114; W.A. Matheson, *The Prime Minister and the*

Cabinet (Toronto 1976), 26, 105; W. Stewart Wallace, *The Macmillan Dictionary of Canadian Biography*, 3rd ed. (Toronto 1963); B.M. Greene, ed., *Who's Who in Canada*, 1932–33 (Toronto 1933)

23 Grant Dexter, 'The Political Situation in Canada,' *Queen's Quarterly* 37 (Autumn 1930): 763; House of Commons *Debates*, 10 Feb. 1936, 67–8

24 R.J. Manion, *Life Is an Adventure* (Toronto 1939), 293–4; Bennett Papers, vol. 483, Samuel Gobeil to Bennett, 24 Jan. 1931; ibid., vol. 484, Arthur Sauvé to Bennett, 4 May 1932

25 'Doctor MacLaren was about as good as a fifth wheel on a coach at Electioneering': Manion Papers, vol. 8, R.B. Hanson to R.B. Bennett, 28 June 1932. Also Stevens Papers, vol. 162A, Munro Interviews 11 and 12; Finlayson Memoir, passim; Manion, *Life Is an Adventure*, 293

26 Meighen Papers, vol. 226A, Manuscript Notes, 56; Bennett Papers, vol. 101, Gideon Robertson to Bennett, 12 Jan. 1932; ibid., Bennett to The Earl of Bessborough, 3 Feb. 1932; Public Archives of New Brunswick (PANB), Hanson Papers, vol. 27, Hanson to R.C. Matthews, 2 Dec. 1933

27 Reid Papers, vol. 1, John Stevenson Interview, Mar. 1931; Bennett Papers, vol. 841, Bennett to Robert A. Reid, 27 Apr. 1937

28 A Politician with a Notebook, 'Backstage at Ottawa,' *MacLean's* 44 (Aug. 1931): 44; Dafoe Papers, vol. 6, Norman Lambert to Dafoe, 19 Oct. 1932

29 *Le Devoir*, 11 Apr. 1933, cited in Marc La Terreur, 'R.B. Bennett et le Québec: un cas d'incompréhension réciproque,' in Canadian Historical Association, *Historical Papers* (CHAP) (1969), 100; Bennett Papers, vol. 480, J.A. Barrette to Bennett, 19 May 1931

30 J.A. Stevenson, 'The Canadian Political Scene,' *Queen's Quarterly* 38 (Spring 1931): 362; Bennett Papers, vol. 484, Armand Lavergne to Bennett, 29 July 1932; Dupré Papers, vol. 8, Thomas Ahern to Dupré, 20 July 1932; Bennett Papers, vol. 102, George Black to Bennett, 14 Nov. 1932; ibid., L.G. Gravel to Bennett, 13 Sept. 1932; Marc La Terreur, *Les Tribulations des conservateurs au Québec de Bennett à Diefenbaker* (Quebec 1973), 40–51

31 House of Commons *Debates*, 30 Jan. 1933, 1657–62; 27 Feb. 1933, 2514–36

32 Bennett Papers, vol. 493, Turnbull to Bennett, 29 July 1933

33 Irene H. McEwen, 'The Senate Appointments of R.B. Bennett, 1930 to 1935,' MA thesis, University of British Columbia, 1978, 5–12

34 House of Commons *Debates*, 29 July 1931, 4278, 4282; Manion, *Life Is an Adventure*, 308

35 PAC, MG 27 III F 16, R.H. Babbage Papers, Bennett to Babbage, 4 Apr. 1932

36 King Diary, 11 Sept 1930; House of Commons *Debates*, 1932, 1282, cited in Finlayson Memoir, 57

37 Dafoe Papers, vol. 5, Grant Dexter to Dafoe, 11 Jan. 1931; vol. 6, Dexter to

Dafoe, 16 Oct. 1932; vol. 7, Dexter to Dafoe, 1933 memo; vol. 5, J.A. Stevenson to Dafoe, 2 Mar. 1931; vol. 7, Dexter to Dafoe, 5 May 1933

38 Christopher Armstrong, *The Politics of Federalism: Ontario's Relations with the Federal Government, 1867–1942* (Toronto 1981), 155

39 House of Commons *Debates*, 8 Sept. 1930, 4–5

40 H. Blair Neatby, *William Lyon Mackenzie King*, II: *1924–1932, The Lonely Heights* (Toronto 1963), 349; Henry Papers, vol. 19, G.D. Robertson to Henry, 27 Sept. 1930

41 House of Commons *Debates*, 12 Sept. 1930, 189; ibid., 16 Sept 1930, 239; C.P. Stacey, ed., *Historical Documents of Canada*, V: *The Arts of War and Peace, 1914–1945* (Toronto 1972), 204–6; S.D. Clark, *The Canadian Manufacturers' Association: A Study In Collective Bargaining and Political Pressure* (Toronto 1939), 93–5; Robert B. Bryce, *Maturing in Hard Times: Canada's Department of Finance through the Great Depression* (Montreal 1986), 72–3

42 Stacey, ed., *Historical Documents*, V, 482–4; C.P. Stacey, *Canada and the Age of Conflict*, II: *The Mackenzie King Era, 1921–1948* (Toronto 1981), 137–9; Hanson Papers, vol. 1, Bennett to Hanson, 18 Dec. 1930

43 Bennett Papers, reel M-1060, J.T.M. Anderson to Hon. George Perley, 11 Nov. 1930; ibid., 18 Nov. 1930; ibid., Perley to Anderson, 27 Nov. 1930; ibid., Bennett to Perley, 10 July 1933; Bryce, *Maturing in Hard Times*, 54–5; Vernon C. Fowke, *The National Policy and the Wheat Economy* (Toronto 1957), 248–64

44 House of Commons *Debates*, 12 Mar. 1931, 1–3

45 Bennett Papers, vol. 489, J.D. Chaplin to Bennett, 26 Jan. 1931; Ferguson Papers, vol. 2, R.A. Stapells to Ferguson, 7 Apr. 1931; O. Mary Hill, *Canada's Salesman to the World: The Department of Trade and Commerce, 1892–1939* (Montreal 1977), 351; Bryce, *Maturing in Hard Times*, 87

46 Bennett Papers, reel M-1046, Bennett to Ross McMaster, 6 Feb. 1931

47 Ibid., reel M-1060, Bennett to M.N. Campbell, 22 Oct. 1931; Fowke, *Wheat Economy*, 260

48 Kenneth Bryden, *Old Age Pensions and Policy-Making in Canada* (Montreal 1974), 7–8, 61–2, 86—7

49 Struthers, *No Fault of Their Own*, 53–9

50 Ferguson Papers, vol. 18, Ferguson to Bennett, 10 Sept. 1930; ibid., Ferguson to L.A. Taschereau, 10 Sept. 1930; Cahan Papers, vol. 8, Cahan to Archbishop Georges Gauthier, 9 Apr. 1931; Bennett Papers, vol. 172, Press Statement, 8 Apr. 1931; *Round Table* (Sept. 1931), 875; Armstrong, *Politics of Federalism*, 146–8; Stacey, *Historical Documents*, V, 477–88

51 *Canadian Annual Review*, 1932, 28

52 Henry Papers, vol. 27, R.B. Bennett to Henry, 9 May 1932; Clark, *Canadian Manufacturers' Association*, 95; 'Ottawa and the Trade Agreements,' *Round*

Table (Dec. 1932), 53–4; Stevens Papers, vol. 162A, Interview No. 10, 15; Finlayson Memoir, 154–7; Dafoe Papers, vol. 6, Grant Dexter to Dafoe, 16 Oct. 1932

53 *The Economist* (18 Jan. 1936), in Stacey, ed. *Historical Documents*, V, 212–13

54 Ian M. Drummond, *Imperial Economic Policy, 1917–1939* (Toronto 1974), especially 191–289; Tim Rooth, 'Imperial Preference and Anglo–Canadian Trade Relations in the 1930s: The End of an Illusion?' *British Journal of Canadian Studies*, Dec. 1986: 205–22; Dana Wilgress, *Memoirs* (Toronto 1967), 92–6; Hill, *Canada's Salesman*, 520–9; *Canadian Annual Review, 1932*, 319–26. Canadian textile producers believed their interests had been sacrificed in the Ottawa Agreements: QUA, Donald M. Sutherland Papers, vol. 2, A.O. Dawson to Murray MacLaren, 27 Apr. 1934.

55 House of Commons *Debates*, 21 Mar. 1933; Cahan papers, Cahan to Archbishop Georges Gauthier, 13 May 1933; Hill, *Canada's Salesman*, 541

56 House of Commons *Debates*, 20 Feb. 1933, 3207; PAC, Richard H. Babbage Papers, Bennett to Babbage, 22 May 1933; 'The American Road,' in Robert Bothwell and Norman Hillmer, eds., *The In-Between Time: Canadian External Policy in the 1930s* (Toronto 1975), 61–5; W.D. Herridge Papers (Private Collection), File S 5, Herridge to Cordell Hull, 14 Nov. 1934; Stacey, *Age of Conflict*, II, 169–70

57 *Canadian Annual Review, 1932*, 371–8; Stacey, *Age of Conflict*, II, 145–9; Bennett Papers, vol. 276, Herridge to Bennett, 13 Sept 1933; King Diary, 16 July 1932

58 House of Commons *Debates*, 10 Oct. 1932, 49; 1 June 1931, 2142

59 Ibid., 12 Mar. 1931, 2; 6 Oct. 1932, 2; 21 Mar. 1933, 3223

60 *Canadian Annual Review, 1932*, 42; Bennett Papers, vol. 131, Bennett to Perley, 26 June 1933; Manion Papers, vol. 18, R.J. Manion to James Manion,27 Jan. 1934; Rhodes Papers, vol. 1131, Address by R.B. Bennett to the Toronto Board of Trade, 23 Jan. 1933; Bennett Papers, reel M-965, Bennett to H.J. Barber, 7 Apr. 1933

61 Bennett Papers, reel M-965, Edgar N. Rhodes to ... (form letter), 30 Mar. 1933; ibid., reel M-986, Department of Finance Memorandum: Salary Deduction Act, 23 Feb. 1932; Finlayson Memoir, 127; Bryce, *Maturing in Hard Times*, 75–9

62 Bennett Papers, reel M-1206, R.K. Finlayson memorandum to Bennett, 12 Feb. 1934; House of Commons *Debates*, 24 Feb. 1933, 2450

63 Bennett Papers, vol. 276, Herridge to Bennett, 10 Feb. 1933; Stacey, ed., *Historical Documents*, V, 240–2; David Ricardo Williams, *Duff: A Life in the Law* (Vancouver 1984), 149–56

64 Bryce, *Maturing in Hard Times*, 104–10

65 House of Commons *Debates*, 26 Apr. 1932, 2391; 6 Apr. 1932, 1749

66 A.E. Safarian, *The Canadian Economy in the Great Depression* (Toronto 1970), 88–92; Bryce, *Maturing in Hard Times*, 124–30

67 Manion Papers, vol. 4, Manion to Bennett, 1 July 1931; House of Commons *Debates*, 29 July 1931, 4278; 1 Feb. 1933, 1688. J.S. Woodsworth read Bennett's 'iron heel' statement into Hansard from an article in the Toronto *Mail and Empire*, 10 Nov. 1932.

68 House of Commons *Debates*, 29 July 1931, 4278; Stacey, *Historical Documents*, v, 126–9; Barbara Roberts, *Whence They Came: Deportation from Canada, 1900–1935* (Ottawa 1988), 125–94; Lita–Rose Betcherman, *The Little Band: The Clashes between the Communists and the Political and Legal Establishment in Canada, 1928–1932* (Ottawa 1982), 127, 143, 172–211

69 Manion Papers, vol. 4, Manion to Bennett, 1 July 1931; James Eayrs, *In Defence of Canada, I: From the Great War to the Great Depression* (Toronto 1964), 124–36; Struthers, *No Fault of Their Own*, 80–2; Lorne A. Brown, 'The Bennett Government, The Single Unemployed and Political Stability, 1930–1935,' PhD thesis, Queen's University, 1980, 523

70 House of Commons *Debates*, 14 Feb. 1933, 2102; Montreal *Gazette*, 4 Mar. 1932

71 Bennett Papers, reel M-3174, Bennett to Borden, 17 Apr. 1918; ibid., reel M-1069, Bennett to Rev. F.G. Hardy, 2 Jan. 1934; QUA, H.A. Bruce papers, vol. 1, Bennett to Bruce, 25 July 1938; Bennett Papers, reel M-1069, Bennett to F.B. Fetherstonhaugh, 15 Feb. 1932

72 House of Commons *Debates*, 16 Feb. 1932, 236–7

73 Ibid., 6 May 1932, 2709–12; 18 May 1932, 3035–6

74 Margaret Prang, 'The Origins of Public Broadcasting in Canada,' *Canadian Historical Review* 46 (Mar. 1965): 1–29; E. Austim Weir, *The Struggle for National Broadcasting in Canada* (Toronto 1965), 130–7

75 House of Commons *Debates*, 29 Apr. 1931, 1099–1104; Bennett Papers, reel M-1459, Irvine to Bennett, 29 Apr. 1931; Henry Papers, vol. 22, Ferguson to Henry, 9 Mar. 1931; 'Unemployment Insurance,' *Canadian Forum* 11 (June 1931): 324

76 Finlayson Memoir, 233–4; Bennett Papers, reel M-1459, W.C. Clark to Bennett, 18 Jan. 1933; Armstrong, *Politics of Federalism*, 149–52

77 Bennett Papers, reel M-961, Bennett to Sir George Perley, 10 July 1933; Finlayson Memoir, 208; Bryce, *Maturing in Hard Times*, 135–7; Douglas H. Fullerton, *Graham Towers and His Times* (Toronto 1986), 41–5

78 Bennett Papers, reel M-1180, H.H. Wrong to Bennett, 17 May 1933; ibid., reel M-1182, Silver Treaty Agreement, 22 July 1933; House of Commons *Debates*, 26 Feb. 1934, 952; Bryce, *Maturing in Hard Times*, 134

79 Bennett Papers, reel M-1182, Secretary of State for External Affairs to High Commissioner for Canada in Great Britain, 27 May 1933; reel M-1180, W.D. Herridge to Bennett, 10 Apr. 1933

80 House of Commons *Debates*, 12 Mar. 1934, 1423–6; Bennett Papers, reel M-1182, G.H. Perley to W.D.Herridge, 5 July 1933; ibid., H.W. Wood to Bennett, 1 June 1933; ibid., Perley to High Commissioner, 26 June 1933; ibid., reel M-1183, R.K. Finlayson to M.A. MacPherson, 19 Dec. 1933; Fowke, *Wheat Economy*, 260–1; Finlayson Memoir, 196–202

81 Bryce, *Maturing in Hard Times*, 108–9; Safarian, *Canadian Economy*, 89

82 Manion Papers, vol. 4, Manion to Bennett, 24 Aug. 1933; Stevens Papers, vol. 22, Memo: 'A New National Policy,' 2 Sept. 1933; Bennett papers, vol. 488, R.D. Morand to Bennett, 10 May 1933; ibid., vol. 433, Finlayson to Bennett, 12 Sept. 1933; ibid., vol. 276, Herridge to Bennett, 13 Sept. 1933; ibid., reel M-1182, Grote Sterling to Bennett, 28 Aug. 1933; *Canadian Annual Review*, 1934, 28

83 Bennett Papers, vol. 841, Bennett to Robert A. Reid, 11 Jan. 1938; Daly Papers, vol. 2, autobiographical note: Bennett, n.d.

84 Rhodes Papers, vol. 653, Redmond Code to Rhodes, 26 July 1930; ibid., Rhodes to Code, 30 July 1930; Bennett Papers, vol. 472, Rhodes to A.D. McRae, 30 July 1930; ibid., McRae to Rhodes, 5 Aug. 1930

85 Ibid., Redmond Code to Bennett, 23 Aug. 1930

86 Ibid., vol. 475, Robert Lipsett to Bennett, n.d.

87 PC Party Papers, vol. 406, file – The Canadian, 1930–1935

88 Bennett Papers, vol. 472, Robert Lipsett to Bennett, 21 Sept. 1930; ibid., vol. 475, Lipsett to Bennett, 18 Mar. 1931; *Canadian Parliamentary Guide, 1934*, 324; *Ottawa Journal*, 7 Mar. 1938, in PC Papers, vol. 423; Daly Papers, vol. 2, autobiographical note: A.D. McRae

89 Bennett Papers, vol. 485, J.J. Gibbons to Bennett, 22 Dec. 1930; Stevens Papers, vol. 12, Stevens to Bennett, 8 Dec. 1931; Manion Papers, vol. 18, R.J. Manion to James Manion, 12 Jan. 1934; Bennett Papers, vol. 953, Arthur Sauvé to Sir George Perley, 9 Aug. 1933

90 Stevens Papers, vol. 15, Bennett to Stevens, 15 Mar. 1932; Bennett Papers, vol. 480, Bennett to Ivan Sabourin, 16 Sept. 1931; Manion Papers, vol. 4, Bennett to Manion, 22 Nov. 1933

91 Bennett Papers, vol. 472, Memo of Temporary Organization Committee, 17 Nov. 1932; vol. 954, Stevens to Bennett, 28 Dec. 1933

92 Ibid., vol. 472, J. Earl Lawson to Bennett, 2 Oct. 1933; vol. 486, Lawson to Bennett, 4 Nov. 1933

93 Manion Papers, vol. 8, J.D. Chaplin to Manion, 16 June 1933; R.B. Hanson to Manion, 16 June 1932

94 Bennett Papers, vol. 952, W.C. Pitfield to Bennett, 9 Oct. 1930; vol. 954, Stevens to Bennett, 28 Dec. 1933

95 Ibid., vol. 480, D.M. Dorion to Bennett, 26 Apr. 1932; ibid., vol. 472, Arthur Sauvé to Bennett, 13 Oct. 1932; ibid., vol. 480, Alfred Duranleau to Joseph Rainville, 11 Oct. 1932; ibid., vol. 481, Georges Laurin to Bennett, 22 Apr. 1933;

Meighen Papers, vol. 187, Ted Meighen to Arthur Meighen, 26 Apr. 1932

96 Bennett Papers, vol. 475, Senator P.E. Blondin to Bennett, n.d.; J.H. Bender to Bennett, 18 Sept. 1933; Senator Lorne Webster to Arthur Meighen, 27 May 1933

97 Henry Papers, vol. 27, Home Smith to Henry, 3 June 1932; Manion Papers, vol. 5, W.G. Clysdale to Manion, 8 Apr. 1931; Henry Papers, vol. 27, Arthur Ford to Henry, 3 Aug. 1932; Ferguson papers, vol. 2, R.A. Stapells to Ferguson, 7 Apr. 1931; Bennett Papers, vol. 952, William H. Price to Bennett, 4 May 1932; ibid., vol. 486, J. Earl Lawson to Bennett, 4 Nov. 1933; Archives of Ontario (AO), George Drew Papers, vol. MU3549, Harold M. Daly to W.G. Clysdale, 17 Mar. 1933

98 Bennett Papers, vol. 472, Bennett to Alice Millar, 4 June 1932; ibid., vol 491, Dr H.C. Hodgson to Bennett, 16 July 1932; ibid., vol. 492, Robert Weir to Bennett, 19 Feb. 1932; ibid., vol. 102, Edgar R. Teed to Bennett, 18 Nov. 1933; Stevens Papers, vol. 15, H.R. Drummond-Hay to Stevens, 1 Aug. 1933

99 Manion Papers, vol. 10, Manion to Charles McCrea, 30 Oct. 1930; House of Commons *Debates*, 16 Feb. 1934, 651; Stevens Papers, vol. 29, Stevens to F.D. Pratt, 29 Feb. 1932; Ferguson Papers, vol. 2, R.A. Stapells to Ferguson, 7 Apr. 1931

100 Bennett Papers, vol. 480, Thomas Maher to Bennett, 11 May 1931; vol. 489, A.E. Ross to Sir George Perley, 19 Dec. 1932

101 Bruce Papers, vol. 1, Bruce to Dr Peter McGibbon, 20 Oct. 1932; Stevens Papers, vol. 12, Stevens to Bennett, 4 Nov. 1931; Sutherland Papers, vol. 2, Murray MacLaren to Bennett, 2 Sept. 1933

102 Manion Papers, vol. 18, R.J. Manion to James Manion, 5 Oct. 1932; Henry Papers, vol. 27, Arthur R. Ford to Henry, 3 Aug. 1932

103 *Canadian Parliamentary Guide, 1934*, 320–22

104 House of Commons *Debates*, 8 Feb. 1932, 41

CHAPTER 6

1 Toronto *Globe*, 8 July 1935

2 Ibid.; also Montreal *Gazette* and Winnipeg *Tribune*, 8 July 1935; Stevens Papers, vol. 125, Warren Cook et al., petition to Stevens, 5 July 1935

3 Montreal *Gazette*, 9 July 1935; *Vancouver Province*, 9 July 1935

4 Stevens Papers, vol. 41, text of Montreal speech by Stevens, 4 Dec. 1934; ibid., Stevens to Editor, Brockville *Recorder-Times*, 24 Nov. 1934; ibid., vol. 74; H.H. Stevens, 'Big Business,' *Winnipeg and Western Grocer*, Apr. 1935

5 Stevens Papers, vol. 222, Address by H.H. Stevens to Conservative Members of Parliament, 17 May 1933; House of Commons *Debates*, 30 Apr. 1934, 2653

6 Bourassa Papers, reel M-721, C.H. Cahan to *Le Devoir*, 6 Sept. 1926; Cahan

papers, vol. 6, text of Montreal speech by Cahan, 12 Sept. 1935

7 The term *'laissez–faire* conservatism' is ably explained in the American context by Clinton Rossiter in *Conservatism in America: The Thankless Persuasion*, 2nd ed. (New York 1962), 131–62.

8 House of Commons *Debates*, 21 Jan. 1935, 58

9 R.B. Bennett, 'Democracy on Trial,' *Canadian Problems as Seen by Twenty Outstanding Men of Canada* (Toronto n.d.), 11–31; House of Commons *Debates*, 19 June 1935, 3810

10 Bennett, 'Democracy on Trial,' 16; House of Commons Debates, 22 Jan. 1935, 82

11 Andrew D. MacLean, *R.B. Bennett* (Toronto 1935), 77; PC Papers, vol. 239, Verbatim Report, 269; *Winnipeg Free Press*, 6 July 1938

12 Gad Horowitz has written of 'three Conservative ideological streams: right–wing liberalism, orthodox toryism, and tory–radicalism,' in *Canadian Labour in Politics* (Toronto 1968), 22. David Bell and Lorne Tepperman see the same tripartite division of Canadian Conservatism in *The Roots of Disunity: A Look at Canadian Political Culture* (Toronto 1979), 214. William Christian and Colin Campbell describe *'laissez–faire'* and 'tory populist' elements evident in the Conservative party, but they apply the term 'corporatism' to Bennett's position, in *Political Parties and Ideologies in Canada*, (Toronto 1983), 104–7.

13 Michiel Horn, *The Great Depression of the 1930s in Canada*, CHA Booklet No. 39 (Ottawa 1984), 10

14 Finlayson Memoir, 342; House of Commons *Debates*, 18 Apr. 1934, 2267–93; Robert B. Bryce, *Maturing in Hard Times: Canada's Department of Finance through the Great Depression* (Montreal 1986), 108–11

15 Toronto *Globe*, 20 Jan. 1934; Montreal *Gazette*, 24 Oct. 1934; Rhodes Papers, vol. 1182, Sir George Perley to the provincial premiers, 13 July 1934; ibid., L.A. Taschereau to R.B. Bennett, 31 July 1934; James Struthers, *No Fault of Their Own: Unemployment and the Canadian Welfare State, 1914–1941* (Toronto 1983), 109–26

16 House of Commons *Debates*, 25 June 1934, 4273; ibid., 26 June 1934, 4299; Bennett Papers, vol. 203, Bennett to D.M. Duggan, 25 July 1934

17 House of Commons *Debates*, 30 Jan. 1934, 84; 22 Feb. 1934, 827; 27 June 1934, 4358

18 Bennett Papers, reel M-961, Bennett to W.M. and H.S. Southam, 9 May 1934; ibid., reel M-1040, W.C. Clark to R.K. Finlayson, 27 June 1934; King Diary, 27 Feb. 1934; Douglas H. Fullerton, *Graham Towers and His Times* (Toronto 1986), 41–55

19 House of Commons *Debates*, 16 Apr. 1934, 2204–5; ibid., 19 Apr. 1934, 2353–5; 5 June 1934, 3664–5; *Round Table*, June 1934, 633–8; *Canadian Forum* 14

(May 1934): 283–4. The Judicial Committee of the Privy Council declared the Natural Products Marketing Act unconstitutional in 1937.

20 House of Commons *Debates*, 30 Jan. 1934, 83; 4 June 1934, 3639–40.

21 Bennett Papers, reel M-959, Statement by E.N. Rhodes, 24 Aug. 1935; ibid., H.F. Gordon Memorandum to E.N. Rhodes, 10 Sept. 1935; Bryce, *Maturing in Hard Times*, 160–2

22 Bennett Papers, reel M-959, H.F. Gordon to E.N. Rhodes, 10 Sept. 1935; Finlayson Memoir, 238

23 R.G. Smails, 'The Dominion Companies Act, 1934,' *Canadian Journal of Economics and Political Science* 1 (Feb. 1935): 53–63; *Canadian Annual Review*, 1934, 87–9

24 House of Commons *Debates*, 29 Jan. 1934, 7; ibid., 27 Feb. 1934, 979; ibid., 5 Mar. 1934, 1195; ibid., 6 Mar. 1934, 1228; Bennett Papers, reel M-1338, Cahan to Bennett, 25 Sept. 1933; ibid., F.J. Lafleche et al. to Bennett, 31 Jan. 1934; Marc La Terreur, *Les Tribulations des conservateurs au Québec de Bennett à Diefenbaker* (Quebec 1973), 44–5

25 House of Commons *Debates*, 26 Feb. 1934, 962–76; ibid., 22 June 1934, 4237–46; King Diary, 22 June 1934; Meighen Papers, vol. 231, Armand Lavergne to Meighen, le 9 juillet 1934; Bennett Papers, vol. 880, Alfred Duranleau to Bennett, 26 July 1934

26 Stevens Papers, vol. 22, R.P. Sparks to Stevens, 11 Aug. 1933; ibid., Warren K. Cook to Stevens, 23 Aug. 1933; ibid., memo: A New National Policy, 2 Sept. 1933; ibid., vol. 206, memo: My Break with Bennett, n.d.; Michiel Horn, *The League for Social Reconstruction: Intellectual Origins of the Democratic Left in Canada, 1930–1942* (Toronto 1980), 49–50

27 Bennett Papers, vol. 435, Stevens to Bennett, 19 Jan. 1934; Toronto *Mail and Empire*, 16 Jan. 1934

28 Stevens Papers, vol. 222, H.H. Stevens to Francis Stevens, 24 Jan. 1934; Winnipeg *Tribune*, 16 Jan. 1934; Bennett Papers, vol. 436, A.D. Ganong, MP, to H.H. Stevens, 22 Jan. 1934

29 Stevens Papers, vol. 64, Stevens to Charles Luke, 29 Jan. 1935; House of Commons *Debates*, 2 Feb. 1934, 188

30 House of Commons *Debates*, 2 Feb. 1934, 200; Stevens to Hermiston, 19 Jan. 1934, read into ibid., 19 Feb. 1934, 729

31 *Ottawa Journal*, May–June 1934; *Canadian Annual Review, 1934*, 29; J.R.H. Wilbur, 'H.H. Stevens and the Antecedents of the Reconstruction Party, 1930–1935,' MA thesis, Queen's University, 1960, 100–60

32 Henry Papers, vol. 32, Henry to R.B. Bennett, 15 Feb. 1934; Manion Papers, vol. 9, D.M. Hogarth to Manion, 7 July 1934; Bennett Papers, vol. 436, R.C. Matthews to Bennett, 1 June 1934; Stevens Papers, vol. 162A, interview No. 10, 2

33 Bennett Papers, vol. 436, Stevens to Bennett, 15 June 1934; 21 June 1934. Dozens of telegrams were received by Bennett's office from branches of the Retail Merchants' Association urging the price-spreads inquiry be continued. See Bennett Papers, vol. 434.

34 Stevens Papers, vol. 109, Study Club speech, 26 June 1934; Bennett Papers, vol. 436, Gordon Wilson, MP, to Bennett, 16 Aug. 1934; J.S. Stewart, MP, to Bennett, 11 Aug. 1934

35 Grant Dexter, *Winnipeg Free Press*, 7 Aug. 1934; Arthur R. Ford, *As the World Wags On* (Toronto 1950), 121–2; Dafoe Papers, vol. 7, Dafoe to J.S. McLean, 16 Aug. 1934; Stevens Papers, vol. 109, J.E. Parmelee to Stevens, 10 Aug. 1934; ibid., James Muir to Stevens, 14 Aug. 1934; Bennett Papers, vol. 436, Muir to Bennett, 20 Aug. 1934

36 Stevens Papers, vol. 43, Pamphlet: *Price Spreads and Mass Buying*, 27 July 1934; William Marchington, Toronto *Globe*, 6 Aug. 1934; Bennett Papers, vol. 436, C.L. Burton to Bennett, 3 Aug. 1934; Bennett to Burton, 3 Aug. 1934; vol. 434, Burton to Bennett, 4 Aug. 1934; vol. 436, Stevens to Bennett, 4 Aug. 1934

37 Manion Papers, vol. 5, J.L. Bowman, MP, to Manion, 23 Aug. 1934; ibid., vol. 9, Manion to W.D. Herridge, 8 Aug. 1934; Rhodes Papers, vol. 1193, Rhodes to G.G. Moffat, 18 Feb. 1935; King Diary, 7 Aug. 1934; Bennett Papers, vol. 436, Bennett to John T. Haig, MLA, 13 Aug. 1934; Stevens Papers, vol. 109, Stevens to J.S. Stewart, 7 Aug. 1934

38 Stevens Papers, vol. 62, Stevens to the Editor, *Hamilton Spectator*, 5 July 1935; King Diary, 29 Nov. 1934; ibid., 15 Oct. 1935; 'Special Correspondence,' Winnipeg *Tribune*, 16 Mar. 1935; Stevens Papers, vol. 69, Rhodes to Stevens, 5 Nov. 1934; Richard Wilbur, *H.H. Stevens, 1878–1973* (Toronto 1977), 139–41

39 Finlayson Memoir, 273; Stevens Papers, vol. 61, Stevens to W.R. Givens, 12 July 1935; Lambert Diary, 27 Oct. 1934; Winnipeg *Tribune*, 27 and 29 Oct. 1934; *Ottawa Citizen*, 26 Oct. 1934

40 Bennett Papers, vol. 435, Stevens to Bennett, 26 Oct. 1934; Stevens Papers, vol. 71, Bennett to Stevens, 26 Oct. 1934; Bennett Papers, vol. 947, Bennett to G. Howard Ferguson, 1 Nov. 1934

41 Bennett Papers, vol. 436, Stevens to Bennett, 30 Oct. 1934; Stevens Papers, vol. 71, Bennett to Stevens, 31 Oct. 1934; Bennett Papers, vol. 435, Bennett to Ward C. Pitfield, 8 Jan. 1935

42 Bennett Papers, vol. 436, Lawson to Bennett, 28 Oct. 1934; Toronto *Mail and Empire*, 29 Oct. 1934; Montreal *Gazette*, 29 Oct. 1934; Toronto *Telegram*, 29 Oct. 1934; *London Free Press*, 29 Oct. 1934

43 Bennett Papers, vol. 434, Bennett to E. Sherry, 22 Dec. 1934

44 Ibid., vol. 276, W.D. Herridge to Bennett, 12 Apr. 1934, 18 July 1934, 20 Aug. 1934

45 Finlayson Memoir, 251–6

274 Notes to pages 154-9

46 *Canadian Annual Review, 1934*, 32–3; Manion Papers, vol. 9, Herridge speech, 15 Dec. 1934; ibid., Herridge to Manion, 17 Dec. 1934; Robert L. Borden, *Letters to Limbo* (Toronto 1971), 159–60

47 Bennett Papers, vol. 472, C.R.B.C. to Bennett, 1 Mar. 1935; A Politician with a Notebook, 'Backstage at Ottawa,' *MacLean's* 48 (Mar. 1935): 15, 54; Finlayson Memoir, 262

48 Stevens Papers, vol. 58, First Bennett Address, 2 Jan. 1935

49 J.R.H. Wilbur, *The Bennett New Deal: Fraud or Portent?* (Toronto 1969), 83–90

50 Bennett Papers, vol. 487, Arthur Ford to Bennett, 8 Jan. 1935; Public Archives of Canada (PAC), MG 26 M, John G. Diefenbaker Papers, vol. 1, Diefenbaker to Robert Weir, 10 Jan. 1935; Finlayson Memoir, 261; Manion Papers, vol. 18, R.J. Manion to James Manion, 10 Jan. 1935

51 Meighen Papers, vol. 226A, Meighen to W.R. Graham, 22 May 1956; Dafoe Papers, vol. 8, Grant Dexter to Dafoe, 4 and 7 Jan. 1935; Montreal *Gazette*, 4 Jan. 1935; Borden, *Letters to Limbo*, 164

52 Bennett Papers, vol. 713, C.C. Ballantyne to Bennett, 8 Jan. 1935; Alvin Finkel, *Business and Social Reform in the Thirties* (Toronto 1979), 36–8

53 King Diary, 9 Jan. 1935; Dafoe Papers, Dexter to Dafoe, 14 Jan. 1935; Frank H. Underhill, 'A Socialist Analysis,' *Canadian Forum* 15 (Feb. 1935): 168–9; H. Blair Neatby, *William Lyon Mackenzie King*, III: *The Prism of Unity, 1932–1939* (Toronto 1976), 88–9; Kenneth McNaught, *A Prophet in Politics: A Biography of J.S. Woodsworth* (Toronto 1959), 252

54 For slightly different accounts of the Canadian New Deal's launching, see the following: Donald Forster and Colin Read, 'The Politics of Opportunism: The New Deal Broadcasts,' *The Canadian Historical Review* 60 (Sept. 1979): 324–49; W.H. McConnell, 'The Genesis of the Canadian "New Deal,"' *Journal of Canadian Studies* 4 (May 1969): 31–7

55 Stevens Papers, vol. 62, Stevens to W.D. Herridge, 17 Dec. 1934; vol. 31, Stevens to C.E. Disher, 8 Nov. 1934

56 Bennett Papers, vol. 435, L.B. Pearson memo, 9 Nov. 1934; ibid., vol. 434, Bennett to J.W. Crawford, 20 Nov. 1934; Winnipeg *Tribune*, 30 Oct. 1934; Wilbur, 'Stevens and Antecedents of Reconstruction,' 211

57 Dafoe Papers, vol. 8, Dexter to Dafoe, 14 Jan. 1935; Stevens Papers, vol. 70, Norman Sommerville to Stevens, 19 Feb. 1935; Winnipeg *Tribune*, 16 Mar. 1935; House of Commons *Debates*, 12 Apr. 1935, 2667; King Diary, 9 Apr. 1935; Stevens Papers, vol. 69, R.M.A. handbill, 'The Stevens Programme,' 30 Mar. 1935

58 *Report of the Royal Commission on Price Spreads* (Ottawa 1937), 5–13

59 Ibid., 264–5

60 Ibid., xviii–xxv

61 Ibid., 276–307; Stevens Papers, vol. 125, Stevens to W.D. Stewart, 9 May 1935

62 Bennett Papers, vol. 276, Herridge to Bennett, 18 Jan. 1935; ibid., Herridge to R.K. Finlayson, 23 Jan. 1935; Finlayson Memoir, 267; Manion Papers, vol. 9, Herridge to Manion, 23 May 1935; Dafoe Papers, vol. 8, Chester Bloom to Dafoe, 17 June 1935

63 House of Commons *Debates*, 17 Jan. 1935, 3–4, 28–60

64 It was actually Sir William Mulock who first suggested to King the strategem he was to follow so masterfully: King Diary, 15 and 16 Jan. 1935. Bennett let slip to Grattan O'Leary that the reform bills were not even drafted at the time of the broadcasts: Dafoe Papers, vol. 8, Dexter to Dafoe, 4 Jan. 1935.

65 Bennett Papers, reel M-1459, W.C. Clark to Bennett, 18 Jan. 1933; ibid., Sir George Perley to Bennett, 7 Sept. 1934; ibid., C.H. Cahan to Bennett, 2 Feb. 1935; Finlayson Memoir, 233–4; House of Commons *Debates*, 29 Jan. 1935, 280; King Diary, 18 Feb. 1935; Finkel, *Business and Social Reform*, 81–93

66 *Canadian Annual Review, 1935 and 1936*, 28–45; C.A. Curtis, 'Dominion Legislation of 1935: An Economist's Review,' *Canadian Journal of Economics and Political Science* (CJEPS), 1 (Nov. 1935): 599–608; J.R.H. Wilbur, 'R.B. Bennett as a Reformer,' CHA *Papers* (1969), 104–8

67 King Diary, 23 Jan., 9 Feb., 28 Feb. 1935; Manion Papers, vol. 18, R.J. Manion to James Manion, 18 Mar. 1935

68 Bennett Papers, vol. 276, Herridge to Finlayson, 24 Jan. 1935; *Canadian Annual Review, 1934*, 31; Manion Papers, vol. 18, R.J. Manion to James Manion, 8 Feb. 1934; King Diary, 25 Apr. 1934, 3 Feb. 1935

69 PAC, Bennett Papers, reel M-3173, E.W. Beatty to Bennett, Feb. 35; Ferguson Papers, vol. 3, Bennett to Ferguson, 7 Mar. 1935; Bennett Papers, vol. 949, Bennett to John McNally, 6 Mar. 1935; Lambert Diary, 3 Mar. 1935 (Lambert's informant was R.K. Finlayson); King Diary, 15 Mar. 1935 (King's informant was C.H. Cahan); Manion Papers, vol. 84, personal memo, 13 Mar. 1935; ibid., vol. 18, R.J. Manion to James Manion, 13 May 1935; King Diary, 20 May 1935 (King's informant was Bennett); House of Commons *Debates*, 11 Mar. 1935, 1572; Bruce Papers, vol. 1, Bennett to Bruce, 28 May 1935; Bennett Papers, vol. 486, Herbert Bruce to F.D.L. Smith, quoted in Smith to Bennett, 15 July 1935; King Diary, 5 Sept. 1935 (King's informant was Manion)

70 Rhodes Papers, vol. 1199, Rhodes to Borden, 12 Mar. 1935; ibid., vol. 1194, James MacGregor to H.R. Milner, 16 Mar. 1935; Bennett Papers, reel M-1096, Finlayson Memoranda for Sir George Perley, 21 and 22 Mar. 1935

71 Rhodes Papers, vol. 1187, Rhodes to Edouard Cloutier, 26 Mar. 1935; House of Commons *Debates*, 22 Mar. 1935, 1960–89; *Canadian Annual Review, 1935 and 1936*, 19–25; Bryce, *Maturing in Hard Times*, 108–13

72 Queen's University Archives (QUA), C.G. Power Papers, vol. 7, Power to E.M.

Macdonald, 29 Jan. 1935; Bennett Papers, reel M-1479, Bill 39 – Economic Council

73 House of Commons *Debates*, 17 Jan. 1935, 3–4; *Canadian Annual Review, 1935 and 1936*, 44; King Diary, 6 Mar. 1935

74 Struthers, *No Fault of Their Own*, 130; Manion Papers, vol. 9, Manion to Herridge, 8 Apr. 1935; vol. 84, Manion personal memo, 9 Apr. 1935

75 House of Commons *Debates*, 12 March 1934, 1423; ibid., 12 June 1935, 3577; *Canadian Annual Review, 1935 and 1936*, 37–41, 50–2; Rhodes Papers, vol. 1196, Canadian Chamber of Commerce to R.B. Bennett, 18 June 1935; Vernon C. Fowke, *The National Policy and the Wheat Economy* (Toronto 1957), 256–65

76 Bruce Papers, vol. 1, Bruce to Bennett, 23 Apr. and 10 Aug. 1934, 8 Jan. 1935; Bennett to Bruce, 5 Nov. 1934, 2 Feb. 1935

77 Bennett Papers, reel M-1488, Explanation of Dominion Housing Act, Edgar N. Rhodes, 17 Aug. 1935; *Canadian Annual Review, 1935 and 1936*, 42–3; Bryce, *Maturing in Hard Times*, 163–6; John Bacher, 'One Unit Was Too Many,' *Journal of Canadian Studies* 22 (Fall 1987): 50–61

78 *Canadian Annual Review, 1935 and 1936*, 34–5

79 House of Commons *Debates*, 19 June 1935, 3810, 3796; Bennett Papers, vol. 772, Gagnon to Bennett, 14 June 1935; Kennedy to Bennett, 8 June 1935

80 House of Commons *Debates*, 29 May 1935, 3166–8; ibid., 14 June 1935, 3653–4; Dafoe Papers, vol. 8, Dexter to Dafoe, 3 June 1935; Finlayson Memoir, 266–7; King Diary, 27 May 1935

81 Bennett Papers, vol. 772, Kennedy to Bennett, 8 June 1935; House of Commons *Debates*, 19 June 1935, 3796–801; 'Canada: The Parties and the Election,' *Round Table* 100 (Sept. 1935): 808–9. In the end, the courts struck down unemployment insurance and the three labour–convention laws, along with the Natural Products Marketing Act. The trade and industry commission, Guthrie's Criminal Code amendments, and the Farmers' Creditors' Arrangement Act were all declared *intra vires*: Wilbur, *Bennett New Deal*, 192–9.

82 Bennett Papers, reel M-1096, Bennett to Ralph Webb, 12 Dec. 1934; reel M-1430, Bennett to Gordon Hill, 14 June 1935

83 House of Commons *Debates*, 21 Jan. 1935, 58

84 Bennett Papers, vol. 467, Cahan to Bennett, 3 Dec. 1934; Dafoe Papers, vol. 8, Dexter to Dafoe, 4 Jan. 1935; King Diary, 21 Feb. 1935; Bennett Papers, vol. 467, Bennett to Cahan, 5 Feb. 1935, 4 Dec. 1934

85 Manion Papers, vol. 4, Manion to Bennett, 14 Feb. 1935; Stevens Papers, vol. 58, Stevens to C.E. Disher, 31 Jan. 1935; Leon Ladner to Ernest Watkins, n.d., reprinted in Watkins, *R.B. Bennett: A Biography* (London 1963), 209–13; Bennett Papers, vol. 495, H.C. Hodgson to Bennett, 15 Feb. 1935

86 Dafoe Papers, vol. 8, Dexter to Dafoe, 12 Jan. 1935; Manion Papers, vol. 4,

Manion to Bennett, 14 Feb. 1935; Bennett Papers, vol. 276, Herridge to Bennett, 8 Mar. 1935; Ladner to Watkins, in Watkins, *Bennett*, 209–13; Dafoe Papers, vol. 8, Dexter to Dafoe, 4 Jan. 1935; Stevens Papers, vol. 125, Stevens to Bennett, 25 Feb. 1935

87 Manion Papers, vol. 18, R.J. Manion to James Manion, 11 Mar. 1935; Stevens Papers, vol. 125, Cook to Stevens, 15 Mar. 1935; Stevens to Cook, 16 Mar. 1935

88 King Diary, 15 Mar. 1935; House of Commons *Debates*, 15 Mar. 1935, 1745–7; ibid., 12 Apr. 1935, 2668–75; Charles Bishop, Winnipeg *Tribune*, 13 Apr. 1935; Manion Papers, vol. 18, R.J. Manion to James Manion, 15 Apr. 1935; King Diary, 12 Apr. and 27 May 1935; King Papers, Series J1, vol. 204, C.H. Cahan to King, n.d.

89 Manion Papers, vol. 5, Manion to H.A. Bruce, 5 June 1935; King Diary, 20 May 1935; Rhodes Papers, vol. 1199, Rhodes to D.R. Cameron, 25 Mar. 1935; ibid., Rhodes to G.H. Murphy, 17 June 1935; Lambert Diary, 12 May 1935; King Diary, 5 and 7 June 1935; Dafoe Papers, vol. 8, Dexter to Dafoe, 11 July 1935; Manion Papers, vol. 18, R.J. Manion to James Manion, 4 June 1935; Harry W. Anderson, Toronto *Globe*, 5 June 1935. According to Grant Dexter, Bennett thought Manion was 'a rattle pate': Dafoe Papers, vol. 8, Dexter to Dafoe, 3 June 1935.

90 King Diary, 15 Oct. 1935; Bennett Papers, reel 416, Bennett to Thomas S. Grant, 18 Dec. 1935; ibid., vol. 841, Bennett to R.A. Reid, 4 Nov. 1935; Stevens Papers, vol. 58, Stevens to John Anderson, 10 June 1935

91 House of Commons Debates, 19 June 1935, 3792–810; F.C. Mears, Montreal *Gazette*, 20 June 1935; Dafoe Papers, vol. 8, Dexter to Dafoe, 3 June 1935

92 Charles Bishop, Winnipeg *Tribune*, 20 June 1935; Stevens Papers, vol. 61, Stevens to W.R. Givens, 12 July 1935; ibid., vol. 65, Stevens to R.L. Maitland, 22 June 1935; Bennett Papers, vol. 435, Bennett to William H. Price, 17 July 1935

93 House of Commons *Debates*, 13 June 1935, 3592; ibid., 24 June 1935, 3900–1; Victor Hoar, 'The Regina Riot,' in Ronald Liversedge, *Recollections of the On To Ottawa Trek* (Toronto 1973), 231–50; Michiel Horn, *The Dirty Thirties: Canadians in the Great Depression* (Toronto 1972), 306–89

94 Bennett Papers, vol. 952, Bennett to A.E. Ross, 8 Mar. 1938

CHAPTER 7

1 Charles Bishop, Winnipeg *Tribune*, 12 Oct. 1935; Stevens Papers, vol. 132, Form letter to Reconstruction candidates, 4 Oct. 1935

2 M.C. Urquhart and K.A.H. Buckley, eds., *Historical Statistics of Canada* (Toronto 1965), 616; Howard A. Scarrow, *Canada Votes* (New Orleans 1962), 90–101

3 Winnipeg *Tribune*, 15 Oct. 1935; King Diary, 14 Oct. 1935

4 James Struthers, *No Fault of Their Own: Unemployment and the Canadian Welfare State, 1914–1941* (Toronto 1983), 137; W.A. Mackintosh, *The Economic Background of Dominion-Provincial Relations* (Toronto 1964), 137

5 A.L. Normandin, ed., *The Canadian Parliamentary Guide, 1937* (Ottawa 1937), 385 and 553

6 Bennett Papers, vol. 495, J.A. Clark to Bennett, 30 July 1935; Charles Bishop, Winnipeg *Tribune*, 12 Oct. 1935; Dunning Papers, vol. 10, Dunning to E.M. Macdonald, 21 Aug. 1935

7 Bennett Papers, vol. 276, W.D. Herridge to R.K. Finlayson, 18 Sept. 1935; Herridge to Bennett, 14 May 1935; Herridge to Finlayson, 3 Oct. and 23 Sept. 1935

8 Dafoe Papers, vol. 8, Dafoe to Grant Dexter, 17 July 1935; King Diary, 26 June 1935

9 Grace MacInnis, *J.S. Woodsworth: A Man to Remember* (Toronto 1953), 286–7; Stevens Papers, vol. 162A, Interview No. 11; ibid., vol. 132, Form letter to each Reconstruction candidate, 4 Oct. 1935; John McMenemy, 'Fragment and Movement Parties,' in Conrad Winn and John McMenemy, eds., *Political Parties in Canada* (Toronto 1976), 29–48

10 Manion Papers, vol. 18, R.J. Manion to James Manion, 20 July and 26 Aug. 1935

11 Toronto *Globe*, 7–16 Sept. 1935; Bennett Papers, vol. 276, Herridge to Finlayson, 18 Sept. 1935; Montreal *Gazette*, 10 Oct. 1935; Public Archives of Canada (PAC), MG 30 E 133, A.G.L. McNaughton Papers, vol. 105, W.D. Herridge to McNaughton, 20 Sept. 1935

12 Montreal *Gazette*, 1–8 Aug. 1935; W.L. Mackenzie King, 'The Issues As I See Them,' *MacLean's* 48 (15 Sept. 1935): 10, 29–31

13 Owen Carrigan, *Canadian Party Platforms* (Toronto 1968), 119–21; J.S. Woodsworth, 'The Issues As I See Them,' *MacLean's* 48 (15 Sept. 1935): 11, 31–2

14 Carrigan, *Platforms*, 130–4; H.H. Stevens, 'The Issues As I See Them,' *MacLean's* 48 (15 Sept. 1935): 11, 32; Winnipeg *Tribune*, 20 July 1935; Montreal *Gazette*, 12 Oct. 1935

15 J.M. Bliss, ed., *Canadian History in Documents, 1763–1966* (Toronto 1966), 297–9

16 Montreal *Gazette*, 4 Oct. 1935; R.B. Bennett, 'The Issues As I See Them,' *MacLean's* 48 (15 Sept. 1935): 10, 26, 28; King, 'The Issues,' 10; PC Party Papers, vol. 356, Speakers' Handbook: Supplement, 1935

17 Montreal *Gazette*, 5 and 11 Oct. 1935; King, 'The Issues,' 31. See also Research Committee of the League for Social Reconstruction, *Social Planning for Canada*, rev. ed. (Toronto 1975), 477–86.

18 Montreal *Gazette*, 14 and 1 Oct. 1935

19 Winnipeg *Tribune*, 15 July 1935; Stevens, 'The Issues,' 11
20 Bennett Papers, vol. 276, Herridge to Bennett, 8 Oct. 1935; Dafoe Papers, vol. 8, Chester Bloom to Dafoe, 18 Sept. 1935; Montreal *Gazette*, 1 Oct. 1935; C.P. Stacey, *Canada and the Age of Conflict*, II: *The Mackenzie King Era, 1921–1948* (Toronto 1981), 169–73
21 King Diary, 7 Sept. 1935; C.P. Stacey, ed., *Historical Documents of Canada*, V: *The Arts of War and Peace, 1914–1945* (Toronto 1972), 110; Bennett Papers, vol. 199, Bennett to Perley, 22 Sept. 1935; R. Bothwell and J. English, 'The Riddell Incident,' in Robert Bothwell and Norman Hillmer, eds., *The In-Between Time: Canadian External Policy in the 1930s* (Toronto 1975), 122–5
22 Bennett Papers, vol. 276, Herridge to Finlayson, 18 Sept. 1935; Montreal *Gazette*, 14 Oct. 1935; Finlayson Memoir, 195
23 Manion Papers, vol. 18, R.J. Manion to James Manion, 29 Sept. 1935; Hackett Papers, vol. 7, Hanson to Hackett, 10 Sept. 1935; Correspondence, R.A. Bell to the author, 4 June 1984
24 Manion Papers, vol. 18, R.J. Manion to James Manion, 17 Oct. 1935; Hackett Papers, vol. 7, Hanson to Hackett, 10 Sept. 1935; Meighen Papers, vol. 215, Bennett to Meighen, 30 Sept. 1935; ibid., Meighen to Bennett, 30 Sept. 1935; A Politician with a Notebook, 'Now It Can Be Told,' *MacLean's* 43 (1 Aug. 1930): 42
25 Manion Papers, vol. 9, Manion to D.M. Hogarth, 30 July 1935
26 Cahan Papers, vol. 8, Cahan to Grattan O'Leary, 16 Aug. 1935; Dafoe Papers, vol. 8, A.R. Cameron to Dafoe, 16 Aug. 1935; Bennett Papers, vol. 102, Bennett to Senator R.H. Pope, 16 Aug. 1935; vol. 199, Cahan to Bennett, 29 Aug. 1935; vol. 472, L.W. Fraser to J.E. Lawson, 25 July 1935
27 King Diary, 31 July–12 Oct. 1935; Toronto *Globe*, 9 Oct. 1935; Dunning Papers, vol. 10, Dunning to E.M. MacDonald, 30 Sept. 1935
28 Montreal *Gazette*, 12 Oct. 1935; Stevens Papers, vol. 131, Stevens to William Savage, 21 Oct. 1935; King Diary, 15 Oct. 1935, based on a chat King had with the Canadian Press reporter who was assigned to Stevens's campaign
29 Kenneth McNaught, *A Prophet in Politics* (Toronto 1959), 275
30 *Canadian Annual Review, 1935 and 1936*, 67
31 Bennett Papers, vol. 472, J.E. Lawson to Bennett, 11 Dec. 1934; Manion Papers, vol. 13, Home Smith to Manion, 14 Jan. 1935; Bennett Papers, vol. 487, Arthur Ford to Bennett, 8 Jan. 1935; vol. 495, H.C. Hodgson to Bennett, 15 Feb. 1935; vol. 480, Senator R.H. Pope to Bennett, 29 Mar. 1935
32 PC Party Papers, vol. 310, memo for Dr Robb re Office Accommodation, 15 Nov. 1938; Rhodes Papers, vol. 1193, Lou Golden to Rhodes, 26 June 1935; Dafoe Papers, vol. 8, Dexter to Dafoe, 4 Jan. 1935; Lambert Diary, 12 Jan. 1935; Hackett Papers, vol. 6, R. Edwards to Hackett, 30 Jan. 1935; Private Corre-

spondence, Hon. Richard A. Bell to the author, 4 June 1984

33 Rhodes Papers, vol. 1193, R. Edwards to J.R. MacGregor, 14 Mar. 1935; ibid., vol. 1194, W.R. Campbell to M.A. MacPherson, 15 Feb. 1935; ibid., vol. 1193, J.E. Lawson to Rhodes, 1 Apr. 1935; PC Party Papers, vol. 356; ibid., vol. 406; Rhodes Papers, vol. 1193, Lawson to Rhodes, 14 Feb. 1935

34 Bennett Papers, vol. 276, H.R. Milner to Herridge, 5 Feb. 1935; Manion Papers, vol. 10, J.E. Lawson to Manion, 15 May 1935

35 Stevens Papers, vol. 22, Stevens to R.L. Maitland, 8 June 1934; Bennett Papers, vol. 476, Bennett to J.R. MacNicol, 13 Feb. 1934; Dafoe Papers, vol. 8, Dexter to Dafoe, 4 Jan. 1935; King Diary, 28 May 1935; Manion Papers, vol. 12, W.H. Price to Manion, 5 June 1935

36 Bennett Papers, vol. 480, Georges Laurin to Sir George Perley, 15 Mar. 1935; ibid., J.C. Dussault to Bennett, 12 Apr. 1935; J.A. Whitaker to Perley, 5 Apr. 1935; vol. 481, Maurice Dupré to Perley, 3 May 1935; Ward Pitfield to Bennett, 1 Nov. 1934; Alfred Duranleau to Bennett, 18 Feb. 1935

37 Ibid., vol. 486, W.H. Price to Bennett, 3 Nov. 1934; Rhodes Papers, vol. 1193, J.E. Lawson to Rhodes, 1 Apr. 1935; Bennett Papers, vol. 435, Price to Bennett, 11 June 1935; vol. 490, R.C. Matthews to Perley, 20 Sept. 1934

38 Stevens Papers, vol. 15, W.H.S. Dixon to Stevens, 28 Sept. 1934; Bennett Papers, vol. 473, F.W. Turnbull to R.K. Finlayson, 10 Nov. 1934; Diefenbaker Papers, vol. 3, L.W. Williamson to Diefenbaker, 18 Feb. 1935; Bennett Papers, vol. 495, H.C. Hodgson to Bennett, 15 Feb. 1935; vol. 474, J.E. Lawson to Bennett, 15 Jan. 1935

39 Correspondence, R.A. Bell to the author, 4 June 1984

40 Ibid.; Bennett Papers, vol. 474, Bennett to Meighen, 30 Sept. 1935; vol. 472, Webb to Bennett, 23 Aug. 1935; vol. 199, Hanson to Bennett, 26 Aug. 1935

41 Correspondence, Bell to author, 4 June 1984

42 Bennett Papers, vol. 957, MacNicol to Bennett, 22 July 1935; ibid., vol. 199, Robinson to R.A. Bell, 29 Sept. 1935; Hackett Papers, vol. 6, Hackett to Lou Golden, 28 Sept. 1935; ibid., Adrien Arcand to W. Hackett, 27 Sept. 1935; PC Party Papers, vol. 314, J.E. Denison to R.B. Bennett, 5 Aug. 1937

43 PC Party Papers, vol. 356, *The Canadian*, 2/4 (15 Aug. 1935): 40; 'The Speakers' Handbook,' 1935; French-language publicity

44 Bennett Papers, vol. 205, Lawson to Finlayson, 31 Oct. 1935; Correspondence, Bell to author, 4 June 1984; Bennett Papers, reel 416, Bennett to Hector Charlesworth, 2 Mar. 1936; George B. Foster to Bennett, 18 Mar. 1936

45 Ibid., vol. 474, 'Mr Sage' Broadcast No. 2, script, 14 Sept. 1935; Austin Weir, *The Struggle for National Broadcasting in Canada* (Toronto 1965), 200–2; Hector Charlesworth, *I'm Telling You: Further Candid Chronicles* (Toronto 1937), 122; King Diary, 23 June 1936; House of Commons Debates, 11 Feb. 1936, 118–20

46 Bennett Papers, vol. 474, memos re election broadcasts, n.d.; King Papers, Series J4, vol. 162, 'Memorandum of Radio Broadcasts,' 31 July – 14 Oct. 1935

47 Ibid., 'Liberal Publicity Campaign,' 1935; Reginald Whitaker, *The Government Party: Organizing and Financing the Liberal Party of Canada, 1930–58* (Toronto 1977), 28–84

48 Stevens Papers, vol. 132, Reconstruction Party Memo, n.d.; vol 131, George Wright to Stevens, 21 Oct. 1935; vol. 133, Reconstruction Bulletin Number 1, n.d.

49 Walter D. Young, *The Anatomy of a Party: The National CCF, 1932–61* (Toronto 1969), 138–48; John A. Irving, *The Social Credit Movement in Alberta* (Toronto 1959), 119–44

50 John R. Williams, *The Conservative Party of Canada: 1920–1949* (Durham, NC 1956), 150; K.Z. Paltiel, *Political Party Financing in Canada* (Toronto 1970), 30. See also J.L. Granatstein, *The Politics of Survival: The Conservative Party of Canada, 1939–1945* (Toronto 1967), 7; and Granatstein, 'Conservative Party Finance,' *Studies in Canadian Party Finance* (Ottawa 1966), 257–61

51 'We are not any too well supplied with funds,' Dunning observed in August: Dunning Papers, vol. 10, Dunning to E.M. MacDonald, 21 Aug. 1935. See also King Diary, 11 Sept. 1935; Dafoe Papers, vol. 8, Dexter to Dafoe, 18 Sept. 1935; King Papers, Series J1, vol. 270, N.P. Lambert to King, 24 July 1939.

52 Manion Papers, vol. 9, Hogarth to Manion, 10 Oct. 1935; Bennett Papers, vol. 206, Price to Bennett, 15 Oct. 1935; (PAC), reel M-3173, Atholstan to Bennett, 13 Oct. 1935

53 Bennett Papers (UNBA), reel 416, George B. Foster to Bennett, 18 Mar. 1936. The largest donors were: Atholstan, $100,000; CPR, $50,000; Bank of Montreal $30,000; Royal Bank, $25,000; Dominion Steel & Coal, $25,000; National Breweries, $25,000; Canadian Industries, $20,000; and Dominion Textiles, $15,000. A further eight donors made gifts of $10,000, meaning sixteen contributors accounted for $370,000. It is interesting to speculate on the relationship between these funds, collected in the final 'three or four weeks before election day,' and Bennett's veer to the right in his speech-making, as the campaign wound down: ibid., G.A. Campbell, Chairman of Montreal Collection, to Bennett, 6 Feb. 1936.

54 J.L. Granatstein, 'Financing the Liberal Party, 1935–1945,' in Michael Cross and Robert Bothwell, eds., *Policy by Other Means: Essays in Honour of C.P. Stacey* (Toronto 1972), 183; Lambert Papers, vol. 13, 'Financial Statement' by E.G. Long, 31 Mar. 1936; King Papers, Series J4, vol. 162, 'Liberal Publicity Campaign,' 1935; Bennett Papers, vol. 205, J.J. Gibbons to J.E. Lawson, 8 Oct. 1935; ibid., C.R.B.C. invoice, 9 Nov. 1935; ibid., reel 416, Memo for Miss Miller [sic] from Conservative Alberta Headquarters, n.d. The budget allo-

cated $43,300 to Alberta, of which $13,800 had been paid at the time of this memo. Lambert was only able to send $8,300 to Alberta Liberals.

55 Manion Papers, vol. 9, Hogarth to Manion, 24 July 1935; Bennett Papers (PAC), reel M-3173, Atholstan to Bennett, 13 Oct. 1935. R.A. Bell recollects that when his boss, J.E. Lawson, went to Montreal to ask His Lordship to divert some of his funds to support the publicity activities of party headquarters, Atholstan's answer was to instruct his butler to 'show this man to the door': Correspondence, Bell to author, 4 June 1984.

56 Bell to author, 4 June 1984; Bennett Papers, reel 416, George B. Foster to Bennett, 18 Mar. 1936; Runge Press to Bennett, 9 Feb. 1938

57 Stevens Papers, vol. 131, George Wright to Stevens, 21 Oct. 1935; ibid., vol. 130, Leslie Bennett to Stevens, 23 Oct. 1935; King Diary, 15 Oct. 1935

58 Howard A. Scarrow, *Canada Votes* (New Orleans 1962), 90–101

59 Ferguson Papers, vol. 3, Ferguson to Beaverbrook, 2 Nov. 1935; Bennett Papers, reel 416, Bennett to C.H.J. Burrows, 9 May 1938

60 Bennett Papers, vol. 487, Ford to Bennett, 13 Aug. 1935; Carman Carroll, 'The Influence of H.H. Stevens and the Reconstruction Party in Nova Scotia, 1934–35,' MA thesis, University of New Brunswick, 1972, 124–45

61 Scarrow, *Canada Votes*, 90–101

62 Certainly the new parties' policies were aimed at these two classes.

63 Escott Reid, 'The Canadian Election of 1935 – and After,' *The American Political Science Review* 30 (Feb. 1936): 111–20

64 'Canada: The Parties and the Elections,' *Round Table*, 100 (Sept. 1935): 815–17; John Cripps, 'The Canadian Elections,' *The Political Quarterly* 6 (1935): 569; Stevens Papers, vol. 131, J.R. Martin to Stevens, 22 Oct. 1935; ibid., vol. 162A, Interview No. 11; *The Globe*, 15 Oct. 1935; Bennett Papers, vol. 205, Plunkett to Bennett, 16 Nov. 1935

65 Archives of Ontario (AO), M.F. Hepburn Papers, vol. 234, Hepburn to A.W. Roebuck, 24 Sept. 1935; Bennett Papers, vol. 883, F.W. Turnbull to Bennett, 30 July 1935

66 Montreal *Gazette*, 7 Oct. 1935; Bennett Papers, vol. 205, Andrew Davison to Bennett, 28 Oct. 1935; D.B. Plunkett to Bennett, 16 Nov. 1935

67 Bruce Papers, vol. 1, Bennett to Bruce, 18 Oct. 1935; Bennett Papers, vol. 473, Bennett to 'Dear Supporter,' 12 Nov. 1935; vol. 205, Bennett to W.E. Tummon, 15 Feb. 1936; vol. 206, Bennett to Hugh Clark, 25 Oct. 1935; vol. 841, Bennett to Robert Reid, 7 Nov. 1935; (PAC), reel M-3174, Bennett to Borden, 31 Oct. 1935

68 Bennett Papers, vol. 841, Bennett to R.A. Reid, 4 Nov. 1935; Stevens Papers, vol. 130, Stevens to T.R. Grant, 18 Nov. 1935; King Papers, Series J1, vol. 204, C.H. Cahan to King, 16 Dec. 1935

CHAPTER 8

1 General description of the convention is based on four newspapers: *Ottawa Citizen*, Toronto *Globe and Mail*, Montreal *Gazette*, and Winnipeg *Tribune*, 1–9 July 1938.

2 PC Party Papers, vol. 417, Proceedings of the Convention of the National Conservative Party of Canada, July 5–7 (Convention Proceedings)

3 John C. Courtney, *The Selection of National Party Leaders in Canada* (Toronto 1973), 149

4 Convention Proceedings, 303–14

5 A Politician with a Notebook, 'Backstage at Ottawa,' *MacLean's* 51 (15 Aug. 1938): 8; King Diary, 7 July 1938

6 'Canada: Political Affairs,' *Round Table* 103 (June 1936): 603; A Politician with a Notebook, 'Backstage at Ottawa,' *MacLean's* 49 (15 July 1936): 37; King Diary, 12 June 1936; Bennett Papers, vol. 956, Bennett to Mark Irish, 27 Sept. 1937; reel 416 (UNB), H.N. Streight to R.K. Finlayson, 1 May 1936; reel M-1480, Bennett to Glidden Traders, 20 Feb. 1937

7 Dafoe Papers, vol. 10, T.A. Crerar to Dafoe, 17 Apr. 1937; King Diary, 16 June 1938

8 House of Commons *Debates*, 10 Feb. 1936, 63

9 Ibid., 19 June 1936, 3919; 20 June 1938, 4058; 19 June 1936, 3941

10 Ibid., 16 June 1936, 3781; Bennett Papers, vol. 947, Maurice Dupré to Bennett, 26 June 1936. The lone francophone in the Tory Caucus was Jules Wermenlinger of Verdun, until Georges Héon won a by-election in Argenteuil in 1938.

11 House of Commons *Debates*, 1 July 1938, 4526–8

12 PC Party Papers, vol. 314, J.E. Denison to R.B. Bennett, 21 July 1936; vol. 306, Denison to R.K. Finlayson, 30 Jan. 1937; vol. 314, Denison to Bennett, 5 Aug. 1937, 11 Jan. 1938; vol. 310, Memorandum for Dr Robb, 15 Nov. 1938

13 Bennett Papers, vol. 841, Bennett to E.J. Gott, 6 Aug. 1936; ibid., vol. 957, John R. MacNicol to Bennett, 13 Mar. 1937; ibid., reel 416, J. Earl Lawson to Bennett, 23 Dec. 1937; Lambert Papers, vol. 2, Lambert to Mackenzie King, 30 Dec. 1938

14 Bennett Papers, vol. 840, Bennett to Ralph Webb, 10 Feb. 1938; vol. 947, Bennett to Maurice Dupré, 7 Jan. 1936; vol. 946, Bennett to George A. Drew, 14 July 1938; reel 415, Bennett to F.W. Turnbull, 26 Jan. 1937; vol. 840, Turnbull to Bennett, 11 Jan. 1936

15 Stevens Papers, vol. 153, Paul Miquelon to Stevens, 7 Mar. 1938

16 Bennett Papers, reel 416, George C. Nowlan to Bennett, 21 May 1936; ibid., vol. 840, John G. Diefenbaker to Bennett, 31 Dec. 1937; Convention Proceedings,

124; Meighen Papers, vol. 218, Meighen to General J.A. Clark, 10 May 1937; A.L. Normandin, *The Canadian Parliamentary Guide: 1939* (Ottawa 1939), passim

17 Toronto *Globe and Mail*, 7 Aug. 1937; Bennett Papers, reel 415, Bennett to George Challies, 13 June 1936; Public Archives of Canada (PAC), Hanson Papers, vol. 1, Hanson to R.J. Manion, 28 Oct. 1936; King Diary, 8 Apr. 1937

18 Charles Bishop, Winnipeg *Tribune*, 9 Aug. 1937; Bruce Papers, vol. 1, Bennett to Bruce, 24 Aug. 1937; Manion Papers, vol. 18, R.J. Manion to James Manion, 31 Aug. 1937; Bennett Papers, vol. 840, Bennett to H.N. Streight, 8 Feb. 1938; Diefenbaker Papers, vol. 1, E.E. Perley to Diefenbaker, 18 Aug. 1937

19 PC Party Papers, vol. 416, Minutes of Conference, 4 and 5 Mar. 1938; Montreal *Gazette*, 2 Mar. 1938; ibid., 7 Mar. 1938; Diefenbaker Papers, vol. 1, J.H. Gillespie to Diefenbaker, 8 Feb. 1938; 'One clear united call, one resolution of loyalty and affection, might have meant his staying. The hard-bitten realists who met in Ottawa in March issued no such call ... Bennett resigned': M. Grattan O'Leary, 'Who'll Succeed Bennett?' *MacLean's* 51 (1 May 1938): 10

20 K.R. Wilson, *The Financial Post*, 12 Mar. 1938, clipping in Power Papers, vol. ·80; Meighen Papers, vol. 156, Policy and Convention Committee Report, 5 Mar. 1938; Winnipeg *Tribune*, 1 Mar. 1938, 9

21 Convention Proceedings, 60–7; PAC, MG 27 III C 16, John Bracken Papers, vol. 138, Minutes of National Conservative Convention Committee Meeting, 9 Apr. 1938; Bennett Papers, vol. 957, John R. MacNicol to Bennett, 21 June 1938; PC Party Papers, vol. 240, Memorandum – Organization 1938 National Convention, Conservative Party

22 PC Party Papers, vol. 418, Auditor's Report of 1938 Convention; ibid., vol. 423, MacNicol to G.B. Foster, n.d.; Bennett Papers, reel 416, R.K. Finlayson to Harry Hatch, 17 May 1938; ibid., Bennett to G.B. Foster, 27 Apr. 1938; ibid., J.M. Macdonnell to Bennett, 5 May 1938; PC Party Papers, vol. 423, H.A. Stewart to J.R. MacNicol, 22 July 1938; Bennett Papers, reel 416, George B. Foster to Bennett, 7 June 1938. Rail fare alone would cost each Saskatchewan delegate sixty dollars: Diefenbaker Papers, vol. 1, Diefenbaker to Alex H. Reed, 18 June 1938.

23 Bracken Papers, 9 Apr. 1938 Minutes; Ruth M. Bell, 'Conservative Party National Conventions, 1927–1956: Organization and Procedure,' MA thesis, Carleton, 1965, Table V; PC Party Papers, vol. 418, List of Ballot Books Issued

24 Meighen Papers, vol. 236, H.R. Milner to Meighen, 21 May 1938; Diefenbaker Papers, vol. 1, Diefenbaker to Errick F. Willis, 4 May 1938; Public Archives of New Brunswick (PANB), Hanson Papers, vol. 7, Maurice Dupré to John R. MacNicol, 20 Mar. 1939

25 Winnipeg *Tribune*, 8 July 1938; King Diary, 8 July 1938

26 Bennett Papers, reel 416, Sir Thomas White to Bennett, 13 June 1938; PC Party Papers, vol. 416, Memo re Organization of Ottawa Convention, 5–7 July 1938; Bennett Papers, reel 416, Joseph Harris to Bennett, 29 June 1938, 2 July 1938

27 PC Party Papers, vol. 417, Minutes of Meetings of the Resolutions Committee, 5–7 July 1938; Convention Proceedings, 234–87

28 Arthur Meighen, 'The Defence of Canada,' 5 July 1938, in *Unrevised and Unrepented* (Toronto 1949), 312; F.C. Mears, Montreal *Gazette*, 6 July 1938; Convention Proceedings, 93–9

29 Convention Proceedings, 154; Harold Dingman, Toronto *Globe and Mail*, 7 July 1938; Mears, Montreal *Gazette*, 7 July 1938; Bennett Papers, reel M-1480, Bennett to J. Leonard Apedaile, 14 July 1938

30 PC Party Papers, vol. 417, Resolutions passed at the National Conservative Convention, 5–7 July 1938 (Convention Resolutions); ibid., Resolutions Committee Minutes; Bennett Papers, reel 416, Joseph Harris to Bennett, 2 July 1938; Convention Proceedings, 237–49; King Diary, 7 July 1938

31 Bennett Papers, reel 416, Harris to Bennett, 2 July 1938; A Politician with a Notebook, 'Backstage at Ottawa,' *MacLean's* 51, (15 Aug. 1938): 8; PANB, Hanson Papers, vol. 31, Hanson to F.R. MacMillan, 21 July 1938; Convention Proceedings, 260–73; King Diary, 7 July 1938

32 Convention Proceedings, 148; Toronto *Globe and Mail*, 8 July 1938; Convention Resolutions; Convention Proceedings, 277–9; Bennett Papers, reel 416, Harris to Bennett, 2 July 1938; Mears, Montreal *Gazette*, 8 July 1938; King Diary, 8 July 1938

33 Convention Resolutions; Bell, 'Conservative Party National Conventions,' 154

34 PANB, Hanson Papers, vol. 31, Hanson to F.R. MacMillan, 21 July 1938; ibid., Hanson to John Hackett, 19 July 1938; Bennett Papers, vol. 964, Bennett to Mrs O.R. Campbell, 19 July 1938

35 O'Leary, 'Who'll Succeed Bennett?' 10; PANB, Hanson Papers, vol. 10, John T. Hackett to Hanson, 14 Apr. 1938; Manion Papers, vol. 18, R.J. Manion to James Manion, 26 Mar. 1938; Stevens Papers, vol. 155, Stevens to J.J. Power, 5 May 1938

36 Meighen Papers, vol. 236, Meighen to H.R. Milner, 14 Apr. 1938; PANB, Hanson Papers, vol. 31, Hanson to Milner, 9 May 1938; R.J. Manion, *Life is an Adventure* (Toronto 1936), 292–4; Manion Papers, vol. 18, R.J. Manion to James Manion, 31 Aug. 1937; ibid., 26 Mar. 1938. Plutoria Avenue and Mariposa are the fictional creations of Stephen Leacock: see Alan Bowker, ed., *The Social Criticism of Stephen Leacock* (Toronto 1973), especially xxix–xxxiii.

37 Stevens Papers, vol. 154, Stevens to R.H. Webb, 24 June 1938; Meighen Papers, vol. 236, Milner to Meighen, 19 Apr. 1938

38 Ibid., vol. 156, Mark Senn to Meighen, 1 Apr. 1938; Manion Papers, vol. 18, R.J. Manion to James Manion, 26 Mar. 1938; Meighen Papers, vol. 236, Meighen to H.R. Milner, 14 Apr. 1938

39 *Canadian Annual Review, 1937–38*, 16; PAC, Hanson Papers, vol. 1, Manion to Hanson, 25 Oct. 1936; Meighen Papers, vol. 236, Milner to Meighen, 19 Apr. 1938

40 Stevens Papers, vol. 156, Stevens to Mr Agnew, 2 Mar. 1939; vol. 151, Warren K. Cook to Stevens, 27 Apr. 1938; vol. 153, Stevens to Thomas Lisson, 13 Apr. 1938; Lisson to Stevens, 19 May 1938; vol. 155, telegram to H.H. Stevens, 29 June 1938

41 Ferguson Papers, vol. 1, Senator Iva Fallis to Ferguson, 8 Mar. 1938; Meighen Papers, vol. 236, Milner to Meighen, 19 Apr. 1938; Bennett Papers, vol. 880, M.A. MacPherson to Bennett, 7 June 1938

42 Meighen Papers, vol. 236, Meighen to Milner, 14 Apr. 1938; ibid., vol. 215, Henry Borden to Meighen, 4 May 1938; Manion Papers, vol. 18, R.J. Manion to James Manion, 26 Mar. 1938; Meighen Papers, vol. 236, Meighen to Milner, 26 May 1938

43 Dafoe Papers, vol. 10, Dafoe to George Ferguson, 9 June 1938; Meighen Papers, vol. 156, Meighen to J.A. Clark, 21 June 1938; Bennett Papers, reel 415, Bennett to A.J. Anderson, 21 June 1938; vol 948, Hanson to Bennett, 10 May 1938; vol. 946, Senator W.H. Dennis to Bennett, 1 July 1938

44 Harold Dingman, Toronto *Globe and Mail*, 4 July 1938; W.L. MacTavish, Winnipeg *Tribune*, 4 July 1938; Charles Bishop, *Ottawa Citizen*, 5 July 1938

45 PAC, Hanson Papers, vol. 62, A.R. Landry to Manion, 22 Aug. 1938; Stevens Papers, vol. 151, Stevens to D.F. Glass, 30 June 1938; PANB, Hanson Papers, Hanson to W.H. Grant, 22 Aug. 1938

46 Manion Papers, vol. 10, Charles McCrea to Manion, 13 July 1938; Herridge Papers, File: Conservatives, unsigned – but almost assuredly Herridge to Bennett, 2 July 1938; Charles Bishop, *Ottawa Citizen*, 5 July 1938; Arthur R. Ford, *As the World Wags On* (Toronto 1950), 110; R.C. Mears, Montreal *Gazette*, 7 July 1938; 'Backstage at Ottawa,' *MacLean's* 51 (15 Aug. 1938): 8; Meighen Papers, vol. 226A, Memo for Roger Graham, 103–4; Bennett Papers, vol. 864, Meighen to Bennett, 12 July 1938

47 Toronto *Globe and Mail*, 8 July 1938; Bennett Papers, reel 415, Bennett to Floyd S. Chalmers, 22 July 1938; Convention Proceedings, 225; Meighen Papers, vol. 234, MacPherson to Meighen, 3 May 1940

48 Convention Proceedings, 225–32

49 Ibid., 174–84; Montreal *Gazette*, 5 July 1938; Manion Papers, vol. 18, R.J. Manion to James Manion, 10 July 1938

50 Convention Proceedings, 187–92, 196–204, 210–16; Charles Bishop, *Ottawa*

Citizen, 6 July 1938; Harold Dingman, Toronto *Globe and Mail*, 8 July 1938; 'Backstage at Ottawa,' *MacLean's* 51 (15 Aug. 1938): 8

51 Manion Papers, vol. 18, R.J. Manion to James Manion, 10 July 1938; *Le Devoir* estimate of Quebec's support, cited in La Terreur, *Les tribulations des conservateurs au Québec de Bennett à Diefenbaker* (Quebec 1973), 81; Bennett Papers, vol. 880, MacPherson to Bennett, 22 Aug. 1938; Harold Dingman, Toronto *Globe and Mail*, 5 July 1938

52 Diefenbaker Papers, vol. 3, Diefenbaker to Denton Massey, 10 June 1938; Manion Papers, vol. 18, R.J. Manion to James Manion, 26 Mar. 1938

53 Convention Proceedings, 308

54 King Diary, 7 July 1938

CHAPTER 9

1 Arthur Meighen, *Unrevised and Unrepented* (Toronto 1949), 314–21; M. Grattan O'Leary, 'Who'll Succeed Bennett?' *MacLean's* 51 (1 May 1938): 10

2 Dafoe's letter and Dale's cartoon are both cited in H. Blair Neatby, *The Politics of Chaos: Canada in the Thirties* (Toronto 1927), 50–70.

3 Robert L. Borden, *Letters to Limbo* (Toronto 1971), 258–60

4 Grattan O'Leary, *Recollections of People, Press and Politics* (Toronto 1977), 79

5 Andrew D. MacLean, *R.B. Bennett: Prime Minister of Canada* (Toronto 1935), 76; 1938 Convention Proceedings, 149

6 Bennett to Ross, 1 April 1938, cited in Ernest Watkins, *R.B. Bennett: A Biography* (London 1963), 233

7 Public Archives of New Brunswick (PANB), Hanson Papers, Hanson to Grote Stirling, 23 Apr. 1948; John R. Williams, *The Conservative Party of Canada, 1920–1949* (Durham, NC 1956), 54–60. Another academic who reached a similar conclusion was Richard Wilbur. 'Bennett could have led a charge up San Juan hill; he could not lead a political party': J.R.H. Wilbur, 'H.H. Stevens and the Reconstruction Party,' in Ramsay Cook, ed., *Politics of Discontent* (Toronto 1967), 76.

8 Donald Creighton, *Towards the Discovery of Canada* (Toronto 1972), 19

9 Neatby, *Politics of Chaos*, 69; Richard Wilbur, by contrast, was one of the first scholars to take the reforming side of Bennett's prime ministership seriously: J.R.H. Wilbur, 'R.B. Bennett as a Reformer,' CHA Papers (1969), 102–11.

10 *Winnipeg Free Press*, 6 July 1938; Bennett Papers, reel M-1488, Bennett to W.B. Gemmell, 7 Mar. 1936; reel M-1041, Bennett to J.I. Richmond, 16 July 1935

11 Norman Ward, ed., *A Party Politician: The Memoirs of Chubby Power* (Toronto 1966), 265

12 Flavelle Papers, Flavelle to Hon. R.H. Pope, 14 Jan. 1927

13 Samuel P. Huntington, *Political Order in Changing Societies* (New Haven 1968), 32–9
14 Samuel H. Beer, *British Politics in the Collectivist Age* (New York 1969), 305–8
15 Larry A. Glassford, 'Party Development in Canada: A Case Study of the Conservative Party, 1921–1945,' unpublished paper presented to the Southwest Ontario Comparative Politics Conference, 1987
16 Reginald Whitaker, *The Government Party: Organizing and Financing the Liberal Party of Canada, 1930–58* (Toronto 1977), 28–84
17 Clinton Rossiter, *Conservatism in America: The Thankless Persuasion*, 2nd ed. (New York 1962), esp. 3–19
18 Stephen Leacock set out the broad parameters for a progressive conservatism in 1919 in a series of seven essays collectively titled 'The Unsolved Riddle of Social Justice': Alan Bowker, ed., *The Social Criticism of Stephen Leacock* (Toronto 1973), 71–145.
19 Frank H. Underhill, *In Search of Canadian Liberalism* (Toronto 1960), 236
20 O'Leary, 'Who'll Succeed Bennett?' 52

EPILOGUE

1 Excerpt from F.R. Scott, 'Ode to a Politician,' in J.R.H. Wilbur, *The Bennett New Deal: Fraud or Portent* (Toronto 1968), 249
2 Bennett Papers, vol. 957, Bennett to R.F. McWilliams, 20 Feb. 1936; Bennett to J.H. Warren, Apr. 1937, cited in Ernest Watkins, *R.B. Bennett: A Biography* (London 1963), 231
3 Lord Beaverbrook, *Friends: Sixty Years of Intimate Personal Relations with Richard Bedford Bennett* (London 1959), 88–122; Watkins, R.B. Bennett, 230–3; Public Archives of Canada (PAC), Charlotte Whitton Papers, vol. 4, Bennett to Whitton, 15 Feb. 1939
4 John G. Diefenbaker, *One Canada*, I: *The Crusading Years, 1895–1956* (Toronto 1975), 155–6, 166–7
5 George C. Perlin, *The Tory Syndrome: Leadership Politics in the Progressive Conservative Party* (Montreal 1980)

Sources

ARCHIVAL COLLECTIONS

Public Archives of Canada
 Richard H. Babbage Papers
 Baron Beaverbrook Papers
 R.B. Bennett Papers
 Sir Robert Borden Papers
 Henri Bourassa Papers
 John Bracken Papers
 C.H. Cahan Papers
 Co-operative Commonwealth Federation
  and New Democratic Party Papers
 J.W. Dafoe Papers
 Harold M. Daly Papers
 John G. Diefenbaker Papers
 Maurice Dupré Papers
 Roderick K. Finlayson Papers
 Sir George Foster Papers
 R.B. Hanson Papers
 W.L. Mackenzie King Papers
 Armand Lavergne Papers
 Liberal Party of Canada Papers
 A.G.L. McNaughton Papers
 R.J. Manion Papers
 Arthur Meighen Papers
 Sir George Perley Papers
 Progressive Conservative Party of Canada Papers

J.L. Ralston Papers
Escott Reid Papers
H.H. Stevens Papers
F.H. Underhill Papers
Charlotte Whitton Papers
J.R.H. Wilbur Papers
J.S. Woodsworth Papers
Public Archives of New Brunswick
R.B. Hanson Papers
Public Archives of Nova Scotia
E.N. Rhodes Papers
Archives of Ontario
T.L. Church Papers
George Drew Papers
G. Howard Ferguson Papers
George S. Henry Papers
Mitchell F. Hepburn Papers
Queen's University Archives
Herbert A. Bruce Papers
T.A. Crerar Papers
Charles Dunning Papers
Sir Joseph Flavelle Papers
John T. Hackett Papers
Norman P. Lambert Papers
James M. MacDonnell Papers
C.G. Power Papers
Norman M. Rogers Papers
Donald M. Sutherland Papers
University of New Brunswick Archives
R.B. Bennett Papers

PRIVATE COLLECTIONS AND CORRESPONDENCE

W.D. Herridge Papers, Toronto
Richard A. Bell Correspondence with the author 1984

GOVERNMENT OF CANADA DOCUMENTS AND PUBLICATIONS

House of Commons. *Official Report of Debates*. Ottawa 1926-38
Report of the Chief Electoral Officer. Ottawa 1931 and 1936

Report of the Committee on Election Expenses, 1966. Ottawa 1966
Report of the Royal Commission on Price Spreads. Ottawa 1937
Seventh Census of Canada, 1931. Ottawa 1932
Studies of the Royal Commission on Bilingualism and Biculturalism, VI: Cabinet Formation and Bicultural Relations, ed. by Frederick W. Gibson. Ottawa 1970
The Canadian Parliamentary Guide, ed. by A.L. Normandin. Ottawa 1926–39

CONTEMPORANEOUS NEWSPAPERS AND MAGAZINES

Canadian Forum
Edmonton Journal
Halifax *Herald*
London Free Press
MacLean's
Montreal *Gazette*
Montreal *Le Devoir*
Montreal Star
Ottawa Citizen
Ottawa Journal

Queen's Quarterly
Round Table
Toronto *Globe*
Toronto *Globe and Mail*
Toronto *Mail and Empire*
Toronto *Telegram*
Winnipeg Free Press
Winnipeg *Tribune*
Vancouver Province

Index

ship bid, 33; key member of
caucus, 47; party fund-raising, 61,
71, 87, 93; and Quebec Conservatives, 63, 64; as member of cabinet,
103, 105; acting prime minister,
143, 162–3; and economic policy,
118, 173; and party office, 128;
opposed Stevens inquiry, 150;
re-elected in 1935, 207; succeeded
by Héon, 218
Pitfield, Ward, 30, 63, 64, 65, 131, 189
Plunkett, D.B., 201
Political Quarterly, The, 201
populism, 139, 141, 171, 241, 245
Power, Charles 'Chubby,' 100, 109,
237
Prairie Farm Rehabilitation Act, 163,
172, 236
Price, J.H., 65
Price, W.H., 66, 67, 132, 189, 194, 195
Price Spreads Inquiry: establishment,
149–53; report, 157–9; implementation, 154, 155, 163, 165–6, 170,
173; alienated big business, 172;
key part of Reconstruction
platform, 181
prime minister, powers of, 100
Privy Council, Judicial Committee of
the, 124
Progressive Conservative Party.
See Conservative party
Progressives: origins of party, 14;
alliance with Saskatchewan
Conservatives, 68–9; government
of Manitoba, 70, 177, 245; led by
Crerar, 78; cooperation with
Liberals, 91, 94; and Reconstruction Party, 198
Prophetic Bible Institute, 187
Provincial Party (B.C.), 49

provincial rights, 140
public works: Stewart as minister,
103; as part of emergency relief,
111, 114, 119; as part of recovery
plans, 127, 128, 143, 163, 164, 181;
as part of Conservatives' convention platform, 221

Racey, A.G., 85, 192
radio: coverage of 1927 convention,
43; use during 1930 election, 58, 72,
79–80, 86, 87; political issue, 124–5,
135, 160, 172; New Deal broadcasts, 154–5, 167; use during 1935
election, 184, 186, 192–3, 196
Radio League, 125
Rainville, Joseph: Quebec organizer
for 1930 election, 64–6, 83, 87, 93;
supporter of Duranleau, 104;
appointed to Montreal Harbour
Board, 131; organizer for 1935
election, 189, 191, 211
Ralston, J.L., 193
Raymond, Donat, 195
reaction: hard-line Depression
policies, 118–24, 142–3, 171–3;
dialectic struggle with reform, 136,
156, 204, 220–1, 241; views of
Cahan, 139–40; part of Bennett's
philosophy, 180, 209, 235, 236;
modern versions, 245
realignment, voter, 202–3
reciprocity, 9, 11, 12, 74
Reconstruction Party: formation,
137–8, 171; election campaign, 179,
180–1, 182–3, 186–7, 193–4, 195–6;
voting analysis, 175–7, 197–8, 239;
eventual demise, 203, 224, 241
reform: Borden's Halifax platform,
11; Winnipeg convention platform,

DATE DUE

GAYLORD			PRINTED IN U.S.A.